Lonesome Melodies

American Made
Music Series

LONESOME MELODIES

The Lives and Music of the

STANLEY BROTHERS

DAVID W. JOHNSON

University Press of Mississippi ✳ Jackson

www.upress.state.ms.us

Designed by Peter D. Halverson

Cover photograph by John Cohen

The University Press of Mississippi is a member of the Association of
American University Presses.

First printing 2013
©
Library of Congress Cataloging-in-Publication Data

Johnson, David W. (David William), 1946–
Lonesome melodies : the lives and music of the Stanley Brothers /
David W. Johnson.
p. cm. — (American made music series)
Includes bibliographical references, index, and discography.
ISBN 978-1-61703-646-0 (cloth : alk. paper) — ISBN 978-1-61703-647-7
(ebook) 1. Stanley Brothers. 2. Bluegrass musicians—United States—
Biography. I. Title.
ML421.S73J66 2013
781.642092'2—dc23   2012029580

British Library Cataloging-in-Publication Data available

To Mike Seeger

CONTENTS

ACKNOWLEDGMENTS

It takes a community to write a biography. That much I learned during my ten-year effort to revisit the lives and music of two brothers from southwestern Virginia whose legacy will last many times longer than their twenty professional years together.

I am grateful to editor and folklorist Judith McCulloh for her early encouragement of this project. I owe much to Ralph Stanley, who granted me two interviews in 2003 and a third in 2005. Ralph's nephews Carter and Bill Stanley spoke with me about their father, Carter Stanley. Their sisters, Doris Stanley Bradley and Jeanie Stanley Allinder, shared memories of their father and mother, as did their cousin Roy Sykes Jr.

Fred Stanley of Abingdon, Virginia, spoke with me about his father, Lee Stanley. The late Mike Seeger gave me permission to use interviews he conducted with Carter and Ralph Stanley in 1966. For recordings of these and Mike's interview with fiddle player Leslie Keith, I am grateful to the staff of the University of North Carolina's Southern Folklife Collection. The special collections room of the Portsmouth, New Hampshire, Public Library proved the perfect place to revise a manuscript.

After the project began as an article on Ralph in the *Mars Hill Review*, a conversation with Nolan Porterfield, biographer of Jimmie Rodgers and John Lomax, led to my decision to focus on the two decades Carter and Ralph performed together. Professor William R. Ferris of the University of North Carolina, Chapel Hill, has been supportive of my writing since 1991. Stanley Brothers historian Gary B. Reid provided guidance when I was uncertain how to proceed, as did bluegrass historian Fred Bartenstein. Both shared unofficial recordings from their collections that would have been difficult to obtain elsewhere.

Former Clinch Mountain Boys Lester Woodie, George Shuffler, Melvin Goins, and Larry Sparks took time to answer my many questions and share recollections of performing with Carter and Ralph from the

1940s through 1960s. Current Clinch Mountain Boy guitarist James Alan Shelton responded to e-mails about cross-picking and relayed my questions to Ralph. The late Jack Cooke spoke with me briefly about his role in John's Gospel Quartet. Bluegrass musician Bill Clifton offered insights into the personality of Carter Stanley, as did Larry Ehrlich, who recorded the brothers in 1956.

Books by Professors Bill C. Malone, Neil V. Rosenberg, and John Wright were the foundation of my research. Malone's *Country Music U.S.A.*, Rosenberg's *Bluegrass: A History*, and Wright's *Traveling the High Way Home: Ralph Stanley and the World of Traditional Bluegrass Music* sat at my elbow throughout the writing process. In addition to their significant contributions as historians, Professors Malone and Rosenberg had met the Stanley Brothers and were willing to personalize accounts contained in their books. Professor Wright compiled an invaluable oral history of Ralph Stanley. Books and articles by Professors Ronald D. Cohen, Ivan M. Tribe, and the late Charles K. Wolfe were vital to my research. Each of these scholars generously answered questions.

Dr. Christopher P. Holstege of the University of Virginia Medical Center shared his expertise on alcoholism related to moonshine and the probable nature of Carter Stanley's treatment at the University of Virginia Hospital in 1966.

Members of the Stanley Brothers community shared their memories, writings, fan club publications, and photographs. Don Morrell of Abingdon, Virginia, gave me access to his collection of Stanley Brothers songbooks. Jeffrey Fox, editor of *The Clinch Mountain Express*, collected several of his interviews with Ralph into a booklet that was a valuable source. Mary Bruce Mazza loaned me her father Dr. Bruce Mongle's collection of Stanley Brothers memorabilia. Linda Shaw, managing editor of *Bluegrass Unlimited*, located articles that I requested to complete my research. Bill Jones of Norton, Virginia, sent photographs of radio station WNVA. The late Charles L. Perdue, professor at the University of Virginia, supplied background on the song "Man of Constant Sorrow," as did country music expert Richard K. Spottswood. Richard Rose, artistic director of the Barter Theatre in Abingdon, sent me the script of the play *Man of Constant Sorrow*, written by Dr. Douglas Pote. Scott Sanders, archivist at Antioch University, researched important campus appearances by the Osborne and Stanley Brothers in 1959 and 1960.

Moe Lytle, president of Gusto Records, allowed use of the King-Starday photograph files for this project; art director Chuck Young was able to find unpublished images. Photographer and musician John Cohen allowed me to include his photographs of the Stanley Brothers on stage. Roy Sykes Jr. loaned photos that had belonged to his father, bandleader Roy Sykes. Jordan Loupe got them from Virginia to New Hampshire. Hazel Lambert, widow of Darrell "Pee Wee" Lambert, lent me a photograph she took of the Stanley Brothers and Clinch Mountain Boys in 1947. Fannie Steele provided photos of the Stanley family from her personal collection.

Many others who knew Carter and Ralph shared recollections in interviews that are the heart of this book. Their names appear in these pages. I am deeply grateful. I would like to thank four women whose help was especially important to my understanding the lives of girls and women in southwest Virginia in the 1940s and 1950s: Exie Rose, June Suthers, Hazel Lambert, and the late Thelma Bruzdowski. Carter and Ralph's boyhood friend Carl Hammons helped me gain a similar understanding of the lives of boys coming of age on the ridges of Clinch Mountain.

At the University Press of Mississippi, assistant director/editor-in-chief Craig W. Gill's belief in the book has been instrumental in my completing it. Managing editor Anne Stascavage oversaw manuscript preparation. Copy editor Will Rigby contributed to style and accuracy—any lapses being the author's. Tyrone Nagai compiled the index. Senior production editor Shane Gong Stewart took the book through production. Art director John Langston and designer Peter Halverson designed its handsome cover and interior pages. Marketing director Steven B. Yates, publicist Clint Kimberling, and marketing assistant Courtney McCreary supported the result. Editorial assistant Katie Keene helped throughout.

Finally, I am grateful to my father, the late Dr. William E. Johnson, who enjoyed my writings about music, and my good friend Denise Stanley, who expressed her confidence from the beginning that I could write a book about the Stanley Brothers.

David W. Johnson
Stratham, New Hampshire
June 7, 2012

Lonesome Melodies

1. THE HILLS OF HOME

On a map, the far southwest corner of Virginia is shaped like a wedge. Driven into a mountainous region of the mid-Atlantic states, the wedge divides West Virginia to the north, Kentucky to the northwest, and Tennessee to the south and southwest. To the southeast, beneath four-fifths of Virginia (from the city of Bristol on the Tennessee border to the coast of the Atlantic Ocean) is North Carolina. This five-state region unites sections of the states that share common physical and cultural attributes, two of the most prominent being the presence of mountains and the pervasiveness of music. In the original sense of the term "country music"—music made by people in rural locales—this is the heartland.

Ignoring the political boundaries of the states are mountain ranges that form the region's topographic spine. The mountains stiffen the terrain of most of West Virginia, central and southwestern Virginia, western North Carolina, and trace the edge of eastern Tennessee. The ranges go by different names in different states. They are called the Blue Ridge Mountains in Virginia, the Cumberland Mountains in Tennessee, the Alleghenies in Pennsylvania, the Catskills in New York, the White Mountains in New Hampshire, and the Green Mountains in Vermont. Yet, as links in a geologic chain, they combine to form a single range that extends from central Alabama north through New England and into the Canadian provinces of New Brunswick, Newfoundland, and Quebec. Collectively, the mountains are the Appalachians.

By world and even North American standards, the Appalachians are not towering—the highest among them, Mount Mitchell in North Carolina, rises 6,684 feet—but they loom large in American history During the Revolution, Vermont's Green Mountain men fought for their state's independence. West Virginia became known as the Mountaineer State after the combative people who first settled it. The feud between

the Hatfield and McCoy families along the border of West Virginia and
Kentucky accounted for thirteen murders.

Today, in less belligerent times, the United States National Park Service
maintains a trail that runs from Mount Katahdin in Maine to Springer
Mountain in Georgia—a continuous footpath of 2,174 miles. Thousands
of hikers traverse the length of the Appalachian Trail as a measure of en-
durance or a spiritual quest—though such modern tests pale in comparison to the rigors that European settlers and their descendants faced.

Well before there was a Trail, the explorer Daniel Boone migrated with
his family from North Carolina to the Clinch River valley in Virginia. His
mission was to rendezvous with a prominent Virginian, Captain William
Russell, in Russell's settlement called Castle's Wood. From Castle's Wood,
Boone and Russell planned to lead a party of more than thirty men on an
expedition to settle the region that would become Kentucky.[1] Local legend maintains that in Virginia, in what was then named Wolf Hills and is
now the town of Abingdon, Boone descended into a cave to destroy the
wolves that had killed his dogs. For Boone and those who traveled with
him, there would be more serious threats on the frontier than wolves.

On October 9, 1773, Boone's eldest son James, Captain Russell's son
Henry, and five other members of a supply party rendezvousing with the
first Kentucky expedition had the bad luck of camping under the hostile
eyes of nineteen Native Americans. Belonging to three different tribes,
the Native Americans were on their way back from a meeting to discuss
the tribes' mutual concerns about the European settlers moving into the
region. "Seeing this as an opportunity to send a message of their opposi-
tion to settlement," wrote historian John Mack Faragher,[2] "at about dawn
the Indians fired down into the sleeping group." The bullets killed two
young brothers and wounded James Boone and Henry Russell, who were
tortured before being killed by blows to the head. The raiders captured
a slave, whom they killed with a hatchet forty miles from the site; and
bones believed to be those of a sixth victim were found twenty years later.

Since Daniel Boone and William Russell were well-known men, the
killings sparked an outbreak of Indian hating that claimed victims from
the Cherokee and Mingo tribes who were killed after being tricked
into visiting settlers. Other settler families decided to return to North
Carolina, but the Boones accepted an offer to live in a borrowed cabin on
the Clinch River in Castle's Wood (now Castlewood), about thirty miles
west of what is now Abingdon. Before choosing the ill-fated camp site,
young James Boone had followed the trail of his father's advance party to

where it crossed the Clinch River at Hunter's Ford, near the contemporary community of Dungannon.[3] About thirty miles north of where the raid took place is the near-vanished mountain community of McClure, a logging center during the late nineteenth and early twentieth centuries when logging and farming constituted the economic basis of the region.

The prominent people who passed through former frontier settlements such as Abingdon, Castlewood, Dungannon, and McClure, and the significant events that occurred in these places, testify to the fact that this isolated area once was a central path for settlers emigrating through the mountain frontier to what would become the midwestern and western territories of the United States. Rather than believing that they lived in a backward region that time had forgotten—a stereotypical view of Appalachia during the nineteenth and early twentieth centuries—residents in the mid-twentieth century were likely to believe they inhabited a region that had seen a great deal of history and been a gateway to the American West.

This may explain why two young brothers who were musicians stopped by the roadside in the late 1940s to have their picture taken as they stood behind a white wooden sign with black lettering that identified the location as the Cumberland Gap.[4] The older brother, Carter Glen Stanley, had been born on August 27, 1925, near the lumber camp of McClure, Virginia, and Ralph Edmond was born on the same small farm eighteen months later on February 25, 1927. The distance from McClure to the Cumberland Gap in Kentucky is about 100 miles.

By publishing the picture in their first booklet of song lyrics, the brothers invoked the symbolism of the Gap in relation to their own journey. The photo caption reads, "Stanley Bros. looking into three states at historic Cumberland Gap." They were documenting the fact that they stood near a famous departure point in American history and, though they had only an inkling of what was to come, were about to embark on a series of road trips, country recordings, adventures, and mishaps that would last twenty years and make an enduring contribution to the history of American music.

In considering the region that shaped Carter and Ralph's personalities and character, it is worth remembering that the Dickenson County where the brothers spent their boyhoods was only 150 years removed from the killing of the Boone party near the Clinch River—roughly the same passage of time that separates the writing of this book from the Civil War. Dickenson County's history as frontier would have been part of the region's consciousness in the 1920s and 1930s. Those with firsthand experience would have passed away, but grandparents of the Stanley brothers' generation would have known people who had fought battles with Native Americans, just as my grandfather told me stories about the Civil War that he had heard from his stepfather, who had been a drummer boy in the Union Army.

Settlers who followed in the footsteps of early explorers such as Daniel Boone would have migrated down the Great Valley of Virginia on a southwesterly diagonal from what is now Wytheville. Before reaching the rolling foothills and lowlands that allowed the cultivation of farms,[5] the migrants would have to find low points where they could cross the precipitous New River Gorge etched into the topography of what later became West Virginia.

The paths of rivers and streams created the most fertile soil while supporting farmers and livestock with necessary water. When population growth in the extreme southwest region of Virginia demanded it, the Virginia General Assembly in 1880 carved Dickenson County from portions of Russell, Wise, and Buchanan counties, naming it after delegate William J. Dickenson, who sponsored the resolution. The county's first settlements—Haysi, Holly Creek (now Clintwood), Nora, and Sandlick—each developed along a stream.[6] The Stanley family's farm was located near the Big Spraddle Branch stream that fed down Smith Ridge into the McClure River between McClure and Stratton about two miles northeast of Nora, where Carter and Ralph attended high school.

The opening in 1915 of a line of the Carolina, Clinchfield, and Ohio Railway into this region of abundant natural resources created the infrastructure for dramatic growth. Though mining and logging had taken place in the region, these industries remained small in scale, meeting the needs of the local population—until the arrival of the railroad. In anticipation of Dickenson County's development, lumber and mining companies purchased mineral rights in the late 1800s, and cashed in on these claims when the rails provided transportation to the markets to the east. Between 1910 and 1920 the county's population increased almost 50 percent as workers arrived to take jobs in lumber and coal mining companies. Mining towns such as Trammel, Clinchco, and Splashdam sprang up along the rail line, while McClure and Fremont developed as centers of the timber industry. Agriculture continued to play a central role in the region as farmers cultivated more than half the county's land until the mid-1930s.[7]

Though they appear not to have been aware of the specific history of either side of the family beyond two generations, Carter and Ralph grew up with a sense that they were descended from longtime inhabitants of the rugged hills they called home. "I don't know when or why my people came here," Ralph recalled.[8] "Don't know why they decided to stay. All I know for sure is we've been in these mountains as long as anybody can remember." Had they been interested, he and Carter could have traced the Stanley roots deep into the Virginia soil. Their paternal ancestor William Standley was born around 1720 and lived in Orange County, Virginia.[9] The family name had emerged from Anglo-Saxon people living on the lands of Stoneley in the Cumberland region of northwest England in the early eleventh century.[10] Derived from an Old English word meaning a stony clearing or field, the name and its variations served to identify people who lived near such a place. The name was unusually suited to a family who chose to settle in mountainous, rocky Appalachia.

More than 700 years removed from the original name bearers, the ninth child of William Standley was Joseph (or Josses) Standley, born around 1762. Only the first name of his first wife, Judith, survives; his second wife may have been Sarah Hatcher. He lived in Franklin County. His fifth child and fourth son, George, was born around 1793, dropped the *d*, and settled in a part of Russell County that later became Wise County.

George Stanley married Winifred (Winney) Roberts around 1816 in Russell County. The county's 1850 census lists 57-year-old George as a farmer, with his father Joseph (whose age now was given as 93 rather than 88)[11] living with him and his wife at what later became Stanley Gap near Georges Fork. The fork is believed to have been named for an earlier George Stanley, a long hunter who settled in the area.[12] Long hunters took trips lasting months, skinning hides from animals such as bear and elk while surviving on the abundance of animals and fish found in what then was the wilderness. Some would return with their families to homestead in the most suitable locations they had discovered in their travels.

James, the third child of George and Winney Roberts Stanley, served in the Confederate army during the Civil War.[13] He was a private in Company C of the 48th Virginia Infantry, enlisting on May 1, 1861, at age 37.[14] A blurry photo of James's wife, Rebecca Beverly, appears in the shared Crabtree-Stanley genealogy. She is a solemn, dark-haired woman. The couple returned to Russell County, living near George and Winney. Their seventh child, Nathan, was born around 1863 in what had become Wise County. A smiling Nathan, dressed in coat and tie, and a kindly-looking Stacy Stanley are the first couple of this family line whose photograph appears in the genealogy. They were married on August 26, 1881,—forty-four years almost to the day before the birth of grandchild Carter. Their fourth of seven children, born on May 15, 1888, was Fitzhugh Lee Stanley, the father of Carter and Ralph.

Though portrayed—even in their own words and those of their kin— as rustics who somehow tumbled from the Appalachians into the music business,[15] Carter and Ralph Stanley were the progeny of two established families. Their recent ancestors included veterans who had served on both sides of the Civil War. From their expressions and attire, paternal grandparents Nathan and Stacy appear to have been respectable farmers. On the maternal side, Lucy Smith Stanley's parents, Noah and Louisa McCoy Smith, tended to their farm on Smith Ridge and raised eleven children. Several were (or married) farmers and coal miners, one served in the United States army in the Philippine Islands, and another was a police officer.[16]

The Stanley parents both were descendants of the stoic, self-sufficient Scotch-Irish who settled much of the Appalachian region, carving farms out of an impossible landscape of vertical terrain and rocky soil. They raised their own crops, bred their own livestock, went on Sunday to churches they had built, and made their own entertainment by singing traditional songs and playing musical instruments like the banjo and fiddle.

The marriage of Lee Stanley and Lucy Jane Smith Rakes was the second for each. They had eight children from their first marriages who became half brothers and sisters to Carter and Ralph. Lucy had been married to Watson Rakes. When Watson died, she was left to support their young daughter, Ruby. Lucy "did a little bit of everything to make ends meet as a single mother, including nursing," recalled Doris Stanley Bradley, the older of Carter's two daughters.[17] Carter and Ralph's half sister Ruby Rakes (Eubanks) came to play an important role in the boys' lives. "We took care of the kids," Ruby recalled.[18] "Ralph was the one I looked after and my stepsister Georgia took care of Carter." She described young Ralph as "mischievous."

Lee Stanley's first marriage had been to Lottie Ellen McCoy Vance, whose husband had died in a logging accident.[19] When Lottie became gravely ill, Lee looked for a nurse to care for her. He and his wife had seven children and needed full-time help. Having heard through friends and neighbors that Lucy Rakes was the best nurse available, he arranged for her to live in his home to provide Lottie with around-the-clock care. Despite Lucy's constant attention, Lottie died on March 14, 1924. Soon afterward, Lee and Lucy became husband and wife. Lucy gave birth to Carter the following August when she was near 40. When Carter and Ralph were young boys, she and Lee purchased the Smith family home on Smith Ridge when it was put up for auction after the murder-suicide of its owners, Lucy's brother Emery Smith and his wife Lena.

Lee and Lucy Smith Stanley encouraged their children to participate in music from childhood. Though he did not play a musical instrument, Lee liked to sing in church with his brother Jim Henry Stanley, who was a preacher, as well as sing in the home. "[Jim Henry] worked for Dad . . . used to drive a team of horses for him in the woods logging," Ralph recalled. "And he would come home with Dad now and then and they would set up late at night and sing a lot of the old songs."[20] Songs that the brothers learned all or in part from their father included "Man of Constant Sorrow" and "Pretty Polly," and remained in their repertoire from their earliest years through Ralph's solo career into the twenty-first century. "He couldn't play a thing as far as an instrument, but his voice was just the same as ours," said Ralph.[21]

Prompted by his mother, Ralph recalls lining out a hymn in church as early as age five.[22] The term "lining out" means that the preacher or person leading the singing would recite the words in a rapid sing-song fashion so that the congregation would be reminded of the words and be able to put them to the melody of the hymn. In a 2002 interview on the National Public Radio program *Fresh Air*, Ralph described the experience to host Terry Gross:[23]

> *[The church] was a little old white building and had home-made benches in it. And, of course, it had a stand for the preacher to preach. And way back in the early days I've been told . . . [that] I lined some songs sometimes, and I got that from the preacher. And I've heard the reason the preacher lined it, they didn't have the money maybe to print a songbook for each singer, so he would line that song, and then all the congregation would hear the words and sing.*

In 1993 he told the *Washington Post*, "I remember singing those hymns around the house to myself when I was only 5 or so."[24]

In a separate interview, Ralph explained that "the churches I was raised up in don't use music"—meaning instruments. "They do all their singing without any music. I guess the type singing I do comes from the old churches, maybe modernized a little. It's still got some of the old-time sound to it." A sound that particularly impressed him was the moment when the women's voices would enter a hymn. "They all sang . . . the same part. Everybody actually sung lead, but there usually would be three or four men and three or four women, and the women would come in higher, just an octave higher or something, and they really blended well."[25] A vocal effect similar to Ralph's description of the women's voices can be heard in his falsetto singing on several sacred songs recorded by the Stanley Brothers, such as "A Voice from on High."

The influence of church music was a repeated theme in the Stanley brothers' early publicity. "At about the age of ten, [Carter] became interested in old-time music," reported the brothers' first souvenir song book. "Being reared in a Christian home, his love for sacred songs grew; and, today, Carter will say the old hymns are the most beautiful of all."[26] A later song book stated that "The boys are Baptist by religious training, and they know and sing many of the old religious tunes they learned at their mother's knee and at the country tent meetings."[27]

Around the time Ralph was learning to sing hymns, his mother was teaching him to play the banjo. Ralph remembered learning his first tune, an instrumental melody, when he was 11. "My mother tuned the banjo the first time I ever had one in my hand and she played this tune," Ralph recalled, "and I think first time I ever tried it, I could play it a little bit."[28] The name of the tune was "Shout Little Lulie"—a fast-paced Appalachian breakdown suitable for dancing. North Carolina banjo player Samantha Bumgarner called a dance over it when she recorded the tune as "Shout Lou" for Columbia Records on April 23, 1924, in New York City.[29] In 1928 she appeared at the inaugural Mountain Dance and Folk Festival in Asheville, North Carolina; her playing at the 1936 festival inspired 16-year-old Peter Seeger to take up the five-string, extending her legacy into the folk revival of the 1950s and 1960s.[30]

Around 1939 Carter ordered his first guitar from the mail-order house Montgomery Ward. Mailman Woodrow Owens not only delivered the guitar in a long box wrapped in brown paper, but tightened the strings to the correct tuning and taught Carter the rudiments of playing his new instrument. Small in stature but nicknamed Toughy "because he would get drunk and get into fights," according to the brothers' friend Carl Hammons, Owens would play the harmonica on his mail route when he had been drinking. "You could hear him coming from a long way away," said Hammons.

Ralph already had been given an inexpensive banjo, but only after making a choice between the instrument and an animal:

[M]y aunt lived about a mile from where we did, and she raised some hogs. And they called the mother a sow, a hog, and she had some pigs. Well, the pigs was real pretty and I was going to high school and I was taking agriculture in school. And I sort of got a notion that I'd like to do that, raise some hogs. And so my aunt had this old banjo, and my mother said, "Which do you want, the pig or the banjo? And each one of 'em's five dollars each." I said, "I'll just take the banjo."[31]

Soon after Carter's guitar arrived, Ralph wanted a mail-order banjo, which his uncle Dewey Baker ordered from the Spiegel catalogue. Ralph paid back his uncle for the hundred-dollar instrument in monthly five-dollar installments.[32]

The brothers began to practice together and with friends. Schoolmates in Dickenson County became their first audience outside the family. Jim Owens, whose grandmother was a cousin of Lucy Stanley, recalled the brothers playing on stage at Ervinton High School.[33] When I asked Ralph about early performances, he was typically understated. "I hadn't done any performing except little social gatherings like high school plays and stuff like that," he said. "There were different settings in the plays, when they'd change the stage and pull the curtains. I would keep them satisfied when they would do that. I was 15 or 16 and playing a little bit."[34] Asked if he had planned on music being his career, he responded, "I was hoping it would, but I didn't know what would happen. I was young and green and didn't know anything, really."

Ralph's reticence suggested that there would be more to the story. Working at the University of Virginia's College at Wise, one town over from where Ralph lived, I was in a good position to locate others who had attended Carter and Ralph's earliest performances. A colleague from Berea College in Kentucky said that her mother had attended high school with the Stanley boys. "She said they were always singing at events at school but no one would have dreamed of their success," Diana Taylor recalled. "Mom said she actually thought Carter may have been the more talented one."

When I called her, Trulah Counts Taylor wanted to make clear was that her high school days were "a long time ago." A resident of Haysi, Virginia, not far from where the Stanley boys grew up, Mrs. Taylor graduated with Carter from Ervinton High School in 1943. Up until 1945—the year that Ralph graduated—high school in southwestern Virginia ended after the eleventh grade. "I was very young back then," Trulah Taylor said.[35] "When we graduated I wasn't quite 16. Carter was very nice looking. Carter seemed to get along with people very well. Of course, we would have little programs in the gymnasium like all schools have or used to have. They would just happen to be on the program. Carter and Ralph would play music. There might be telling stories . . . dancing. We enjoyed that we got out of class. Their type of music was the type of music I was used to. My husband and brothers all played bluegrass music. Ralph was not as outgoing. He was much shyer. Carter was good looking. He just had a wonderful personality." I asked what sort of songs they played. "Of the type that Ralph does today," she said. "Of course, Carter was the lead singer. He did most of the singing."

By all accounts—including his own—Ralph was quiet other than when he played the banjo. "He was just a little old standoffish boy, playing his music," said a cousin. "He didn't have the personality Carter had. Carter was more outgoing."[36] Ralph may not have been as extroverted as his older brother, but he made loyal friends. One of them, Alice Nunley, was in the same class as Ralph from seventh grade until their junior year in high school, when her family moved. "I always got him in trouble for talking," she recalled.[37] "It was always me doing the talking, not him. He didn't talk much. The teacher would punish us by making us each write 500 times, 'I will not talk in school.' I'd write mine and then I'd write his, too. Since we wrote so much alike, she couldn't tell the difference." Ralph added that Alice covered for him when he was absent. "I was kind of bad for missing school," he said. "But if I missed a day, when I came back, I'd find all my lessons in order and turned in just like I was there. She's the one that got me through." Carter lacked such a helpful classmate. "He was on his own," said Ralph. "If he didn't do his own lessons, they just didn't get done."

The brothers had considerable opportunities at home, in church, and in school to develop their musical talents before they "come out of the hollers." As in most of Appalachia, electricity and radio arrived late on Smith Ridge (some houses on neighboring Bad Ridge did not have running hot water until 2004), but in time to influence the young brothers' musical tastes. "I know we was about the first family in that area that ever had a radio and a lot of people would gather around on Saturday night to listen to the *Grand Ole Opry*," Ralph recalled, adding that radio gave the brothers their start as performers. "We would get those kindling sticks . . . like we had a fiddle or guitar or something, and we'd play on them sticks with the music we heard on the radio like we had instruments and the neighbors that come in, they enjoyed it."[38] The presence of an audience did not bother the congenial Carter, but at first Ralph would insist that the brothers remove themselves to the kitchen. "I was too bashful to play before them."[39]

Their rapid progress as musicians was evident when Carter and Ralph began to give local performances outside of school, making their radio debut as teenagers. When asked if he remembered the first song he learned, Ralph responded: "I can tell you the first song I sung on the radio: 'I Called and Nobody Answered.' I heard Roy Acuff do that. I heard him on the radio on the *Grand Ole Opry*. This [radio debut] was in Bluefield, West Virginia. We were young. That was with my brother. We were both teenagers. I don't remember where I learned that from Acuff or not. I know I heard him sing it. I believe I heard it before him, but I don't remember where."[40] Acuff built his reputation as "the King of Country Music" by frequent touring and regular appearances on the *Opry*. He recorded "I Called and Nobody Answered" in Chicago on April 30, 1941.[41] The Stanley Brothers' rendition was broadcast on Bluefield radio station WHIS.

The teenaged Stanley Brothers performed more than once on the radio. In an interview, Ralph said that he and Carter had made their radio debut on the Saturday morning program *Barrel of Fun* on WJHL in Tennessee.[42] "It was at the Bonnie Kate Theatre in Elizabethton and Speedy Clark was on the show," Ralph said. "I was absolutely scared to death." Three years older than Carter, Manuel "Speedy" Clark began his professional career in 1938 as a performer in Doc Hauer's Medicine Show—the same troupe that had given Roy Acuff his start.[43] Clark played banjo and danced the buck and wing. *Barrel of Fun* had been a popular radio program since the 1930s; it was no wonder that Carter and Ralph were intimidated. Ralph recalled performing another Acuff song "When I Lay My Burden Down," which Acuff had recorded on April 11, 1940. On this one, it was Carter who was nervous.[44] "He always liked to cut up a little bit . . . and holler maybe during a song. And I know the first time that we played on the radio, why he tried to holler and it wouldn't come out. He was scared so bad it wouldn't come out."

From the songs they chose to sing on radio, it is apparent that Acuff
was an early influence on the Stanley boys—a fact that Carter would acknowledge in an interview many years later.[45] Both of the "debuts" are
early expressions of the brothers' professional ambitions that sometimes
were downplayed in later recollections. "We had hopes, you know," Ralph
would say. ". . . We'd listen to the *Grand Ole Opry* stars and we'd listen
to the people on the radio and we would just think in our mind how we
would like to be people like that."[46]

Their first public appearance outside of radio and Ervinton High
School took place at a Republican Party gathering in the Greenwood,
Virginia, elementary school. Ralph remembered that "county officials,
they come by and got us, and I think we rode in the back of a pickup truck
and went to this school where they had their meeting that night . . . and
played and they brought us back home. Just the two of us."[47]

Like many families in the region, the Stanley family made its living
through a combination of working the land and logging. In later years,
Ralph often was asked about his childhood. His responses varied, and accounting for the differences might have been ambivalence about how to
represent the circumstances of a boyhood that changed dramatically because of a single event.

In a 1975 article in the folk music magazine *Sing Out!*, Ralph recalled
his boyhood activities while working on an expansion of his festival
grounds in McClure. "[We would] Walk down the hill there to school,
about two mile each way. We had plenty of chores to do around here. We
sort of made our living farming. Raise a garden—hay, corn . . . we usually
had a busy schedule. Of course in the wintertime we had our milking to
do, usually kept three or four horses, chickens, gather eggs, cut kindling,
carry coal, we just about had a full-time job."[48]

Ralph gave a different response when *Fresh Air* host Terry Gross asked
him how his family had made a living. "My father was a logger," he said.
"He cut timber and hauled it out of the woods and had a saw mill. He
sawed it into lumber."[49] In one of her typically disarming questions, Gross
asked him if his father had lost any fingers in accidents. "No. He never did
any of that kind of work," said Ralph. "He was the boss, so he hired men

to do all of that." So he must have made a decent living? "He did. We were maybe just a little bit ahead of maybe some of the neighbors and the folks. He did well with it."

When Jeffrey Fox, editor of Ralph's fan club newsletter, the *Clinch Mountain Express*, asked Ralph about his father's occupation, his answer was more detailed: "Our dad would take the saw mill and move it to the boundary [of a logging operation]. He bought boundary timber all over and had a crew working for him. Where the timber was, there he'd set up his saw mill. He sawed his lumber and hauled out the logs with a team of horses. He'd take them to the mill that way. If they wanted logs, he'd give them whole logs. If they wanted them sawed, he'd saw 'em. Then they'd load 'em on trucks and take 'em to market."[50] Log-laden trucks are a common sight on the steep, narrow highways of southwestern Virginia.

The impression left with most interviewers was that life on the Stanley farm was hard, but not oppressive. Putting the boys' circumstances in a harsher light was Benny Steele, a relative who paid occasional visits to Lee Stanley's roadside store on Smith Ridge and once asked Lee for a job cutting lumber. He recalled knowing Carter and Ralph "ever since they's little bare-footed boys."[51] As the boys grew older, he noticed them working on both the farm and at the saw mill. The latter particularly struck him. "Carter, them big logs, he'd get down there under them and roll them up for his brother to saw in the skidway there, and Ralph, he was out there taking lumber from the big saw, him and brother Doc. . . . Big Lee, their daddy, was standing there. He said, 'Boys, get to moving them slabs out of there.' He never let them stand. They had to keep on the go. And I sat there on the rock . . . and shook my head in shame that them boys had to do a hard work like that and was good as music players as they was."

Ambivalence about the early days also may have stemmed from the private nature of the man being interviewed. Soft-spoken, with clear blue eyes and a well-combed mane of white hair, Ralph in an interview situation did not give away much of what he might be thinking or feeling. On occasion, an interviewer would have a difficult time determining if Ralph had misheard a question (as in his response to my asking him about the first song he learned) or shaped an answer in the way that he thought the questioner might want to hear. For example, in the *Sing Out!* interview, musician and filmmaker John Cohen asked Ralph, "When you and Carter started, where were the first places you played?"[52] Cohen's question was straightforward, yet instead of mentioning their performances in school, on radio, or even their first professional job, Ralph answered in a way that framed his and Carter's status as rural amateurs rather than aspiring professionals.

"We done our rehearsing and learning round in the barn, out in the corn field, in the shade of the apple tree," he said. "Then we'd go out to a friend's house and play a little while, maybe they'd come into our living room and listen to us play." Perhaps the answer was influenced by the locus of the conversation near the old Stanley family home. Ralph's half-brother Lance Stanley, who was helping him work on the festival site, completed this rustic picture. "The old house used to sit out yonder, and him and Carter would sit on the porch of an evening, after we'd worked to the day. They'd play their guitar and banjo when we were boys goin' to school. Ralph was a little white-headed boy, wasn't over 8 or 10 years old."

In the *Fresh Air* interview, Ralph responded to the same question about first performances by mentioning the school appearances. "You know, they have these senior plays at the high school where we went, and they would have one scene and they have to pull the curtains and change the scenes around. Well, a lot of times we would go out in front of the curtains and pick and sing for the people until they got ready to go—got the stage ready for the next part." There was no mention of the brothers' radio appearances in Bluefield, West Virginia, or Elizabethton, Tennessee.

Though varying in the details, Ralph's descriptions of a childhood in the mountains were less stark than those of writers seeking to describe the conditions of his and Carter's early lives. That did not prevent writers from expressing themselves with considerable certainty. In an interview with the *Washington Post*, Robert Cantwell, author of *Bluegrass Breakdown: The Making of the Old Southern Sound*, told freelance writer Eddie Dean (later the co-author of Ralph's autobiography) that "The fact of the matter is that, growing up, Carter and Ralph had a wretched life and they were deeply poor."[53] Dean offered his own explanation of the Stanley brothers' career choice: "During the Depression, when the Stanleys were growing up in a place called Big Spraddle Creek, music offered a chance to escape a life sentence of hard labor."

As with accounts of the Stanleys' sudden emergence as polished musicians after World War II, the image of the brothers enduring abject poverty in their youth appears to be as much mythology as history. If true, the image would seem to include them in Walker Evans's Depression-era photographs of Appalachia that captured sad-eyed, barefoot families sitting on the porches of ramshackle cabins. Those disturbing images were real enough, yet the day-to-day lifestyle of the Stanley family would not be found in Evans's pictures. For almost two-thirds of their boyhoods, Carter and Ralph grew up on a family farm, doing chores, and attending school. Their impoverishment began with a domestic disturbance that shattered the household. Years later Ralph Stanley would title a banjo number "Hard Times." The title referred to financially lean times he and Carter experienced as musicians, yet could have applied as well to life on the Stanley farm after 1939.

2. MANY DAYS OF MY CHILDHOOD

The event that ended the relative normalcy of the "many days of my child-hood" that Carter later would idealize in song was Lee Stanley's leaving the family when Carter was 13 or 14 and Ralph was 12. Lee and Lucy had been married for fifteen years. Lucy was 53. She and the two boys never got over the fact that Lee abandoned them to be with a younger wom-an—a red-haired witch, in the opinion of Carter's older daughter, Doris.[1] Lee's departure was both an emotional and financial blow. "The boys nor their beloved mother ever recovered from his desertion of the family and struggled constantly to keep the wolf from their door," Doris wrote. Lee's decision to leave and start a new family created a permanent void in his sons' lives, especially Carter's. A family member confided, "I don't think he ever got over his parents' divorce. He told [his wife] that he had to be-come the man of the house. I think it tore him up inside."[2]

In an interview published in the Ralph Stanley fan club newsletter, boyhood friend Carl Hammons recalled that after the divorce, Carter continued to be more under his father's influence than Ralph did.[3] Ralph seemed to agree. When the newsletter editor asked Ralph if he had helped his father at the saw mill, Ralph replied: "I worked a few days for him. . . . I'd take a wheelbarrow and roll the sawdust out of that hole where the saw blade ran. It was hard work. Carter did more than I did for Daddy."

Carl was in the same high school class as Ralph, but became Carter's best friend. In the newsletter, Carl summed up his friendship with Carter in a few sentences: "Me and Carter was wild. Ralph wasn't. We didn't hurt nobody but ourselves. We walked to school in thirty minutes. Me and Carter would go out at recess to smoke and pitch pennies with the other guys. We'd always win at penny flipping. Carter would rub his head or give me some signal so I'd know if it was heads or tails. You could take three or four pennies to the store and get a pocketful of candy."

Candy was not all the boys consumed. A tall, angular man who became a regular at Ralph's festivals, Carl chuckled when I asked him what "wild" meant: "We smoked cigarettes. People didn't like it when kids smoked. We drank alcohol and got drunk. Dad made moonshine. A lot of people did. In the 1930s it was tough to make a living."[4]

During the day, Ballard Hammons was a mail carrier, delivering it on horseback as Woodrow Owens had done before him. He picked up the mail in Stratton, and his morning route took him along Smith Ridge and neighboring Ramsey's Ridge. "It was a seven mile circle," Carl recalled. "Then he would go home to Flat Top and change horses and have lunch. He would deliver the mail to Tom's Creek, which [was] about a seven or eight mile circle. He was paid a dollar a day."

Carl began drinking as early as age 10 or 11. If Carter had not tasted moonshine before meeting Carl, he did after they met. Moonshine was a staple of the local economy. When their father left, Carter and Ralph contributed to the family income by delivering moonshine for their uncle Dewey Baker. Ralph recalled, "We'd walk along the Clinchfield railroad tracks a ways, and then cross over the creek to an old house where we delivered the whiskey. We'd bring it in gallon jugs and they'd sell it in pint bottles."[5]

Carl's recollections touched on a cornerstone of the Appalachian economy: barter. "We were always tradin' something: eggs for candy, squirrel dogs, pocket knives, rabbit dogs," said Carl. "We'd grow corn and hoe it by hand. We all hoed corn. We'd take it to the mill—one or two bushels and trade it for flour, then it wouldn't cost us any money for groceries." To which Ralph added, "I peddled a few things, too"—a reference to one of his most consistent traits.[6] Throughout his life, Ralph has liked to raise and trade horses. When Ralph bought a horse for several hundred dollars, he paid for it in twenty-dollar bills taken from a wad of twenties that he carried in his pocket. A relative who accompanied Ralph was curious why he would carry so many twenties. I suggested that the source of the cash was the CDs Ralph sold at festivals and performances for twenty dollars—five dollars higher than the going rate. As one musician said to me, "Only Ralph gets twenty."

In their teenage years, learning the music business was preferable in the eyes of the Stanley boys to working with Lee at the saw mill or finding a job in the mines. Recalling one of his early band mates, Ralph noted that he "was of the same mind as me and Carter about the mines, he didn't want to spend his life down in those dark holes."[7]

Throughout his youth, Lucy was Ralph's primary influence; and Carter appeared to take after his father. Illustrating these parent-child relationships is an undated photo published in the Crabtree and Stanley families' shared genealogy that shows Lucy and Lee Stanley flanked by their two children, who appear to be from around 12 to their early teens.[8] Ralph stands next to his diminutive mother, perhaps an inch or two taller, with the blond hair that his half-brother Vance described. Standing next to his father, long-legged Carter wears a fedora that brings him almost to Lee's height. Though the photo shows shared family features, what is most striking is how much Ralph appears to be his mother's son and Carter his father's. The paired-off arrangement of parents and children provides visual evidence of the connection that Carter lost when Lee abandoned the family for Della Meade Moore of Pound, Virginia (whom he later married)— and the degree to which Ralph's close relationship with his mother may have sustained him through the split—and vice versa. "I knew I had to help my mother because she didn't have nobody else," Ralph recalled.[9] "So while Carter'd be out fighting chickens, I'd be back home feeding chickens with my mother. We'd milk the cows and churn the butter, and I'd help her hoe out the garden, put in the crops, and bring in the harvest." In Ralph's opinion, Lee "left my mother high and dry on Smith Ridge, without a penny of help."[10]

Fred Stanley was born to Lee and Della in 1957. Fred recalled Lee as "a well-respected person in the community. A lot of people in southwest Virginia knew him."[11] By the late 1940s Lee's involvement in lumber included saw mills and a lumber supply business in Coeburn. In the early 1950s he was one of three men who started the public water system in Castlewood. Of medium build and 5' 11" in height, Lee was "a very businesslike person," Fred recalled, "certainly caring for his family. His word was his bond, as he used to say." He brought sons Lansing and Edward into the lumber business.

Lee and Della would take time away from home to book Carter and Ralph into schools and theaters, sometimes taking Fred with them. On the road, Lee was the brothers' "spokesperson." Fred recalled Carter and Ralph "coming to the house several times, and sometimes they would bring some of members of the band. My dad always liked to hear them come into the living room and play." Lee suffered from asthma. Della "took very good care of him until the final day that he died."

As much as the dissolution of the family might shape the future relationships of Carter and Ralph, the fourteen years that the family lived together on Smith Ridge provided the crucible for the brothers' music. Lucy's banjo playing and Lee's ballad singing melded with the hymns learned in church. In one corner of the living room stood a Victrola with "a pile of records" on its bottom shelf.[12] Though hand-cranked and a bit scratchy-sounding, these cabinet-sized consoles produced by Victor did not require electricity and put forth full, lifelike sound. It was almost as if the listener were in the same room with the musicians. Among the 78-rpm discs that Carter and Ralph "wore . . . out" were recordings by the duo Grayson and Whitter, the Carter Family, and Fiddlin' Cowan Powers and Family—all of whom came from within a hundred miles of Smith Ridge.[13] In 1936, Lee brought home a battery-powered Philco radio that Ralph recalled vividly: "It was one of those big console models with wooden legs, like a nice piece of furniture, one of the first radios ever seen in our neighborhood. . . . There weren't many radio stations we could pick up, as far back as we were in the mountains. But the ones we did came in loud and clear, and it was all country music."[14] Among the stations were WHIS in Bluefield, West Virginia; WSM in Nashville, the home of the *Grand Ole Opry*; and the 500,000-watt XERA in Villa Acuña, Mexico, across the border from Del Rio, Texas. Soon Carter and Ralph were exposed to the songs and styles of old-time country performers such as Molly O'Day, Cousin Emmy and her Kin Folk, Roy Acuff, Charlie and Bill Monroe, and Mainer's Mountaineers. "Country music was like a great big family back in them days," Ralph recalled. "The groups were mostly kin to each other, they grew up playing together, and the closeness came through in the music, especially in the singing. . . . This was important for Carter and me, because we were brothers singing together, just like Charlie and Bill and all the rest. It gave us hopes maybe we could make it big someday, too."[15]

Asked about professional musical activity in the area when he and Carter were growing up, Ralph said: "They've not been too many musicians right in this particular part of the country. On over the hill, in Kentucky, there are more than around here."[16] Still, both brothers remembered hearing the music of the southwestern Virginia string band Fiddlin' Cowan Powers and Family, which recorded instrumental tunes with dance calls from 1924 to 1927.[17] In the twilight of his career, James Cowan Powers would work with the Stanley Brothers.

Carter recalled listening to a duo near McClure known as Doc and Carl, the Virginia Boys. "There was two boys who worked at the saw mill some for my dad," he recalled.[18] "Doc Addington was Maybelle Carter's brother, and Carl McConnell was a barber in Gate City, Virginia." Doc was a guitar player and Carl played banjo. There are no recordings of the duo, but it is worth noting that Doc and Carl played the same two instruments as the Stanley Brothers.

With the purchases of the guitar and banjo, Carter and Ralph could put their hands on playable instruments anytime they wanted. They wasted no time in realizing the childhood fantasies that they had mimed with kindling sticks. Their enthusiasm was a mixed blessing for the adults in the Stanley household. "We used to play at home a lot, on Sunday, and of a night before we'd go to bed," Ralph recalled.[19] "And our daddy, he usually had business to take care of. He worked men in his job, and he was a little nervous and he'd usually run us out of the house. Couldn't stand that noise. We'd go to the woodshed or the woods or the barn or wherever and practice. We'd go anywhere we could get to play and sing a little. Carter got a guitar before I did the banjo, and immediately after we got them, I'd say we was trying to sing some together. I always sang tenor." Alice Nunley's brother Richard and schoolmate Jewel Martin sometimes joined them on fiddle and mandolin. "We just played wherever we could, under apple trees, whatever. No pay. Just a apple or two. When they'd fall off."

After the Virginia Boys left McClure to play on the radio in Louisville, Kentucky, a number of amateur musicians remained in Dickenson County, particularly banjo players. "Most of the music around here was just the five-string banjo," Ralph recalled, "maybe a fiddle here and there. About all they used it for was to play for old-time dances. It had faded out some when I was growing up. Wasn't too many dances at that time." But like the singer of the song "O Susanna," Lucy Smith Stanley often had the instrument on her knee. "Mother had an old banjo," recalled Ralph. "Just a few of the neighbors had something. My mother's people all played music. She had eleven brothers and sisters, and they all played the five-string banjo."[20]

The song Ralph Stanley is most closely identified with, "Man of Constant Sorrow," has the old-time sound. "The first time I heard the 'Man of Constant Sorrow,' my father, he knew one verse of it," recalled Ralph.[21] "I don't know where he got it, but he sung it. And Carter and me got together and put some words on it, enough to start singing it, make a song out of it." He described it as "another song that's probably a couple hundred years old."[22] The other song he recalled learning all or in part from his father that he later recorded was "Little Bessie." From sitting on the steps as his mother played clawhammer-style banjo, Ralph remembered learning "Little Birdie" and "Pretty Polly."[23]

Before leaving the subject of what Ralph called "the old ones,"[24] it would be useful to consider the origin of "Man of Constant Sorrow" and how it entered the Stanley Brothers' repertoire. According to a leading historian of old-time country music, the late Charles Wolfe, a blind Kentucky musician named Dick Burnett performed a version of "Man of Constant Sorrow" under the title "Farewell Song" around 1912.[25] In 1913, Burnett collected his best-known songs in a small book of lyrics that he arranged to have printed in Danville, Kentucky. Burnett's transcription of the lyric referred directly to his blindness. According to Wolfe, the melody of "Farewell Song" was based on an old Baptist hymn called "Wandering Boy," and the lyrics were almost identical to those recorded by the Stanley Brothers in 1951. Wolfe interviewed Burnett in 1973 and 1974.[26]

The question arises: How did a song performed by a blind man in Kentucky make its way into the repertoire of two aspiring musicians in Virginia? The answer to the question provides a roadmap of the three paths along which songs could travel in the 1920s and 1930s. First, songs could move with the singers who sang them. Burnett and his partner, fiddle player Leonard Rutherford, traveled throughout the South. "There isn't a town this side of Nashville, from Cincinnati to Chattanooga, that's any size, what we have been in," Burnett told Wolfe.[27] Their travels took them to the mining camps of eastern Kentucky and southwestern Virginia—the heart of Stanley country.

Second, songs could travel from musician to musician through the medium of phonograph records. Though Burnett and Rutherford recorded at least twenty-four songs together between 1926 and 1930, they did not record "Farewell Song"—or if they did, the recording does not survive.[28] However, one of Dick Burnett's neighbors in south central Kentucky was Emry Arthur, whose family was well-known in the region for its singing. According to Wolfe, Burnett "routinely exchanged songs with the Arthurs" and taught Emry "Man of Constant Sorrow," which he recorded in 1928 and again in 1931.[29] Once again, the lyrics were the same as those later recorded by the Stanley Brothers, with minor variations. Lee Stanley may have known only a verse of the song, as Ralph recollected, yet when the brothers "put some words on it" in the 1930s or 1940s, they managed to arrive at nearly the exact words that had existed as far back as 1912.

In his notes to the Emry Arthur compilation CD *Man of Constant Sorrow, Volume One*, Charles Wolfe identified the hymn "The White Rose" and a version of "Down in the Tennessee Valley" as sources for

"Man of Constant Sorrow." Wolfe's reference to different sources in the book and CD notes illustrate the difficulty that even the most knowledgeable of music historians might encounter trying to trace a song as it transformed through what folklorists call "the folk process." Wolfe did not include in his discussion of "Man of Constant Sorrow" the potential economic benefit of owning the copyright to the song. It appeared that neither Dick Burnett nor Emry Arthur copyrighted it, which made it available for Carter Stanley to copyright as his own work in 1951. Some fifty years later, with the song's inclusion in the popular film *O Brother, Where Are Thou?*, the value of the Stanley Brothers' 1959 arrangement of the song to the children of Carter Stanley was approximately $500,000 in a one-time buyout by the music publisher peermusic (formerly Peer Music). When the brothers recorded the song in 1951, Ralph sang solo; and of all the Stanley Brothers' songs, "Man of Constant Sorrow" is the one most closely identified with him rather than Carter, becoming the title of Ralph's autobiography in 2009.

The third route by which "Man of Constant Sorrow" could have reached the Stanley Brothers was radio. The relatively new medium does not appear to have played a part in the process, yet this does not mean that the songs heard on their father's radio, acquired in 1936, had an unimportant role in the continuing education of Carter and Ralph as musicians. "We heard the *Grand Ole Opry* some, and there was a station opening up in Norton and one coming up in Bristol, and we come to think we could make a career out of playing," said Ralph. "We knew we didn't want farm work and we darn sure didn't want the mines."[30] As was the case with Roy Acuff on the *Opry*, radio was the way they first heard the music of another significant influence, North Carolina banjo player and singer Wade Mainer, co-leader with his brother J. E. of the popular recording group Mainer's Mountaineers. J. E. and Wade had an early-morning radio show originating from Asheville, North Carolina, that the Stanley boys listened to as they prepared to do their farm chores.[31]

In background and relationship, J. E. and Wade were much like the Stanley brothers, only a generation earlier. They were born in mountainous Buncombe County, North Carolina, near Asheville—J. E. in 1898 and Wade in 1907. In both duos, the older brother seems to have had his choice of instrument (J. E. chose fiddle and Carter Stanley guitar) while the younger brother learned the banjo. J. E. and Wade Mainer co-led the band for several years, becoming an influential act. According to country music historian Ivan M. Tribe, "Their radio programs, sponsored by Crazy Water Crystals, made them a household name throughout the Carolina Piedmont, and their Bluebird disc of 'Maple on The Hill,' cut [without J. E.] in August 1935, spread their fame even wider."[32] The Mainer brothers became important figures in the transition from the Appalachian string band sound (fiddle, guitar, mandolin, and banjo playing as an instrumental ensemble) to the sound of bluegrass (similar instrumentation, but increased emphasis on vocals and individual instruments playing brief solos).

Wade Mainer was one of the few musicians whom Ralph Stanley has identified as an influence. When I interviewed Wade in 2005, he was living in Flint, Michigan.[33] In a parallel with the Stanley brothers, Wade had moved north to work for General Motors. Carter and Ralph tried automotive work in Michigan during a brief period in the early 1950s when bookings were scarce. Unlike Wade, who worked with GM until his retirement in 1972, the Stanley brothers stayed in Michigan only a couple of months before returning home.

When I asked Wade if he had met Ralph Stanley, thinking that they might have crossed paths early in the Stanley Brothers' professional careers, his answer surprised me. He recalled that he had met the brothers when they were young boys or teenagers. "It's strange how that happened," he said. "Ralph Stanley and his brother lived over there just over the mountain. They were running around over there in Bristol [Tennessee/Virginia], and I was on air in North Carolina on WWNC. That's when I formed my band. It went over in his direction, and he got to listen to it—him and his brother both. They asked a lot of questions. Ralph wasn't playing back then." You met Ralph *before* he was playing? "I'm not for sure if those boys were playing any music. I think they come to my shows a couple of times. I think I met 'em there as young kids."

Since old-time music historians consider Wade Mainer a key figure in the transition from string band music to bluegrass—second only to Bill Monroe, who is credited with creating bluegrass as a sound that became a style—the fact that young Carter and Ralph Stanley may have been able to learn Mainer's style directly from the playing of the musician and his band is significant. As those who play an instrument know, it is one thing to hear music on record or the radio, and quite another to hear the music in person, where a trained eye can learn how the musician is playing what the listener is hearing. If Wade's memory is correct, Ralph would have been able to observe Wade's style of banjo picking, which was a two-fingered transitional approach between the older thumb-and-fingers scrape of the clawhammer style that Ralph learned from his mother and the more contemporary three-fingered (actually thumb and two fingers) picking style practiced by North Carolinians Snuffy Jenkins and Earl Scruggs.[34] Wade developed his precise two-fingered approach after he discovered that plucking individual notes with his thumb and forefinger was more pleasing to his ear than the full chords of the clawhammer style.[35]

The Stanley Brothers "learned a lot of my music," Wade maintained. "Ralph recorded just about everything I made.[36] Of course I didn't get anything out of it, royalties or anything . . . I didn't get to copyright it, and so I lost all of that." The Stanley Brothers, on the other hand, would "pick them songs up along the way and put them on a record"—the act of recording being an important first step toward a copyright claim. Many musicians of Wade Mainer's generation either did not know how to copyright their material, did not take the time to copyright it, or hesitated to copyright material that they had not written. Carter and Ralph adopted the casual approach to copyright that had been successful for their neighbors to the southeast among the gentle hills of Poor Valley in Scott County, Virginia: the Original Carter Family.

From 1927 to 1941, the vocal and instrumental trio composed of A. P. Carter, his wife Sara, and sister-in-law Maybelle Carter (who was Sara's cousin) claimed authorship of almost everything they recorded, regardless of its source. Talent scout and record producer Ralph S. Peer encouraged these claims because they constituted a statement that the compositions were "original." In exchange for this statement, early recording artists such as the Carter Family would receive about 25 percent of the income generated by sales of a recorded song. This was an improvement over a flat fee of $25 to $50 for a recording, yet 75 percent went to the publishing company, which made it easy to understand why publishers such as Peer did not look closely at an artist's copyright claims.[37] In the words of one expert, "Pressured to produce material that was new (i.e. copyrightable) yet somehow authentic to their temperament and traditions, aspiring rural artists . . . fell back on two obvious sources: either they dredged up old, half-forgotten relics of the past, or they composed original songs that sounded like old ones. . . ."[38]

Given the wealth of traditional material from which performers could draw their repertoires and the talent scouts' lack of familiarity with the material, this loose interpretation of copyright was easy to practice in the early days of field recording in the South. When the Stanley Brothers began making records in 1947, they claimed authorship of traditionally derived material in the manner of Carter's claiming "Man of Constant Sorrow" and the Carter Family before him. Contrary to their image as a couple of country boys who knew little except picking and singing until their return from military service in 1946, the brothers had used the many days of childhood in the 1930s and early 1940s to learn the business of music as well as the craft. Graduating from Ervinton High School in the classes of 1943 and 1945, they would receive a call to learn a new set of skills.

3. BROTHERS IN ARMS

During the Civil War, residents of far southwestern Virginia found themselves pressured to declare their loyalty to either the Union or the Confederacy. Though connected in 1856 by a 204-mile railroad extension from Bristol, Tennessee, to Lynchburg, Virginia, that proceeded east to the future Confederate capital of Richmond,[1] a sizeable segment of the population would have preferred to remain independent from either side. By character and geography, they were self-sufficient people whose primary loyalty was to the survival of the family in a subsistence environment. But the warring armies forced the mountain folk to choose sides.

On November 4, 1864, the war struck close to the southwestern Virginia home of the Stanley family when a clash with trained Confederate soldiers took the life of a family member, Charles Hibbitts. A Stanley who bore his mother's name, Hibbitts had may have been part of a paramilitary unit called the home guards, composed of men who had been recruited to protect Union sympathizers and their property from outlaws and supporters of the Confederate army.[2] Accounts of the circumstances of his death differ; one was that an informer revealed the location of a home guards camp to Confederate soldiers. The accounts agree on one point: Confederate soldiers killed Hibbitts and other Union sympathizers in a pre-dawn encounter that became known as the Battle of Cranesnest.[3]

In the late 1930s, the approach of war in Europe may not have darkened daily life in Appalachia much more than the Great Depression had done through most of the decade, yet its ominous clouds soon cast shadows of uncertainty on a young person's prospects for the future.

Growing up in these times, Carter and Ralph Stanley learned at an early age that society expected certain things of a male child, just as it had strict expectations of female children. If a boy's family lived on a farm, as the Stanley family did, he had to contribute to the enterprise by performing a variety of routine tasks. "We called it doing up the work," recalled Carter to Mike Seeger in 1966.[4] Carter and Ralph "would get up about 5 o'clock in the morning to feed the cows and chickens, then walk two miles up Pilot Knob to the one-room school there, then walk back to more chores and bed."[5] When school was in session, Ralph recalled, "We'd leave before dark and get home after dark, sometimes climbing up and down through those dark woods in 18 inches or more of snow." The question remains whether life was oppressively hard for Carter and Ralph, or typical of farm life in most rural areas during the 1930s. In a documentary film made on around the time of his fiftieth anniversary as a performer in 1996, Ralph's description of a boyhood spent rising before dawn to milk cows before walking to school sounded as bucolic as it was demanding, though this pleasant image could be a difficult past viewed through the filter of time.[6]

In the 1930s another expectation of a boy growing up in a region that once had been the frontier was the ability to hunt. A boy's mother might teach him to play banjo—as Lucy taught Ralph—but chances were that his father or grandfather or uncle would show him how to use the family rifle. Though animal populations had decreased from the effects of human settlement and despoiling of the land by logging and mining, deer, raccoons, opossum, and the occasional moose were plentiful in southwestern Virginia during Carter and Ralph's youth.

Of the two boys, Carter had the greater interest in hunting. A few years after he returned from the army, he was known well enough as an avid sportsman and hound breeder to be introduced on the radio as "that big coon hunter from Dickenson County."[7] Ralph was more interested in taking care of animals than hunting them. While in high school, he expressed an interest in becoming a veterinarian—though he later qualified the statement by saying that he was "full of notions" at the time.[8] He and Carter's best friend, Carl Hammons, were in the same year at Ervinton High School. Hammons recalled high school agriculture teacher Orville Deel introducing the two young men to veterinary medicine as part of his farming classes. Deel was a demanding teacher. He required students to conduct a summer project for the Future Farmers of America. The two classmates decided to raise pigs. For Ralph, the experience was a big improvement over his earlier time at the saw mill. "There wasn't no comparison," he said. "We'd go out and work on sick animals. I learned to castrate hogs. I castrated a few bulls, too."[9] His interest in veterinary work might explain why he appended the title Dr. to his name after he received an honorary doctorate in music from Lincoln Memorial University in Harrogate, Tennessee, in 1976.

A third expectation of a young man growing up in the 1930s was that when his country called, he would be willing to serve. Though southern men historically seem to gravitate to military service with more enthusiasm than many of their peers in other parts of the country, enlistment anywhere in the United States required little persuasion after the Japanese bombed the American fleet at Pearl Harbor on December 7, 1941. Eighteen months older, Carter was the first to answer the call, enlisting in the Army Air Forces after graduating from high school in 1943. Ralph joined the army on May 16, 1945, two weeks after his own graduation. One of the brief songbook biographies reported that Ralph served "as an infantryman in the late General Patton's Third Army in Europe,"[10] but his actual duty assignment was more mundane. As it did for the majority of military men and women, Carter and Ralph's service consisted of playing support roles. Carter never left the United States, becoming an aircraft armorer in 460 Base Unit of the AAF at Kingman Army Airfield in Arizona. Ralph was sent overseas, serving as a clerk in Germany.

Clerk or not, Ralph took part in postwar military actions. After training for the infantry in Camp Gordon, Georgia, he was sent to Germany as part of the occupation. "I had it pretty good in Germany," he recalled. "The war was over when I got over there but we done a lot of disarming."[11] That meant searching house to house in German villages for people in possession of weapons—an operation that sometimes turned ugly. "I've seen them take . . . rifles and just knock the men and women down in the corners and just take what they had and everything," Ralph remembered.[12] When I asked him if he played banjo in the army, he said "Not too much. Special service, you know. I got a banjo from them, and just played around for my own deal. Some of the officers like to hear me pick and sing a little bit. I guess that helped me get through easy."[13]

As is often the case with Ralph's recollections, there was more to the story. His banjo playing caught the ear of two officers in his battalion, who knocked on the door of his room to ask him to play a couple of tunes.[14] They liked what they heard and promoted Ralph to mail clerk. Soon he made sergeant. "I'd play the banjo for them now and then," he recalled. "They really liked me." One day the colonel yelled over to his sergeant that orders had arrived making all soldiers who had served overseas for eighteen months eligible for discharge. "You're a God-damned liar," Ralph shot back, thinking the colonel was pulling his leg. On the contrary, the colonel wanted to send Sergeant Stanley to officers' training school, but Ralph was not tempted. His only wish was to go home.

After serving for thirty-two months, Carter was discharged in March 1946, seven months before Ralph. He returned to Smith Ridge and began playing music as a professional. Ralph was discharged from service on October 16, 1946,[15] and was anxious to get his music career going, too. "I planned to start playing as soon as I got out the army," he said. The brothers' first songbook biographer, James A. Baker (identified as their agent), wrote that before Ralph's return, "Carter worked in radio, singing solos. . . ."[16] Carter may have made a few solo appearances, but his steady musical job was as guitar player and vocalist with Roy Sykes and the Blue Ridge Mountain Boys—an association that began when Carter and Sykes met at Fort Meade, Maryland, as they were being discharged from the army.[17]

Born on March 8, 1921, Roy Sykes graduated from Honaker High School in May 1937 and began to organize an early version of his band. According to Roy Sykes Jr., his father's band was the first to play on radio station WNVA in Norton, Virginia, beginning on July 1, 1946. Publicity photographs taken outside the station's transmitter building on the outskirts of Norton show a tall, smiling Roy Sykes in a pose resembling bluegrass pioneer Bill Monroe, though playing fiddle rather than mandolin. Carter stands behind Sykes, showing off his guitar.

During my conversations with Roy Sykes Jr., it became clear that he felt that his father could have achieved much wider recognition had he continued his musical career with—or even without—the involvement of the Stanley brothers. According to Roy Jr., his father was only eight when he first played on radio station WOPI in Bristol in 1929 as part of a family band. Since the station went on the air on June 15, 1929,[18] the Sykes family would have been one of WOPI's earliest groups of performers. The decision that his son thought limited his career occurred much later in his life: "My mom wanted to get married, and mom talked dad into coming off the road. He had a recording contract in New York. He was going to record at RCA. Piggly Wiggly [stores] would broadcast him and his band once a week." Instead, the couple married in February 1946 and Roy Sr. remained a local musician. His band became Carter and Ralph Stanley's first musical showcase when they returned to southwestern Virginia in 1946.

As a musician and mentor, Roy Sykes played a significant role in the life of Carter Stanley. According to Roy Sykes Jr., before World War II, his father traveled to Maryland, where he got a job building houses in a Baltimore subdivision near an aircraft factory—most likely the Middle River, Maryland, housing development for workers at the Glenn L. Martin Company aircraft plant.[19] With some of his wages, he purchased a professional-level guitar, even though he was primarily a fiddle player. "He stopped in Baltimore and got that D-28," Roy Jr. said, referring to a vintage instrument he had shown me in Virginia. "[My father] paid $189 with case and it was bought June 1, 1941." At the time he joined the Blue Ridge Mountain Boys, Carter still played an inexpensive guitar. Roy Sykes loaned his new band member the D-28; Roy Jr. pointed out scratches left on the instrument by Carter's distinctive playing style. The guitar is now owned by Ralph Stanley's guitar player, James Alan Shelton.

Carter's original mail-order guitar from Montgomery Ward was far from professional quality—a beginner's instrument at best. By contrast, the D-28 model, made in limited quantities by C. F. Martin & Co. of Nazareth, Pennsylvania, was the industry standard for a utilitarian professional instrument. Big and boxy (the D is for dreadnaught, after a warship of the British navy), the D-28 was loud enough to compete with the high notes of fiddle, banjo, and mandolin, yet mellow enough to provide an underpinning for vocals and instrumental solos.

The new guitar would not be the only influence Roy Sykes had on the Stanley Brothers' guitar sound. In 1946 or 1947, Sykes brought Jesse McReynolds from Carfax, Virginia, into his band as an electric guitar player. McReynolds was 14. He was so shy that Sykes's wife brought him food as he waited in the car.[20] Jesse (who with brother Jim would form the successful country duo Jim and Jesse) later developed a style of mandolin playing called cross-picking that influenced not only other mandolin players, but North Carolina guitar and bass player George Shuffler. During the time Shuffler accompanied the McReynolds brothers, he paid close attention to Jesse's cross-picking technique and later adapted it to guitar as a member of the Clinch Mountain Boys.[21]

The bond between Roy Sykes and Carter Stanley that had been forged by music became even stronger when the two men married sisters. The connection lasted until Carter's death. Roy Jr. described his father and Carter as being "as close as brothers." Like Carter, Roy Sykes had experienced loss early in his life: his brother Giles had died in a car crash. Though he never recorded, Sykes maintained a long musical career with his own and other groups. "He played music for 54 years when he passed" on April 1, 1985, said his son.

Rather than continue with Roy Sykes after their return from military service, in 1946 Carter and Ralph decided to form their own band. The decision launched the brothers' musical star into the constellation of similar fraternal duos that were a staple of old-time country in the 1920s and 1930s. These brother acts, as they were called, provided a more compact version of the many family string bands that formed in a culture that placed high values on family, self-sufficiency, and music. A brother duo's frequent instruments were guitar and mandolin, sometimes accompanied by a fiddle.

As did the generations described in the Old Testament, one duo often begat another. For example, J. E. and Wade Mainer were two of the most successful brothers in the early to mid-1930s, though they augmented their sound with additional personnel. One of these was North Carolina neighbor, guitar player, and singer Zeke Morris, who joined the Mainers for several years before forming the Morris Brothers with his brother Wiley.[22] As happened with both the Mainer and Morris siblings, brothers would split up to start their own bands or join another musician's group. The Stanley Brothers stayed together for twenty years, with only a couple of brief interruptions in the musical partnership. The personnel surrounding them changed frequently, yet the brothers' sound remained consistent because Carter and Ralph's vocal harmonies and instrumental blend were central to it.

In addition to the Mainers, who played within groups, two brothers who performed as a duo may have influenced the early Stanley Brothers. Born in Elkmont, Alabama, Alton and Rabon Delmore began recording in 1931 and joined Nashville's *Grand Ole Opry* the following year.[23] Their presence on the *Opry*'s diverse roster of country entertainers (a variety of talents ranging from African American harmonica player DeFord Bailey to banjo-twirling former vaudevillian Uncle Dave Macon) meant that the Delmore Brothers could be heard in the Stanley home on Smith Ridge during radio station WSM's regular Saturday night broadcasts. Having gone on the air in 1925 with a cast of amateur performers, the *Opry* professionalized its standards over time to become a weekly entertainment highlight for families throughout the South. Sitting by the radio, the Stanley brothers would have heard the Delmores' smooth harmonies on many occasions.

Carter and Ralph heard the Delmore Brothers in person at the first "hillbilly show"[24] they ever attended. Carter was 11 and Ralph was 9. At the show, Alton and Rabon gave the young Virginians their first taste of what a successful brother act looked and sounded like. The performance took place in October 1936 at Ervinton High School in Nora, Virginia, which both brothers were to attend in the next few years.[25] According to Alton Delmore in his autobiography, *Truth Is Stranger than Publicity*, he and Rabon toured that year with old-time fiddle player Clayton McMichen, one of the founders of the seminal North Georgia string band, the Skillet Lickers. McMichen was a musician of considerable reputation in the South, having shared billing in 1929 with Mississippi country star Jimmie Rodgers.[26]

Questions of influence aside, attending the Ervinton High School show was a pivotal event in the lives of the Stanley boys. Recalling the show thirty years later, Carter said it was the catalyst behind his decision to become a professional musician: "We just wanted to play music always. We was just little boys. There was just something about it. The curtains opened, they started playing, and I said that's for me."[27]

Another brother act whose path would cross that of the Stanley Brothers, Ira and Charlie Louvin, experienced a similar epiphany at a concert, but under very different circumstances. When *Grand Ole Opry* star Roy Acuff arrived in an air-cooled Franklin car to appear at the Spring Hill School that they attended in Henagar, Alabama, the Loudermilk brothers (who later changed their name for the stage) were unable to afford the twenty-five-cent price of admission. It was a hot night, so they stood outside in the schoolyard with a crowd as big as the one inside. "That was our first stage show," recalled Charlie. "But . . . when we saw Acuff pass in his car that day, we knew that's what we wanted to do. It was just a matter of how to do it."[28] In early 1955, after several frustrating auditions, the Louvin Brothers made their debut on the *Opry*.[29]

When interviewed by Mike Seeger in 1966, Carter did not mention that the Delmore Brothers were part of the Ervinton High School show with Clayton McMichen. The omission could be taken to mean that the Delmores made little impression on the Stanleys. Another possibility is that the oversight was a conscious one. There would have been a powerful reason for the latter to be the case: For a member of one old-time country brother duo to cite the influence of an earlier brother duo would create the risk of being accused of stealing their style, if not their material.[30] The tracing of artistic influences in old-time country and bluegrass can be a subjective task, especially if those who are influenced are as reticent as the two Stanleys. Though his public persona on stage and radio was effusive,

Carter could be distant; and from his youth, Ralph was known for being tight-lipped and shy. Identifying influences on the Stanley Brothers leaves much to the ears of the individual listener.

The tight harmony on the Delmore Brothers' recording of the traditional song "The Lover's Warning" in February 1936 (only months before the Stanley brothers heard them at Ervinton High School, so the Delmores may have sung it that night) sounds very similar in style to the traditional "East Virginia Blues" on an informal tape the Stanley Brothers made in 1956.[31] At the urging of the fan who recorded them, the tape focused on songs they had learned or performed in their earliest years. Aside from a couple of times when they sang different words, the brothers performed the song well, though when Carter said it was the first time they had sung the song in fifteen years, Ralph corrected him: "First time I ever sung it." Carter amended his remark to "the first time I guess we ever sung it all the way through." Separately or together, there must have been some rehearsing since instead of playing banjo, Ralph added a lovely mandolin part to the song using fingerpicks.

Carter and Ralph's early vocal harmonies resemble those of another brother duo that preceded them and with whom they later worked on radio: Bill and Earl Bolick of East Hickory, North Carolina. When Bill and Earl were about to make their first record in 1936, their producer suggested they come up with a different name[32]—an idea that made sense if the producer took into account that the Germanic "Bolick" did not match the Scotch-Irish ancestry of most acts in country music at the time. Taking their name from the slogan "Blue Ridge Mountains, land of the sky," Bill and Earl became the Blue Sky Boys. Carter recalled listening to them on the radio and later meeting them at WCYB.[33]

"Their intricate yet simple harmonies, their perfectly matching voices, and their unadorned mandolin and guitar instrumental backing set them off from the competition," an anonymous critic wrote on the country music Web site CMT.com, "so much so that two generations of subsequent duet singers echo them, some without realizing it." An example of their possible influence on the Stanley Brothers is the murder ballad "In the Hills of Roane County," which the Bolicks recorded in 1940. Based on a murder that took place in east Tennessee in 1884 (though not brought to trial until 1909), the purported author of the song was the murderer himself, who wrote the lyrics as a poem while serving a life sentence. Residents of the region recall hearing the song on the 1930s and 1940s.[34]

Though the Stanley Brothers did not record "Roan [sic] County" until January 29, 1963, for their *Folk Concert* album, Ralph later recalled the song as one of the first he and Carter learned and performed.[35]

The description of the Blue Sky Boys' "perfectly matching voices" identifies a crucial element in the distinctive sounds of sibling harmony: voices that match like bookends. An outstanding characteristic of brothers and sisters singing together is the blend of individual voices—whether pitched high, low, or in the middle—into what becomes something like a separate voice. This is what the listener often hears in the recorded music of the Delmores, Bolicks, and the Stanley Brothers. In general, the Delmore Brothers featured more of a unison sound, while the Bolicks exemplified those "intricate yet simple" harmonies. I learned how true the description of the latter was at Ralph Stanley's annual bluegrass festival on Smith Ridge in late May 2006. After I complimented her on being able to satisfy an audience request for a Blue Sky Boys' number, songwriter and singer Gillian Welch told me how difficult the song had been for her and partner David Rawlings to perform.[36]

Before beginning the song, Welch made a humorous show on stage of inhaling several deep breaths. She later explained that the breaths were necessary on a practical as well as theatrical level because the overlapping phrases in the Blue Sky Boys' harmonies gave the singers fewer opportunities to breathe than in most songs. That raised an interesting possibility: Challenging vocal duets might be easier to perform for biological brothers or sisters who share the same speech and breathing patterns. The special qualities of the sound may account for the durability of the niche market of sibling and family harmony occupied by performers in country music from the Delmores to the Everly Brothers to the Whites, who—like the Delmores sixty years before them—became regulars on the *Grand Ole Opry*.

Another pair of brothers who influenced Carter and Ralph's style were western Kentucky natives Charlie and Bill Monroe. Older brother Charlie and younger brother Bill learned to play music from family members. Their mother played fiddle and sang, and her brother, Pendleton Vandiver, was a well-known local fiddler. Charlie and Bill continued their musical education in singing schools held every summer at the Baptist and Methodist churches, and with Arnold Shultz, an African American guitarist and fiddle player. When their father died in 1928, Bill moved in with Pendleton Vandiver, whom he had been accompanying at local dances from age 12 or 13. Living in Uncle Pen's cabin, Bill began to transpose the older man's wealth of fiddle tunes to his chosen instrument: mandolin. As the youngest in such a musical family, Bill had few options but to choose an instrument that no sibling was playing.[37] The Monroe Brothers performed as professionals for two years before they first recorded on February 17, 1936, and made sixty recordings as a duo before parting company in 1938. Each went on to lead his own group.

By the time Carter and Ralph Stanley heard Bill Monroe in person in early September 1940,[38] Bill had joined the *Grand Ole Opry* with a group he called the Blue Grass Boys. The name of the band became the descriptor for the new genre. Bluegrass featured the same instruments that were to be found in string band music—guitar, mandolin, banjo, fiddle, and bass fiddle—but was played at a driving pace. Wrote Charles Wolfe, "To the casual listener, the main difference was speed: Monroe's music demanded new standards of musicianship and was taken at tempos twice or even three times as fast as normal. When the older string bands strove for an ensemble sound, Monroe let instrumentalists trade leads and even tried improvised solos."[39]

As aspiring professionals, Carter and Ralph attended Bill Monroe and the Blue Grass Boys shows, falling under the spell of what they heard. "About 1939 Bill Monroe began to appear around [Dickenson County] some and we had a chance to see him once in a while," Carter recalled. "When we saw him, in our opinion that was the way we wanted to play."[40]

Tennessean Joe Wilson encountered the Stanley Brothers several times in their careers. As a native of the five-state region, Wilson had special insight into their early sources since he had been exposed to them himself. He identified the old-time duo of G. B. Grayson and Henry Whitter—a fiddler from North Carolina and guitar player from Virginia, respectively—as a strong influence on Carter. According to Wilson:

> . . . he used a lot of Grayson's melodies and songs. Obviously he had been exposed not only to all the Victors but all the Gennett Records. One of the things we talked about was how we could get them, who had good copies of them. I gave him a tape. I don't think it ever affected anything he recorded, it was after he had recorded some of the early things that had—he used some Grayson and Whitter tunes, melodies, and he recorded some of the songs. . . .
>
> But he was eager to have all of that material. I remember we sat down and took an envelope and he wrote down the names of all the songs he knew that Grayson and Whitter did and says, "Now if there

are any other that you could give, and you got—" and I responded
to it by giving him a little reel tape that probably had ten or twelve
more songs.[41]

Though he felt that Carter had more of an interest in Grayson and
Whitter than in the Mainers, Wilson credited Wade Mainer's sound as an
important influence. "Musically, on the balance, though there was obviously more of an ensemble sound with Mainer. And the Stanleys really
were patterned after Mainer when they first went to the radio much more
than they were after Monroe or any of those people. That came later."[42]

Clarence "Tom" Ashley, who played guitar with Grayson but never recorded with him, was an old-time country influence on Carter and Ralph
whom Wilson had seen when Ashley worked with the Stanleys:

Tom was a great entertainer. He had the kind of sense of humor that
tickled the hell out of Carter, which was the kind—we think of black-
face stuff as being real rough, pie-in-the-face kind of stuff. It really
wasn't, not the way that Tom did it. I've seen them. He had Carter
doing straight man stuff on that. He had the whole band involved in
some of those things, you know.[43]

The elements of minstrelsy were present, though for the most part
blackface had disappeared by the postwar years—to be replaced by "rube"
comics who remained in country music into the 1950s. Prior to the war,
it was not uncommon for photographs of old-time country acts to include a member in blackface. A publicity photo of the Monroe Brothers
shows the comic Rusty Scott in blackface kneeling in supplication at Bill
Monroe's feet as Monroe appears ready to strike him with his raised
mandolin.[44] Wilson characterized the type of blackface humor that the
Stanley Brothers used in their act as "light stuff." Carter would ask Ashley,
who was in character as Rastus Jones from Georgia, "Rastus, is your pants
too short?" Ashley would respond, "No, they not. I'm just down in them
too far."[45]

Carter placed a high value on his friendships with old-time musicians.
In the early 1960s, he included a warm reference to Tom Ashley while
introducing a song at the Ash Grove in Los Angeles, where Ashley and
other Appalachian performers appeared during the folk revival.

Within the world of old-time country, the music was evolving more
quickly than the stereotypes. Bluegrass was revolutionary—much like

bebop was to jazz, which it was about to revolutionize during those same years. Before finishing high school and joining the military, the Stanley brothers had caught a glimpse of a tradition-based music that was becoming cool. When they returned home in 1946, they were more than ready to become active participants in what their eyes and ears told them was their old-time music's future.

4. A BAND ON THE RUN

The weather in southwestern Virginia can be very pleasant during October. The leaves turn yellow, orange, and bright red, and there is an invigorating chill in the night air while the days remain warm enough to be comfortable. In 1946, as the Greyhound bus carrying Ralph Stanley hummed southward through Virginia, the newly discharged veteran must have experienced a deep sense of comfort as he looked out the window to see flat farmland giving way to the gentle foothills and sheltering, tree-studded spines of the Blue Ridge Mountains. One only can imagine the surging emotions the home-loving 19-year-old felt at the prospect of being reunited with his mother, father, brother, and other members of his family after seventeen months in the army, much of it spent overseas. He was not disappointed. When the bus pulled into the Bristol, Virginia, terminal at around 1 p.m., Ralph spotted the smiling face of Carter and the stoop-shouldered figure of Lee Stanley waiting for him. Carter showed Ralph his new gold tooth and tattoos on both arms: one combining a dagger and the words "Death before dishonor," the other "Mother" next to a heart pierced by an arrow.[1] Excited as he was to be back in the Clinch River Valley and wanting to see his mother on Smith Ridge, the enjoyment of Lucy's home cooking would have to wait as Carter and Lee took him to a different sort of homecoming.

Since leaving the army in March, Carter had joined the band of fellow returning veteran Roy Sykes. According to published schedules from September and October 1946, Roy and the Blue Ridge Mountain Boys performed live shows twice a day on radio station WNVA in Norton, Virginia, from 7:00 to 7:15 a.m. and noon to 12:15 p.m.[3] The station's business office was located downtown, and the studio and transmitter facility stood outside town on Route 23 toward Kentucky in a section of Norton called Josephine.

A photograph from that time shows Carter and Roy in shirts and ties standing on a downtown sidewalk outside WNVA. Sykes wears the natty jodhpurs that were an integral part of the image of Bill Monroe and the Blue Grass Boys. The two men lean together with an arm around each other, looking more like a father and his son than two near contemporaries.[4] Similarly clad but with the addition of jaunty Stetson-style hats, the men posed for a photograph in the park in Big Stone Gap, Virginia, where the Blue Ridge Mountain Boys played during the summer of 1946. A relaxed Carter has a cigarette in his right hand; he was a lifelong smoker. A more musician-like photo shows the two men standing outdoors under trees that are coming into foliage in the spring of 1946. Carter holds the big Martin guitar that Sykes bought in Baltimore in 1941, while the bandleader cradles his violin. Beside them is the 1938 Pontiac that advertised the band as "Radio and Stage Artists."

The Sykes band was a popular ensemble in 1946. An undated publicity photo taken inside radio station WNVA shows seven members, including four guitarists—one on lap steel and another with an electronic pickup placed across his acoustic guitar's sound hole so that the guitar could plug in to an amplifier. Publicity photos taken outside the studio show a six-member band: Ray Lambert on bass, Pee Wee Lambert on mandolin, Roy Sykes on fiddle, Carter on acoustic guitar, and brothers Gains and Jack Bevins on lap steel and amplified acoustic, respectively. They are nattily dressed with the exception of "Pickles" Lambert, who stands astride his bass with the costume and expression of a hick—the bass player's customary comedic role. The bandleader employs a different sort of showmanship as he trick fiddles behind his back. After his wartime service with the military police of the 82nd Airborne Division, Roy had gained radio experience working for the Armed Forces Network in Frankfurt. Having introduced songs and celebrities on the air, he was well acquainted with his role as bandleader when he returned to the United States, and an ideal mentor for future emcee Carter Stanley.

Adding a special dimension to Carter's time with the Sykes band was the friendship he developed at the radio station with one of the first generation of recording musicians from the region, Fiddlin' Powers. James Cowan Powers and his wife Mathilda, who played fiddle and banjo, played music at dances in the Castlewood area of Russell County as they raised a son and three daughters. "Daddy would bring home an instrument for each child," recalled their daughter Ada. His gifts resulted in the creation of a family string band. In 1916, when Mathilda died of tuberculosis, Cowan made the decision to turn the family band professional, possibly so that he would not have to leave the children alone while he worked.[5] Cowan's history was not lost on Carter, who was respectful of his musical forebears. Of his time in Sykes's Blue Ridge Mountain Boys, he recalled: "I believe I was about the youngest one in the group and seemed like nobody else in the whole bunch had any time for the old man except me. I made a friendship there that lasted till he died. I've always been very glad that I did."[6]

On the day Ralph returned home from the army, Carter's attention was divided between playing with the band and greeting his younger brother. With his father's help, he managed to do both. It was a powerful moment for the men of the family when Ralph stepped into the WNVA broadcast studio in time for the band's afternoon show. Ralph joined the band for a personal appearance that night.

For all practical purposes, this day in the third week of October 1946 marked the debut of the Stanley Brothers playing together as professionals. Their debut as an independent act did not take place until Ralph quit the Sykes band a few weeks later, persuading Carter to join him. "I decided that [playing with Sykes] wasn't for me," Ralph recalled in 2003, "so I told Carter that if he wanted to organize our own group, I would be glad to, but if he wouldn't, I was gonna pursue something else. So he agreed with me real quick."[7] One reason for Ralph's decision was that Sykes—primarily a fiddle player—played banjo well enough to take the instrument out of Ralph's hands for the banjo numbers that brought the most applause. The young banjo player resented that Sykes's showmanship upstaged him. Carter remembered the Stanley Brothers making their debut under their own name on November 2, 1946, when they began the first of four or five weeks of live broadcasts on WNVA. They performed on a Saturday morning *Hayloft Capers* program that showcased local talent.[8]

If not personally upset by these departures, as his son says he was not, Sykes had a difficult time professionally because following Ralph and Carter was Sykes's multi-talented mandolin player, Darrell "Pee Wee" Lambert. Born August 5, 1924, in Thacker, West Virginia, Lambert was a year older than Carter and two and a half years older than Ralph.[9] He was the first of several West Virginians to play a prominent role in the lives and music of the Stanley Brothers. Ralph described Pee Wee as "a fine mandolin player. He played a little bit like Bill Monroe—just a bit more plainer, more simple."[10] Ralph recalled that Pee Wee "had a good high tenor voice, too, and could sing like Monroe." He and Ralph became close personal friends. When the band's second souvenir song and picture book was published (selling for fifty cents), the editorial copy noted that Pee Wee "is considered a right hand man with the Clinch Mountain Boys."[11]

As was the case with Carter, Ralph, and Roy Sykes, almost all the young men in Dickenson County either had enlisted or been called to military service in World War II. With so few men left in the labor-intensive landscape of Appalachia, life for women in the mountains was especially difficult during the war years. One such woman was Exie Rose. "I was born way over from Haysi in Dickenson County," she recalled. ". . . I had four brothers and no sisters. I was the oldest one and daddy's pet. I helped with them a lot when I was grown enough . . ." She paused. "Guess it was kind of rough growing up at that time, but we didn't know any better so we enjoyed our life."[12]

I met Exie Rose in October 2004 at the concert before the opening of the Ralph Stanley Museum and Traditional Music Center in Clintwood, Virginia. Seated at the merchandise table, Ralph solemnly signed CDs, photographs, T-shirts, hats, and other paraphernalia. He brightened when a woman about his age approached him. "Dancing girl," he said softly, with a rare public smile. I thought there must be a story behind Ralph's greeting and asked Mrs. Rose if I could interview her. When we spoke months later, she said she remembered well the return of the Stanley brothers and the other men of Dickenson County from the war. "Oh boy, it was something," she said. "We could go to Haysi and we had plenty of boys to pick from. I believe Carter and Ralph was just getting out of service and were around Haysi. They was friendly. Carter was a lot more talky than Ralph is. I always liked Ralph anyways."

She recalled running into Ralph in Haysi. "It's just a little small town, not as big as Clintwood," she said. "I was walking down the street. . . . I met him and Carter and I believe it was Curly Ray Cline [possibly Pee Wee Lambert] that was with them.[13] We stopped and talked several minutes. They asked me what I was doing. I said, 'I'm not doing anything.' Carter said, 'You're waiting on a call to Hollywood then, are you?' We had a good little talk there." The conversation shows Carter's flirtatious behavior with women, yet Exie Rose's recollections suggest that Ralph was the brother she preferred. "After that he got into the [roller] skating rink up near Tarpon, between Haysi and Clintwood," she said. "Ralph and Carter got to making their music up there on Saturday night and we got to having square dances up there, and we had the best time there ever was. They would stay there and play for us as long as they would play. We got to have a big gathering . . . thirty or forty people. Ralph was the highlight of our life back then. Back then there wasn't no cars much, and girls didn't drive and we had to go to the closest place we would find. I guess we walked. But it's not too far from my house." I asked her how long the Saturday nights continued. "For right onto a year," she said. "Then he got a place on the radio station where he made music at, but we would see him around Clintwood. . . . He said his mother taught him how to play banjo, he told us one time. She taught him to play 'Pretty Polly.'" I asked what she thought of his banjo playing as a young man. "I thought he was pretty good. Everybody else seemed to think that, too. We did square dancing. That was all we knew. We had a real good time. You had to make your own fun back then."

Except to family members and friends like Exie Rose, the Ralph whose personality emerged after he continued on his own was little known for most of two decades following his return from the service. Whether this was a product of Ralph's shyness or attention being drawn to the extroverted Carter (or a combination of the two) was important in the on- and off-stage relationship of the Stanley Brothers. When I had the opportunity to ask Ralph about Carter in an interview at his home in 2003, he was direct about the differences in their personalities, though asserting, "We were very close."

"Carter was really interested in getting in this business and he loved to do it, and he was really out front more than me," Ralph said.[14] "He done emcee work and things like that while I was doing booking and the business end of it. We made a pretty good pair that way, you know. He was forward, and I was very backward back at the start. I helped him sing and everything like that, but he did the emcee work." Ralph appeared to be understating his roles in the band. In a musical genre characterized by vocal harmony, he was an excellent high harmony vocalist and occasional lead singer, with a piercing, rough-edged voice that grew more distinctive over time. He was accomplished on the banjo, mastering two-finger style before making a transition to three-finger. He played traditional drop thumb, or "clawhammer," style as well. Carter, meanwhile, possessed a sweet, soulful voice—pitched between tenor and baritone—that delivered lead vocals and harmonies in a natural, unaffected manner. Though not flashy, his guitar style was well suited to the task of playing rhythm, and he displayed smooth multi-note runs as he changed keys. "His ensemble guitar playing was beautiful," remembered one listener.[15] "As I recall, he played with thumb and finger, like Charlie Monroe and Lester Flatt."

During our interview, I felt that I should tread carefully in sensitive territory. I asked Ralph open-ended questions about Carter, beginning with what it was like to work professionally with his brother. "It was great. Brothers always have a few differences. Every difference we ever had was over with as quick as it started. We just had a few words and that was it. I know all families, sisters, brothers has a few disagreements, so we got on great." In response to a general question about Carter as a songwriter and musician, Ralph expressed the highest regard for his brother. "He was one of the great songwriters that has ever been, and he was good at his work . . . great at his work. He was natural and he never put on. He believed in his work and that makes it much easier to do than just a put on. He was interested in it, and it was his life."

I asked whether there was a special quality about Carter that people might not know unless Ralph told them. "He was forward. He never met a stranger," Ralph said. "He'd just as soon tell president of United States what he thought as he did with me. He was just out front that way. I think that was good in a way because he told people what he thought. He was a good crowd-pleaser who could satisfy a Christian on stage or a drunk. . . ."

I phrased my next question carefully, asking if Carter's health had deteriorated toward the end of his life. "Oh yeah," he said. "Carter failed in the last couple of years. His voice didn't stay as good, but his voice still had that feel. He couldn't use it as well, but he still had the touch."

After splitting from Roy Sykes in the fall of 1946, the brothers wasted little time in assembling a band. As their first fiddler, they recruited 22-year-old Bobby Sumner from Vicco, Kentucky. Ralph remembered Sumner as "a real good fiddle player," but less reliable in terms of his commitment to the band. Ralph said Sumner "was actually the first, but he didn't stay but a couple of weeks and came in and out. I always called Leslie Keith our first fiddle player."[16] The Stanley Brothers and the Clinch Mountain Boys' second songbook mentioned Sumner, reporting that "Bobby has been doing radio work for four years." Sumner's radio career included performing with other groups besides the Stanley Brothers. He rejoined Carter and Ralph in early 1949 and played on their first major-label recording session that March.[17]

Sumner's successor in early 1947 was Leslie Keith, who came from Harrisonburg, Virginia, 275 miles to the northeast of Smith Ridge. "I heard him on a radio station at Bluefield, West Virginia," Ralph said. "I

liked his fiddle playing. . . . He had an old-time sound, a very lonesome
style the people loved." Keith was older than the brothers and had professional experience that the younger musicians lacked. During World War
II, he served in Special Services in Europe, where he entertained wounded soldiers in the hospitals by playing old-time country music in the hospitals. "He'd been in the business for years," Ralph recalled. "We weren't
experienced at all."[18] Keith already had made a name for himself among
Appalachian fiddle players. In 1937, fiddler and bandleader Joe Woods
invited Keith to join his band. The following year, the two men rented
Glenwood Park between Bluefield and Princeton, West Virginia, for fifteen dollars to stage a fiddling contest. Keith demonstrated his promotional skills by calling the *Grand Ole Opry* and persuading star performer
Fiddlin' Arthur Smith to participate in the contest for $100 and bus fare.[19]
Publicizing the contest for two weeks on local radio—as Smith did on
the *Opry* broadcasts—Keith and Woods attracted twenty-seven fiddlers
and a paid attendance of 9,000. Keith and Smith were the finalists. When
the applause meter used to judge the contestants registered the same
response four times running, the sponsors "Just left it at that," recalled
Keith. Years later, he and a young fiddle player named Lester Woodie employed the contest device to draw crowds to the Stanley Brothers.

During the band's early weeks, Carter's smooth-talking leadership of
the Stanley Brothers on stage was formative, and Ralph's eventual role
as business manager had not begun. To launch the band's career, someone more comfortable with business than the brothers had to act as their
manager and agent, arranging bookings and negotiating payment. That
person was Lee Stanley. "Our daddy booked quite a few shows for us,"
Carter recalled.[20] "He was about halfway in retirement. He liked music as
well or even better than Ralph and me. He'd even go with us a lot of times
at night. He was getting up there in years, but he'd manage to go with us."
     Having survived the Great Depression as a saw mill owner in the
timber industry, Lee had plenty of experience with the give and take of
business in southwestern Virginia. Though Ralph may have liked Leslie
Keith's fiddling, it was Lee and Carter who placed telephone calls to the
veteran about joining the band.[21] In late 1946, Lee booked the band's first
public appearance, which took place in November or December in an

elementary school near Big Stone Gap, Virginia.[22] Ralph recalled that only eight or ten people were on hand. "We split the proceeds between us," he said drily, ". . . two dollars and fifty-five cents apiece." A percentage of the proceeds went to the school. Pee Wee Lambert's widow, Hazel, recalled that after the performance, "They come in one night a-laughing" over the amount of their pay.[23] Small payday or not, the beginning of the brothers' careers as professional musicians must have produced elation in the Stanley family.

For the first months, the band performed without a bass fiddle, whose booming low notes provide both rhythmic and harmonic foundations for other instruments. Working without a bass came from necessity rather than style. "Most of the other bands had one," said Ralph. "It just took us a few months to find one."[24] The musician necessary to complete the band was Ray Lambert from nearby Clinchfield, Virginia. The addition of Lambert dealt another blow to Roy Sykes, who employed Lambert in the Blue Ridge Mountain Boys. Ray was no relation to Pee Wee Lambert. "Pickles" Lambert played the comedic role of the hick that often fell to the bass player in old-time country bands. Barnyard humor replaced the vestiges of blackface comedy that carried over from minstrel and medicine show entertainers. According to Ralph, Ray Lambert "dressed up in a monkey suit [tuxedo] and blacked his teeth out, and called himself 'Cousin Wine-Sap.'" When Ray was unavailable, Carter assumed the role of resident hayseed in the brothers' evolving stage act.

The months of October and November 1946 were life-changing for the Stanley brothers. In the space of six weeks, Carter and Ralph made the transition from returning soldiers to a pair of professional musicians at an exciting time for American music. As evidenced by the success of Bill Monroe and the Blue Grass Boys, whose definitive personnel lineup came together in 1946, old-time country and bluegrass were on the verge of wider popularity. Prior to the early 1920s, country musicians would have been familiar only to audiences who heard them in person; the pre- and postwar growth of recordings and radio made it possible for millions to hear their music. Bill Monroe had achieved that level of success recording for Columbia Records and performing on weekly radio broadcasts of the *Grand Ole Opry*. By contrast, Carter Stanley had played and sung for a few months on local radio, and Ralph for only a few weeks. With a career consisting of performances in one or two schoolhouses in southwestern Virginia, the Stanley Brothers were far behind Monroe. But when a new radio station began to broadcast in late September 1946 from Bristol,

Virginia, Lee Stanley inquired whether the station could use a country band on its program schedule. In December and the months to follow, the response to Lee's query would propel the Stanley Brothers from a couple of personal appearances near their home to regional stardom.

5. RADIO, RECORDS, AND COPYRIGHTS

Three elements crucial to the development of country music in the 1920s through 1950s were the rapid growth of radio, the popularity of phonograph records, and the availability of traditional song material that could be copyrighted. Each element provided an additional source of income for performers and the nascent country music industry. Most important to the career of the Stanley Brothers was their daily presence on a powerful radio station—Bristol, Virginia's WCYB. Without the regional celebrity they acquired almost overnight on WCYB, Carter and Ralph might have spent years building a following, if they managed to survive in the music business long enough to do so.

In the late 1930s Roy Hall and His Blue Ridge Entertainers struggled to make a living before the group progressed from small radio stations in North Carolina to a large one in southwest Virginia. In North Carolina, "The musicians slept five to a room in a boardinghouse, ate meals together, and rode to show dates crammed tight in one car, five dudes wedged shoulder to shoulder, everybody smoking unfiltered cigarettes, their instruments packed in the trunk."[1] After April 1940, when the soft drink company opened a bottling plant in Roanoke, regular Dr. Pepper–sponsored appearances on Roanoke's WDBJ led to the group being booked for performances in Virginia, West Virginia, and North Carolina—a pattern for regional success that the Stanley Brothers would duplicate in 1947.

The medium of radio was well suited to overcoming the geographic and economic challenges of Appalachia. Foremost was radio's ability to span distances in a part of the country whose population had settled in remote communities and on farms. People living in Appalachia came to depend on the new medium as an important source of news and entertainment—types of content that were not on the minds of radio pioneers such as Italian inventor Guglielmo Marconi, who developed a radio telegraph system.

The inventors' goals were practical. Given the medium's ability to over-come distance and convey basic information such as latitude and longi-tude, the primary use of early radio was for communication from ship to shore and ship to ship. Canadian Reginald Fessenden pioneered con-tinuous wave transmission of audio that enabled him, on Christmas Eve 1906, to broadcast his playing "O Holy Night" on the violin and reading a passage from the Bible to ships at sea; yet the potential of radio for broad-casting voice and music in the form of scheduled programs went unreal-ized for a decade.

On the other hand, the value of wireless ship-to-ship transmission was dramatized to the public on the night of April 14–15, 1912, with the sink-ing of the passenger liner *Titanic*. Without the *Titanic's* "Marconi room" having the ability to transmit Morse-coded distress signals across the North Atlantic, one of which was received by a wireless engineer on the *Carpathia* passing 58 miles away, the outcome of the *Titanic's* fatal col-lision with an iceberg might have been the loss of all aboard. Having re-ceived the sinking liner's coordinates, the *Carpathia* steamed through an ice field to rescue the 700 survivors who had managed to board lifeboats, and transport them to safety in New York. Ernest V. "Pop" Stoneman's 1924 recording of "The Sinking of the Titanic" became the first country music record to sell a million copies—and was heard all over Appalachia on the radio.

The geographic challenge of Appalachia to radio lay in the region's mountains, which interfered with signals broadcast from stations in the valleys. The same challenge faced television in the 1940s and 1950s, lead-ing to the development of cable TV as a way to bring television to isolated areas. The economic challenge was that potential advertisers were fewer in the agricultural and coal-mining counties of Appalachia than they were in cities such as Pittsburgh, where licensed commercial broadcasting be-gan over station KDKA on November 2, 1920.[2]

Instrumental to the arrival of radio in southwest Virginia and east Tennessee was William A. Wilson from Caney Branch, Tennessee. Wilson took a correspondence course in telegraphy that, by 1920, landed him a job as head of the testing and traffic departments of the Western Union office in Bristol.[3] By 1923, while keeping his Western Union posi-tion, Wilson transformed his interest in radio from hobby to business by opening Bristol's first retail radio shop. This was an act of faith because the nearest commercial radio station was KDKA, whose signal was re-ceived sporadically and not during the summer.

After a fire destroyed his shop in January 1924, Wilson reopened at a new location with one salvaged receiver. On February 3 history lent a helping hand in the form of a presidential death that was broadcast. A crowd gathered in his shop and on the street outside to listen to the dying words of Woodrow Wilson. "Everyone had to stand real still," he recalled.[4] "If a person moved at all, the set would fade out." He soon sold the first home radio in Bristol, a three-tube Westinghouse model costing $165. By the next year, Wilson's Bristol Radio Company had grown to a point where he could leave Western Union; and by the day in 1927 that he relocated the renamed Wilson Radiophone Service to Bristol's busy intersection of Piedmont and State Streets, he had sold 5,000 radio sets.

For musicians and listeners alike, a parallel technological revolution was taking place in sound recording. On the Tennessee side of State Street in Bristol, the field recording of regional musicians that began in 1923 in Atlanta came to town from the last week in July 1927 through the first week in August. Working with the Victor Talking Machine Company of Camden, New Jersey, freelance recording director Ralph S. Peer and his engineers installed their equipment on the second floor of a vacant warehouse for women's hats at 408–410 State Street.

Peer was a powerful figure in both southern music and field recording. He set up shop in Bristol on the recommendation of Virginia recording artist Ernest V. Stoneman, who said there were an abundance of talented musicians in the region. Inviting musicians to audition with an advertisement in a Bristol newspaper on July 24 (the paper followed up on July 27 with a front-page story), Peer began the sessions on July 25 with Stoneman and his Dixie Mountaineers. Having recorded "The Sinking of the Titanic" and other successful titles, Stoneman was a proven commodity.

On August 1, three of the aspiring new faces entered the studio. Their tall, sharp-featured leader A. P. Carter had corresponded with Peer about the possibility of recording in Bristol. With his wife, Sara, and sister-in-law Maybelle, A. P. had driven thirty miles over a rough mountain road the day before from Maces Springs, Virginia, repairing several flat tires in the process. Years later, Peer offered this recollection of his first glimpse of the Carter Family: "They wander in. He's dressed in overalls and the women are country women from way back there. They looked like hillbillies. But as soon as I heard Sara's voice, that was it. I knew it was going to be wonderful."[5] A country music historian disputes Peer's description, saying that self-respecting performers such as the Carters would dress for a session in nothing less than their Sunday best[6]—but there is general agreement in regard to the results of the session: The recorded songs not only were exceptional in quality, but seminal in the history of country music. By the time the Carter Family stopped recording in 1941 (performing until 1943), they had made almost 300 recordings—250 separate titles including country standards such as "The Wildwood Flower," "Keep on the Sunny Side," and "Can the Circle Be Unbroken?"

Similarly prolific once his six-year recording career began in Bristol in 1927 was Jimmie Rodgers. Soon the industry's biggest star, the Mississippi native struggled to record two songs on August 4, the second-to-last day of the sessions. His two and a half hours of studio time required more takes than any other musician. Though an experienced solo performer, Rodgers was unprepared. While rehearsing the previous night, his band split from him over the issue of whether to record under its original name, the Tenneva Ramblers, or as the Jimmie Rodgers Entertainers—the name used when Rodgers booked performances.

Since the recording sessions were open to audition, both parties were able to record on August 4. In contrast to the confidence he displayed on later recordings, Rodgers sounded tentative as he accompanied himself on guitar, singing a World War I song, "The Soldier's Sweetheart," and an old lullaby "Sleep, Baby, Sleep." On the latter he recorded the yodel that became his trademark. The Tenneva Ramblers recorded three songs, including "The Longest Train I Ever Saw." This song fell into the gray area between folk authorship and copyright ownership as practiced by the Carter Family and Stanley Brothers—but not by all performers. Roy Hall at first assigned one of his Blue Ridge Entertainers the "tedious task . . . [of] researching the music copyrights for the next week's radio programs," yet later "taught them how to copyright material that existed in the public domain."[7]

According to folklorist Judith McCulloh, "Longest Train" and its lyrical and melodic twin, "In the Pines," are products of the folk tradition that preceded copyright. They developed over time from a succession of performers rather than from a single singer or songwriter. "My sense is they were cobbled together from bits of verse," McCulloh said, "into loose configurations that were never very stable but somehow stuck together enough—held together by the music as much as anything—that people came to identify them as this or that song."[8]

McCulloh explained the basis on which musicians in the early decades of recording had few reservations about claiming ownership of songs that predated them.

A different attitude prevails in folk communities from what prevails in the commercial marketplace. A traditional singer may add or change a verse or two and feel entirely justified in claiming to be the author of the whole thing. If the community comes to associate that version of the song with that singer, it is in their view entirely appropriate to say, Oh yes, that's X's song, X did write that song. Within this elastic concept of authorship, they're right. But the copyright lawyers . . . would proclaim that A wrote the song and X can claim only the new bits (if sufficiently different from A's) and has to pay A for use of the original if it comes to publication or recording. These matters have surfaced more in recent times, especially since the folk revival [of the 1950s and 1960s], when there was money to be made from traditional materials.

When McCulloh asked Bill Monroe—the originator of bluegrass music—about his source for "In the Pines," he was careful to reply that fiddler Clayton McMichen "has the copyright on that one." Monroe sang a traditional version, while McMichen had written new words to the traditional tune. "Monroe was aware of copyright and . . . didn't want to take any chances of being accused of infringement," said McCulloh. Ironically, Roy Hall was blocked from releasing the first recording of the now-classic fiddle tune "Orange Blossom Special" because the composers, Ervin and Gordon Rouse, would not allow his record company to use the tune.[9]

The issue was money. The earning power of musicians in the south was slim, and came from the few sources available. This explains why there was so much competition to play on the radio and to make records. Radio shows and recordings were routes that enabled musicians to generate income in addition to in-person performances. Sponsored radio shows might give the impression of being profitable for musicians, but often were unpaid. Station managers used the argument that performers were rewarded for doing a radio show in the form of free advertising for in-person performances. This was the argument that the Stanley Brothers faced in December 1946 after they passed the audition for a show on Bristol's new station WCYB. "The station's vice president, Fay Rogers, called us into his office and he got right to the point," Ralph recalled.[10] "We had the job but there was no salary or money for meals or nothing like that. The only thing WCYB was offering was the chance to make our name."

Since Carter was 21 and Ralph 19—both recently out of the army, with little professional experience—they had no leverage. "We didn't know whether we could make it or not," Carter recalled.[11] "They said they couldn't promise us a dose of medicine. I'll never forget that. Clay Rogers, he was the vice president . . . he said, 'Fellas, I won't promise you a dose of medicine. You might starve to death up here.'"

Carter recalled the audition taking place on Christmas Day or the day before, and both brothers recalled December 26 as their start date. There had been considerable competition for the two available slots. After going on the air on September 23, 1946, WCYB auditioned a total of thirty-five "rustic string bands," as *Billboard* magazine termed them in 1947.[12] The other successful band was Curly King and the Tennessee Hilltoppers, who were on the air when the Stanley Brothers arrived. The station management's strategy was to select groups that would appeal—in name as well as in musical style—to residents of both Tennessee and Virginia.

Curly King and his band were featured on the *Thrift Supply Company Show* broadcast in the late afternoon. The station offered the Stanley Brothers the *Farm and Fun Time* slot, which aired six days a week at 12:05 p.m. Honaker Harness and Saddlery in Honaker, Virginia, sponsored *Farm and Fun Time*.[13] The early shows were described as "fifteen-minute programs of country music, which featured fiddle music, hymns, 'heart songs,' and early bluegrass tunes."[14] Ralph recalled *Farm and Fun Time* as expanding to 55 minutes until 1 p.m.[15] Both the *Thrift Supply Show* and *Farm and Fun Time* were able to reach the radio sets of many listeners because the Federal Communications Commission[16] had granted WCYB a 1,000-watt license that was increased to 5,000 watts about a year later. The station's reach extended into five states: Tennessee, Virginia, West Virginia, North Carolina, and Kentucky—the heartland of old-time country music.

By contrast to WCYB, station WNVA in Norton, where Carter and Ralph had played with Roy Sykes and the Blue Ridge Mountain Boys, broadcast on a 50-watt signal that limited its audience to the immediate area. Sponsoring the Blue Ridge Mountain Boys' shows on the same principle as the WCYB shows (free performances on air would lead to paying appearances in the listening area) were Piggly Wiggly grocery stores. Roy Sykes Jr. believed that the Piggly Wiggly Corporation had big plans for his father until he decided to marry and forgo touring. Even if Roy Sr. had such sponsorship, he would have needed a more powerful station to provide the platform for his musical ambitions. By deciding to leave the Sykes band to form their own group, the Stanley Brothers were able to find that platform, bypassing Bristol's original radio station, WOPI, in the process.

WOPI had begun broadcasting seventeen years before on June 15, 1929, after W. A. Wilson had asked east Tennessee Congressman Carroll B. Reese for help in securing a license. When Wilson visited Washington, Reese took him to see the judge who was chairman of the Federal Radio Commission. His office was in the Department of Commerce—a reflection of the way the government envisioned the new medium of radio. Recalled Wilson: "... after Mr. Reese informed the judge of our mission, the judge said, 'wait a minute,' then came back with a four page form and said to fill it out and mail it back to him and he would see what could be done. In a couple months time, the permit was received."[17] Broadcasting from the corner of State and 22nd Streets in Bristol, Tennessee, WOPI had 100 watts of power and was on the air from 7 a.m. to 10 p.m. in two-hour intervals so that that the motor-generators would be able to cool. By the 1940s, it was on the air from 6 a.m. to midnight.

WOPI's inaugural half-hour program was broadcast by remote from the Hotel Bristol. A sponsorship cost $10. Uppermost in Wilson's mind was seeking advertisers to meet his $140-per-week payroll. Almost as soon as he found them by broadcasting from east Tennessee communities such as Kingsport, Johnson City, and Greeneville, the Great Depression that began in October 1929 came close to silencing the new signal. The indefatigable Wilson found enough sponsors to stay on the air; and by 1935, economic conditions had improved to the point that he could originate all his broadcasts from Bristol.[18]

While conducting business and studio operations from 1933 to 1945 at the same 410 (and later 412½) State Street location where the 1927 Bristol sessions had taken place, WOPI began a weekly country music broadcast that became known as the *Saturday Night Jamboree*, drawing studio audiences of fifty to sixty people. WOPI was able to capitalize on the popularity of the popularity of the Saturday night country show by renting more space,[19] selling tickets to some 350 people in the new auditorium that the station dubbed the Radiotorium.

On February 24, 1945, fire damaged the station, destroying equipment, offices, and the Radiotorium. Forced to relocate, Wilson moved down the street to the Union Trust Building at 310 State Street, less than a hundred yards from the train station. With the success of the *Saturday Night Jamboree* , the city once again became a popular destination for old-time country performers as well as the newer country bands. In 1942 a publicity photograph of twenty-seven performers on the *Jamboree* stage set (designed to simulate a barn) included the original members of the Carter Family in the center, with Maybelle's three daughters to their right.[20] Standing in the back row is a solemn-faced young man with slick black hair who began working at WOPI while in high school. He became known in Bristol and later in Nashville as Tennessee Ernie Ford, whose biggest hit was the coal mining song "16 Tons."

WOPI increased its signal to 250 watts as the Depression was ending in 1939, and applied for the region's first FM (frequency modulation) license, superior to AM (amplitude modulation) for broadcasting music. Locating its transmitter near the peak of White Top Mountain in Virginia, WOPI-FM went on the air on Christmas Day 1946 with a signal that could be received for 100 miles around—a potential audience of up to 4 million people. Technical advances took precedence over local programming, however, and by 1947 NBC network shows such as *The Fred Waring Show* and *The Grand Ole Opry* had replaced *Saturday Night Jamboree*. Before the end of 1947, WCYB capitalized on its more powerful signal and popularity of local programming to reach out to a much larger listening area and potential audience base.[21] The new station in town had become the market leader—and the Stanley Brothers' springboard to regional success.

6. "COME ON ALONG, JOIN IN THE SONG"

A farmer living in radio station WCYB's listening area toward the end of December 1946 or in January and February 1947 would have completed much of his work by noontime, since winter was removed from the planting and harvesting seasons. He would be more than ready to sit down for his noon meal and a break from the never-ending chores. If he lived near the city of Bristol, whose combined population of 25,000 in the mid-1940s resided on both sides of the Virginia and Tennessee state line, he might have heard about a new radio station going on the air. Even if he had not, he might be turning his radio dial to find a program to entertain him as he ate. This may have been the one time each day he was in contact with the world outside his farm. As he rotated the radio dial, his ears perked up when he heard the familiar sounds of old-time country music, but at a musical tempo that was excitingly unfamiliar. Not only were the musicians playing at breakneck speed; they were whooping and yipping as if it was some kind of Saturday evening social. He had experienced this surge of energy from time to time when musicians got into the music at barn dances and pie suppers, but he had never encountered anything like it on local radio. Before long he discovered that he could listen to this show every day but the Lord's Day, so he left his radio tuned to WCYB and made the new show a daily ritual—a welcome respite in a life of hard work and unbreakable routine. Even the program's name, *Farm and Fun Time*, made it sound as if the show were produced with him in mind.

Larry Gorley, host of WOPI's *Bluegrass Jamboree* program, recalled:

I remember listening to the radio show as a boy and my most vivid memory is visiting my grandparents' home during summer vacation from school. They would stop whatever work was being done and gather around the kitchen table for lunch. After the blessing was said, they would turn the family radio on to WCYB and Farm and

Fun Time. *Listening to the program gave them great pleasure as well
as the latest farm news and it was only in my later years that I found
that so many others made it a point to be tuned in to the show that
could be heard in several states.*[1]

The WCYB studios were located on the Virginia side of Bristol in the
General Shelby Hotel at 100 Front Street,[2] not far from the train depot
where musicians had debarked in 1927 to audition for Ralph Peer. In
the winter of 1946–47, the four members of the Stanley Brothers and
the Clinch Mountain Boys[3] would arrive shortly after 10:00 a.m. to tune
their instruments and rehearse several numbers for that day's program.[4]
Within a few minutes of show time, they would gather around the large-
headed, single microphone bearing the station's call letters, pluck a few
notes and clear their throats one last time before going on the air. The
engineer in the glassed-in booth would cue the group with the time remaining—fifteen seconds . . . ten . . . five—and signal with his hand that
the group was on the air. Above his glass window, the red light would go
on, and at the same moment, Carter, Ralph, Pee Wee, and Leslie would
jump into their theme song: "Moving along, singing a song / singing a
song of home sweet home / Come on along, join in the song / singing
our troubles away." The song lasted about twenty-four seconds, catching the audience's attention so that Carter could introduce the first full
number.

In the years before tape recording, WCYB and other radio stations featuring live music had to solve the problem of what to do on the occasional
day when the group might not be able to perform in the studio. The solution was a 16-inch-diameter transcription disc that could record about a
third of the 55-minute show. Three discs could reproduce a full program.
Fortunately for those interested in the career of the Stanley Brothers, a
transcription disc from 1947 survived to be issued on vinyl in 1988 and
reissued on compact disc in 1997.[5] The disc offers listeners an aural snap-
shot of what *Farm and Fun Time* sounded like on a program that would
have been similar to so many others. Included in this 18-minute, 50-sec-
ond slice of early WCYB content are three vigorous fiddle tunes played
by Leslie Keith, two duets sung by Carter and Ralph, two covers of Bill
Monroe songs performed by Pee Wee Lambert, and a sacred number
sung by the four musicians as harmonizing quartet.

Introducing the first of his and Ralph's duets, Carter said, "Right here's
a number that Ralph and me introduced just lately on WCYB, and it

seems like a lot of folks enjoy it everywhere." A listener had sent a poem to the Stanley Brothers care of the radio station, and the group arranged it as lyrics to a melody they composed in the traditional style, though they kept the song to three verses (suited to the length limitations of recording and radio), titling it "Our Darling's Gone."

Playing energetic fiddle on "Cotton Eyed Joe" and "Orange Blossom Special," Leslie Keith sounded more like an excited newcomer than the experienced professional he was. Pee Wee Lambert covered songs he had learned by listening to Bill Monroe on the *Grand Ole Opry*—the traditional horse race song "Molly and Tenbrooks" and Monroe's classic "Blue Moon of Kentucky." Lambert sang in a high, thin tenor similar to Monroe's voice while playing melodic, Monroe-like mandolin breaks. Carter dedicated the hymn "Lonely Tombs" to infirm listeners: "We'd like to do it especially for all you folks that's not feeling well." The older brother did the talking, with the exception of Ralph's chipper response "Yes, sir, Carter!" to the question of whether Ralph was ready to play his "fancy banjo"—a phrase Carter lifted from host George D. Hay's introductions of Earl Scruggs on the *Grand Ole Opry*.[6]

In terms of impact on the brothers' careers, the most significant of the eight songs transcribed that day is one of the first compositions that Carter and Ralph claimed as their own, "Little Glass of Wine." John and Elizabeth (Lyttleton) Lomax had recorded a Kentucky guitar player named Bill Bundy singing a similar song, "Poison in a Glass of Wine," on October 13, 1937, while on a Library of Congress song collecting trip. In theme, the song adheres to a traditional ballad narrative in which a young man pressures a young woman to marry him. When she says they are too young and asks for more time, he becomes jealous and plots to kill her. His motive is that if he can't have her, no man will. In similar Appalachian ballads, such as "Banks of the Ohio," the suitor turned murderer surrenders himself to the law to let justice take its course. The plot twist in "Glass of Wine" occurs when the young man drinks from a poisoned glass of wine after poisoning the wine of his intended—similar to the ending of Shakespeare's *Romeo and Juliet*.

Though sometimes identified as the first song the Stanley Brothers wrote, "Glass of Wine" was the third. When I interviewed Ralph in 2005 about a reissue of the brothers' earliest recordings,[7] he set the record straight for me. "The first song that Carter and me wrote was 'Mother No Longer Awaits Me at Home.'" I asked if there was an event that had inspired that first song. "No," he said. "That [loss of mother] hadn't happened to us, but it was something that could have . . . you had to read between the lines . . . something that very easily could happen."

Written to the melody that eventually became "Glass of Wine" was another narrative in which a young man falls in love with the barmaid, only to have her jealous lover stab her in the back as the young man is walking her home. This song, which Ralph told me was written around the same time as "Mother No Long Awaits Me at Home," was titled "The Girl behind the Bar." Of the three, "Glass of Wine" was the regional hit. Introducing it on the transcribed *Farm and Fun Time*, Carter said it was the song that drew the most requests.

In an earlier interview, Ralph described "Girl behind the Bar" as "like 'Little Glass of Wine.'"[8] The brothers learned a portion of the "Glass of Wine" lyrics from a lumber worker near McClure. "We got part of that song from a fellow by the name of Otto Taylor," Ralph recalled. "There used to be the Ritter Lumber Company around here. We met him at a camp where he lived. He had part of that song, and we just finished it out and claimed it."[9]

Founded in 1901, the W. M. Ritter Lumber Company harvested both hardwood (such as oak, hickory, and ash) and softwood trees (such as pine and maple) throughout southern Appalachia, purchasing lumber rights from the railroads that had penetrated the region or from the resident owners—often for as little as twenty-five cents a tree.[10] Workers such as Otto Taylor lived in mobile campsites composed of modified railroad cars. Workers and their families would pack up a camp about once a year so that their living quarters and belongings could be moved a few miles down the railroad line to the next growth of timber.

Dickenson County was dense with these camps. Before World War I, eighteen lumber companies had opened for business in the county.[11] From Ralph's description, it sounded like the Stanley boys were no strangers to the camps, where workers would gather near the social car to share music and songs after a communal supper. In the camps, two young men who were considering careers in music could find experienced musicians and fascinating characters, as well as catchy new material such as "Little Glass of Wine." As far as ownership of a song was concerned, the rights often would attach to the person or group who popularized it, rather than serving as reliable identification of the person who wrote it. Ralph's explanation of hearing part of "Glass of Wine" and "finishing it out" is consistent with his description of having heard a verse or so of "Man of Constant Sorrow" from his father before he and Carter "finished" that song. The unanswered question is whether finishing a song would be described more accurately as learning it from a prior performer such as Otto Taylor. Among musicians and audiences at the time of "Glass of Wine," this distinction seemed to matter little. As musicologist Judith McCulloh explained, a traditional singer adding or changing a verse in a song would feel entitled to claim the composition as his or her own. As stated simply by Ralph, he and Carter found "Glass of Wine" and "claimed it."

With the success of their radio show, the Stanley Brothers had every reason to expect 1947 to be an exciting year. When they took a room in the city to meet their daily performance schedule, Bristol was a stimulating place for the young musicians to live. In the two decades since the remarkable field recording sessions of 1927, the city that linked Virginia and Tennessee had become a crossroads for musicians from all over Appalachia. Nashville had yet to establish itself as the capital of country music recording, though that would change within a few years. Along with Atlanta, Georgia, and Charlotte and Asheville, North Carolina, Bristol was one of the centers of old-time country activity as the music incorporated a variety of new sounds, from the brisk precision of bluegrass to the crying steel guitars of more commercial country. For Carter, Ralph, and Pee Wee Lambert, popularity on a powerful regional radio station must have felt like being promoted to the major leagues of baseball after spending just a few months in the minors. Even though Leslie Keith had been in the business for a much longer time, the number of listeners hearing his fiddle over WCYB represented a significant increase over that of the station in Bluefield, West Virginia, on which Carter and Ralph first had heard him.

During an interview, I asked Ralph about these earliest months in his career. He sketched the chronology.

The first year went really well. We played about three weeks at a radio station, WNVA, in Norton, Virginia. We'd heard of a new radio station in Bristol that would start a midday program. We were first to start this show. We were on the air live. It was 55 minutes . . . an hour . . . and we played that program an hour a day six days a week for something like two or three years. And that program began getting popular everywhere, and some more groups moved in. And they had so many sponsors waiting in line to get in the show that they had to move it up to two hours, and then other groups moved in and helped us out for two hours.[12]

The popularity of *Farm and Fun Time* led to a steady flow of requests for personal appearances that the new band—with Lee Stanley as manager—kicked off by arranging what appears to be its first performance outside of Dickenson County, in neighboring Russell County. "[The radio show] helped us build an audience," Ralph recalled, "and we would advertise for shows at high schools and theaters, and we got so many invitations to come to a school at a certain place or theater or something that we would just pick through 'em and pick the best. So we played six nights a week. We were booked all the time. It was bigger than we expected. It was real good for us. I think we played like six days on *Farm and Fun Time*, and we booked a little school . . . a grade school . . . out from Bristol in a place called Belfast, and that was the first where we played out of Bristol. We had two packed houses on a Saturday night, and we had to play two shows to take care of the people, and that was the way it was for several years. We thought we had a career then."

Many members of the radio audience arrived at the same conclusion: Seeing the Stanley Brothers in person was worth the price of admission, even if they hardly could afford it. Max K. Powers attended the Mount Rogers School in Whitetop, Virginia, on the same mountain where pioneering Bristol radio station WOPI had built its transmitter. "This was a night show and I was there early to make sure I got a seat for the first of two shows," Max told me one afternoon at Emory and Henry College in Virginia, where we worked together in 2001–2002. "We did not have an automobile back then, so I walked a mile or more up and down hills. I believe admission was somewhere in the twenty-five to fifty cents range. If it had been more, I probably wouldn't have been there."[13]

As were many who attended the Stanley Brothers' early shows, Max was drawn back to his school that evening by the lively music and banter he had heard over WCYB. "I had been listening to Carter and Ralph on radio, but this was my first live bluegrass show," he remembered. "I was so impressed by their performance that I sat through the second show." He remembered with certainty three of the band members and their respective roles: Carter Stanley on guitar and lead vocals; Ralph Stanley on five-string banjo and tenor vocals; and Leslie Keith on fiddle and blacksnake whip. "The mandolin player may have been Pee Wee Lambert, and I don't recall the bass player's name," Max continued. "It would be near impossible for me to name songs they did then, because I have listened to the Clinch Mountain Boys ever since."

As one might gather from the presence of Leslie Keith's whip, music was not the only entertainment that old-time country bands could provide. This was before the demand for authenticity that accompanied the folk music revival of the late 1950s and early 1960s began to treat the music as an artifact. In the case of the Stanley Brothers, their bassist Ray Lambert portrayed the comedic hick Cousin Winesap, while solemn-faced fiddler Leslie Keith made use of his Native American heritage by transforming into an Indian chief who was skilled with a blacksnake whip. They were the first of several minstrel-style acts that the Stanley Brothers added to their shows.

"The act by Leslie Keith sticks in my mind," Max Powers recalled. "He was very accurate in clipping either a cigarette or a piece of paper from someone's fingers." Keith had learned the routine from Lester Vernon Storer, another reputable fiddler whose stage name was Natchee the Indian. In regard to the music, Powers remembered the Stanley Brothers' "tight singing, with Carter's lead and Ralph's high tenor and fierce banjo breaks. Mount Rogers was a four-room school," he said. "Two of the rooms had a partition of folding doors between them, and the auditorium was created by unfolding those doors. Can you imagine Carter and Ralph performing for an audience of forty to fifty people?"

Having graduated from high school in 1952, Max estimated that he saw the Stanley Brothers and the Clinch Mountain Boys sometime between his fifth- and seventh-grade years, placing the show around 1947 or 1948. Listening to his recollections that day in my office, I could almost hear the crack of the whip and Ralph's equally crackling banjo breaks.

7. MAKING RECORD TIME

As the wax disc revolved under the cutting lathe, the wax cut by the lathe spun away from the disc in strips called "swarf." Wade Mainer remembered the swarf because when he and Mainer's Mountaineers recorded in the 1930s, the lathe stood near the musicians. "It was kind of like a turntable," he said.[1] "The wax was cut into a record, and somebody had to brush the wax to keep it from getting tangled up." According to Mainer, this was the reason "a lot of those records don't have that good a sound." Mainer's recollections of the wax disc process and two of its predecessors—metal wire and wax on top of a tin base—prompted me to ask how a musician would discover a new tune or song before records and radio existed as sources. "We learned it from somebody else," he said. "Back then in mountains of North Carolina especially, old people lived in farms and houses on the mountains and would get down and sing and go to one another's houses and play music. I learned a good lot of my music from my brother-in-law." Simple though the question was, I had wanted to ask it of a musician who had grown up in the years before records and radio made it possible for music to travel outside the range of the community and the next couple of towns. Mainer's answer showed how personal contact among musicians was the connection that permitted old songs and tunes to continue to exist for generations.

This had been the state of music in the mountains for two hundred years before talent scouts such as Ralph Peer arrived in Appalachia with weight-powered machines that could capture the music and package it as a product. Before recording, songs had been something singers in that part of the country shared with their kinfolk and neighbors for entertainment. The recording process transformed the old ballads into commodities. Though developed to preserve the human voice for the transcription of business dictation—much as radio was developed for the utilitarian purpose of ship-to-shore and ship-to-ship communication—early recording technology soon was used to capture the sounds of music. This created a demand for recorded content that could be played in the home. Because of the size of the first record players, which was necessary to include the winding tube of an internal amplification system, furniture dealers sold the early appliances. It made business sense for the same dealers to sell records. As was the case with all mass media prior to the World Wide Web, a strong economic relationship developed between the systems of distribution (the distributors and sellers of record players and records) and the providers of content (the companies that recorded and manufactured records). Without the Victrola or equivalent appliance to play the group's songs in living rooms throughout North America, there would not have been a practical reason for the Victor Recording Company to seek to preserve the sounds of the Carter Family, or for a northeast Tennessee entrepreneur to want to make records of the Stanley Brothers.

Known as Jim or Hobe, Hobart Stanton ran a small recording business out of Johnson City, Tennessee, twenty-six miles south of Bristol and well within range of WCYB's signal. Whether it was their radio popularity or a personal pitch to him that led Stanton to sign the Stanley Brothers to his Rich-R-Tone label remains a matter of debate. According to Stanton, the brothers initiated the contact. "First time I ever met 'em, they came to Johnson City to see me and honestly I wasn't that impressed," he told an interviewer.[2] Stanton said he had been keeping his ears open "for something tight like Lester and Earl"—referring to singer and guitarist Lester Flatt and banjo player Earl Scruggs, who were members of Bill Monroe's Blue Grass Boys in 1947, but left to form an influential group that was known for its breakneck playing and precise sound. Stanton continued, "like all artists, [the Stanley Brothers] pursued me to impress me to record them." He recalled Carter and Ralph making a return visit to Johnson City with a mail sack in their car full of requests sent to the radio station for them to sing "Little Glass of Wine."

The Stanley Brothers maintained in separate interviews that Stanton had done the pursuing. While writing an article on a 2005 reissue of the brothers' earliest recordings, I asked Ralph about it. "He came to Bristol and asked us to record," Ralph said. "I notice he wrote something different [in the reissue booklet]. To my remembrance, he came to Bristol and approached us 'cause we didn't know anything about him. He heard us on the radio." Fred Congdon had worked with Stanton in the 1960s. He was the business manager of Rich-R-Tone at the time of the reissue by

Rounder Records. His memory supported Ralph's. "It is my understanding that Jim Stanton was quite the entrepreneur in the early days of the recording industry and in fact until his death," he wrote.[3] "Jim contacted different groups performing their music in and about the Johnson City area . . . and took his recording equipment to where they were. I am told that he also recorded a considerable amount of music at his home on Pine Street in Johnson City and in the local radio stations."

To record the Stanley Brothers, Stanton brought them into the studio of rival Bristol radio station WOPI, which was located a few blocks from WCYB at 310 State Street.[4] His reasons were both practical and personal. "We sort of called WOPI our home base for recording because . . . we liked Russ [Robinson, the station's engineer] and they had a right good facility there," recalled Stanton.[5] ". . . [T]hey had a good disc cutter, and it was handy for the Stanley Brothers 'cause they were living in a rooming house there and working on WCYB. . . ." The station most often used the disc cutter to create transcription discs to preserve programs for later airplay. Given the presence of adequate technology in the studio, Stanton must have known that the single most important component in the success of the recording process was an experienced engineer. The engineer's combination of technological expertise and ability to arrange and balance a wide range in sounds of voices and instruments was critical to determining the quality of the final product. In Stanton's opinion, Russ Robinson possessed what people in the recording business liked to call "good ears."

Stanton may not have had good ears himself (in Ralph's opinion, "when it came to hillbilly music, Hobe didn't know his ass from a hole in the ground"),[6] but he had an eye for talent. In early 1947 he traveled to Asheville, North Carolina, to record the husband and wife team of Wilma Lee (Leary) and Dale Troy "Stoney" Cooper. Wilma Lee and Stoney performed on Asheville radio station WWNC. As with the Stanley Brothers, Stanton first recorded the Coopers at the radio station. Wilma Lee recalled a second session in December. She and Stoney released two records in 1947 with the band listed as the Clinch Mountain Boys before learning that the Stanley Brothers had claimed the name.[7] The Coopers' connection to Clinch Mountain in southwest Virginia is unclear. By contrast, the Stanley Brothers adapted the Clinch Mountain Boys moniker from one of their sponsors during their brief stint at WNVA in Norton: the Clinch Valley Insurance Company,[8] located near the Clinch River that runs through southwest Virginia.

The Coopers soon changed their radio affiliation to WWVA in their home state of West Virginia and the name of their band to the Clinch Mountain Clan. In 1947 WWVA was a 50,000-watt station that hosted the *World's Original WWVA Jamboree* (known as the *Wheeling Jamboree*), on which the Stanley Brothers were to appear toward the end of their career. In 1954 the Coopers became members of the *Grand Ole Opry*.

Like the brothers, the Coopers irritated Bill Monroe by releasing one of his songs on record before he did. They recorded "The Wicked Path of Sin" after hearing the Blue Grass Boys sing the song on the radio under the name the group used when performing gospel numbers: the Blue Grass Quartet. (Monroe had named his group after the nickname of his native state, Kentucky.) A stenographer, Wilma Lee took down the words in shorthand. Rich-R-Tone released the Coopers' recording in September 1948—a month before Monroe's own recording was issued.[9] The Coopers maintained they were unaware that "Wicked Path of Sin" was a Monroe composition and that his record label was about to release it. Crossing paths with Monroe on a Saturday night at the *Opry*, Stoney Cooper told him he liked the song he had heard Bill sing so much that he had recorded it. "Yeah, I know," responded Monroe. "Don't it seem to you a little that when you sing other people's songs, after a while you sort of get yourself patterned like them?" Recalled Cooper, "That really hurt me, you know."[10]

The Coopers' recording sixteen songs for Rich-R-Tone in one or two sessions was exceptional. The common practice was to record four songs, which provided material for two double-sided 78 rpm[11] records that the record company could release during the next six months before arranging another session.

The first four songs the Stanley Brothers cut at WOPI were divided between gospel quartets and the brothers' original compositions. Ralph Stanley's vague recollection of the source of the gospel quartets—"Death Is Only a Dream" and "I Can Tell You the Time"—is that ". . . we got 'em from old songbooks that we found somewhere."[12] Joined by Pee Wee Lambert, Leslie Keith, and Ray Lambert, the brothers followed the gospel arrangements that Bill Monroe had been using since 1940 by featuring four voices in harmony, accompanied only by Carter's guitar and Pee Wee's mandolin.[13] Monroe-influenced Pee Wee sang the tenor part; Ralph, the customary tenor vocalist, sang baritone; Carter sang the lead part; and Ray sang bass. The recorded results seemed a little hurried for gospel, but possessed an affecting youthfulness. The careful arrangements of the songs reflected the trouble the band members took to get each part the way they wanted it. Leslie Keith recalled early band rehearsals in which he and Carter would take turns standing in front of the group to hear how the individual sounds blended together.[14]

Both of the originals, "Mother No Longer Awaits Me at Home" and "The Girl behind the Bar," are credited to Carter, though when Ralph referred to them in our interview, he seemed to indicate that he and Carter co-wrote them. In lyrics and melody, "Mother No Longer Awaits Me at Home" is a reworking of "Mother's Only Sleeping," recorded by Bill Monroe and the Blue Grass Boys in Chicago on September 16, 1946, and the same month by Charlie Monroe—six months before the Stanley Brothers stepped into the studio. The Stanley Brothers' version contains lines identical to the Blue Grass Boys' recording, which Monroe had copyrighted, though there is a slight variation in the events of this sentimental narrative of a young man's mother being "called to heaven." The Clinch Mountain Boys' several similarities to the Blue Grass Boys here and on the WCYB radio transcriptions help explain why Monroe's initial impression of the Stanley Brothers was imitators who were invading his musical turf. This was only the beginning of the rivalry.

The second Stanley composition recorded that day, "The Girl behind the Bar," sounded more original, though it employed the same melody as "The Little Glass of Wine," which Ralph acknowledged learning from lumber worker Otto Taylor. Carter's (or Carter and Ralph's) lyrics may be original. In both songs, the melody supports a story with a sad ending. In "Girl behind the Bar," a jealous lover stabs the girl when she walks home from the bar, and the tragic lovers of "Glass of Wine" are "bound to die." Carter and Ralph sang both numbers as duets.

Though not as heartfelt as some of their later material—especially songs written by Carter that are among the most poignant in any genre of country music—the Rich-R-Tone recordings hold special significance because they identified the roots of the Stanley Brothers' music. Taking place at WOPI in late 1947 or early 1948, the second Rich-R-Tone session included both "Little Maggie," which Ralph said he learned from Mainer's Mountaineers, and "Our Darling's Gone," whose melody comes from the Carter Family. Two other songs recorded that day were "The Little Glass of Wine" and "The Jealous Lover," another sad ballad with a fatal ending that, in this case, the brothers learned from a neighbor but copyrighted to Carter.[15] As sung by the 20- or 21-year-old Ralph Stanley, "Little Maggie" is compelling. The blend of Ralph's driving banjo and piercing voice sounds foreboding. The effect is heightened by an echo that resonated in the studio itself. I asked Ralph where he had learned "Little Maggie" and a similar song, "Little Birdie," recorded for Rich-R-Tone in the middle of 1952. "I think I heard 'Little Birdie' and 'Little Maggie' both from Wade Mainer and Steve Ledford," he said. "I forget which one of them sung it and the other one played it. I guess Steve played the fiddle and Wade sung it."[16]

Ralph appeared to be referring to Wade Mainer's 1937 Bluebird releases of "Little Birdie," done before Ledford joined Mainer, and "Little Maggie," on which Ledford played fiddle and sang harmony. Ralph's version of "Little Maggie" sounds very similar to that of G. B. Grayson and Henry Whitter, who met at a fiddlers' convention in Mountain City, Tennessee in 1927, and recorded together for two productive years. Mainer's band likely learned "Little Maggie" from Grayson and Whitter, thus passing it along to Ralph through the folk process. Ralph may have forgotten the Grayson and Whitter recording. The only differences between the two are that Ralph played the melody on banjo rather than fiddle and dropped a couple of verses. The Stanley Brothers certainly were familiar with Grayson and Whitter's material. They came from the same mountainous wedge of Tennessee, Virginia, and North Carolina; and on the two Rich-R-Tone takes of "Little Glass of Wine," Carter exclaimed the title over an instrumental break exactly as Grayson or Whitter had on their recording of "Handsome Molly." No matter what the source, there was a stark power in Ralph Stanley's recorded performance of "Little Maggie" that became his signature in old-time country music.[17]

"Our Darling's Gone" developed from quite different sources. A woman whose husband was killed in a mining accident sent a poem about her and her children's feelings of loss and faith to the brothers in care of WCYB. The brothers turned it into one of their most requested numbers by grafting the widow's poem to the melody of the Carter Family's "Can the Circle Be Unbroken?" Despite the fact that the words came from one identifiable source and the melody from another, the brothers copyrighted the song as co-writers. This creative appropriation demonstrated an attribute vital to the Stanley Brothers' long-term survival in the music business: the ability to generate and cultivate a constant stream of new material. In total, they would record nearly three hundred songs and tunes. Many came from the Appalachian tradition, others from personal inspiration, and still others—such as the poem and melody that became "Our Darling's Gone"—from a combination of serendipity and tradition.

In their final session at WOPI in mid-1948, the Stanley Brothers and
the Clinch Mountain Boys recorded "The Rambler's Blues" and "Molly
and Tenbrook." Mandolin player Pee Wee Lambert sang lead vocals on
both numbers. On the former, Leslie Keith added new words to a melody the Carter Family had recorded almost twenty years before, with lyrics that mentioned rambling: "I did not like my fireside / I did not like
my home / I have a mind for rambling / so far away from home";[18] and
the Clinch Mountain Boys learned the latter song about a famous horse
race from a Bill Monroe radio or personal appearance and recorded it.
The fact that Rich-R-Tone released "Molly and Tenbrook" at the same
time as Wilma Lee and Stoney Cooper's version of "The Wicked Path of
Sin" helps to explain why Monroe was so annoyed when he confronted
Stoney Cooper at the Opry.[19] Bluegrass historian Neil V. Rosenberg gives
the Stanley Brothers' version of "Molly and Tenbrook" a special place in
the evolution of the genre as "the first direct evidence that the 'sound' of
Monroe's band was being imitated by other bands. . . . This imitation . . .
is important because it marks the transition from the sound of Monroe's
[1945–48] band to the style known as Bluegrass."[20]

According to Rosenberg, the musical components of early bluegrass
were: "All the instrumentalists . . . took solos at various times, while the
rest of the band provided rhythmic and melodic background. . . . Within
this framework of soloist and band, Monroe's virtuoso musicians performed a variety of songs: slow and medium tempo blues, fast break-
downs, religious pieces, medium to fast tempo love songs, and waltzes."[21]
The Clinch Mountain Boys did not match the repertoire and virtuosity
of the Monroe musicians, but took advantage of energetic instrumental
work and Pee Wee Lambert's Monroe-style singing to narrow the gap in
performance. As we will see, the Stanley Brothers often were willing to
work within the framework of the most popular style of the moment—a
trait that would sustain their careers but mask their originality. Historical
arguments aside, I asked Ralph in 2005 what it had felt like to have those
first records out. "We thought that we had reached the top," he said.[22]

8. IN SEARCH OF A SOUND

In the language of baseball, the Stanley Brothers and the Clinch Mountain Boys hit a home run in their first time at bat. *Farm and Fun Time* created an immediate demand for personal appearances, and their records sold well in the hardscrabble environs of southwestern Virginia and eastern Kentucky. Soon after cutting "Little Glass of Wine," the group made a much-publicized appearance at Honaker Harness and Saddlery, the *Farm and Fun Time* sponsor. The owner gave each band member a new pair of black boots to complement sport coats and homburg hats the musicians had bought in Bristol. "Outside the store and all the way down the street was the biggest crowd we'd ever seen," Ralph said. "People came from out of the mountains and all over. . . . Hobe drove up with a thousand copies of the record and by noon he'd sold out. He could have sold another thousand."[1] The hillbilly band in homburgs were on their way to becoming regional stars; yet the Stanley Brothers of 1947 and 1948 were very much a group in search of its own sound, with little time to develop one. Driven by radio popularity, personal appearances proceeded at a hectic pace with little time for introspection.

The path to success in the music business dictated that the band travel constantly, most often performing its segments of the radio show in the morning and early afternoon before driving to and from an engagement the same night. The pressures and temptations of life on the road became the brothers' reality for most of the next two decades, though their earliest ventures were day trips that allowed them to return to their own beds at night or in the early hours of the morning. The distance to the appearance determined their departure time from Bristol: "sometimes as soon as we got off the program" and other times as late as 6:00 p.m. "We'd usually get home anywhere from 10 to 1, 2, 3 o'clock."[2]

Their travels took them along the winding two-lane roads that traversed familiar mountainous terrain.[3] Their vehicle was a 1937 black four-door Chevrolet sedan purchased from a brother-in-law. Most often, Ralph would sit behind the wheel. At 5 feet, 6 inches tall, he was physically and temperamentally a better fit in the driver's seat than lanky Carter, who stretched out in the front passenger seat while Pee Wee Lambert and Leslie Keith hunkered in the back. The musicians packed all their instruments and a small public address system into the trunk until Ray Lambert joined them in 1947. When the bassist traveled with the band, he strapped his bass fiddle onto the roof of the car. Anticipating a transportation upgrade, the group did not paint its name on the first car, but even in those days the Stanley Brothers and the Clinch Mountain Boys in transit were easy to spot. "You knew it was us when you saw a packed sedan with the bass tied to the top," said Ralph.[4]

There were frequent sightings. Ralph Stanley and Leslie Keith both described their personal appearances after the first two or three weeks of *Farm and Fun Time* as a series of full houses and turn-away crowds. The immediate success of the radio program helped the band build an audience overnight, Ralph recalled, "and we would advertise for shows at high schools and theaters. We got so many invitations to come to a school at a certain place or theater or something that we would just pick through 'em and pick the best. So we played six nights a week. We were booked all the time."[5]

Most early performances took place in schoolhouses and the occasional theater, with flatbed trailers and the roofs of drive-in movie refreshment stands serving as stages in the summer months. Kerry Hay, who was born on Backbone Ridge, about fifteen miles as the crow flies from the brothers' home place on Smith Ridge, heard Carter and Ralph when they played noontime at the Turner School in Martha Gap on a Saturday around 1947.[6] "With all due respect to Ralph, Carter was the real talent of this duo," he said, expressing an opinion common among those who heard the Stanley Brothers at this stage in their career. "I can't even remember whether they had sidemen with them."

Accompanied by his mother, grandfather, and younger brother, Hay walked to his elementary school and each family member paid the twenty-five cents admission. A chalkboard divider separated the elementary school into two rooms; the divider could be retracted to accommodate a greater number of people in a single large room. Hay recalled:

> *There was a fairly good-sized crowd, probably owing to the fact that the Stanley Brothers were already enjoying some measure of*

popularity. The show lasted an hour or so, and both Carter and Ralph exhibited good signs of professionalism.[7] Carter asked my grandpa, who was an accomplished Baptist church singer, to come up on stage and sing "The White Dove" with them, which he did. Assuming that the crowd numbered forty people, which I think is a fair guess, the guys grossed ten dollars. Of course, in today's dollars, that wasn't such a bad payday.

If the Turner School show was as early in the Stanley Brothers' career as it sounds, it predates the recording of "The White Dove" and Hay heard a more familiar song, such as a gospel or sacred number.[8] The requests for bookings often came from parent-teacher associations attempting to raise money for their respective schools.[9] A common arrangement called for PTA and band to split the proceeds along an agreed percentage, so the Martha Gap payday may have been more like five dollars.

Many small paydays added up, and depending on the crowds and number of shows the band played on a given night, some of the paydays were substantial. The steady income was necessary because Carter had followed his friend Roy Sykes in courting one of the intelligent and pretty Kiser sisters from Carterton, Virginia. The youngest of the four sisters, Janice Kay, became valedictorian at Castlewood High School. Sykes married Norma Jean Kiser on Valentine's Day, 1946. Not long after, Carter became enchanted with one of Norma Jean's younger sisters, Mary Magdeline, and the couple married on November 11 of the same year. A photograph taken around that time shows a smiling Carter with his arms wrapped around the lovely, dark-haired Mary; he liked to tell her that she looked like the actress Lana Turner. Together they made a very attractive couple. Early in their marriage, they lived in an apartment in Norton. After moving to Bristol for a time, Carter built a four-room house near the home place on Smith Ridge, and Mary soon gave birth to the first of their five children, a son named Carter, after his father, and Lee after his grandfather. Carter now had the responsibility of a family, while Ralph, who was single, continued to live with his mother at the home place and at a boarding house in Bristol.

During the winter of 1947–48, the brothers rented a house on Carolina Avenue in Bristol along with Pee Wee Lambert and his wife, Hazel. The Lamberts had met while Pee Wee performed with Roy Sykes on WNVA. Living nearby in Wise, Virginia, Hazel had begun a new job at the soda fountain of the Passmore Pharmacy in Norton. The drugstore was located

on the first-floor corner of the building that housed the station. Carter
and Pee Wee passed the drugstore's wraparound window on their way
to the side street entrance to the station. They noticed the new girl at the
counter and decided to find out more about her. That was in 1946. On
March 25, 1947, Pee Wee and Hazel were married and soon moved to
Bristol, where Carter and Mary were living.

Carter and Ralph brought Lucy to the Carolina Street house because
the winter was very cold. "I just wanted to get her where we had some
good heat in the house," Ralph recalled.[10] "Hazel and my mother got along
great, and my mother done most of the cooking for us. It was just like
we were back at the old home place and we'd all eat together like family."
Lucy and Hazel joined forces to take care of the increasing volume of mail
the brothers were receiving at WCYB. Most of the requests were for the
songbooks that the group sold on the air. The two women would open
the mail, write the names and addresses of the intended recipients on the
books, and take a walk downtown to mail the books they had addressed.
"We had so much fun," recalled Hazel.[11] On one occasion, the mail led to
one of Hazel's occasional disagreements with Carter. The women opened
a letter written to him by a female fan whose open expression of her sentiments led Hazel to show it to Carter's wife. "I give it to Mary. Oh God,
Carter come . . . He said 'Hazel, I am mad at you.' I said, well, you shouldn't
have been talking or whatever you was doing" with the female fan.[12]

A percentage of the letters—as many as twelve to fourteen in a single
day, said Carter—were requests for personal appearances. The writers
would be members of a PTA, women's club, the Veterans of Foreign Wars,
or similar organization, asking if the band could appear at a specific time
and place or that the band name the date. The brothers would take their
pick of the most desirable of these venues, and de facto business manager Lee Stanley would handle the rest of the arrangements, distributing
handbills advertising *Farm and Fun Time* as he visited the sponsoring
organizations to finalize bookings.

Lee's system provided valuable marketing support for the newly popular band. "By him being so interested, I think that give us a little push,"
Carter recalled, "but we didn't have it rough really like some had. Things
started going pretty quick for us, and pretty soon we started making a
little money."[13] At one point, Lee's "little push" kept the band working for
more than ninety days in a row, Carter remembered. "Our dad kept a
record of it. I'll never forget that we really wanted a day off . . . just one
day off would have been fine. We finally took it." From this frenzied first

round of appearances arose a number of repeated and regular engagements—the bread and butter of a band working regionally. One of these
brought the Stanley Brothers to the Morgan Theater in Grundy, Virginia,
on Saturday nights for several years.

These engagements made a private problem more visible. According to
a town resident, Carter would arrive at his destination early and obtain a
ride into the surrounding hills where he could purchase some moonshine
liquor. After consuming the 'shine, he would return to play the gig—or
not. Sometimes he would be late getting to the stage; on other occasions
he would miss the performance altogether, leaving his brother and the
sidemen to carry on without him. Since Carter served not only as lead
singer and rhythm guitarist but also as master of ceremonies, introducing the songs and overseeing the show's continuity, these situations were
awkward for the other members of the group. The resident's account
dates from around 1950 and contradicts the common assertion that the
older brother's drinking did not affect the quality of his performances until the final years of his career.

Tall and handsome, Carter was bound to attract the attention of wom-
en, as was his younger brother, who was good-looking but shy. "Now we
used to like pretty girls . . . and there was plenty of pretty girls on the
road," Ralph recalled.[14] "Now with these girls you'd see on the road, you
can look at them and not get in trouble. But, sometimes . . . you get with
one and maybe go a little too far." Such attention is not unusual for musicians in any genre, including the postwar generation of old-time country
and bluegrass performers. Bluegrass historian Neil Rosenberg described
performing hillbilly music as "A way of seeing the world and sowing wild
oats. . . . It led to prestige and status in the community similar to that
which came with the glamorous railroad or professional baseball jobs."[15]

With his slicked-back hair and engaging manner, Carter exuded status and charisma. One of the southwestern Virginia women who found
him hard to resist was Thelma Easterling of Norton. Raised by her mother's sister after her mother had died when she was two, Thelma did not
know who her father was.[16] As a teenager, she began to follow the Stanley
Brothers after her girlfriends brought her to one of their performances. "You know how young girls are," she said. "They had a radio show.
We liked the music. We listened to the show and went to a lot of their
events."[17]

A concert in the spring of 1948 gave 18-year-old Thelma the opportunity to meet her idols in person. Her recollection of the performers she

saw that night included Bristol radio regulars who were on their way to becoming stars: the Stanley Brothers, Lester Flatt and Earl Scruggs, and Jim and Jesse McReynolds. The McReynolds brothers hailed from Carfax in the Coeburn area, twenty-two miles from the Stanley home place on Smith Ridge. "We had our own band there [in Bristol]," recalled Jesse, "and we were playing on one radio station, and Flatt and Scruggs were on the other, and the Stanley Brothers. So we were all trying to get started at the same time, in the same town. So we had a lot in common there."[18] Thelma and her friends chatted with the musicians before and after the performance. "We were just fans," she said. After the show, the musicians invited Thelma and several other women to join them at the motel where they were staying. She said two of her girlfriends were among the group, which she described as "a whole bunch." She remembered Carter and Ralph being at the motel, along with two members of their band and other performers from the show.

Once back at the motel, the musicians offered drinks to the girls. "I wasn't used to drinking," Thelma said. "Everybody paired off." When the couples formed, she said that her partner was Carter. "It wasn't a love triangle," she volunteered—perhaps a reference to the fact that Carter was married. "I couldn't wait to get out of there." When I asked why her wish to leave was so urgent, she said she did not like the way the musicians treated the women. "They were a little bit intimidating," she said, "like we had to do something or we weren't getting out of there."

When her period was two months late, she realized that she was pregnant. "It was my fault," she said. She refused to reveal the identity of the father to anyone other than her cousin and cousin's husband. She did not tell Carter. "I didn't want him to know," she said. When Thelma's aunt learned that her niece was pregnant, she made arrangements for Thelma to leave Norton for the Florence Crittenton Home for unwed mothers in Lynchburg, where residents washed dishes, helped in the kitchen, and cleaned toilets.[19] Recreation consisted of instruction in sewing and knitting. Thelma believed correctly that most of the women at the home gave up their babies for adoption. After World War II, maternity homes became "a place to sequester pregnant girls until they could give birth and surrender their child for adoption."[20] Against the prevailing philosophy, Thelma decided to keep her child. She gave birth to a girl on January 18, 1949.

I learned of Thelma's story from her daughter, Sandra, who e-mailed me in the summer of 2005 after seeing an article I wrote for the *Bristol*

Herald Courier about Carter's daughter Jeanie, who had recorded a tribute album to her father.

My mother is from Norton, Virginia, and told me she was with Carter for one night in 1948. I gather she is ashamed and will tell me only that it was a mistake. . . . I always thought something was amiss and overheard my aunt and mother talking one night and my aunt admonishing my mother for not telling me the truth. . . . Mother finally told me when I was 43 years old. That's when I went to Virginia as all my mother's kin are still there and went snooping. I visited Smith Mountain and my father's mausoleum and tried to glean as much as I could from all the tombstones . . .[21]

Her search led to meetings with cousins on the Smith side of the family who "were very welcoming and told me I was a sure daughter of his (look like him, walk like him, built like him . . .)."[22]

Thelma told me that she had saved a poster of the concert where she met Carter for years before giving it to Jim and Jesse's parents through a mutual friend. She died on September 19, 2007.

For much of 1948 Carter, Ralph, and the Clinch Mountain Boys were on the road. With earnings from early appearances, the brothers were able to trade in the 1937 Chevrolet after about two months for a white 1939 Cadillac "I wish I still had that one," said Ralph decades later. "It would really be worth something now."[23] By summer, they had paid cash for a new 1947 Cadillac, cementing their status as a successful young band. Their tour schedule pushed the vehicle to the limit, but the Cadillac's comfort was a major improvement. The spacious interior gave Carter more elbow room to write. He had begun to make use of the time spent driving to and from performances to compose original songs that were suited to what was about to become the band's new sound. "A lot of time traveling . . . nobody saying much, your mind wanders, one thing to another," he said. "I guess you'd call it imagination."[24] Sometimes he would throw a line out to the group for suggestions. Though he was in his early twenties with a high school education, Carter's songwriting demonstrated a way with words. The best of his early writing combined popular images of the rural South, such as loving parents and the home place, with sentimental lyrics that were similar to the elegiac style of England's Graveyard poets.

One of the earliest examples of Carter's developing skills as a songwriter was "The White Dove," written one night while returning from a show. "We was coming home from Asheville, North Carolina, to Bristol, Tennessee, and I had the light on because I wanted to write it down, and Ralph was fussing at me for having the light on," he recalled. "He was driving and he said the light bothered him, but he hasn't fussed anymore about that."[25] By the time the band arrived in Bristol, Carter had composed a verse and chorus.[26] The images of mourning resemble the poet T. S. Eliot's concept of the objective correlative—the use of a concrete image to evoke a particular emotion.

In the deep rolling hills of old Virginia
There's a place that I love so well
Where I spent many days of my childhood
In the cabin where we loved to dwell

Chorus
White dove will mourn in sorrow
The willows will hang their heads
I'll live my life in sorrow
Since mother and daddy are dead

We were all so happy there together
In our peaceful little mountain home
But the Savior needs angels up in heaven
Now they sing around the great white throne

As the years roll by I often wonder
If we will all be together someday
And each night as I wander through the graveyard
Darkness finds me as I kneel to pray

The two-lane highway that wound from North Carolina over the mountains to Tennessee and Virginia would suggest "deep rolling hills"; Carter's feelings of loss at his parents' divorce could transform in song into the death of both parents; the final verse gains power from an internal alliteration ("wonder" and "wander") and the forlorn image of an orphan praying at his parents' graves. The young writer accomplished a great deal within the three verses and chorus allowed by this standard song form, demonstrating a depth of feeling that was characteristic of his best work.

The combination of imagination and circumstances may have colored some of Carter's songwriting, but the pressure to write songs came from musical peers. Carter began writing songs in earnest after several musicians connected with Bill Monroe protested to the management at WCYB about the Stanley Brothers covering the songs of Monroe and his former bandmates. One source of complaint was Bill's brother Charlie. "Charlie come to the station one time," Ralph recalled.[27] "Carter and myself, we went out and talked to him. He shook hands with both of us and said you do a good job and I appreciate you doing my numbers, and the next week—he was in Knoxville at that time—the station got a letter from him asking the station to not allow us to do any of his numbers."

A similar protest took place after guitarist and lead vocalist Lester Flatt and banjo player Earl Scruggs joined *Farm and Fun Time* in May 1948, having left Bill Monroe's Blue Grass Boys to form the Foggy Mountain Boys (after the title of a Carter Family song). "Flatt and Scruggs come to Bristol and about all we was doing then was Bill Monroe tunes," Ralph recalled. "Well, Lester didn't like that so he tried to ground us. He tried to stop us from doing any of Monroe's tunes, which didn't do much good. There were some words over it. . . ."[28] The argument took place outside the WCYB studio and resulted in punches being thrown. "[Lester] got right in Carter's face and told him flat-out we can't be playing their songs," Ralph recalled.[29] "Carter gave it right back to him, and they were close to blows over it. He got pretty smart with Lester and told him a word or two. . . . Then Lester said something against me, and Carter popped him." This blow in defense of his younger brother was the first in a feud that would haunt Carter for the rest of his life. According to musician Bill Clifton, who knew both men, "Carter could hold a grudge once he became angry at somebody, and he disliked Lester Flatt terribly. There were a lot of fistfights that went on between those two."[30]

While Flatt and Scruggs were working at a Knoxville radio station, Earl Scruggs joined the rivalry by sending WCYB station manager Bill Lane a letter objecting to Ralph's performing the banjo tune "Cumberland Gap," which was a banjo showcase for Scruggs. Lane was loyal to his hometown friends. He wrote to Scruggs that if he cared to listen to WCYB during the next week, Ralph would not only perform "Cumberland Gap" on every show but the brothers would dedicate it to him. Ralph wondered what all the fuss was about: "That tune is older than me and Earl Scruggs and three or four of our grandpas put together."[31]

Beyond loyalties, the issue of the Carter, Ralph, and Pee Wee Lambert relying too much on Monroe material was based in fact. Bluegrass historian John Wright noted the early Clinch Mountain Boys' systematic approach to copying other performers' songs in an essay separate from his oral history *Traveling the High Way Home: Ralph Stanley and the World of Bluegrass*:

> *In their early years the Stanley Brothers used writing as part of a unique method of "collecting" extra material. . . . The two brothers and two of their band members would buy tickets to the performance of a rival group. . . . Each of them would have a pad of paper and each of them would have an assignment. As soon as a new song would begin, brother 1 would write the first line, brother 2 the second, sideman 1 the third, and sideman 2 the fourth. (It helps that the typical verse and the typical chorus are each four lines long.) The next day at noon the new song would be featured on the Stanley Brothers' radio program—as often as not before it had been recorded or even broadcast by the source band.*[32]

Rival radio station personnel entered the fray. "At the time the Stanleys were in Bristol, we had a new record out," recalled Lester Woodie, the band's fiddle player from 1949 to 1951.

> *There arose a pretty stiff competition between several radio stations there. Station WFHG was jealous of WCYB because of the success of their live shows. This disk jockey was doing a show on WFHG and he played the Stanley Brothers' new record. He followed it with Bill Monroe, saying "Now this is what it is supposed to sound like." Carter got so mad that he went down there and got that disk jockey by the collar and pulled him out of that studio and had his words. And that just fueled the flame between the two stations. They never came to actual blows, but there were some pretty strong words.*[33]

Despite their obstinate attitude in the face of the comments from their peers, the Stanley Brothers absorbed the message to find their own material. According to Ralph: "The feud with Charlie [Monroe] was bad, but this here spat with Flatt and Scruggs was even worse. Lester was a rival calling Carter out, man-to-man, right there on the street. . . . Carter was so proud about his music that he took it as a blow to his honor. It shook him up and gave him a challenge. I believe it helped turn him into the songwriter he became." In the year after the letters from Charlie Monroe and Earl Scruggs and the vocal objections of Lester Flatt, Carter wrote what Ralph estimated to be fifty to sixty of his own songs. "That's when we began singing Stanley Brothers [songs], so I guess it was a help after all," Ralph concluded.[34]

As the group's music evolved from the sweet harmony of brother duos toward the flashier instrumentation and quicker tempos of bluegrass, national record labels began to express an interest in signing them. Though making records for Rich-R-Tone, they were free to sign elsewhere because the arrangement was only a handshake agreement. "At that time we didn't know A from B," said Ralph. "We didn't know about things like that. And [Jim Stanton] didn't pay us anything: just promised us some royalty on the record. We were glad just to get some records out."[35] Carter hinted that Stanton took advantage of them.[36] Someone later told Ralph that "Little Glass of Wine" sold 100,000 copies[37]—a doubtful figure when sales of 5,000–8,000 would have been good for a local label.

Carl Sauceman, who with his brother J. P. fronted the Green Valley Boys on *Farm and Fun Time*, recalled that in the late 1940s, the Stanley Brothers "were hot."[38] Sauceman held a part-time job selling records for Jim Stanton, who distributed records on the Mercury label in addition to his own Rich-R-Tone products. Sauceman reported, "Every time I walked into a record store and they found out I was selling Rich-R-Tone, they'd holler for me to bring them a load of Stanley Brothers records." Salesmen from other labels took notice. "One day a salesman for RCA walked into a record store in Harlan, Kentucky, with his supervisor," Sauceman recalled. "The salesman asked who the biggest selling artist was, thinking it would be [country star] Eddy Arnold. When the dealer said it was the Stanley Brothers, the supervisor rared [sic] back like a judge and said, 'Who are the Stanley Brothers?' The reply was that they were the hottest thing in the country."[39]

Sauceman overstated the geographic boundaries of the Stanley Brothers' market, which was regional with pockets of popularity. "We could sell like 5,000 Stanley Brothers in Kentucky and absolutely not give one away in Georgia," recalled Stanton.

I've gone into department stores, like in Atlanta, Georgia, and to a salesgirl I knew well, and if I put a bluegrass sound on her turntable, it would embarrass her to the point that she would look around

to see who was listening and in turn it would reflect back on me, I
would be embarrassed for doing it. . . . People tied a banjo and fiddle
with Kentucky, with coal mining, with rural hillbillies and, socially,
people that were more educated, maybe more socially prominent,
they turned their nose down at it. [40]

Even in their own market the Stanley Brothers were aware that they
had a distance to go to match up with the high level of musicianship found
in the Monroe and Flatt and Scruggs bands. Recalling when Earl Scruggs
tried to prevent him from playing "Pike County Breakdown" on WCYB,
Ralph said: "I don't know why. I couldn't touch him on it."[41] Indeed, the
arrival of Lester and Earl and their Foggy Mountain Boys on *Farm and
Fun Time* in the spring of 1948 was the event that brought home to Bristol
musicians the disparity between originators and imitators. "The Stanleys,
they'd always copy Bill [Monroe]," recalled Jim McReynolds of Jim and
Jesse, "and Flatt and Scruggs, they came in with the more or less original
sound, 'cause they'd been with Bill and recorded on everything that he
had out. And so when Flatt and Scruggs came to Bristol why they just
snowed 'em under as far as the real sound of bluegrass, 'cause Earl, he was
the top banjo man. . . . And everything [the Stanley Brothers] done, Flatt
and Scruggs come in on the same program, just about, with the original thing."[42] Confronted by two of the originators at uncomfortably close
quarters, the imitators were determined to develop a sound of their own.

9. LONESOME MELODIES

———◆◆▸✕◂◆———

In the background was the whine of the tour bus changing gears. In the foreground were the voices of an enthusiastic young interviewer and a tired-sounding country performer. Musician and folklorist Mike Seeger was interviewing Carter Stanley as they toured England and Europe together in March 1966. Seeger was a founding member of the revivalist old-time music group, the New Lost City Ramblers. Carter and Ralph were traveling as a quintet with a fiddler, bassist, and their favorite guitarist, George Shuffler. Rounding out the folk tour roster were the Mamou Cajun Band, led by brothers Cyprien and Adam Landreneau; Kentucky mountain singer Roscoe Holcomb, who shared a fondness with Ralph for harmonizing on the old hymns on the bus; and Cynthia May Carver, known professionally as Cousin Emmy, an entertainer with a fine mountain voice who not only could pick banjo but played "You Are My Sunshine" using an inflated rubber glove.

During this strenuous, country-hopping tour, Seeger somehow found the energy to record separate interviews with Carter and Ralph on consecutive days. During his interview with Carter, one of Seeger's questions led the weary singer to reflect on the diminishing importance of making a record. At one time, Carter opined, the opportunity to make a record was a significant milestone in the life of a musician; but the process had become cheapened to the point where all a musician had to do was pay someone a couple of hundred dollars to put out a recording.

Carter's reflections in 1966 provided a marked contrast to his cavalier behavior as a young man in 1948 in Bristol who seemed to give scant consideration to the significance of a record deal. In fact, he played so hard to get with one of the leading record labels, RCA, that the label lost interest. After the RCA sales supervisor who visited Harlan, Kentucky, learned how many records the Stanley Brothers were selling in his territory, RCA began to woo the brothers to sign a contract. This was not a one-man label out of Johnson City, Tennessee; RCA was the Radio Corporation of America and future record label of rock 'n' roll star Elvis Presley. "But Carter Stanley was a very independent individual," Carl Sauceman recalled.[1] "RCA wanted them to come to Nashville, but Carter told them he didn't have the time and if they wanted to talk to him, they could come to Bristol."

The mighty corporation decided not to pay a visit to the hillbilly songwriter, so the Stanley Brothers continued to make records under their handshake agreement with Rich-R-Tone until Columbia Records approached the brothers. "We hadn't signed a contract [with Rich-R-Tone]," recalled Carter. "We had a gentleman's agreement. It didn't turn out that way, money-wise anyhow."[2] In the play *Man of Constant Sorrow*, when Carter answers a phone call from Columbia Records, a frustrated Ralph shouts at him that he had better do a better job responding to this one than he did with the call from RCA.

Carter and Ralph did in fact do better, which may have been because Columbia was willing to come to the Stanley Brothers. "Six months after we'd been in Bristol, we got a call from Art Satherley of Columbia and he wanted us to record," said Ralph.[3] "A little time collapsed [*sic*] and I believe the next radio station we went to was [WPTF in] Raleigh, North Carolina, and that was about 1948. Art Satherley flew down to Raleigh and signed us up. At that time we had Pee Wee Lambert, Art Wooten, Carter, and myself, and he rented a room or two in the hotel. We went to see him there and we signed the contract, and I think he pulled out of his coat pocket a couple of hundred dollars and said, 'You might need a little money. I'm gonna give you this.'" According to Ralph, Satherley was anxious to record four songs that the brothers had been performing: "Pretty Polly," "Little Maggie," "The White Dove," and "Little Glass of Wine."[4]

Born in Bristol, England, the son of an Episcopal minister, Satherley had been a significant force in recording country music, both black and white, from the mid-1920s onward. During the time he had been in the business, the music of rural black performers had come to appear on what the labels called race records, while labels released the music of rural white performers on what were called hillbilly records. Satherley scouted and produced recordings of musicians in both categories. When he signed the Stanley Brothers, he was head of country artists and repertoire (A&R)[5] for Columbia's parent company, American Recordings. "ARC, through the transplanted Englishman Art Satherley and other talent scouts, was very much in the country business" and had been so since

1924, according to a history of Columbia.[6] Talent scout Ralph Peer, whose 1927 field recording trip to Bristol, Tennessee, had led to the discovery of the Carter Family and Jimmie Rodgers, described Satherley as "the re-cording genius for Columbia Records for a good number of years. . . . [H]e was a good judge of what the market needed."[7]

Satherley decided the market needed the Stanley Brothers enough to justify risking the loss of one of the performers already on Columbia's roster, Bill Monroe. Monroe had warned Columbia that he would leave the label if it signed the Blue Grass Boys' most blatant imitators. By the summer of 1948, the Stanley Brothers had gone so far as to ease fiddle player Leslie Keith out of the group to make room for former Blue Grass Boy Art Wooten so that the Clinch Mountain Boys would sound more like the Monroe band and Flatt and Scruggs. Keith understood the rea-son for his replacement. "On . . . the records, we wasn't too bluegrassy at that time," he recalled. "It was kinda bluegrass and old-time mixed, on the fiddling end of it and also on the singing end of it. . . . Monroe's type of stuff was coming up real fast, and they wondered if I'd consider letting them get a faster fiddler. . . ."[8] Keith formed his own band before joining WCYB performers Curly King and the Tennessee Hilltoppers. When the Stanley Brothers signed the contract with Columbia in October, Monroe proved true to his word, fulfilling the requirements of his existing con-tract and leaving for rival Decca.[9] In his final Columbia recording ses-sion on October 22, 1949—in the same Nashville studio that the Stanley Brothers used—the proud originator of bluegrass recorded the contrac-tual minimum of four songs.

Personnel changes and other occurrences unfolded among the Clinch Mountain Boys over the next several months. An American Federation of Musicians' recording ban that began on January 1, 1948, prevented the group from recording for Columbia until after the labor dispute was re-solved in mid-December. During that time Art Wooten left the group, to be replaced by the brothers' original fiddler from 1946, Bobby Sumner. Sumner's style was more old-time than Wooten's. Wooten stayed long enough to play on a mid-1948 Rich-R-Tone session that produced "The Rambler's Blues" (sung to a tune resembling Grayson and Whitter's "Short Life of Trouble") and the cover of Monroe's "Molly and Tenbrook," both sung by Pee Wee Lambert. Though they played their instruments, Carter and Ralph kept their voices off these recordings made during the ban; on "Molly and Tenbrook," Ralph recorded three-finger banjo in the style of Earl Scruggs for the first time. When the Stanley Brothers finally set foot in the studio located in Nashville's Tulane Hotel on March 1, 1949, to record for Columbia, they were in disbelief. "To us that would have been impossible," Carter said. "They had Bill Monroe."[10]

Though it was home to the *Grand Ole Opry* and Acuff-Rose Music, which published country and gospel music exclusively, Nashville in the spring of 1949 was a long way from the Music City it became in the 1950s and 1960s. According to fiddle player Lester Woodie, who played his first session with the Stanley Brothers on November 20, 1949, Castle Studios were "like your back room compared to today's studios. It wasn't elaborate. They had . . . good equipment, but it wouldn't be compared to the equipment today. About all I remember about the studio is just there wasn't much there except the mike and the guy with the controls behind the glass."[11]

At the first two Nashville sessions, Satherley and his associate Don Law positioned the group's instruments and voices around a single microphone. By the third session, the producers employed three microphones: one for the brothers, a second for Pee Wee Lambert, and the third for the fiddle player. The bass player worked a few feet behind the rest of the group, standing to the left as the musicians faced the microphones. The man behind the glass was the engineer, who used the audio controls to capture the sound as cleanly as possible. "I was really surprised—or maybe amazed is a better word—to see both these Columbia executives attend our sessions," recalled Woodie. "They really liked the Stanleys."[12] For their part, the Stanley Brothers had invested considerable time and effort in rehearsing the new vocal style they had developed, which consisted of trio harmonies by Carter, Ralph, and Pee Wee that were arranged differently from the familiar trios of old-time country music. The customary trio consisted of a lead vocalist, a tenor who sang harmony at a pitch above the lead vocalist, and a baritone who sang harmony below the lead vocalist. The new trio form that the Stanley Brothers and Pee Wee Lambert were pioneering pitched both of the harmony voices above that of the lead singer, with the baritone singing his part above the tenor. The name they gave to the style was "high baritone." Three of the first four songs recorded that day utilized the distinctive configuration of vocal parts, introducing a new option for vocal arrangements into the world of old-time country and bluegrass that soon would influence other groups. Since each of the songs was a Carter Stanley composition, the original material and an identifiable sound had come together at last. The producers let the musicians run with their new sound. "They pretty much left the music to us," said Woodie.[13]

During the 1966 interview, Carter explained the origins of the innovative trio sound to an interested Mike Seeger:

> . . . [W]e had Pee Wee Lambert that sung this high part. . . . What we was trying to do was get a sound [that harmonized] three parts—tenor, lead, and high baritone. Now Maybelle Carter and her daughters use that arrangement. As far as I know I never heard that arrangement until we got it. I don't mind to tell you who suggested us. Art Wooten played fiddle with us, felt that would be a good sound for us. As records will tell, we worked some at it but didn't perfect it, of course. It's been done much better by others.[14]

During his 2002 interview with Terry Gross on *Fresh Air*, Ralph provided his own explanation of the route by which the new trio harmonies had entered into the group's music. To demonstrate the harmonies to listeners, Gross played the Columbia recording of Carter's "The Lonesome River," recorded in 1950.

GROSS: On that recording we just heard, your brother's singing lead; you're singing harmony. And also singing harmony is Darrell "Pee Wee" Lambert. Talk about those harmonies that you sang together . . . how you arranged it . . . who was singing which part.

STANLEY: Pee Wee Lambert, he started out when we first started our group in 1946, and Carter done the lead singing, and I done the tenor singing, and we developed a new sound before anybody else called the high baritone, and Pee Wee Lambert did that. And that's just become . . . real popular through the years. About everybody uses that now, but we were the first to do that particular sound with the three parts together. High baritone—you know, everybody had been used to doing a low baritone. We did a high baritone, tenor, and lead.

GROSS: How did that work out? How did you come up with the idea?

STANLEY: We were just practicing . . . and it just—but things like that come to you. And we'd never heard it before. We was just feeling around, rehearsing the song, and just happened to find it.

GROSS: So by the high baritone, does that mean he's singing the
part that a baritone would be singing, except he's singing it an
octave higher?
STANLEY: Right.[15]

Seventy-five years old at the time of this interview, Ralph may have
forgotten the influential role Art Wooten played during his brief initial
tenure with the Stanley Brothers. In general, Ralph seemed more guarded than Carter in regard to identifying early influences, though neither
brother referred to Bill Monroe and the Blue Grass Boys' recording of "I
Hear a Sweet Voice Calling" during an October 1947 session in Chicago.
On the Monroe composition, vocalists Monroe, Lester Flatt, and bassist
Howard Watts (who adopted the stage name Cedric Rainwater) sang a
harmony similar to the high baritone; yet on the Monroe recording, the
desired effect appears to be to create an ethereal chorus for the phrase
"way up in heaven," different from the soulful trio harmony of the Stanley
Brothers and Pee Wee Lambert. Monroe used vocal trios less often than
other bluegrass performers. While noting the similarity of style, bluegrass
historian Neil Rosenberg does not appear to dispute the fundamental accuracy of Carter and Ralph's claim to the high baritone, writing that ". . .
although Monroe, Flatt, and Rainwater had recorded a similar trio for one
song for Columbia in 1947 . . . the high baritone trio became identified
with the Stanley Brothers."[16]

When unveiled on their first Columbia recordings, the Stanley
Brothers' use of three male voices singing in tight, high harmony created
a tension on the choruses that would release after a song returned to an
instrumental break or the lead voice. In addition to "The White Dove," the
group used the trio sound on two other of Carter's originals, "A Vision
of Mother" and "The Angels Are Singing (in Heaven Tonight)." As with
"White Dove," the subject of both "Vision" and "Angels" was the death
of a loved one. Though voicing the songs' lyrics, the high baritone harmonies created the emotional effect of a mournful keening well suited
to the nature of the subject matter. On the fourth song recorded during
the afternoon of the first session—"Gathering Flowers for the Master's
Bouquet"—Carter and Ralph sang a traditional duet.

Contributing to the keening of the high baritone trio sound was a subtle vocal effect that consisted of the three voices sliding from one note to
another. "We call it a slur," said Carter. "Slur your voice . . . that's just the
way we sing. There's no effort there. We do it without even knowing it."[17]

Given the careful attention to detail in rehearsals that Leslie Keith had experienced as member of the Clinch Mountain Boys, Carter's description
of the slur as he offered it to Mike Seeger in response to Seeger's question sounded more than a bit disingenuous. As he did with his comment
about others performing the trio harmonies better, Carter knew how to
deflect a line of questioning with a self-deprecating blend of humility and
humor. "I don't think anyone would want to copy [the slur] and I doubt if
anyone could," he joked.[18]

The evening of the first Columbia session included two more of
Carter's original compositions. Lyrically, "It's Never Too Late" and "Let
Me Be Your Friend" both fell somewhere between songs of love and
friendship—an unusual gray area in relations between the sexes (as expressed in the country genre) that Carter revisited several times in his
songwriting. "Never Too Late" was a mid-tempo waltz, while "Let Me Be"
raced along in duple meter (2/4 or 4/4)—faster and louder than anything
else recorded on the session. The sound of "Let Me Be" was straight bluegrass, featuring wailing fiddle and rattling banjo solos. Bill Monroe had
recorded the same melody with the same instrumentation for Columbia
on "It's Mighty Dark to Travel" on the October 1947 session that produced "I Hear a Sweet Voice Calling." As he had done with other melodies, Carter added a new set of lyrics. The brothers borrowed from their
own songbook on the session, recording a new version of their regional
hit, "Little Glass of Wine," so that Columbia would benefit from future
sales.

During the same waiting period before the first Nashville session that
led to the evolution of the high baritone sound, a similar cross-pollina-
tion process changed the instrumental sound of the Stanley Brothers.
Having begun to play banjo in the strumming clawhammer style taught
to him by his mother, Ralph had developed a basic picking style patterned
after another early influence. "I played with one finger and thumb until
after I got out of the army . . . I sort of picked up that style from Wade
Mainer . . ."[19] The next step in his evolution as a banjo player was to adopt
a style of playing with thumb and two fingers (called three-finger) that
appears to have originated among the banjo pickers of North Carolina.
"When we started playing professionally, I started playing—or trying
to—with three fingers. It was in about 1947. The first three-finger I heard
was Snuffy Jenkins, and I heard [Snuffy's nephew] Hoke Jenkins play it.
And I heard another boy . . . in North Carolina. And then when I was
discharged [from the army] I heard Earl Scruggs play it. . . . On the radio

with Bill Monroe . . . But actually, what decided me was Earl, because Earl did take the three-finger and do something with it. He improved it so much than when Jenkins or any of them had. I really liked his way of playing. And still do better than anybody I've ever heard."[20]

The expanded possibilities of the three-finger style included the ability to play rolls and rapid cascades of notes that allowed the player to syncopate the tempo or to erupt in the ear-dazzling bursts that many listeners have come to associate with bluegrass. A related technique was to play single notes slightly muffled by the player's hand to generate the effect of popping behind and around the voice of the lead singer and the solos of other instruments—a staccato sort of accompaniment that gave the music a bubbly, lighthearted feel. Through his radio exposure on the *Grand Ole Opry* with Bill Monroe and the Blue Grass Boys and later formation of his own group with Lester Flatt, Earl Scruggs was the acknowledged master of the instrument, playing with a dexterity and clarity that were unequalled in the recordings of the time. As he had been with Wade Mainer, Ralph was a follower, yet he found ways to make each style his own. "Anything I ever heard on banjo, I always tried to get it, but a little different," he recalled. ". . . I never did try to copy anybody."[21]

Emerging from the shadow of their reputation as imitators of Bill Monroe, the Stanley Brothers were prepared to discover new markets for their music. That is how their story would appear to be unfolding; yet beneath the apparent successes were the economic forces that would drive the Clinch Mountain Boys and other old-time country and bluegrass acts to stay on the move throughout their careers. The first such force was competition. The arrival of Flatt and Scruggs and their new group in Bristol in May 1948 created some serious competitive pressure. As Jim McReynolds commented, Lester and Earl led a hot band. Joe Morrell, who was a member of the other charter group on WCYB, Curly King and the Tennessee Hilltoppers, went further in describing the impact of the former Bill Monroe sidemen. He said Flatt and Scruggs "shook things up . . . . It was like rock 'n' roll . . . like Elvis Presley shook things up, but not with as broad appeal."[22]

When I interviewed Ralph in 2003, he gave this account of the evolution of *Farm and Fun Time*:

We'd heard of a new radio station in Bristol that would start a mid-day program. We were the first to start this show. We were on the air live. It was 55 minutes . . . an hour . . . and we played that program

an hour a day six days a week for something like two or three years.
And that program began getting popular everywhere, and some more
groups moved in. They had so many sponsors waiting in line to get in
the show that they had to move it up to two hours, and then other
groups moved in and helped us out.

The key phrase, repeated twice with an important change of context, is
moved in. With their reputation enhanced by *Grand Ole Opry* appearances with Bill Monroe and the Blue Grass Boys, Flatt and Scruggs found a
WCYB station management that was pleased to make room for their new
sound. Where once they could count on half of the program's musical
airtime, the new format reduced the Stanley Brothers to a single fifteen-
minute performance during each of the expanded program's two hours.

A second economic force was supply and demand. As the program's
original and only old-time country group, the Stanley Brothers had that
market all to themselves for almost a year and a half. Curly King and the
Tennessee Hilltoppers played in a popular country style, without the old-
time mountain influences that shaped Carter and Ralph's music. In a region where to travel in any direction for a few miles from the center of a
town meant to be in the middle of farms, barnyards, barking dogs, and
entire families that played instruments, the music of the Stanley Brothers
most closely matched the tastes of the audience whom Carter unabash-
edly addressed on the radio as "friends and neighbors." The trembling pa-
triarch of old-time music, A. P. Carter,[23] might appear on the air for five
minutes to sell Bibles containing an inserted picture of the Carter Family,
but the Carters had disbanded in 1941. By contrast, Flatt and Scruggs
fronted an active young band, hungry for the cash and adulation of personal appearances.

In an area where many groups and organizations already had sponsored the Stanley Brothers, the law of supply and demand joined forces
with the law of diminishing returns. Carter, Ralph, and their sidemen had
been wearing out the territory. There were only so many schools, court-
houses, theaters, drive-in theaters, and flatbed trailers at auto dealer-
ships where they could play . . . and had not already played once, twice,
or more. Hearing their repertoire on the radio every day but Sunday and
having seen them in person, audience members welcomed the opportunity to hear a new act with new material. In addition, Flatt and Scruggs had
the advantage of being famous outsiders rather than familiar insiders like
Carter and Ralph in a region where the last name *Stanley* was almost as

common as their mother's maiden name of Smith. Having become popular over the airwaves of WSM in Nashville, Flatt and Scruggs could satisfy the audience's understandable desire for novelty and celebrity.

Given the economic forces at work and the tug of their own ambitions, the Stanley Brothers pulled up stakes in July 1948 to begin working at radio station WPTF in Raleigh, North Carolina, which is where Columbia's Art Satherley caught up with them. A new station meant a new audience and new territory in which to book personal appearances. This was the first of several similar moves that the brothers made in the next two and a half years. They returned to the familiar environs of Bristol and *Farm and Fun Time* in early 1949, spending most of the year on the program before moving in the fall to radio station WTOB in Winston-Salem, North Carolina, where they worked from October through December. Other sojourns during this period extended from July to September 1950 at radio and television station WSAZ in Huntington, West Virginia; October 1950 on the *Louisiana Hayride* program that originated from radio station KWKH in Shreveport, Louisiana; and November and December 1950 on radio station WVLK in Versailles, Kentucky, near Lexington. In between forays into new listening and performing areas, they remained welcome on WCYB.

Fiddle player Lester Woodie was a band member for most of this period. While in high school in Valdese, North Carolina, he had played in a youthful outfit called the Melody Mountain Boys that included George and John Shuffler, both of whom would join the Stanley Brothers. After graduating in June 1949, Les Woodie took a job on the night shift at a bakery. The Stanley Brothers came to town to persuade former Bill Monroe fiddler Jim Shumate to replace the departed Bobby Sumner. "He wasn't able to join them, but he recommended me," Woodie recalled. "So there they were, asking me to join them. I didn't debate about it too long, because I wanted to get out of that bakery."[24] Ralph and Pee Wee were the recruiters; Woodie met Carter the next day in a room at the Hickory Hotel in Hickory, North Carolina, that the group had reserved for the audition. Despite not having heard any of their records, Woodie became a member of the group after playing two or three fiddle tunes and singing backup on "Little Glass of Wine."

Having listened to the music of the Louvin Brothers, Blue Sky Boys, and Sons of the Pioneers, Woodie had a little trouble getting used to the Stanley Brothers' tempo and pitch. "Back in those days, they played and sang most everything high and fast," he recalled. "If Pee Wee couldn't get up high enough, Carter would get on him. 'Oh, you can do it,' Carter would say. 'Get on up there!' The only thing that really bothered me about playing with the Stanley Brothers at first was their speed. They played everything so fast. But when you're eighteen years old, it's not too hard to get your speed up. It wasn't long before I fell in with them. It did take me a while, though, to learn their songs." At an early appearance, he became nervous when the group was about to play a gospel number. "I told Carter I didn't know the words, so Carter told me to just fake it. So I jumped in there and sang . . . If I was lucky, I'd hit a word right here and there. But since they were going so fast, it really didn't make much difference."

Between the Stanley Brothers' active performing and recording schedules, the recent high school graduate soon became a veteran. An astute observer, his recollections offered invaluable insight into a band in transition. He recalled a shy Ralph "content to sit back and play the banjo and let Pee Wee do all of the singing." During all-night automobile rides to get to a show, he had an early exposure to the singer Ralph would become. "There it was, 2 o'clock in the morning," Woodie recalled, "and everyone trying to sleep with Ralph at the wheel keeping himself awake by singing the old Primitive Baptist hymns. He really used to sing some weird songs. To me, the lonesome sound of those Baptist hymns is what gave the Stanleys their identity." At the same time, he could see that they "worshiped Monroe and his music. Pee Wee, especially, just idolized Monroe. In fact . . . Pee Wee even looked a little like Monroe. When he put his hat on, it was uncanny." Woodie was aware that the respect was not mutual. "Monroe didn't take kindly to other groups using his material and copying his style," he recalled. "Since the Stanleys were Bill's biggest challenge, there grew up quite an animosity between them. At the time . . . it was quite intense."

Woodie's recollections of Carter's songwriting methods are significant. He played with the group during the time when Carter wrote several of his most enduring songs. "I feel like I was rather fortunate," he recalled. "Carter was really coming into his own as far as his writing ability, and I worked with Carter on several songs."[25] Woodie believed he may have contributed to the desolate "The Lonesome River," the heart-rending "Let Me Love You One More Time," the regretful "The Fields Have Turned Brown," and an upbeat declaration of love titled "Hey! Hey! Hey!"

"I still think 'The Fields' and 'Lonesome River' are some of his best work," he said. "I don't remember specifically the words or phrases I threw at him. You know, I may suggest two or three things . . . he may not write it in at that moment, then use it before the song was finished. In no way would I try to take credit for any of his writing, but I feel privileged to have been with him during that time."[26] In a separate interview, Woodie reflected, "You know as a writer sometimes you need a little different idea or you need a thought or maybe a word to rhyme with what you got going and so on, and Carter and I would banter back and forth."[27]

The three months in residence at radio and television station WSAZ appears to have been a particularly productive period for Carter. Perhaps it was the change of scene to West Virginia or the loneliness of being away from his wife and family that sparked his creative output—or the novelty of being on the new medium of television. WSAZ-TV began broadcasting on November 15, 1949, the seventy-second station in the United States. Since early network and syndicated programming left a number of hours on the schedule for local shows and almost all of television's early content derived from the formats that had been successful on radio—from news to situation comedies—the new station filled some of the available slots with the proven popularity of local music programs. Having played a pioneering role on WCYB in Bristol, the Stanley Brothers were one of three groups that introduced country music to WSAZ-TV—the others being Texas Slim and his Prairie Buckaroos and Richard Cox and the Harvesters.[28]

What was unusual about the Stanleys' daily program was that it was broadcast in an early-evening time slot, rather than during the early morning or noon hours when country music usually was scheduled on radio. Though country music would establish itself on WSAZ-TV and television in general, the Stanleys' program lasted only about three months. Their limited run was not for lack of trying to appeal to a variety of tastes. Woodie recalled:

> As far as the music is concerned, we played a lot of the standards . . . Carter Family songs, some of Monroe's songs. I remember Pee Wee was covering Bill with the then-popular "Prisoner's Song." Carter was doin' "Wanderin' Boy." Ralph did "Pretty Polly," "Man of Constant Sorrow," some old gospel songs, songs from Ralph's Primitive Baptist church, including some of the old "lined songs" such as "Amazing Grace." . . . Of course Ralph played "Little Maggie," "Cripple Creek," [and] "Shout Lula." I was playin' "Bill Cheatham," "Cricket on the Hearth," "Black Mountain Blues," "Orange Blossom Special." . . . And

*they were beginning to have some of their own material, such as
"White Dove," "I Love No One But You," and we were just trying out
Carter's songs as he wrote them.*[29]

The group delivered the music in a variety of combinations, with
Carter, Ralph, and Pee Wee performing solos, and Carter and Ralph duets. "All three made a fine trio," Woodie added. "I thought [this was] their
strong point. Then I joined them singing bass for the Clinch Mountain
Boys Quartet." Perhaps the barrier to long-term success was more fundamental. According to country music historian Ivan Tribe, "Despite the
quality music and the effort, the show seemed a bit ahead of its time. Not
enough people had television sets as yet . . ."[30]

Given a break from the hectic pace of traveling every night, Carter
wrote several songs in Huntington. Woodie recalled details of the process.
"I remember we were living on the eighth floor of a hotel in Huntington
for a while. I watched the tugboats out on the Ohio River. Carter was writing and I was eighteen years old—not a lot of experience, but I did have a
knack for phrasing and rhyming words. He would be searching sometimes
and would throw me a word or line and I would suggest something."[31]

The view from the eighth floor overlooking the Ohio during the late
months of summer certainly resonates in the verses and chorus of "The
Lonesome River."

*I sit here alone on the banks of the river
The lonesome wind blows the water rolls high
I hear a voice calling out there in the darkness
I sit here alone too lonesome to cry*

*Chorus
Oh the water rolls high on the river at midnight
I sit on the shore to grieve and to cry
The woman I love she left me this morning
With no one to love or kiss me goodnight*

*We met there one night by the banks of the river
Sat there holding hands and making our vows
Swore we'd never part and be happy together
But a new love she's found she's gone from me now*

Short though the lyric content might be, the song evokes a forlorn mood in the first line and sustains it throughout. The mournful keening of the high baritone trio on the chorus lends additional power to the objective correlative-like poetics of "Oh the water rolls high on the river at midnight." Use of an image similar to the objective correlative appears in the title of "The Fields Have Turned Brown."

I left my old home to ramble this country
My mother and dad said son don't go wrong
Remember that God will always watch o'er you
And we will be waiting for you here at home

Chorus
Son don't go astray was what they both told me
Remember that love for God can be found
But now they're both gone this letter just told me
Four years they've been dead, the fields have turned brown

For many long years this world I have rambled
No thoughts of the day when I would return
Now as I go home and find no one waiting
The price I have paid to live and to learn

As with "The White Dove," the theme is the loss of one's parents, linked this time to the metaphor of a farm's fallow fields—a more subtle image than willow trees that hang their heads. Written later than "White Dove," "Fields" is more compact than its predecessor, illustrating Carter's growing command of language in his lyrics. Composed of two verses and chorus, the song's structure parallels "Lonesome River."

For the young songwriter—turning 25 at the time the lyrics were written—"The Lonesome River" and "The Fields Have Turned Brown" represented a stylistic advance beyond the more explicit narrative of "The White Dove." Theme, structure, and language in the more recent songs unified to create an emotional impact that was supported by the instrumentation and vocal harmonies. Carter's lead singing is soulful and sincere. As captured by the engineer in the well organized (if less than luxurious) recording studio in the Tulane Hotel in Nashville, these songs have remained in the old-time country repertoire long enough to demonstrate that they possess the enduring quality that is one characteristic of art.

10. THE ROAD TURNS ROCKY

———————

Expectations ran high for the Stanley Brothers and the Clinch Mountain Boys as they drove to Shreveport, Louisiana, in the fall of 1950 to join the cast of radio station KWKH's *Louisiana Hayride*. In the four years that had passed since Ralph had ridden the bus back to southwestern Virginia after being discharged from the army, he and Carter had accomplished things they only could have dreamed of in the years prior to their return home. They had organized their own band, starred six days a week on a radio show that could be heard in five states, made their first records for a small regional label only to be signed by a prestigious national label, and completed three months of television broadcasts in West Virginia on one of the first TV stations in their part of the country. If the upward spiral of the recent past was any indication of what the future held, the brothers were bound for stardom . . . sooner rather than later.

In shifting their base of operations to Shreveport, they appeared to be going in the right direction to realize their potential. Only two years before, in August 1948, a tall, scrawny country singer from Alabama named Hank Williams had used his *Hayride* performances as the springboard to catapult onto the stage of the *Grand Ole Opry*. Hank's yodeling version of the song "Lovesick Blues" created a sensation with the studio audiences of both programs,[1] launching a meteoric career that ended on January 1, 1953, when he died in the back seat of his Cadillac on the way to a New Year's Day appearance in Canton, Ohio. Residents of Bristol, Virginia, claimed that the young man driving Hank through a snowstorm made one of his final stops at a diner a few blocks from the studios of radio station WCYB.

That lay in the future. In the fall of 1950, the lesson of Hank Williams to young musicians was about the fast-track to stardom that regular appearances on the *Louisiana Hayride* could provide. In April and May 1949, live performances and radio airplay of "Lovesick Blues" broadcast over

KWKH's 50,000-watt signal helped Williams sell 48,000 copies of the record in seventeen days, making it the number one country song.[2]

The first thing the Stanley Brothers had to do when they arrived in Shreveport was buy new clothes. When the band decided to break up the trip by staying overnight at a hotel in Birmingham, Alabama, a thief broke into their car. "About 2 o'clock in the morning the phone rang," Lester Woodie recalled. "It was the Birmingham police. They asked if we owned a 1950 Buick. Carter told him 'yes.' They said he needed to come down . . . someone had broken the window, took all our hats, our clothes, but thankfully they didn't get to our instruments."[3] The instruments remained safe in the trunk.

Louisiana Hayride was a relatively new member of a type of program patterned after a rural barn dance. Texas listeners were the first to hear the musical variety program that included country comedy on January 4, 1923, when Confederate Civil War veteran and fiddler Captain M. J. Bonner hosted such a show on radio station WBAP in Fort Worth.[4] The following year, Chicago station WLS gave a name to the new genre by inaugurating the *National Barn Dance*; WSM in Nashville joined the trend in 1925 with its first broadcasts of what would become the *Grand Ole Opry*. Local and regional radio soon followed suit. Bristol station WOPI's *Saturday Night Jamboree* and the *World's Original WWVA Jamboree* in Wheeling, West Virginia, were direct descendants of these on-air hoedowns that enlivened the early days of radio.

Shreveport came as a culture shock to the newcomers from the mountain states. Situated on a bluff above the Red River, the city took its name from Henry Miller Shreve, who supervised the dislodging of a 200-mile logjam that had clogged the river's main channel for four centuries.[5] In 1839, Shreve succeeded in opening the 1,300-mile length of the Red River to commerce, connecting the Red River Valley to the Mississippi River as it flowed from Natchez down to New Orleans. An influx of traders brought their cultures and music to the city; the growth of the cotton trade brought slaves who, in 1840, outnumbered the white population of Caddo Parish, of which Shreveport was the parish seat.[6] History and heritage created in Shreveport a musical melting pot, mixing traditions transported not only on the river but over the land. A trading post near the future site of Shreveport had been a stopping point for settlers migrating through Georgia and Louisiana along a route called the Texas Trail.[7] Musical influences felt in the city came from traveling minstrel shows, white and African American crews working on the river boats and docks,

pianists and fiddlers who entertained aboard the steamboats, and musicians who accompanied medicine shows that sold cure-all tonics and
body-purging laxatives.

Another side of Shreveport's music could be heard in the bars and
brothels along Fannin Street that provided venues for barrelhouse pia-
no players such as Sycamore Slim and Chee-Dee, whose bass-driven
rhythms influenced the guitar style of young Shreveport-area native
Huddie Ledbetter.[8] Ledbetter became famous as the blues and folk musician Lead Belly. In 1930, a producer for Okeh Records held recording sessions in Shreveport similar to those organized by Ralph Peer in Bristol in
1927. The Shreveport sessions recorded an African-American string band
from Jackson, the Mississippi Sheiks, whose song "Sitting on Top of the
World" would become a standard among blues and bluegrass musicians,[9]
including Bill Monroe and Texas band leader Bob Wills.

When it came to string-band ensembles, the 1950 edition of the Clinch
Mountain Boys were more accustomed to the highly structured fiddle
tunes of Fiddlin' Powers and Family than the bluesy repertoire of the
Sheiks. The sights, sounds, smells, and foods of Shreveport—not to mention a good percentage of the people—all seemed strange. When they arrived at the Municipal Auditorium to play on the *Hayride*, the Stanley
Brothers and their sidemen felt intimidated by the gaudily dressed country singers. Used to attentive audiences who were familiar with their spare
mountain sound, the Virginia-based musicians found it disconcerting to
play in front of Louisiana audiences who were more raucous in response
to livelier acts rather than respectful of tradition-based music. In 1954,
the *Hayride* audience would go wild over Elvis Presley. The overall effect
was to make Ralph, especially, feel homesick.

Reflecting on the abrupt departure from Shreveport, Lester Woodie
offered this insight: "Ralph thought the world of his mother and couldn't
be that far away from her."[10] Evidence of the special bond appeared often
in Ralph's early life. During the time when Carter had left for the army
and Ralph was finishing high school, the younger son and his mother
formed their own musical duo, with Ralph on the fiddle. He recalled:

*Carter left and went to the army a long time before I did, and our
mother plays some banjo. Well, during that time me and Carter—I
don't remember which one—sold some of these garden seeds and
flowers and so forth, and as a premium for it we got a fiddle. While
he was gone, I tried to learn to fiddle a little. My mother played*

*banjo and I played fiddle, and a lot of neighbors would invite us in
on weekends and we'd go around and play some. . . . She'd play the
banjo and I'd try to play the fiddle.*[11]

Their repertoire included string-band standards such as "Old Joe
Clark," "Bile Them Cabbage Down," and "Cripple Creek."

In addition to homesickness, another possible reason for the band's
departure from Shreveport was Ralph's brush with the law. He and a local
woman were brought before a judge for violating a city ordinance against
unmarried couples occupying the same hotel room. The woman entered
a plea of not guilty, but changed her mind when Ralph decided to plead
guilty. Though Ralph later would laugh about the episode, his embarrass-
ment may have contributed to the band's decision to leave town after only
three weeks—not much longer than it had taken Hank Williams to promote "Lovesick Blues" to number one.

While based in Shreveport, the band performed daily on one of
KWKH's morning music programs as well as on the *Hayride* itself, and
opened for popular *Hayride* performer Slim Whitman at performances
in east Texas. The morning radio show began at 8:30, preceding similar
programs by the Wilburn Brothers and Red Sovine, whose somber recita-
tions over music in the 1960s such as "Phantom 309" helped to popularize
the sub-genre of country truck-driving songs. In 1950 Slim Whitman was
beginning to stand out among KWKH's roster of talent. Born in Tampa in
1924, he had mastered the yodeling style of Jimmie Rodgers and learned
to play guitar despite having lost two fingers of his left hand while working as a meat packer in Jacksonville.

Discovered by Elvis Presley's future manager, Colonel Tom Parker,
who secured him a record contract with RCA in 1948, Whitman had
worked his way to the *Louisiana Hayride* through local performances on
Tampa radio stations and national network exposure starting in 1949 on
Smoky Mountain Hayride.[12] By the fall of 1950, he was on the verge of
becoming a star with his recordings of "Love Song of the Waterfall" and
"Indian Love Call." Like Hank Williams, Whitman was an example of the
Hayride's ability to claim its slogan "Cradle of the Stars." Leaving a prominent showcase such as the *Hayride* may have been a fork in the road for
the Stanley Brothers.

Toward the end of the Louisiana sojourn came the offer of a new job.
Radio station WVLK in Versailles, Kentucky, near the bluegrass country
of Lexington, needed to replace Flatt and Scruggs. The Stanley Brothers

made their final appearance on KWKH on October 25. The band would travel to Nashville for a recording session and then to Kentucky, where Carter placed a call to another musician from Valdese, North Carolina, to join the group on bass.

One of nine children in a musical family, George Shuffler played guitar and mandolin as well, and was a fine baritone vocalist. Knowing that the Stanley Brothers had a waiting list of musicians who wanted to play with them, he quickly accepted Carter's offer. From November through early 1951, this edition of the Clinch Mountain Boys performed daily over WVLK and appeared every Saturday night on the station's *Kentucky Mountain Barn Dance* held at the Clay Gentry Arena.[13] The group also entertained tobacco merchants. Shuffler recalled performing around the first of the year in tobacco barns as burley was sold. "We did a lot of [radio] remotes," he said.[14] From this beginning as a last-minute addition to the band, he would perform off and on with the Stanley Brothers through 1966.

WVLK was the group's seventh station affiliation in four years, and the band followed the by now familiar pattern of working a new territory until they wore out the local income potential. The Stanley Brothers had plenty of company as they station-hopped; almost all of the country groups did the same as a matter of economic survival. The winter was the most difficult season in which to earn a living, interrupted by holidays and with weather requiring that all performances take place indoors. Carter and Ralph and their sidemen managed to squeeze brief visits with their families into the transition times; and the families were forced to live close to, or move in with, kinfolk during the months that their husbands and fathers were on the road.

"I'd go to my mom's all those times," recalled Pee Wee Lambert's wife, Hazel. "I stayed there and Mary [Kiser Stanley], she'd go to her mom's. Here we go, dragging two children . . . mercy."[15] Carter and Mary now had a second son, Billy (born William Edmond Stanley on July 3, 1949), and the Lamberts had welcomed a second child not long after—a continuing pattern of births that caused some good-natured needling between Carter and Pee Wee over the years. After the Lamberts had moved to Columbus, Ohio, in the late 1950s, Hazel recalled, "Carter come by one time . . . that's when Jeanie was born. . . . He was always such a big tease. He said, 'Well Pee Wee, I got one on ya.' Mary would have a baby and then I'd have a baby. Mary had a baby and I had a baby, down to the four. I stopped at four and Mary went on to five." Carter and Mary's first daughter, Doris

Jane, was born November 10, 1953. Another son, Bobby James, arrived on June 4, 1955. The fifth and last child, Norma Jean, was born April 30, 1962.

Before the migration from station to station began, the two young mothers were able to wheel their first-born children in strollers to the WCYB studios, where they could watch their husbands perform on *Farm and Fun Time*. By fall 1950 the camaraderie of those early Bristol days must have seemed like a distant memory. The husbands had to travel farther to feed their growing families, and the wives had to make do with an irregular income and the long absences of their men. To the Stanley and Lambert children, their daddies seemed more like familiar visitors than resident parents. There was almost no such thing as time off. It was not until early 1951 that Carter had time to build the four-room house on Smith Ridge where Mary and the children stayed when not spending their time with Lucy Smith Stanley.

Relocating from Shreveport to Versailles at the end of October 1950, the band members may not have had the chance to return home because on November 3 they were due at the recording session in Nashville—their first in almost a year.

At its previous Nashville session on November 20, 1949, the group recorded six songs—enough material for three records. Two of the songs employed the high baritone harmony; the other four were duets—three by Carter and Ralph and one by Carter and Pee Wee. Supporting the vocalists were Lester Woodie on fiddle and Nashville session musician Ernie Newton on bass. For Woodie, the Stanley Brothers' third Nashville session—and his first—was memorable.

It was the first time that I'd made any records, and I was quite young at the time and amazed by it all. One thing that impressed me, on all the sessions we did for Columbia, [was that] Art Satherley and Don Law, they . . . took the time to fly in from New York[16] to those sessions and sat right in there. Don was quite active in the sessions and making suggestions and so forth. They took a big interest in it. . . . they would suggest a mandolin break would be good here or a-doing a certain type of arrangement on it. . . . They went to great lengths to talk it out.[17]

As would many people in the future, Satherley and Law envisioned the Stanley Brothers as scions of the old-time tradition in which they performed—authentic mountain folk in contrast to Bill Monroe's more polished, jodhpur-clad Blue Grass Boys. "They were fascinated evidently by the style of living the Stanleys were used to," said Woodie. At one session, Carter rewarded his producers' fascination by bringing Art Satherley a genuine country ham.

The post-Shreveport session on November 3, 1950, reunited the same musicians and producers in the same Castle Studio setting in Nashville. Despite the identical personnel and place, the four songs recorded in two hours that morning suggested that the format of the group's records had changed. The first song to be recorded—"Hey! Hey! Hey!"—was a brisk celebration of love on which Woodie's fiddle accelerated into double time. Years later Woodie confessed, "At first I thought 'Hey! Hey! Hey!' was a bit weak." He told Carter that the songwriter must be repeating the words of the title because he couldn't think of anything else to write.[18] Woodie's kidding was on target since Carter also repeated a line in one of the verses; but Woodie came around to liking the number. "After we started working it up and playing it a few times, I rather liked it. The tempo was good. I wanted to do something with the fiddle that would help it, so one day I had tuned the fiddle in A to play [Leslie Keith's] 'Black Mountain Blues,'[19] and Carter started the 'Hey' song. I started shuffling the bow behind their singing and Carter stopped and asked, 'What are you doing?' I said, 'Just tryin' to fill up the background.' His remark was: 'I like it!' And he insisted that I do that on the recording." Fiddlers call what Woodie played on his second break a double shuffle. Ralph sang harmony on the chorus. The song jumped.

The recording of "The Lonesome River" followed, incorporating the mournful sound of high baritone harmony. The next two numbers recorded that morning provided a contrast with earlier Nashville sessions. "I'm a Man of Constant Sorrow" and "Pretty Polly" were the first solo vocals by Ralph since his forceful rendition of "Little Maggie" for Rich-R-Tone in late 1947 or early 1948. These traditional ballads would become significant additions to the band's recorded catalogue. The Columbia producers must have had a hand in the choice of material, since each of the traditional songs was combined with one of Carter's compositions on the two records that resulted from the session. "Hey! Hey! Hey!" was the flip side of "Pretty Polly," and "Lonesome River" paired with "Man of Constant Sorrow." There was reason for a change. Earlier records for the national label "weren't selling as much as we'd hoped and what Columbia had hoped they would," said Ralph.[20] "That was a big disappointment for Carter . . ."

For many years Woodie continued to receive compliments for his fiddle introduction and solo on "Man of Constant Sorrow," though he remained modest about his intentions. "I was just trying to come up with something that fit the song," he recalled. "There wasn't much out there to copy, so I just did the best I could."[21] Yet Ralph held up Woodie's playing on the song to a later generation of Clinch Mountain instrumentalists as an example of what could be achieved by taking time to "work out something on [songs] that people'll notice."[22]

On the world stage in 1950, the beginning of the Cold War was a development that the Stanley Brothers and the Clinch Mountain Boys could not help but notice. Tremors in the new balance of power that followed World War II had led to the first confrontation—albeit indirect—between the United States, China, and the Soviet Union. The Korean War began on June 25, 1950. Though the military draft had been allowed to expire in 1947, President Harry Truman sought to reinstate it in 1948, and by mid-1950 the numbers of young men being drafted were increasing. Having served in World War II, Carter and Ralph were exempt from the draft, but their sidemen—Les Woodie and George Shuffler's younger brother John on bass—were not. After finishing the year on radio in the Lexington area, the band faced a difficult stretch during which work was sparse. As Ralph recalled, "One time . . . business got a little bad in the winter time and then Lester Woodie, he was playing fiddle, he got his call to the army, and we went home and Carter built him a house on the old home place. Naturally, I was single at that time and I stayed with my mother."[23] Years later, Ralph revealed how exhausted and uncertain he was at the time: ". . . I was all give-out from the road. I was running on empty . . . I told Carter I was heading back home to Smith Ridge. I said it was probably just for a while, just to get some rest and get my strength back up. Deep down inside, I wasn't so sure if I could hack it anymore."[24]

Ralph and a stepbrother built partitions in a store on Smith Ridge that their parents owned so that the Lamberts could live there for the winter. Carter worked on the house for his family. Ralph and Pee Wee took agricultural classes. "I wanted to try for a few months to make a go at being a farmer," Ralph said.[25] As the weather warmed, he and Pee Wee tilled the soil and planted crops on the family farm. "Two horses and a plow, they farmed about a month," recalled Hazel.[26] "They was gonna raise a farm for Mrs. Stanley, I guess. We moved up on the ridge. Me and Pee Wee and two kids lived in a storeroom they had. It was a store . . . a little house . . .

they fixed it up, you know." The family stayed for three months until the experiment was over.

"I saw right away there wasn't much of a future for me in farming," Ralph recalled.[27] ". . . As tired as I was of the road, I missed music too bad to give it up for good." Carter was committed to a career in music. Bill Monroe had invited him to join the Blue Grass Boys, and Carter waited for Monroe to let him know when to begin. While finishing his house, he worked from time to time for Lee Stanley at the saw mill.[28] Together and separately, members of the disbanded group struggled through the winter and may have regrouped to return to WSAZ in Huntington in May. In June, Carter, Ralph, and Pee Wee went their separate ways, with Ralph continuing to reside at home and Carter going on the road with Monroe. Charter member Pee Wee could no longer afford to stay with the group. "There were no hard feelings," recalled Hazel. "We had two children. Times were bad. The band was not playing that much."[29] Pee Wee formed a duo with guitarist Curly Parker. In a separate interview, Hazel said, "This wasn't just about the music. Curly Parker was a civil engineering contractor as well as a guitarist. He offered Pee Wee a steady day job, with a little music on the side."[30] Hazel and the couple's one- and two-year-old children moved in with her mother in Wise, Virginia. Pee Wee continued to play music until 1956. In 1957, he and his family moved to Ohio, where he worked in civil engineering.

With the departure of one of the band's original members, the sound of the Stanley Brothers underwent a major change. Gone were the similarities to Bill Monroe and his Blue Grass Boys. As Ralph said in a 1981 interview, "When Pee Wee left, I think that changed our style altogether. He had sung tenor on some of the songs in a way that made it sound more like Bill Monroe, and Pee Wee played the mandolin a lot like Bill. Without Pee Wee standing there singing in the Monroe style, we just more or less settled down to our natural sound."[31]

Even though he was a band member, Lester Woodie was unsure why the brothers separated. "We had some times that were pretty tough, but I don't think economics was the cause to pause. Actually, things seemed to be getting better about that time. I remember the last date I played with them was a Sunday outdoor show at the Richlands, Virginia, airport. Festivals had not come into play at that time, but I thought that was one of the best gigs, financially, we had played in a long time."[32] After receiving his draft notice, Woodie left to join the air force in mid-July. John Shuffler joined the army, experiencing firsthand the bitter cold and brutal combat conditions in Korea. There was a possibility that the Stanley Brothers had separated for good.

11. HARD TIMES

Among rolling hills and along winding river valleys, the narrow country roads that traversed the southern Appalachians could be dangerous. On the precipitous ridges where Carter and Ralph Stanley grew up, a vehicle sliding off the road into a deep ravine might not be found for weeks. In 1951, a car heading northwest from North Carolina toward Coeburn, Virginia, and Smith Ridge where the Stanley families lived would follow Route 421—a circuitous road that ran between Boone, North Carolina, and Mountain City, Tennessee. Passing through Shouns, Tennessee, Route 421 contained a curve that was on the daily route of a man from Damascus, Virginia, nicknamed the Old Prospector "because he was sure there was gold on top of Long Hope Mountain in North Carolina."[1] Growing up on his family's farm in Trade, Tennessee, Joe Wilson heard the prospector's surplus World War II Jeep early each morning as it passed south on 421 from Virginia, returning north in mid-afternoon.

In August 1951, on the way back from a performance in Raleigh, North Carolina, Ralph Stanley learned the hard way that the Old Prospector's reckless driving could wreak havoc on 421. A truck carrying six workers tried to pass the Jeep at the same time that Pee Wee Lambert dozed at the wheel of the Stanley car. Ralph was asleep in the back seat. The car struck the truck head on. "It knocked me out and I can remember waking up, just staggering along the road, seeing blood and not knowing where I was," Ralph recalled.[2] Facial cuts and a back injury hospitalized him for three or four days. He took several months to recover. Pee Wee was shaken, but not seriously hurt. The workers were "banged up," some with broken bones. The Old Prospector drove on, oblivious to the accident. According to Ralph,[3] "He always shorted the curve, and that's what caused the collision."

The crash occurred at the end of a brief time in which—at Carter's request—Ralph filled in with the Bill Monroe and the Blue Grass Boys.[4]

"Rudy Lyle played the banjo with Bill, and he was called into the service and I was helping them out on the road on some personal appearances until they could get a banjo player . . . ," Ralph recalled. "But I didn't want to go with them regular. And Pee Wee just went along with me on the week, ten days, whatever it was. And so we were coming [home] is when we had the wreck."[5]

Accidents were common on the region's hazardous roads. On August 16, 1930, a near-collision in Damascus took the life of one of the Stanley Brothers' early influences, G. B. Grayson. Grayson, who was blind, had accepted a ride from a neighbor as he walked home from his brother's house in Virginia to Laurel Bloomery, Tennessee. The seat in the roadster was full, so after placing his fiddle inside, Grayson stood on the car's running board. While rounding a curve on U.S. Route 58, the roadster encountered a logging truck driven by yet another neighbor. Thrown from the running board, Grayson was killed. His death came not long after the musician had saved enough money to make a down payment on his childhood home. He was 42.[6]

Growing up to become a folk arts administrator who successfully nominated Ralph for a National Heritage Fellowship in 1984, Joe Wilson was a long-term observer of the brothers' careers. In regard to their separation around the time of the accident, he speculated: "there was always a question of why Carter and Ralph weren't working together at the time, and I think at one point it became convenient to say that Ralph wrecked and therefore [sic]—whereas probably something else was the problem. This gets into the complexities of relationships between brothers and bands. . . ."[7] Years later, Ralph downplayed the break. "We wasn't off very long and I just don't remember where we went to from there . . . probably Bristol I guess. . . ."[8] Before the brothers reunited, Monroe offered his former rival a job that Carter appeared to have sought: "Monroe had always been Carter's idol, and the opportunity to tour with him fulfilled a lifelong dream," wrote Gary B. Reid.[9] When Monroe returned to Nashville for two recording sessions on July 1 and July 7, 1951, Carter became the newest Blue Grass Boy.[10] In his history of the genre, bluegrass historian Neil Rosenberg concluded that what paved the way to the reconciliation was the Stanley Brothers' development of their own repertoire and sound. Monroe no longer saw them as imitators. What's more, "Carter's willingness to step down from the position of bandleader to that of band member was the final move in the resolution of the tensions that had existed between him and Monroe," Rosenberg wrote. "They became fast friends."[11]

According to bluegrass musician Bill Clifton, who knew both men, Monroe developed a special liking for Carter because he was "very genuine and had so much soul in his singing. Nobody had more soul than Carter did." From the perspective of the younger musician, recalled Clifton, "Carter admired Bill tremendously. I'm sure all lead singers did."[12] For Carter, three months in the company of this proud, intense man was a crash course in Monroe's demanding, no-frills approach to music and life. Carter toured with the group from June through August, taking part in the two July sessions that produced six songs. He shared lead vocals with Monroe on "Sugar Coated Love" and "Cabin of Love," and sang on two gospel quartets, "You're Drifting Away" and "Get Down on Your Knees and Pray."

When Carter made his next trip to Nashville in April 1952, it was as lead singer in a new line-up of Clinch Mountain Boys that included George Shuffler on bass and Art Wooten on fiddle. This was Wooten's second time in the band. He had played with the brothers and Pee Wee Lambert on the Rich-R-Tone session in mid-1948 that recorded the cover of Monroe's version of "Molly and Tenbrook" that so irritated the Kentuckian. Mac Wiseman, who became a Blue Grass Boy after performing with Flatt and Scruggs on WCYB when the copycat recording was released, recalled the depth of Monroe's animosity at the time: "When the Stanley Brothers first started, whatever Bill did Saturday night on the *Opry*, they did the next week on the Bristol program that we were on. . . . Bill used to see red. He used to hate the word Stanley Brothers."[13]

In 1951 the Stanley Brothers returned to their familiar slot on *Farm and Fun Time*. They played on the show from September through November. One reason the station management was ready to welcome the Clinch Mountain Boys back was a practice that Jesse McReynolds had observed while he and his brother Jim were beginning their careers on WNVA in Norton. "The Stanley Brothers had a great thing going there, as far as playing show dates and everything," McReynolds recalled.[14] "On the whole, fact was, they started the thing off wrong [. . . .] The Stanley Brothers and a couple more went in there and started giving stations . . . 10 or 15 percent . . . of their show dates [receipts] to be on the station. They started paying off that way and the station actually got rich off it."

Making it clear that he was referring to WCYB, McReynolds added: "for a while there it was as hard to get on that station as it would have been the *Grand Ole Opry*. You just couldn't get on . . . because it was the hottest thing going."[15] When the Stanley Brothers returned to the station in 1951, the demand for airtime had become less competitive than in the early days. The five-state market was becoming saturated. By December 1951, the brothers made another stop at radio station WVLK in Versailles, Kentucky, where they broadcast until early April 1952 before traveling to Nashville to record their final session for Columbia on April 11.

On its last visit to Castle Lab, the group recorded a trio vocal, two duets, and a solo vocal by Carter. The distinctive high baritone harmony that characterized previous Columbia sessions was absent because Pee Wee Lambert had left the group. Instead, the Clinch Mountain Boys sang the trio in the customary fashion, with George Shuffler's baritone vocal underneath Carter's lead and Ralph's tenor vocals. "A Life of Sorrow" turned out to be a lugubrious reworking of both the narrative elements and melody of "I'm a Man of Constant Sorrow" that Ralph recorded solo—and more successfully—in November 1950. "Sweetest Love" and "Let's Part the Best of Friends" were well-crafted compositions by Carter, performed at a comfortable mid-tempo in which Ralph's melodic, understated banjo playing stood out; yet neither captured a listener's attention the way some of the earlier material had.

Carter's heartfelt rendition of the Carter Family song "The Wandering Boy" was significant for two reasons. It demonstrated that the older brother could have achieved success on his own. At age 26, his voice possessed a choirboy purity combined with the sincere country soulfulness that later would so impress Bill Clifton. "Carter was somebody whose vocal style and his empathy . . . his soul went into every song," Clifton said.[16] "He was somebody whose way of writing a song brought in every aspect of one's soul. You couldn't hear a song like 'White Dove' without hearing all his genuine feelings of a song. I don't know if I ever heard anybody then or since that time who had that warm soul vocal pattern." In a scene from the play *Man of Constant Sorrow*, written with the approval of Ralph, a record company executive tries to persuade Carter that he could be the next Hank Williams.

Carter's recording of "Wandering Boy" also showed that the Stanley Brothers were familiar with the Carter Family catalogue. The song was the last recording the Carters made on August 1 and 2, 1927, after driving from Maces Springs to Bristol to take part in Ralph Peer's field sessions; and they recorded it again on October 14, 1941 in their final session in New York City. Possibly because he was repairing a flat tire, A. P. Carter did not take part in the August 2, 1927 session, so there was no male voice on the original recording of "The Wandering Boy." This was appropriate since the song was written from a mother's point of view, just as the second song recorded that day by Sara and Maybelle, "Single Girl, Married Girl," expressed a young woman's point of view. In choosing to sing "The Wandering Boy" as a solo, Carter adopted the role of the wayward son—a persona he would assume in his life.

Despite the pleasing qualities of three of the four songs and Carter's heartfelt vocal on "Wandering Boy," the final Columbia session was a professional bust. Reworking "Man of Constant Sorrow" and covering a Carter Family song, the Stanley Brothers gave the appearance of having little new to offer. With the departure of a member of the original trio, they lost important elements of their sound—Pee Wee Lambert's Monroe-like mandolin playing and high-pitched harmony vocals. Columbia released "Sweetest Love" and "The Wandering Boy" as the band's final record on the label. "Life of Sorrow" and "Best of Friends" went unreleased until 1964 and 1980. It was humbling for the brothers that the most prestigious label in the business—whose chief talent scout for rural music had flown to North Carolina to sign them—had decided not to take advantage of their contract's second option year.[17] The fact that Columbia had signed former Monroe sidemen Flatt and Scruggs added to the insult. Bill Monroe at least had managed to jump to Decca while he still was on the roster of Columbia recording artists.

Without a record label or steady radio show to help promote them, Carter and Ralph had no choice but to relocate to wherever they could find work. In May 1952 they moved to station WOAY in Oak Hill, West Virginia, repeating the pattern of doing radio shows to promote in-person performances. During this period, George Shuffler ended his first stint with the band, returning to North Carolina to work in a factory and build a house for his family. Before leaving, George crossed paths with another group from the first generation of bluegrass performers, native West Virginians Don Stover and the Lilly Brothers. The Stanley Brothers worked at Oak Hill through September, migrating in October to the radio station in North Wilkesboro, North Carolina.

In mid-1952, without a contract, the Stanley Brothers recorded four songs for Rich-R-Tone in a hastily arranged session at radio station WLSI in Pikeville, Kentucky. The studio performances displayed a new rhythmic drive entering into their music—replacing the sedate sounds (other than Carter's vocal on "Wandering Boy") of their final Columbia session. Several developments combined to create the new sound: Carter's apprenticeship with the Blue Grass Boys in which Bill Monroe used sharp strokes on his Gibson mandolin the way a conductor used a baton to control tempo; Ralph's increased comfort with three-finger banjo now that he had been playing in that style for several years; and the band's addition of two new sidemen. Fiddle player Art Stamper joined the group in Versailles, and mandolin player Jim Williams signed on in Oak Hill. Where Pee Wee Lambert had modeled his mandolin playing on the fluttering, melodic side of Bill Monroe's approach to the instrument, Big Jim leaned toward the more staccato, rhythmic aspect of Monroe's playing.

This edition of the Clinch Mountain Boys packed a punch that the earlier group had not possessed, though the band still may have been short on original material. The first song recorded at WLSI was a new Monroe composition that Carter had learned when he was a Blue Grass Boy. Monroe wrote "The Little Girl and the Dreadful Snake" after his niece received a bite from a non-poisonous snake.[18] The song was a moral tale warning parents not to leave children alone. In the hands of the new lineup, the Stanley Brothers' version sounded livelier than Monroe's version, which Monroe recorded on July 18, 1952. Monroe no longer seemed to object to Carter and Ralph using his material. "There were times when the Stanleys would record a song that Bill was going to record and the Stanleys would do it first," Bill Clifton recalled. "If anybody else had done it first except the Stanleys, he would have been incensed. He actually would encourage [Carter]. . . . I know he would make that suggestion to do it."[19] Monroe had good reason to do this: He received royalties from other musicians' recordings of his songs.

The positive energy at the Pikeville session carried into a third version of "The Little Glass of Wine"—equally fast-paced, yet more relaxed in feel than either the original or Columbia versions. The group then converted country balladeer Ernest Tubb's slow reading of "Are You Waiting Just for Me?" into an up-tempo bluegrass number. On the traditional "Little Birdie," Ralph cut loose with bursts of clawhammer banjo in the style that he first had learned from his mother, but fast to the point of sounding frenetic. Carter supported him with quick runs on the guitar that were much more nimble than the single and alternating notes he had used when the brothers made their first recordings. Though not flashy, Carter had become a polished rhythm guitarist in a genre that was difficult to master and later featured lightning-fast strumming and solos. Carter, on the other hand, "had a style of guitar that was very quiet and gentle," recalled Bill Clifton, an accomplished guitar player himself. "He played with a thumb pick and he could play anything at any time no matter how fast it was. I told him: How do you keep up? 'Aw, I just play half time.' Somebody told me he could play in quarter time. He was always right on but didn't try to keep up with the same pace. He showed me how to do it, but I never could do it."[20]

For a group that had lost a major-label recording contract, the Stanley Brothers and the Clinch Mountain Boys sounded buoyant that day in Kentucky. According to Jim Stanton, who was booking the band at the time, the energy in Pikeville was palpable. "They got in a hotel room there one night and started knocking these songs around and they got anxious to cut 'em," he recalled. "WLSI was real strong on giving 'em good radio plugs and their facilities were decent. So we decided to cut the session there to stimulate more interest in the area."[21] The key descriptor of the WLSI facilities was *decent*; the sound quality of the recordings was inferior to the results the group had obtained at WOPI and in the Castle Lab.

The promotion caused genuine excitement. "You know, it was a big thing then to have a record session in your community," Stanton recalled. "We started one morning, seemed to be me like around nine o'clock 'cause they had a show date that night in a little place called Betsy Layne. About noon we had the yard full, the station full, and people trying to do the newscast aggravated at us and all that type of thing."[22] How many of those recordings Stanton was able to sell is impossible to determine, but the community's enthusiasm gave the members of the band a feeling of confidence. So what if Stanton couldn't give away copies of the earlier records in Georgia? The coal-mining region of Kentucky was Stanley Brothers country, where folks loved them and weren't shy about showing it.

Whatever confidence the Pikeville session was able to give the group evaporated in the months that followed. Lack of a record contract was the lesser problem that would be resolved by the spring of 1953, when the brothers signed with Mercury Records. The label's artist and repertoire man in Nashville, W. D. "Dee" Kilpatrick, was partial to their sound, and the timing was right. Mercury had been looking for an established hillbilly act to fill the hole in its roster left by the departure of Flatt and Scruggs. In the summer and fall of 1952, the more serious problem for the Stanley Brothers was the lack of in-person performances. Popular as the band might be in Pikeville and environs, the demand for personal appearances was drying up. By the winter months, the demand had all but disappeared; and soon, so had Carter and Ralph.

Following a path trod by many men from Appalachia, the brothers headed north on Route 23—the Hillbilly Highway—to Michigan to work in the postwar automotive industry. "We were better off than most," Ralph recalled, "because we already had our jobs lined up at the Ford Motor Company outside Detroit."[23] Hattie June (Rasnick) Suthers was a relative whose family helped the brothers make the move to Detroit. Born in the mountains near the Stanley home, June (as she was called) had gotten to know Carter and Ralph when she was a girl growing up in Trammel, Virginia. She was related to the brothers through her aunt Roxie Rasnick, who was Lucy Smith Stanley's cousin. As a child, June listened to the Clinch Mountain Boys on *Farm and Fun Time*. She enjoyed the music and banter as one of the few forms of entertainment available to her and her sisters, and would talk to the brothers whenever they would visit her house, often accompanied by Pee Wee Lambert. "I was just a little tow-head girl of 11 or 12. They'd come around us when they came by that way," she recalled.[24] She described Carter as "an easy-going person. I liked him," adding "Everyone liked both of them." Pee Wee impressed her as "a little old guy [who was] nice looking."

In 1952, her parents had decided to move the family to Michigan in search of employment. Her father, Joe, had been a supervisor in the mines and knew too well the dangers of the work. His son Darrell and wife's brother Junior Phillips were killed in the same mine explosion. At the time of their deaths, both were young men who had been discharged from the army. Darrell was 21. In those days, working families in far southwestern Virginia could not afford a funeral home. June remembered the bodies "laying corpse" in the living room in front of velvet curtains that had been attached to the wall. "The mines were dangerous," she recalled, "but that was all they had to work at except farming, and you couldn't make any money farming to support your family."

Arriving in Detroit, June's father and her brother Kyle went to work for Ford. Married in 1950 at the age of 14, June remained in Trammel before moving to Kingsport, Tennessee. Her only visit to Detroit came when she brought her four-month-old son for her family to see, but she kept in touch. From time to time she heard that Carter and Ralph had dropped by the Rasnick apartment to spend a few hours with old friends from home. On one such visit, Ralph went to the movies with June's sister, Mary, who was 13. June was not sure whether this was a date or not, but one of the girls' aunts maintained social propriety by accompanying Ralph and Mary to the theater.

June's family returned to Virginia in 1956 or 1957. Her brother Kyle and his wife settled near June in Kingsport. The couple had two daughters. In

1966, Kyle became the third member of June's family to be killed in a mining accident. He died in Carbo, Virginia, when the underground car that
was transporting him crushed him against an outcropping of coal. He was
37. "I had very tough parents," June said. "They had to be to have gotten
through all that."

Ralph hated working at Ford. His job on the assembly line was to weld
floorboard pans into trucks. "I worked the night shift, three in the afternoon until midnight," he recalled.[25] "Every time I'd step in the building, I'd
get so sick nearly to where I had to upchuck. . . . For most of the shift, I'd
go hide so the bosses couldn't see me." He lasted for eleven weeks. Carter
stayed three weeks longer. In 1953, Jim Williams had joined the brothers
in Michigan. After the three of them attended a performance by former
Monroe sideman Jimmy Martin and the Sunny Mountain Boys, Big Jim
told Carter and Ralph that they were too talented to be working in a factory.[26] What's more, the sidemen who had recorded with them so energet-
ically in Pikeville were available to regroup for the first Mercury session.
Along with Williams, Art Stamper was ready to go. George Shuffler may
have required coaxing to take time off from his factory job, but Carter
wanted him to play bass.

Carter and George had clicked from the day they met. As a teenager in
North Carolina, George played with his brother John and Les Woodie in a
group called the Melody Mountain Boys. When WCYB bandleader Curly
King hired George's friend Jeff Fullbright to join the Hilltoppers, George
began to visit the radio station in Bristol. On the day he met Carter and
Ralph, the brothers were booked to play that night at a square dance in
Abingdon, Virginia, fifteen miles to the north. "I rode out to that date [in
the same car] with Carter, and we talked all the way, not about music, but
life in general," George recalled.[27]

By the end of the trip, they had discovered that they had a great deal in
common. Not only was George just four months younger than Carter, he
had the same amount of professional experience—possibly more. After
developing his musicianship with the Melody Mountain Boys, George
made it all the way to the stage of the *Grand Ole Opry* with the Bailey
Brothers, and accompanied Jim and Jesse McReynolds for a year in a
band that included Hoke Jenkins—one of the banjo pickers from whom
Ralph learned the three-finger style. Between Christmas and New Year's
Day 1950–51, Carter recruited George to join the Clinch Mountain Boys
at the Versailles, Kentucky, radio station; by the summer of 1953, the raw-
boned North Carolinian was becoming something of a regular. Having

played bass and sung baritone on the band's final Columbia session, he reprised the roles when the group entered the Bradley Studio in Nashville on August 9, 1953, to make the recordings that some consider the Stanley Brothers' finest work.

Carter is credited with writing the four songs recorded that day, though the first, "(Say) Won't You Be Mine," was co-written with Bill Monroe.[28] It set the musical tone for the session: fast, hard driving, and with an edge. Art Stamper and Ralph charged into the introduction on fiddle and banjo, with Ralph introducing bluesy licks to his country style. Jim Williams played his mandolin solo in six-stroke clusters of repeated dah-dah-da-dah-DUH-DUH patterns, with emphasis on the last two strokes. Supporting the lead instruments, George Shuffler played bass in the manner of the guitar player he was, plucking more notes than his brother John or other bassists might have. The result was an intense rhythmic pulse that propelled the music forward.

In the 1975 book *Bluegrass,* one of the first comprehensive accounts of the genre, Bob Artis wrote:

> *To say that the first Mercury session was hot would be a woeful understatement. Carter's lead singing was strong and self-assured, and Ralph was sending his hard, mountain tenor right up through the rafters. The younger Stanley was playing his banjo hard and loud, establishing once and for all the Stanley-style of bluegrass banjo. Williams played some inspired Monroe-style mandolin, and Stamper played breaks and fiddle backup that are still talked about. Giving the session an almost unbelievable forward thrust was bassist Shuffler, playing some of the most complicated bluegrass bass ever recorded.*[29]

The lyrics of the songs were less original than Carter's earlier writing. Though well sung and played, the first verse and chorus of "Won't You Be Mine" consisted of a succession of familiar images.

Can't you hear the night birds crying
Can't you hear that lonesome dove

Chorus
Meet me out on the mountain
Underneath the lonesome pine[30]

Night birds crying, lonesome doves, lovers meeting on the mountain, and the lonesome pine were stereotypical symbols of Appalachian life. Born in Big Stone Gap, Virginia, about twenty miles from Coeburn, novelist John Fox Jr. included the same elements in *The Trail of the Lonesome Pine*, which was among the top ten best sellers of 1908 and 1909 and republished in 1936 to coincide with the film adaptation—the first Technicolor feature to be shot outdoors.[31] Carter and co-writer Monroe would have been familiar with the book, movie, or both. Because the two men had begun writing the song in the summer of 1951 when Carter played with Monroe, the lyrics leaned toward the style of the bandleader. The writers tried to re-create the nostalgic setting that audiences liked.

Recorded next was "This Weary Heart You Stole Away," whose lyrics were enigmatic rather than clichéd.

Wake up sweetheart the night has passed
You slept your troubles all away
Get ready now to love again
This weary heart you stole away

The lyrics leave several questions: whether there are one or two voices speaking in the song; who is waiting for whom; and which member of the couple should be ready to love again. The final two songs, "I'm Lonesome without You" and "Our Last Goodbye," were identical in melody and structure, varying in the lyrics and the fiddle introduction to "Lonesome" being replaced by a banjo introduction to "Goodbye."

The Stanley Brothers returned home to a series of late summer bookings. On August 21, 1953, Carter and Ralph picked up Fiddlin' Powers, an old friend from their days on radio station WNVA in Norton, and drove north on Route 11 to the Moonlite Drive-In in Glade Spring. At drive-in theaters, the band played on the roof of the building that housed the projection booth and refreshment stand, often climbing a ladder to get there, though sometimes there were steps. Carter recalled:

I believe this place just had a ladder. Anyway, we helped the old man up the ladder and down, he played his usual tune . . . as good or better than I ever heard him play it and climbed back down the ladder and got in the car. We closed the show pretty soon after that, five or ten minutes maybe, and by the time we got down to the car there, sitting right beside of the refreshment stand, why he was in awful pain

in his chest and I had a good idea what it was. Course we told him
different. We tried to cheer him up. I reckon it must have been about
twenty miles to the hospital. We took him straight over. We'd rub his
chest. He suffered awful. So we took him, checked him in the hospital
and stayed with him until the doctor done discovered what it was.[32]

The doctor asked Carter to notify the fiddler's family, and Carter and
Ralph waited at the hospital until they arrived. Powers died the next day.
The Stanley Brothers sang at his funeral—the only such occasion at which
they ever performed, despite several requests. Carter reflected that over
the years, his friendship with the old man had grown "stronger instead of
weaker because at first he'd come and stay sometimes two or three days
and then he got so he'd stay two or three weeks with us. Went where we
went, did what we did." Carter hoped that "a man might be rewarded"
for treating one of his musical predecessors with the respect that he had
shown toward Fiddlin' Powers.

The first Mercury session became iconic. In *Bluegrass*, Bob Artis wrote,
"Only four numbers were recorded. . . . All became standards against
which the group would be judged."[33] Carter told Mike Seeger in 1966 that
he thought "we got our best sound on that first session" for Mercury—an
opinion that added weight to their status. However, when I asked Ralph
to identify some of his favorite Stanley Brothers recordings, he extended
his approval to their work on three record labels. "A lot of people said our
Mercury records were the best," he responded. "Some says our Columbia.
Of course we were very new at the business on Columbia, and I think we
had improved a lot for Mercury. I think we recorded a lot of good King
records."[34]

The first five Mercury sessions were held in the Bradley Studio. Using
the model of the Castle Lab, brothers Owen and Harold Bradley built one
of the first independent recording studios in Nashville after Owen's production skills caught the attention of Decca Records.[35] In 1950, he produced a number one country and popular hit—"Chattanoogie Shoe Shine
Boy" by Red Foley—and began working with Bill Monroe after Monroe
arrived at Decca from Columbia. In using the Bradley brothers' studio,
Mercury recorded the Clinch Mountain Boys in the most modern facilities that Nashville had to offer.

Mercury and the Stanley Brothers followed the Bradley brothers
around the city. After completing a seven-song session in April 1955
at the RCA Victor Studio (located in space rented from the Methodist

Television, Radio, and Film Commission at 1525 McGavock Street), the Stanleys returned in mid-December to the Bradley Studio in its new location at 804 16th Avenue South. Installed in a remodeled house, the studio was the first on what would become Nashville's Music Row—home of recording studios, music publishers, and eventually musicians' performance rights organizations such as the American Society of Authors and Composers (ASCAP) and Broadcast Music International (BMI).

The Stanley Brothers had made their first visit to Nashville toward the beginning of the city's rise to prominence as a center for recorded music. Established in 1946 by three engineers from radio station WSM who obtained a $1,000 loan from a local bank, Castle Recording Laboratory was less than three years old when Columbia brought Carter and Ralph to it in 1949.[36] Recognizing the need for a studio to record cast members of WSM's *Grand Ole Opry*, the engineers named their enterprise after the station's claim to being the "air castle of the South." They built the studio on the second floor of the Tulane Hotel at the corner of Seventh and Church Streets. "It was close to WSM," recalled co-founder Aaron Shelton. "We could sneak out the back door and do a recording session and slip back in." Though earlier recording took place in the radio station's broadcast studios, Castle was Nashville's first professional studio, recording country stars such as Red Foley, Ernest Tubb, and Kitty Wells.[37]

While Owen Bradley was perfecting his studio skills at Castle, Harold was becoming one of the top session players in Nashville.[38] The brothers had combined their talents from the time when Harold played amplified guitar in Owen's dance band. As the Stanley Brothers had done at Castle with Columbia, they recorded on Mercury early in the history of the Bradley brothers' studios. Carter and Ralph's third Nashville recording venue was the RCA Victor Studio on McGavock Street—a first-class facility run at one time by guitarist and producer Chet Atkins. As much as their songs and musicianship made the Mercury records special, the brothers would have to share the credit with studios and engineers whose capabilities were evolving, too.

One such evolution—more of a revolution—began July 5, 1954, at Sun Studio in Memphis, Tennessee, when 19-year-old Elvis Presley recorded a fast-paced version of the blues song "That's All Right" by Arthur "Big Boy" Crudup. Presley returned to Sun ten days later to cover Bill Monroe's "Blue Moon of Kentucky," which Monroe had written as a waltz. When Sun Records owner Sam Phillips released the two songs as a 45 rpm[39] single on July 19, 1954, the relative importance of country and popular music began to shift in favor of the latter. With the emergence of Elvis and rise of rock and roll, performers like the Stanley Brothers, who never had financial security to begin with, soon struggled to survive. In 2003, while sitting on Ralph's front patio as the birds sang and his four-year-old grandson mowed the lawn with a toy mower, I asked Ralph about the experience.

> DJ: After this early success, didn't you run into some difficult times?
> RS: It was good for a long time. Then there was a period when it got a little bit lean, and we didn't know what to do. I guess that was about the time rock and roll moved in. That took the attention from old-time music, country, and everything else except Elvis. He was the man there for a few years. The crowds didn't turn out. At first we would draw young people and everything, but all of the young people and a lot of the middle-aged went to this rock and roll. Not only us but bigger country people was hurt.[40]

Even as it appeared that Elvis and his fellow rock and rollers might be a temporary blip on the radar of country music, some reacted quickly to an opportunity to generate additional record royalties. One of these was Bill Monroe. When the Stanley Brothers arrived in Nashville on the eve of their fourth Mercury session in August 1954, Monroe wanted to help produce the session. He had a specific song he wanted the brothers to record. As Carter recalled, "We was in Nashville to record and he said, 'After the *Opry* we'll go eat . . . then I want to come up to WSM studios. There's something up there I want to hear.' He had the record with him: 'Blue Moon of Kentucky' by Elvis Presley. And we had to go up there where there was a machine, you know. So he said, 'I want you to hear something,' and he had never said anything like that to me before. So we went up and that's what we heard: 'Blue Moon of Kentucky' by Elvis Presley. I laughed a little bit and looked around and everybody else was laughing except Bill. He said, 'You better do that number tomorrow if you want to sell some records. It'd be a good idea for you to do that number tomorrow,' and we did it . . . . So I guess he had some vision there that I didn't have. Of course, I probably had vision, too, and then never recorded that. Boy, it was a different sound, there's no doubt."[41]

In 2003, Ralph did not sound enthusiastic either about covering the song, which the group recorded at a medium tempo, or about Monroe's role as producer for the session.

RS: Bill Monroe wrote that song and Elvis made him plenty of money over that. You see, Bill asked us to record it. That was really Bill's idea and Mercury Records'. That's why we recorded that, and we changed things a little bit.

DJ: Do you like your version?

RS: Well, it's all right. I don't like it as good as the way I do it now. We were just trying to see what would happen.

DJ: Was Bill Monroe your producer at that time?

RS: He was in the studio when we recorded it, yeah.[42]

Joining Monroe in the Bradley Studio on August 29, 1954, were two members of his band: bass player Bessie Lee Mauldin, who was involved romantically with Monroe, and fiddle player Charlie Cline. Studio musician Floyd T. "Lightnin'" Chance played bass on the session, while Cline added some finger-picked guitar—the Stanley Brothers' first use of guitar as a lead instrument. Despite Ralph's comment that Monroe was only "in the studio" during the session, Bill persuaded the brothers to record "Close By," a song he had co-written and recorded in June, but had not yet released. As a pioneer of the high, lonesome sound, Monroe would sing as high as he could and appeared to have told the Stanley Brothers to do the same. "Close By" was pitched above their usual vocal range, as was Carter's gospel composition "Calling from Heaven."

Despite the demands placed on them by Monroe, Carter and Ralph managed to record two of their most enduring numbers: one of Carter's finest gospel songs, "Harbor of Love," and one of Ralph's best known banjo instrumentals, "Hard Times." It was ironic that the brothers recorded these two powerful examples of musical expression on a day when their precarious careers as old-time country musicians were in serious jeopardy. The recordings seemed to reflect the brothers' responses to the struggles they were experiencing.

"Harbor of Love" is as direct in emotion as any of Carter's earlier compositions, even if it was written within an entirely different genre.

There's coming a time on the great judgment morning
When the Savior will welcome you home
Will you be prepared for the journey to heaven
On the great ship that carries God's chosen ones home

The song gained power from quartet singing that balanced Carter's straightforward lead and Ralph's falsetto tenor against the baritone and bass vocals of mandolin player Bill Lowe and fiddler Ralph "Joe" Meadows. The interplay of Lowe's mandolin and Charlie Cline's guitar sweetened the instrumental texture. In contrast to the brothers' first gospel recordings on Rich-R-Tone in 1947, the musicians played and sang at a stately pace, as if released from worldly pressure.

Although the span between recordings was months rather than years, a similar contrast in tempo exists between Ralph's first and second banjo instrumentals. He recorded "Dickson County Breakdown" (a misspelling of "Dickenson") at a breakneck tempo in the group's second Mercury session on November 25, 1953. Mandolin player Jim Williams had trouble keeping up with him. He recorded "Hard Times" at a brisk but manageable tempo.

As with several other compositions copyrighted by Carter and Ralph, "Hard Times" had an origin that predated the Stanley Brothers. Fiddle player Les Woodie identified its arrival as a day in 1950 when he and a visiting banjo player began to improvise on a tune that the banjo player brought to WCYB. While not wanting to take credit for lyric suggestions he might have offered Carter, Woodie was willing to claim partial authorship of an instrumental.

> *The only song [or] tune that I did have a part in happened in the WCYB studio on a day off the road. I went over to parties [at the studio] a little and Wiley Birchfield come over with his banjo. Wiley was a pretty good picker. He was between jobs so Ralph took him in to give him some work on the Home Place. That day he said he had one part of a tune and wanted me to play the fiddle with him. I added a second part to it and I kinda liked it. In fact when we got the band together we played it, worked it out and played it on a few shows. We hadn't even given it a name then. A few years later I was in the Air Force and heard their recording of that tune. Ralph called it "Hard Times."*[43]

Ralph played the tune throughout his career until arthritis forced him to give up picking the banjo.

The development of "Hard Times" from musicians jamming for fun in southwest Virginia to a polished recording in a studio in Nashville revealed another way the brothers kept coming up with material: they were close listeners with excellent memories.

In its third Mercury session on May 30, 1954, the group recorded
Carter Stanley composition "Could You Love Me (One More Time)."

Could you love me one more time
With a love that really is mine
I've waited so long they say you've gone wrong
Have I lost you forever this time[44]

Les Woodie remembered Carter working on the song during their
television days in Huntington.

Carter wrote a lot of his songs while we were riding along in the
car. . . . He was working on that song "Let Me Love You One More
Time." I think I helped him with a word or two on that one. Carter
seemed to write on impulse. A lot of times riding along in the car he'd
get a line or two and maybe by the next morning he'd have the rest
of it. He may be riding along and just start singing. He'd sing two or
three lines, or maybe a whole verse. Then that night when we were
warming up for the show, he'd get his guitar and run over it again.[45]

The song became a bluegrass standard covered by artists such as Ricky
Skaggs, who at one time played with future country star Keith Whitley in
the Clinch Mountain Boys.

During the Mercury years, Ralph began to write songs as well as tunes.
He was credited with contributing three songs to the band's fifth Mercury
session on November 28, 1954. Though its lyrics are awkward and rhymes
simple, "I Worship You" contained enough heartache and an emotional kicker in the final line to become a serviceable song for the Stanley
Brothers.

I go back to our home and I lie awake 'til dawn
Still I can't get you out of my life
And my friends say next day what a price you must pay
Last night I saw someone with your wife[46]

After the winter of 1952–53, the Stanley Brothers settled into a pattern
of daily shows on *Farm and Fun Time*, recording sessions two or three
times a year in Nashville, and efforts to be booked into familiar venues
for additional performances. New opportunities were rare. One appeared

in March 1955, when the band was hired to play Richmond radio station WRVA's *Old Dominion Barn Dance* on Saturday evenings. The former capital of the Confederacy was an eight-hour drive from Bristol, but the brothers knew it was worth it. Elvis Presley and rock and roll entertainers were proving to be more than a blip on the radar screen.

Adopting the clever moniker the "Hillbilly Cat" that resonated with both country and blues fans, Elvis made a guest appearance on the *Louisiana Hayride* on October 16, 1954.[47] His leg-shaking performance of the songs on his first record marked the beginning of profound changes in the country music business as the Stanley Brothers had known it. "In sound, in repertoire, and in posture, Elvis Presley of the mid-to-late 1950s represented nothing short of the desegregation of musical aesthetics," wrote Tracey E. W. Laird in her book on the *Hayride.*

This signaled a degree of desegregation of the music business itself, as companies marketed him and rock-and-roll artists like Little Richard, Fats Domino, Carl Perkins, and Jerry Lee Lewis across racial lines. But the implications extended far deeper than a new market category somewhere between white country and black rhythm-and-blues. . . . Although [Elvis] was not the first musician to manifest the rock-and-roll impulse, he touched a cultural nerve as no one had before him.[48]

Thirty- and forty-year-old Caucasian men wearing Stetson hats and string ties, singing songs descended from the exclusively white Scotch-Irish tradition, went overnight from being marketable performers to the least cool musicians on the planet. Younger people in southwestern Virginia snickered at the way the Stanley Brothers looked and sounded.[49]

Next to changing popular tastes, winters continued to be the most serious threat to a country musician's livelihood. Each year the Stanley Brothers had to come up with a new strategy to get through the season. In the winter of 1955–56, a band that included Richard "Curley" Lambert on mandolin, Donald "Chubby" Anthony on fiddle, and George Shuffler on bass toured the Pacific Northwest as far north as Canada to keep working. According to Shuffler, Ralph had to sell thirteen cattle to make the tour possible. "He did that when rock and roll hit so hard," George recalled.[50] "It starved everybody out in country and bluegrass. Ralph was determined to keep band together. He sold twelve big Hereford cows and one big bull. Carter had a family and four real young ones. Ralph was with his mother on her farm, and he sold a lot of it . . . to pay salaries so we could stay on road. I was like Carter. I had a family. I had to have income."

The irony was that the band was playing some of the best music of its career. Not long after the opening of the Ralph Stanley Museum and Traditional Music Center at which George had told me about the sale of the cattle, I asked him when he thought the band had been at its musical peak. "Back during the lean years," he answered. "We was picking hungry, like they say. There wasn't a lot of money. You had to play from your heart to keep from starving to death. We hung together as a group. We kind of get [sic] the best harmony. There were some who could out-pick us, but when it comes to harmony singing, there's no way we could beat the Stanleys and Shuffler—that came to us from some of the top bluegrassers from the people they told it to." Because of the Stanley Brothers' years on the road and time in the studio, the quality of the music had become consistent. What remained problematic was whether the group could string together enough bookings from spring through fall to survive the financial black hole of winter.

12. MERCURY FALLING

During the 1930s, the ultra-powerful signal of border radio station XERA carried all the way from Mexico into Canada. In the red brick tenements of Chicago's South Side, a young boy listened with curiosity to XERA. Broadcast from a transmitter in Villa Acuña, Coahuila, across the border from Del Rio, Texas, XERA was outside the jurisdiction of the Federal Communications Commission, which regulated the power levels of U.S. stations. A program showcasing the down-home voices and instruments of the Carter Family from Maces Springs, Virginia, captured the boy's imagination.

The boy, Larry Ehrlich, became a fan of hillbilly music by listening to old-time performers such as Doc Hopkins, Karl and Harty, and the Monroe Brothers. Hopkins, in particular, was "a storehouse of traditional material."[1] During the Depression, the Kentucky natives had come north to find work. While performing first in the Chicago area as old-time dancers, Charlie, Birch, and Bill Monroe supported themselves by working at the oil refineries in Hammond, Indiana, in the northwest corner of the state near Illinois. Eventually all of the Kentuckians became regulars on Chicago radio station WLS, home of the *National Barn Dance*.

In his late teens, Ehrlich got to know Hopkins when he and his friend Fleming Brown co-hosted a radio program. Around the same time, Ehrlich began to make home recordings. "We were doing . . . *The Midnight Special* every Saturday night on WFMT in Chicago," he recalled.[2] "We would rehearse every Friday night and lots of folks, including Doc and Bill Broonzy, would come over [to Brown's house] to distract us. Everything was very informal and we would listen to each other and record just for the hell of it." In another conversation he said, "That was all pre–Stanley Brothers and that's what conditioned me to the Stanley Brothers. . . . That's why I think I was so receptive to this sound."[3]

The Stanley Brothers became his favorites from the moment he heard a record of "The Lonesome River." Carter's melancholy ballad with the high baritone harmonies "pretty much blew me away," he recalled.[4] Heard on radio, live performances by his favorite group added to his appreciation.

In those days, Ehrlich felt "light years" removed from the steep ridges and broad valleys of far southwestern Virginia—a feeling that led him later to ask a question at the core of the Stanley Brothers' musical appeal: "How . . . did two boys from those ancient mountains reach across time, space, geography and background to touch the very hearts and souls of tens of thousands of seeming strangers such as me?"[5]

Though his estimate of the number of listeners touched by the music was high, his question took note of the trend in the early 1950s in which the Stanley Brothers and other old-time country musicians (along with African American counterparts who played country blues) began to pick up a following among young northern listeners. The northerners were in the vanguard of what would become the urban folk music revival of the late 1950s and early 1960s.

Ehrlich's connection to a geographically and culturally distant style of music illustrated how radio played a significant a role in popularizing folk music. Growing up in a major city in the Midwest where listeners could choose among a variety of stations, Ehrlich was exposed to "a lot of great stuff on the radio." These included live hillbilly programs that were broadcast at five in the morning and four in the afternoon. "I liked the sound of guitars and banjos," he recalled, dismissing much of the later folk revival as "urban crap."

Once his ears became attuned to the music, Ehrlich began discovering new hillbilly performers everywhere. For example, he first heard banjo player Don Reno piped in over the sound system of a drugstore. Soon he was immersed. What separated him from the majority of listeners, who were content to enjoy a program and tune in again the next day or week, was that he began to write letters to the performers. After sending a letter to the Stanley Brothers in care of WCYB, he traveled to Virginia to hear them in person.

Born in 1929, Ehrlich was two years younger than Ralph and four years younger than Carter. "They were in personality and temperament seemingly quite different from each other," he recalled.[6] "Carter was engaging, outgoing and conversational. Ralph, while friendly, was reserved, deferential and rarely said much." Personalities aside, Ehrlich had "never seen two men as close to one another as were the Stanley Brothers. When they sang together the perfection of that closeness was there for the world to hear. And yet their voices were very different. . . . Carter sang with the greatest ease of any singer I have ever watched. His unique, impeccable phrasing and timing were the result. He had the most tender voice I have ever heard. I have never heard a lead singer I would consider his equal. Of Ralph Stanley's voice, what can be said? It is a voice like no other voice."

By the winter of 1955–56, Ehrlich had gained enough of the brothers' trust (he called them "guarded people")[7] to make an informal recording. On March 26, 1956, following a full day around Bristol that included a radio broadcast and a performance at a hog-calling contest, Ehrlich, the brothers, and their band members—Curley Lambert on mandolin and Ralph Mayo on fiddle—returned to the WCYB studios around midnight. Ehrlich turned on his "pathetically antiquated" Webcor tape recorder while the musicians performed full and partial renditions of twenty songs and tunes that the brothers had learned in their boyhoods and early careers. "I did not pay the Stanley Brothers anything for the tape," Ehrlich said.[8] "The thought of doing it just arose spontaneously at the end of a long day. It was just something that we did because we were friends, nothing more, nothing less."

Included in the unrehearsed session that night were songs associated with Grayson and Whitter ("Handsome Molly" and "Train 45"), the Carter Family ("East Virginia Blues" and "Meet Me Tonight"), and the Monroe Brothers ("Drifting Too Far from the Shore"). Carter sang a solo number, "Come All Ye Tenderhearted," learned from an old Baptist hymnal. Ralph contributed renditions of "Shout Little Lulie" and "Little Birdie"; both were banjo tunes that he had learned from his mother. As Ralph fingerpicked the mandolin to accompany "East Virginia Blues," Curley Lambert disappeared from the session, falling asleep. The three remaining musicians performed an instrumental version of the traditional song about steel-driving man "John Henry."

Possibly because of the after-hours use of the borrowed studio, the recording sounds subdued; yet it demonstrated the Stanley Brothers' familiarity with the musical heritage of their region. The recording also provided ample evidence to support Larry's choice of the adjective *tender* to describe a quality in Carter's voice that reflected the vulnerable aspect of his nature. "He was a person of great perception and sensitivity," Ehrlich recalled. "His whole front was a mask. Underneath was a person of great depth and understanding."

Life in the mid-1950s on Smith Ridge provided some stability for Carter and his young family. Listening to Ehrlich's recording at the time of its commercial release in 2004, Doris Stanley Bradley—the older of Carter's two daughters—was reminded of the times that she shared with her father. "I have been to the WCYB studios many times when I was between the age of three [and] five years old," recalled Doris.[9]

It is one of my most cherished memories of my tall, wonderful, handsome, tender, loving Daddy. . . . Each [and] every time they taped a radio show at WCYB stations, it was a wonderful and cherished opportunity for me . . . his little blonde darling whom he treated like a queen and loved beyond all reason . . . to get my hair rolled up on bobby pins (which I had to sleep in because Daddy wouldn't let me go if my hair wasn't curled [and] I wasn't dressed in my prettiest dresses which he himself picked out [and] bought for me, because he said I was "Daddy's beautiful blonde girlfriend, she's my best girl and my only real love, fellers, so just don't go getting no ideas about this one, she's all mine)."

Those weekly WCYB taping sessions were my chance to dazzle Daddy with what he made me feel was my radiant beauty [and] feminine charms, [and] my time to charm him [and] have him [and] his attention exclusively all to myself for 45 minutes or so after each taping session. Only one other person has ever made me feel so beautiful [and] special as I felt accompanying Carter Stanley to WCYB every week for our "weekly milkshake dates." These . . . consisted of Daddy's ordering one vanilla milkshake with two straws [and] pretending to drink half of the milkshake with me out of his straw while I guzzled most of it from another straw from the same big milkshake glass in a silver holder. I'd have to wait sometimes down in the hotel coffee shop with "Roscoe," the man who worked behind the Shelby Hotel Coffee Shop café counter while Daddy [and] Ralph taped the show. Occasionally they'd let me come up [and] sit around on various laps during a taping, or a lull in the activity, but mostly I had to sit [and] not say a word while I was up there because they were taping shows or on live radio.

Those dates and times are memories which will remain alive and treasured as long as I live. . . . I hope they will live on forever as stories of Carter Stanley's love of his children and his respect and admiration for the women in his life. He was such a gentleman and

taught me what being female was all about [and] what kind of re-
spect [and] treatment to demand from the men in my life from my
earliest memory.

While listening to the recording that prompted her memories, Doris
said that "I cried all the way through. . . . I heard the weariness, tender-
ness, and beauty of Carter Stanley performing at his very best. I don't
think either brother expected this recording to be sold at all—they were
candid, spontaneous, [and] wonderful."[10]

Beneath these warm recollections of a loving daughter, Carter faced
serious issues in his personal life. Foremost in terms of impact on him
and his family was that he continued to drink at a debilitating pace. His
alcoholism (though not treated as a disease at the time) had become an
open secret among those who knew him. When we spoke among the guitars and banjos of his Bristol, Tennessee, music store in December 2004,
former Curly King sideman Joe Morrell told me emphatically: "Of course
it was one thing that killed Carter. I knew the man who told Carter he
had to quit or it would kill him. He didn't quit, and it killed him. . . . He
would do it in the morning. I saw him come into WCYB with a bottle in
his guitar case."[11] The man who informed Carter that he needed to stop
drinking if he was to continue living was a respected general practitio-
ner in Bristol, Dr. Bruce Mongle. Whether it was from a tendency toward
self-destructive behavior, as some who knew him suggested, or because
he was caught in the grip of a disease, Carter paid little heed to the doctor's advice.

The professional side seemed as secure as it could be in an insecure
business—until what appeared to be an important musical turning point
in the summer of 1956. Under a contract similar to that with Columbia,
calling for three years plus two option years, the Stanley Brothers had
recorded for Mercury since 1953. They recorded thirteen sides over three
sessions in 1954, eleven in two sessions in 1955, and five in the single session in 1956. During a period that included their Bill Monroe–produced
arrangement of "Blue Moon of Kentucky," the brothers' work reflected
the significant influence of Monroe on their music. The group began its
April 5, 1955, session at the RCA Victor studio on Nashville's McGavock
Street by recording Monroe's "I Hear My Savior Calling" and a seamless
arrangement of a second gospel quartet, "Just a Little Talk with Jesus."
Monroe often played "Just a Little Talk" in the late 1940s on the *Grand
Ole Opry.* Two songs later the band recorded an aggressive warning to

a lover, "You'd Better Get Right," that Monroe and Carter had begun to write in 1951.

"All I knew of the song was the chorus," Carter recalled, "and after I left Bill we wanted to record it. I didn't know the verses that he used, and I just kindly took a word here and there from what I'd heard him do and added a few words to 'em and done our version. Of course I give him credit for the writer of the song because I think that was right. It was his idea; it was his tune and everything. We were always kidding each other about things like that."[12]

At the cost of its own originality, the band tried to emulate the high-pitched vocals of the former critic who had become a mentor. Yet the most successful recording of the seven-song session was the most tra-ditional—an energetic performance of the instrumental tune (with one verse) "Orange Blossom Special" that was cut because there was time left in the day's studio booking. Bass player Bill Lowe exclaimed that "we shoved the damn hell" out of the tune.[13] Featuring the fiddle work of young West Virginian Joe Meadows, whose technique had improved markedly since joining the band the previous year, "Orange Blossom Special" (released July 1955) and "Hard Times" (released January 1955) combined to win the Stanley Brothers and the Clinch Mountain Boys an award as best new instrumental group in a readers' poll conducted by *Country and Western Jamboree* magazine.[14] Though the Stanley Brothers had performed professionally for ten years and were not primarily an in-strumental group, *Bluegrass Unlimited* later considered the award note-worthy because "competition . . . included all the top commercial country and western bands."[15] Bluegrass was not yet a separate category.

"Orange Blossom Special" gave guitarist Bill Clifton a story that illus-trated Carter's quick wit.

It was the same summer as the Stanley Brothers' version of "Orange Blossom Special" came out on Mercury. They didn't have a fiddler at the time when they came to Maryland to do a program on the east-ern shore. They were staying in my family's home. I rode over with them to where they were invited by the wife of the local promoter. She had cooked up a bunch of fried chicken and corn on the cob, feeding all of us at table. Carter was busy eating. She served up all this great meal. She said: I have something I want to tell you all. I'm so excited because my favorite recording is the new record of "Orange Blossom Special." Which one of you plays the fiddle? Carter had a mouthful of food and pointed at me. "Yonder he sits." He always was one for practical jokes.[16]

The time Carter gave Joe Meadows to develop his technique provided another perspective on the bandleader: He enjoyed bringing along promising musicians. "The first professional work he ever done was with us," Carter recalled.[17]

Frankly, I was ashamed for Joe to play with us on stage. I told him to stand way back where people couldn't hear him. I had Chubby Anthony at that time, too. Chubby was getting ready to leave and I broke Joe in that way. And every spare minute that boy had he would work on that fiddle, and he didn't work on somebody else's songs all the time; he worked on the songs that he felt we'd be doing. As a result, Joe Meadows made us one of the best fiddlers we ever had. He was young and he was willing to learn, and he did. I've always admired Joe Meadows for that.

At the April 1955 session the versatile Meadows played lead guitar on "So Blue," a song credited to Ralph. The song used a similar arrangement to the Stanley Brothers' version of "Blue Moon of Kentucky."[18] The search for a more contemporary sound originated with the brothers rather than the record company. Asked if Mercury pushed the group toward the boogie-woogie guitar style popular at the time, Ralph said "No, they never did do that. They liked the old original stuff."[19]

Despite the personal preferences of industry executives such as Mercury's Dee Kilpatrick, the market for old-time country almost disappeared during the rise of rock and roll. Mercury released only one of four numbers the Stanley Brothers recorded at the relocated Bradley Studio on December 19, 1955. The single was another banjo instrumental by Ralph, called "Big Tilda" after Carter's nickname for Ralph's first wife.[20] Playing a newly purchased 1923 Gibson Mastertone, Ralph "got to messing around and come up with a new instrumental with enough forward rolls like to bust down walls; it was the biggest, loudest tune I'd ever stumbled on."[21] The gentle hymn "Angel Band" became one of the Stanley Brothers' best-known performances after it was included in 2000 on the Grammy award–winning soundtrack to the film *O Brother, Where Art Thou?*

While the innovative arrangements of "Blue Moon of Kentucky" and "So Blue" represented an effort to change with the times, questionable production decisions in the Stanley Brothers' one session in 1956 and final two sessions for Mercury in 1957 reflected the struggles of a band to be consistent. As bandleader, Carter was most responsible for the drift. Following the lead of Bill Monroe, who sometimes used two and even three fiddle players, Carter decided to use two for a session on July 16, 1956. They were Chubby Anthony, who replaced Art Stamper after Stamper returned from military service to replace Joe Meadows, and Ralph Mayo, who played with the Stanley Brothers once before. The use of twin fiddles playing in harmony or an octave apart was not a problem, but the use of an echo effect on the fiddles created a distant sound as if the musicians were playing in an empty room. The sound detracted from strong vocals and instrumental work. Compared to earlier recordings, some of the vocals seemed "down" in the mix—a liability for a group known for its singing.

On the first number recorded—the hymn "Cry from the Cross"—Carter or the producer intended to simulate the crying sound suggested by the title. The effect did not fit well in a gospel song that normally would not include either fiddle or banjo. Both instruments were associated with dance music and not considered appropriate to religious music. Echo (also known as reverb) was a trendy effect in 1956. Nashville producer Steve Sholes used it to full advantage on Elvis Presley's first number one hit, "Heartbreak Hotel," recorded in RCA Victor Studios in January 1956. A fluttering reverb heightened the syncopation of Gene Vincent's hit "Be-Bop-A-Lula," recorded later that year. Even with standard recording a fiddle could sound scratchy; the addition of reverb caused the twin fiddles on "Cry from the Cross" to sound shrill. The song proved popular in performance for the Stanley Brothers through the late 1950s, but the recording makes one long for a more listenable version. Echo-effect fiddles were used on three other songs on the session; only Carter's "Let Me Walk, Lord, by Your Side" was recorded without effects.

While Carter was willing to innovate, Ralph preferred the old-time sound. The brothers' differences created disagreements, as Ralph acknowledged when I interviewed him in 2003. Growing up in the same region as Carter and Ralph, Joe Wilson observed that "Ralph Stanley was a brother, so he put up with a lot from a brother. And never a harsh word has fallen from Ralph Stanley's lips about his brother."[22] Acquaintances such as Larry Ehrlich and Mike Seeger noted how close the brothers were, yet some observed that Carter and other band members could be very hard on Ralph. The struggle to survive in the changing musical climate of the mid- to late 1950s increased the potential for friction.

Changes in popular tasted contributed to the demise of perhaps the most successful brother duo of the 1950s, the Louvin Brothers. From humble beginnings in Alabama, Ira and Charlie had risen to become cast members of the *Grand Ole Opry*. In 1958 Capitol Records' Nashville artist and repertoire representative Ken Nelson told Ira that the presence of his mandolin on recordings "was hindering the sales of the Louvin Brothers records."[23] According to Charlie, the combustible Ira—who spent twenty-five years mastering the art of mandolin playing—was "totally destroyed." He remarried three times in seven years before dying in 1965 in a car crash that also killed his fourth wife. In retrospect, Charlie concluded that "the Presley era . . . catching on like wild fire" was responsible for the decreased record sales, not the old-time sound of Ira's mandolin. Charlie said "The pressures in being brothers is insurmountable. I don't believe I can offhand think of a duet that ever made it. Ten years is not long. Ira and I should have sung together for forty years professionally. But we didn't do much . . . after we came to the *Opry*, we only did eight years."[24]

Carter was the critic in the Stanley Brothers. The way with words that made him an exceptional songwriter could take the form of a sharp tongue that did not hesitate to use language as a weapon. One band member recalled a time in the brothers' early days when Carter shut Ralph in a room with his banjo and recordings that featured Earl Scruggs, ordering Ralph to learn to play in the three-fingered style. Whether Ralph acquired the style from records, other players such as Snuffy Jenkins, or Scruggs himself, he did as he was told. The evidence can be heard on two recordings. On "Little Maggie," released in April 1948 shortly before Flatt and Scruggs arrived at WCYB, Ralph played in the two-fingered style. By the time the Stanley Brothers recorded "Molly and Tenbrook," released in September 1948 after Flatt and Scruggs arrived in Bristol, Ralph had switched to the three-finger style. According to bluegrass historian Neil Rosenberg, Ralph's playing "closely resembled that of Scruggs."[25] Rosenberg cited the similarity as one indication that the pioneering sound of Bill Monroe and the Blue Grass Boys was in the process of become a more widespread style.

Carter's criticism of his musicianship stayed with Ralph for years. Ron Thomason, who joined the Clinch Mountain Boys for a year in 1970, described Ralph as ". . . so insecure musically. On the one hand he will project the fact the he believes he has done the great tenor lines and he's the great banjo player and he's done these great things. And they are true. But he doesn't really believe that. Down inside there's a part of him that thinks everybody can play the banjo better and there's a million people that can sing better."[26]

The irony is that, while Carter looked for reasons that prevented the brothers from becoming as popular as Flatt and Scruggs, in the late 1950s Ralph became an increasingly productive contributor to the band, composing tunes and songs as well as singing high harmony and occasional lead. As a key member of the string ensemble that was the basic unit of an old-time country group, he had become adept at backing lead vocalists and instrumentalists soloing on other instruments, playing behind people without getting in their way. When it was his turn to solo, he could play in a range of musical styles, from blistering flurries of notes to a gentle reprise of the song's melody. Just as "Scruggs-style banjo" came to identify the three-fingered picking style of the North Carolina banjo players, there came to be a style associated with Ralph—lacking adornment and forgoing showy effects such as turning the tuning pegs in mid-number, yet well suited to the tradition-oriented material and arrangements of the Clinch Mountain Boys. Musicians and fans would call this "Stanley-style banjo." Beginning with "Dickson County Breakdown" in 1953, Ralph committed to vinyl a string of distinctive banjo tunes, including "Hard Times" and "Big Tilda," that would continue for the next decade.

Former musician Joe Morrell offered a simple explanation for the development of Ralph's style. "He couldn't play as well as Scruggs," Morrell said.[27] "When he switched from old-time to Scruggs style, that's what gave him his own sound. He tried to play three-fingered, but he couldn't get it rolling three-fingered, so he worked it out where he played two-fingered." As he spoke, Morrell illustrated the two picking styles with the thumb and fingers of his right hand. "It was sort of a combination between old-time and Scruggs style," he said. If Morrell's opinion is correct, the evolution of Ralph's style was similar to that of one of his models, Wade Mainer.

In the midst of a diminishing market, one sign pointed to future possibilities for the Stanley Brothers. When Richmond radio station WRVA broadcast the brothers' music to parts of the country well beyond the WCYB listening area, the result was that in spring and fall when the weather was moderate, as well as during summer, the band began to get bookings outside the five states where *Farm and Fun Time* could be heard. Beginning in 1954, outdoor music parks in Maryland, Pennsylvania, Ohio, and Indiana booked the group for performances. For the Stanley Brothers and similar acts, the music parks were an important circuit for the next decade.

In addition to playing the parks, the group departed from its customary territory in the late summer of 1956 to make an extended tour of the Northwest that included a visit to Canada. Idaho Falls served as home base while the band performed shows in Idaho cities as far south as Pocatello, and ventured as far north in the United States as Oregon and Washington. Photographs included in the brothers' songbook from around 1957 show Carter and Ralph standing in front of a "Welcome to Washington" sign and next to "State Boundary, Entering Oregon"—reminiscent of the early photograph taken at the Cumberland Gap. The same songbook reported that "The Stanleys recently completed a very successful Canadian tour," though there is none of the usual photo documentation to support the statement.[28]

Playing the civic auditorium in Idaho Falls as well as appearing on a local television show that featured country music, in one instance the group was billed as stars of the *Grand Ole Opry*, capitalizing on Carter's affiliation with Bill Monroe. The touring band included Chubby Anthony on fiddle, Curley Lambert on mandolin, and George Shuffler on bass. A publicity photograph from the time shows a bug-eyed Shuffler sporting several blacked-out teeth, a checked scally cap (in contrast to the other musicians' Stetsons), and horn-rimmed glasses. The photo left little doubt that Shuffler filled the customary bass man's roles of comedian and rube.

The band considered the six-week tour a success. The only casualty appeared to be Curley Lambert's patience. As quick to launch a verbal needle as he was to bestow a nickname, Carter sometimes could not control himself when he got on a musician's case. During the tour of the Northwest, he rode the mandolin player so hard that Lambert quit the moment the band returned home. The relationship was restored by the following fall because Lambert returned to play bass on the band's final Mercury session.

Struggling through the winter months was hard enough that the brothers sometimes required their band members to work on the family farm.[29] "They got that from Bill Monroe," Joe Morrell said. "He would have his band work all day on the farm until it was time to play." Extra farm hands were not needed on Smith Ridge in 1956–57, but a more serious challenge would face the band and its home region.

Meteorologists know that much of the weather in Virginia, West Virginia, Kentucky, and the Carolinas is the result of a complex

relationship between the Appalachians and the Atlantic Ocean, in particular the Gulf Stream.[30] Because of the topography of its many mountains and river valleys, atmospheric circulation in Appalachia was con-
ducive to floods and droughts. On January 29 and 30, 1957, heavy rain
from a weather system stalled above the region caused one of the most
devastating floods in its history. Water overflowed the banks of the Big
Sandy, New, and Tennessee Rivers in Virginia as well as these and other
rivers that ran through southern West Virginia and eastern Kentucky. The
Virginia floodwaters peaked at the highest level recorded since 1862 on
the North Fork Holston River near Saltville in the same southwestern section of the state.

The flood trapped the Clinch Mountain Boys in their car while they
were returning from a performance. "We'd been playing a show in Grundy
and we were trying to get back through the mountains to Smith Ridge,"
George Shuffler recalled.[31] "And that flood came in and we were looking
to get washed away any minute. We pulled the car up on a high hill above
the flood line and some people took us into their house for the night.
Carter wrote the song there." Carter was so excited about his ballad, "The
Story of the Flood," that he telephoned his music publisher in Nashville,
Wesley Rose, in the middle of the night to sing it to him.[32] Carter's lyrics
were heartfelt and topical, and Rose told him to record the song as soon
as possible to capitalize on the event, which was making national news.
When the waters eased enough for vehicles to travel, the group drove to
Bristol to record "The Flood" at WCYB. The 45 rpm single (backed by the
gospel song "Let Me Walk, Lord, by Your Side," recorded in Nashville)
was released on February 14. Mercury's recent affiliation with a Houston-
based independent label, Starday Records, gave the two labels the ability
to rush the release of a record. According to *The Starday Story*, "With the
advantage of two pressing plants (Chicago and St. Louis) at their disposal,
'The Flood' was a perfect example of how quickly a song could go from
just an idea to hitting the retail shelves."[33]

Come listen good people, wherever you are,
And hear the sad story you've been waiting for,
About the flood of '57, as it happened to be,
In Kentucky, old Virginia, and east Tennessee.

Carter's ballad cemented the bond between the bandleader and members of his audience. When I spoke with former coal miner Jerry E. Powers

at Ralph Stanley's Hills of Home Festival in May 2006, he made this clear. "Carter Stanley wrote that song while I was in the flood," Powers stated,[34] as if the songwriter had him personally in mind.

Working with his brother-in-law in a mine at Grundy, Powers almost died. "We were trying to drain the mine with a sump pump. The water was coming in faster than we could pump it." The water rose to their chests before the foreman told them to abandon the pump. "When the boss man said to get out, we walked half a mile to the mouth of the road," Powers recalled. That distance was from the pump to the mine entrance. Emerging from the mine's internal road, Powers was confronted with a startling new expanse of water. A creek that had a normal breadth of about six feet had overflowed to what seemed like hundreds of feet. He had no choice but to cross the expanse, even though it was not a placid lake but a surging river. "I went under two times and my brother-in-law thought I had drowned," he said. "Each one of us thought [the other] drowned." The river swept both men a considerable distance downstream as they struggled to reach the other side.

Gaining the opposite shore at last, Powers rejoined his brother-in-law, Joe Riley, who had collapsed on the bank and was trying to catch his breath. The men were soaking wet and freezing. They shivered as their bodies battled the numbing cold. Waiting ten minutes to gather what was left of their strength, they began to walk along a railroad track. They could not walk on the adjacent highway because it was under several feet of water. After walking two miles, Powers and Riley came to a house where they found shelter and warmth. On the floors of the house, the mud was a foot deep. Jerry called the experience "one of the fright'ningest times in my life." At age 27, he never went back to the mines.

Carter's song resonated with Jerry and thousands of others who experienced the flood of 1957. The flooding began on January 28, causing millions of dollars on damage. A dozen people died. In some areas, the National Guard was called out to protect what was left of water-ravaged property; in others, Red Cross volunteers ministered to mud-spattered residents through mobile disaster canteens. The headlines of the February 1 *Kingsport* (Tennessee) *News* covered both the national and local impact with the headline "Ike Gets 'Disaster' Request" over the subhead "Man Drowns Near Haysi." On January 31, the federal government declared portions of Kentucky and West Virginia disaster areas, and did the same the next day for Virginia, where twelve counties were affected. On February 14—the day that Carter's song was released—the *New York*

Times reported that the government had allotted the region five million dollars in disaster relief funds.

Little babies were crying, and others were sad,
For in all our lives, we'd seen nothing so bad.
But the brave and the strong were there by the score,
To help the sick and needy to safety on the shore.[35]

In writing about the flood, Carter followed in the topical songwriting footsteps of A. P. Carter, who wrote "The Cyclone of Rye Cove" after a tornado struck a two-story schoolhouse in Scott County, Virginia, on May 2, 1929, killing thirteen of 150 students and injuring dozens of others. A. P. was in a neighboring valley that day and took part in rescue efforts, which included a special train that transported the injured to the hospital in Bristol. The Carter Family recorded "Rye Cove" the same year.

Carter and Ralph met A. P. early in their careers when the older man made one of his visits to WCYB. "The best I recall he just showed up one day at the radio station," Ralph said, "and we saw him watching through the studio window while we played our show."[36] Joe Morrell witnessed a visit a few years later and was bothered by the memory. "He came into the studio one time when I was there," Morrell recalled. "It was almost awful. He was shaking the whole time. He had a cheap guitar and played one song. He was shaking all over—his hand had been shaking all his life. It was almost awful [that] Curly King let him go on the air."

After meeting the Stanley Brothers, A. P. invited them to play on an outdoor stage he had built facing the hill behind his country store. Trying to keep connected to the music business after the Carter Family disbanded, he put on a series of Sunday concerts. "It was supposed to be a one-dollar admission, but he never turned nobody away," Ralph remembered. "There wasn't even a P.A. system. What you call rustic."[37] Writing "The Flood," Carter would have been aware that he acted as A. P. had when faced with a community tragedy; he responded with a record that the outside world would hear.

Carter's expression of the tribulations of friends and neighbors affected by the flood may have enhanced his status as a regional celebrity, but the support of Mercury Records executives was waning. According to Dee Kilpatrick, "The Stanley Brothers were not *really* hot then, but I could at least break even with them. I couldn't do too much with 'em 'cause it was so narrow with bluegrass then. Of course you had the tried and true bluegrass fans, but back then it just wasn't that damn popular."[38] Cutting costs by recording the group in monaural (rather than stereo) sound around a single microphone, Mercury still needed to sell 25,000 copies of a record to begin to make money.

When the band returned to Nashville on February 27, 1957, for a session at the RCA Victor Studio, it recorded another of Ralph's banjo tunes, "Fling Ding," and two new songs by Carter, "I'll Never Grow Tired of You" and "Loving You Too Well." For the banjo number, Ralph reworked a traditional fiddle tune, "Sally Ann." On mandolin was Pee Wee Lambert, who had come to the session at Carter's request to fill in during the absence of Curley Lambert (no relation to Pee Wee).

The Stanley Brothers' final Mercury session took place in RCA Victor Studios on November 15, 1957. It bore little resemblance to the extraordinary first session of August 1953. The weaknesses were in the material and Carter's voice. Now 32, his vocal chords and diaphragm had begun to show the effects of years of drinking and smoking. The shame of the session was that such a high level of talent produced such uneven results. Carter once again adopted the twin fiddle sound, hiring Ben E. "Benny" Martin and Howard "Howdy" Forrester—two of Nashville's top fiddle players. The swaggering Martin was perhaps the finest bluegrass fiddler of his generation. Bill Napier had joined the group on mandolin during the summer and brought to the session "Daybreak in Dixie"—one of the first mandolin instrumentals in the bluegrass repertoire that was not composed by Bill Monroe.

Since the version of "Life of Sorrow" that the Stanley Brothers recorded for Columbia in 1952 had not been released, they re-recorded it as the single from the session, backed with "I'd Rather Be Forgotten" by a friend, E. P. Williams. The most enduring song recorded that day was "If That's the Way You Feel." Ralph's first wife Peggy wrote the lyrics. The version was the band's only recording to feature the hallmark of 1950s Nashville country music, the pedal steel guitar. Carter's vocal was weak and out of tune, and the instrumental accompaniment was tentative, making the song more like a demo than a finished product. For understandable reasons, Mercury did not release it. When the opportunity presented itself, the group tried to duplicate the modest success of "The Flood."

On February 28, 1958, a school bus carrying forty-nine students hit a wrecker pulling a pickup truck out of a ditch on U.S. Route 23 in Prestonburg, Kentucky. After striking the wrecker's left rear bumper and fender—an impact that may have knocked the bus driver unconscious—the bus swerved left toward the Levisa Fork of the Big Sandy River, whose waters were swollen from melting snow. Children screamed as the bus hit a parked car, missed a trailer owned by Floyd County bootlegger Bennie Blackburn, and slid down the riverbank through a grove of willow trees. Resting half in the water, the bus bobbed in the current for a few minutes before being sucked into the river and pushed 250 yards downstream. National Guardsmen and volunteers took fifty-three hours to find the bus. The scene inside was horrific. Terrified small children huddled in the seats, hugging each other. The driver of the wrecker and the bootlegger Blackburn slithered down to the riverbank to save several children. Blackburn described small children clinging to branches of trees submerged in the water before being swept away.

Storekeeper James Goble and his wife Virginia lost two sons and a daughter. In the small communities of Sugar Loaf, Emma, and Cow Creek, six families lost more than one child. The ages of the dead students ranged from 8 to 17. An autopsy determined that the driver, 27, drowned at the steering wheel.

Preceding its article on the accident, *Time* magazine quoted a Cumberland Mountain folk song: "Will the waters be chilly when I'm called to die?"[39] The tragedy demanded a ballad. When the Stanley Brothers gathered in the studio of WCYB, they recorded a song written by Jack Adkins and Buddy Dee, "No School Bus in Heaven." The chorus of the song repeated the image of "little schoolchildren . . . gone on to glory," framing the tragedy in terms of Christian salvation rather than mourning. Mercury released the single on April 30, 1958, backed by "I'll Never Grow Tired of You."

The Stanley Brothers were not the only musicians to record a song about the tragedy. Attorney Woodrow C. Burchett of Prestonburg, who conducted the court of inquiry into the accident, wrote a song that was recorded by country singer Ralph Bowman for the obscure Excellent Records label based in Cincinnati, Ohio. Employing both strings and pedal steel guitar, "Tragedy of School Bus 27"[40] was even more commercial than the Adkins-Dee song, taking aim on tear ducts as it quoted the Bible ("Suffer the little children to come unto me") and noted the coincidence between the bus's number and the number of fatalities.

Because of its diverse population and location on the Ohio River bordering Kentucky, Cincinnati had become home to a number of small record labels such as Excellent. According to a historian at the Rock and Roll Hall of Fame and Museum in Cleveland, "Cincinnati always had one foot in the North and one in the South, with access to blacks in the industrial cities as well as the Appalachians."[41] Having lost a contract with a national label for the second time in six years, the Stanley Brothers would sign with King Records, the independent label located in Cincinnati that was finding success in both the hillbilly and rhythm and blues markets. The label's flamboyant founder would change the sound of the Stanley Brothers for the rest of their careers.

13. SUWANNEE TO CINCINNATI

When Arnold Brim was a boy growing up in Live Oak, Florida, his parents sent him to what he called "music school." He did not want to spend the time to learn how to read sheet music, but his teacher happened to have an old guitar. "Every time he would put it down, I would pick it up," Brim recalled.[1] "I would hit a note, and I thought it would sound like what people were singing. At least that's what it sounded like to me." Before long he wanted to become a musician.

When he was ten, Brim's parents paid three dollars to buy him his first guitar—a Sears and Roebuck Silvertone much like the inexpensive mail-order guitar that Carter Stanley learned to play on. As he grew older, Brim developed a love of old-time country music and skill on two similar instruments: the pedal steel guitar and the dobro. Both used a metal slide to form chords. As a performer, Brim was a late bloomer, making his stage debut around age 30; but he enjoyed performing enough to organize a group called the Suwannee River Playboys—named after the river made famous in song by Stephen Foster that flows just north of Live Oak.

In 1950 an ambitious new manager, Norman Protsman, arrived in Live Oak from Melbourne, Florida, to take charge of radio station. He and one of his on-air hosts, Clarence S. "Cousin Clar" Parker, offered the Playboys the opportunity to play on WNER. Two years later, Protsman bought the station. He decided the time was right to introduce a new program to Live Oak, which was located between Jacksonville and Tallahassee. "Local people would come out and do little skits on the radio," Protsman recalled.[2] "I had the idea to get them all together and put on a little country show . . ." He called his new program the *Suwannee River Jamboree.*

Protsman decided that the most suitable building to host the *Jamboree* would be one of several tobacco market warehouses in the area. "One of the markets was off the ground and had a wooden floor," he recalled. "The others were on the ground and had concrete floors, which would be

143

terrible. We put benches on the wooden floor and made a stage. It was a homemade sort of thing, but it worked."

Cousin Clar [pronounced Claire] Parker loved hosting the *Suwannee River Jamboree*. "We had a great show here for a while," he recalled. "People had to pay a lot of money to get in. . . . I think the admission was fifty cents. Live Oak was a small place then. There were no motels. But people came from south Florida and Georgia. We filled the place every Saturday night."[3] Parker was the resident comedian. On one occasion, he joined cowboy entertainer Smiley Burnett's act without consulting Burnett. "He was on stage telling stories and singing songs. He had his gun slung down low on his hip. I creeped out on stage and lay down on my back and looked right at the barrel of the gun. I made all sorts of faces and the people laughed. Somebody told me later that it bothered him." Parker's antics made him popular with the local audience. When RCA held a contest to see which of the region's disc jockeys could generate the most mail, Cousin Clar finished second despite working in a much smaller market than his counterparts.

Parker joined WNER in 1949 to get the station ready to go on the air in June. It was his first job. Fresh from earning his first-class broadcast license after technical school training in Louisville, Kentucky, and Jacksonville, he thought he would take the job for a little while to build his résumé. As it turned out, he never would need one; he worked for WNER for the next thirty-three years.

During the summer months, when the wooden-floored warehouse was filled with tobacco for the market, the show moved to a new warehouse addition that was not in use. Arnold Brim and the Suwannee River Playboys played on the program from its inception. "At one time there were forty entertainers on the *Suwannee River Jamboree*," Brim recalled. "We had 1,200 people in attendance every Saturday night. It was pretty warm." The *Jamboree* was on the air for three hours, making it Florida's largest and best-known country music show.[4]

At the beginning, the talent was "very local," said Protsman. The station paid the performers from gate receipts and used the income from selling soft drinks to distribute the show around the region. This informal syndication of the *Jamboree* consisted of a tightly programmed thirty minutes of each show that WNER sent without charge to twelve to fourteen stations. "All we asked was that they return the tape," Protsman recalled. The majority of the stations were located in south Georgia and Alabama. Only a couple of north Florida stations broadcast the show. "At the time there was no interest in south Florida in country music," Protsman recalled. "People turned up their noses at it."

Handling much of the production was Aubrey Fowler, whom Arnold Brim described as "a good Christian person who liked country music." During the week, Fowler managed the Production Credit Corporation that specialized in loans to farmers; on Saturday nights he showed a more extroverted side of his personality. "He would help whenever he could," Protsman recalled. "He would get the audience clapping and carrying on. He was sort of a frustrated stage person."[5]

In the mid-1950s, another member of the production team, Jack Henderson, decided that what the *Jamboree* needed was an established professional act. He persuaded the Stanley Brothers' former neighbors from Coeburn, Virginia, Jim and Jesse McReynolds, to headline the *Jamboree*. The move gave a major boost to Jim and Jesse's early careers and expanded the scope of the program to showcase musicians from outside the region as well as local talent.

Jim and Jesse were on the program longer than any other professionals. "I thought they were real nice boys," Protsman recalled. "They were a cut above most of the non-local talent." Besides their musicianship and close harmonies, Protsman (who did not allow drinking on the *Jamboree*) appreciated that they appeared to be clean living. "It was a family show," he said.[6] The station supported Jim and Jesse to the point of making a push to place them on the *Grand Ole Opry*—an effort that proved successful because "Aubrey Fowler knew a lot of people up there." Fowler might have made a similar effort on behalf of the Stanley Brothers. During the time that WNER was producing the thirty-minute segment of the *Jamboree* for distribution, the station managed to place several segments on the *Grand Ole Opry*. The arrangement lasted only four weeks.

Carter and Ralph's time with the *Jamboree* was brief, yet crucial to maintaining their commercial viability. They heard about the *Jamboree* as a performance possibility from Jim and Jesse or from George Shuffler, who had worked with the McReynolds brothers before joining the Stanleys. Jim and Jesse's careers flourished in Florida and Georgia. By 1956 they were performing on television stations in both states.[7] According to Clar Parker, "They went on tour when they were here and never came back. Carter and Ralph came two or three years later."

In 1958, the Stanley Brothers scuffled to make a living by performing at the ballparks and drive-in theaters of their native region and in outdoor music parks with western-sounding names: the Sunset Ranch near

Philadelphia; Silver Creek Ranch in Paris, Virginia; Melody Ranch in Glen
Burnie, Maryland; New River Ranch in Rising Sun, Maryland; and Valley
View Park in Hellam, Pennsylvania. Live recordings from 1956 and 1957
document the group's energetic performances and Carter's folksy ease as
a master of ceremonies even as a the bell from a sledgehammer strength
test rang repeatedly in the background.[8] When their financial situation
came to a head with the loss of the Mercury contract, the brothers were
ready to relocate.

"We needed to move somewhere because we felt like we was wore out
around Bristol," Ralph recalled. "So . . . we talked to [television show host]
Cas Walker some and he wanted us to come down to Knoxville and start,
but we decided to try Florida and if it didn't work out, why we'd go to
Knoxville. But we went down to Florida and we hadn't been there over
three or four weeks 'til this fellow in Live Oak by the name of Aubrey
Fowler . . . contributed a lot to our staying in Florida. He helped us a lot."[9]

Soon after Carter and Ralph moved to Live Oak in November 1958, the
well-connected credit manager recommended that they contact the Jim
Walter Corporation, which built shell homes, to see if the company would
sponsor the musicians on radio and television. Carter had been sold on
the idea of sponsorship during a couple of conversations with fellow
bluegrass bandleader Bill Clifton. Both conversations focused on what
Carter perceived as his competition with Flatt and Scruggs. Clifton said
he thought that Carter's drinking "may have affected his way of thinking
about things."[10]

> One night he called me very late and said he'd found a bus. He want-
> ed to buy a bus and wanted to know if I could help with it. I told him
> I don't think I can, that I'd have to discuss it with my family. Why do
> you want it? I asked. "Flatt and Scruggs have one." That was his rea-
> son. That was important to him: to look as good as they look.
>
> At another time he said "I've finally got it figured out why people
> don't buy our records and come to our performances as much as
> Flatt and Scruggs. They want somebody who plays like Earl Scruggs.
> From now on Ralph is going to play exactly like Earl." I told him I
> didn't think that was a good idea because Ralph has his own unique
> style. I said I thought Flatt and Scruggs do so well because they'd got
> Martha White Flour as a sponsor. Shortly after that they went to
> Florida and got Jim Walter Homes to sponsor them. It wasn't quite
> the same as Martha White Flour.[11]

Few sponsors could match Martha White Flour, whose history began in 1899 when Tennessee mill owner Richard Lindsey named his best brand of flour after his three-year-old daughter, Martha White Lindsey. When the family of Cohen E. Williams of Nashville bought the mill in 1941, the new owners linked the Martha White brand to country music, sponsoring a fifteen-minute radio program, *Martha White's Biscuit and Cornbread Time.* at 5:45 a.m. on WSM. In 1948, Martha White Flour began to sponsor a segment of WSM's flagship program, the *Grand Ole Opry.*[12]

Carter had reason to be jealous. Flatt and Scruggs were flourishing as his band was struggling. Bluegrass historian Neil Rosenberg cites the difference between the career trajectories of the two groups: "Unlike the Stanley Brothers, Flatt and Scruggs did not disband, and their career was marked by one success after another."[13] He was referring to the period from winter 1950 through summer 1951, when Carter, Ralph, and Pee Wee Lambert parted company. By contrast, once Lester and Earl had organized a band, their careers were characterized by steady employment and clear benchmarks of progress—beginning in the Stanley Brothers' own backyard.

In April 1948 WCYB had given the still formative Foggy Mountain Boys a segment on *Farm and Fun Time* that lasted for eighteen months. From there, the band became well known throughout the Southeast as they performed on a succession of medium to large radio stations: Knoxville, Lexington, Tampa, Roanoke, and Raleigh. Because Mercury received twelve fresh recordings when Lester and Earl fulfilled their existing contract in order to sign a new one with Columbia, Flatt and Scruggs records appeared on both labels during 1951–52 at the rate of eight or nine a year. Columbia advertised them as "best sellers."[14]

Another benchmark came in 1953 when a salesman for Martha White Flour attended a Flatt and Scruggs performance and brought the band to the attention of company president Cohen Williams. The salesman convinced his boss that Lester and Earl would sell more flour on the brand's early-morning show on WSM than the western swing band that played the program. Flatt and Scruggs were eager to take advantage of the opportunity, but it was almost denied them when *Opry* manager Jim Denny—sympathetic to Bill Monroe—balked for fear of offending Monroe. WSM decided to allow the arrangement as long as the band would not appear on Martha White's segment of the *Opry.*[15]

Flatt and Scruggs's popularity began to overcome Monroe's blackballing of his former band members in 1955. In January, Martha White Flour and the Pet Milk Company co-sponsored the Foggy Mountain Boys on a thirty-minute show broadcast Saturday at 6:00 p.m. on WSM television. The show generated immediate fan mail. Knowing that WSM paid attention to the volume of mail an act received, Cohen Williams dumped a sack of it on the floor of WSM general manager Jack DeWitt's office.[16] The dramatic gesture set the stage for Williams to threaten to withdraw Martha White advertising from the station if Flatt and Scruggs could not play during its *Opry* segment.

Williams made his point. The Foggy Mountain Boys were allowed to perform on the *Opry*, though WSM did not invite them to join as cast members and would not allow Flatt to serve in his customary role as the band's master of ceremonies. The restrictions disappeared in 1956 when former Mercury Records executive Dee Kilpatrick became *Opry* manager. Having worked with Lester and Earl at Mercury, he made them cast members. This move bothered Monroe, but Flatt and Scruggs were on an unstoppable roll. Martha White sponsored television shows for them in six cities, and the band's spacious blue-and-white bus—bearing the sponsor's name in large blue letters—logged 2,500 miles a week because all the shows had to be done live.[17]

As the Stanley Brothers' sponsors in Florida, the Jim Walter Corporation never enjoyed the reputation that Martha White Flour did. "Jim Walter made a lot of mistakes," observed Bill Clifton, who was from a wealthy Baltimore family and had earned a master's degree in business administration from the University of Virginia.[18] "He thought people would buy shell homes and improve them if he had to take them back. He was wrong. They took shell homes and didn't improve them when they got 'em back. He got into a lot of financial problems."[19]

Before the unimproved homes became a drain on the company, the builder provided the Stanley Brothers with a base for the best income they ever would earn. "We got our television show started for Jim Walter," Ralph recalled. "For three or four years we had about all that we could do playing television and Sunday open houses and so forth. I'd say that from '57 to '61 [*sic*] was really about the best we ever had financially."[20] Even on sideman's wages, guitarist and singer George Shuffler agreed: "Jim Walter was paying us more money than we'd ever seen before."[21]

As country groups would do before videotape became available, the Stanley Brothers traveled to a different city each weekday to perform their program in person. George Shuffler recalled:

The first years we were down there, we started in Jacksonville on Monday night and worked down to the Keys and back up and hit a station every night, and we would wind up in Tallahassee on Friday night. We did that five nights a week and we would do show dates for that area. During that time we didn't tour much out of the state of Florida. We would work within a fifty-mile radius of where our TV show was that day . . . wherever you could get from 6:30, which was when our program ended, to 8 o'clock and set up a PA and go."[22]

Another recurring event on the group's calendar was a fifteen-minute radio program, *The Jim Walter Jamboree*. The company saved about twenty of the shows, which were taped in Atlanta for distribution to other stations. Carter had become an adept announcer. He took advantage of radio as a "theater of the mind" to convey to listeners the impression that he, Ralph, and "all the Clinch Mountain Boys" amounted to a group of diverse ensembles.

Opening the show with the Jim Walter theme song that welcomed "everybody everywhere"—establishing an outsized sense of scale—Carter introduced the band in several different configurations: the Clinch Mountain Boys Quartet would gather around the microphone to harmonize on a gospel song; Ralph would be called on to pick a banjo solo; Ralph and "yours truly" would join voices for a duet; the unnamed trio would step forward to sing a number; and Carter would summon Chubby Anthony to play a fiddle tune. All of these performances would take place in the space of fifteen minutes.

Toward the middle of the show, Carter would launch into a folksy pitch on the advantages of building a Jim Walter home. A customer could begin the process with "scarcely nothing down"; and the company would allow purchasers to "pay for it kinda like the cat eat the grindstone . . . just a little at time." Addressing the audience as "friends," Carter concluded the pitch by reminding potential purchasers: "There is absolutely no substitute for experience. The Jim Walter Corporation has built thousands and thousands of homes all over the country. We don't have *one* dissatisfied customer."[23]

While extolling the virtues of shell homes, Carter settled his family into a comfortable brick and frame house at the corner of Ruby and Main Streets. He and his wife, Mary, arrived in Live Oak with two sons and a daughter: Carter Lee, Billy, and Doris. Mary gave birth to another boy and girl in Florida: Bobby and Norma Jean, called Jeanie. Mary worked as a nurse's aide to help support the family. Ralph purchased a thirty-acre farm outside Live Oak. "I had a few head of . . . cattle and I stocked a little pond with bream and bass," he recalled.[24] "I did some fishing and let Carter do his coon hunting." Joining Carter on hunts were Carter Lee and Billy. Times were better than they had been in Virginia, but the income for any given month could vary. When the Dixie Grill opened in Live Oak in 1959, Peggy supplemented her and Ralph's income by working as a waitress. The Grill became a local landmark where Arnold Brim ate breakfast on the day I interviewed him. He remembered seeing Peggy when she worked at the Grill. He recalled Carter and Ralph attending services at the Westwood Baptist Church where his family worshipped. Sundays were not a day of rest for the Stanley Brothers because the band played at Jim Walter open houses in Florida, Georgia, Alabama, and Mississippi.[25]

George Shuffler lived in Live Oak for four years, at one point renting a house for his wife and three children for part of a year. "They didn't like it and went back to the mountains," he recalled.[26] Though not an avid fisherman, he became one in Florida to relieve the boredom between radio shows and performances. When his family was with him, he took his six-year-old son Steve fishing on the Suwannee River and Lake Louise. After his wife and children returned to North Carolina, he roomed with bass player Henry "Hard Rock" Dockery at a small hotel frequented by truckers. A former bass player, George now played lead guitar in the band.

When the Clinch Mountain Boys were not on the road for four or five days, they could be found at the Amoco gas station across the street from the post office. "They used to make that their local headquarters because the guy that run it played bass with them," Arnold Brim recalled. "His name was Johnny Bonds. He was my first cousin." Brim enjoyed getting to know Carter at the gas station. "Carter was fun," he said. "He would do anything in the world for you. I didn't know him that well, but I would see him when I would run across the street to get a pop. He told interesting stories. He had a lot of history in the music business. He wrote some songs that were played all over the world. If he told you something, you could depend on it. Johnny Bonds thought the world of him."[27] Norm Protsman had similar things to say about Johnny Bonds, who played on the *Jamboree* and would accompany the Stanley Brothers locally on occasion. "He was quiet and unassuming . . . a very calm person . . . I never saw him get mad. You could depend on him."

"The Amoco station was our hangout," George Shuffler confirmed. "We sat around and drank RC's [Royal Crown Cola] and run our mouths." He remembered Bonds, whom he and the Stanley Brothers called Cossie. "He would go with us whenever he could," Shuffler recalled, "but he had the gas station to take care of." Carter would hang out at the gas station for as much as half a day, entertaining Cossie Bonds and whoever else wanted to listen to his stories. Even if there were spells of boredom, the pace of life in Live Oak provided a welcome break for the group. "It was a regular road schedule we could handle, no zigzagging back and forth to the one-nighters, and it didn't tire us out," Ralph recalled.[28]

Between the release of "The Flood" and their relocation to Florida, the Stanley Brothers took part in three recording sessions for two different labels. Before recording for King Records in Cincinnati, Carter and Ralph brought four sidemen into radio station WCYB to conduct a quick session for Starday, whose most successful artist was country and rockabilly singer George Jones.[29] In late 1956 Mercury Records invited Starday to enter into a distribution agreement, because the larger label thought the independent would help expand its country catalogue. There was a difference in status between the labels. According to bluegrass historian Neil Rosenberg, "During 1957 and 1958 the bigger names would be on the Mercury-Starday label while the lesser ones were on Starday. . . ."[30] Since the Stanley Brothers' records were released on Starday, Carter and Ralph now had slipped two rungs on the ladder of label prestige—from Columbia to Mercury and from Mercury-Starday to Starday.

In April 1957 Don Pierce—a California music executive who in 1953 had purchased a one-third interest in Starday for $333—relocated to Nashville to open the Mercury-Starday offices in the suburb of Madison.[31] A year later, having achieved pop music success and ventured into rock and roll, Mercury decided to shut down its country division, keeping future superstar George Jones. The abrupt end to the distribution agreement left Pierce and his Texas-based partners Harold "Pappy" Daily and Jack Starns to operate as an independent once again. In mid-1958 Pierce signed the Stanley Brothers to a contract that was flexible enough to allow Carter and Ralph not only to sign with King but to record for Starday until May 1960. For two years they had records on both labels.

The WCYB session in summer 1958 yielded four numbers. One was a musical makeover: Ralph recorded a version of the instrumental tune "Wild Horse," which dated from the Revolutionary War, that the

label renamed "Holiday Pickin'" when it was chosen to back the song
"Christmas Is Near" on a 45-rpm single.[32] The featured side of the other
single, Carter's "Gonna Paint the Town," consisted of a buoyant chorus
accompanied by verses cobbled together from other songs, including
"Going to the Races," a song Carter had written earlier and given to a
promising new group—the Country Gentlemen—to record as one side
of its first record.[33] Though not as original as the songs that would follow, "Paint the Town" offered a preview of the confident old-time country
sound that would characterize the band's first album for King.

In 1958 the long-playing record was relatively new in popular music.
Most often, a popular LP was a collection of singles or a hit single or two
surrounded by songs and tunes that were little more than filler.[34] When
Columbia released its first bluegrass LP in the late summer of 1957—
Foggy Mountain Jamboree by Flatt and Scruggs—the album was most like
the former: a collection of six instrumental tunes and six songs by the duo
and their sidemen that producer Don Law had compiled from as far back
as 1951. Opening with Earl Scruggs's distinctive banjo playing on "Flint
Hill Special," the record alternated tunes featuring Scruggs and songs featuring Lester Flatt, all of consistent high quality.

So pervasive was Scruggs's influence among banjo players that his
name appeared in the title of the first bluegrass LP even though he did
not play on it. When Northwestern University classicist and banjo player
John Wright heard about the three-finger style in the 1950s, ". . . everybody called it Scruggs Style, so much so that I initially thought that the
word 'scruggs' was some sort of common noun or adjective that I'd never
heard of rather than the name of a human being. I suspect that Ralph and
Carter thought of it as Scruggs Style, too, but I also suspect that nobody's
ever going to get Ralph to admit that."[35]

In early 1957, the independent label Folkways released *American Banjo:
Three-Finger and Scruggs Style*. Producing the thirty-two-song sampler
was musician and musicologist Mike Seeger. King Records entered the
bluegrass LP market in February 1958 when it issued two albums by Don
Reno and Red Smiley, *Sacred Songs* and *Instrumentals*.

Forty-year-old Sydney Nathan launched his record label in September
1943 by taking country musicians Louis "Grandpa" Jones and Merle
Travis, who were under contract to Cincinnati's 50,000-watt radio station
WLW, to Dayton, Ohio, to make records under assumed names.[36] After
working in a variety of marginal businesses (from a pawnshop to shoot-
ing galleries) in the healthy climate of Arizona, the asthmatic Cincinnati

native returned home to open Syd's Record Shop in 1938. He mostly sold popular music until a jukebox outlet owner who owed Nathan six dollars offered to pay the debt with "300 hillbilly, western, and race records, old ones from his jukeboxes, at two cents a platter. He figured that I could sell enough of them for ten cents each to get back my six bucks."[37] Nathan sold the record shop in 1939 and moved to Florida to be near his brother and open a photo-finishing business. An historic winter of sleet and snow ruined his business plan. Returning to Cincinnati in 1939, Nathan reopened the record shop at a location where many of his customers were African American. He stocked blues, gospel, and jazz. Soon the owner of a radio store that stocked hillbilly records offered to sell Nathan his inventory. With it, Nathan acquired a hillbilly clientele. Two of these were Grandpa Jones and Merle Travis, who performed along with the Delmore Brothers on WLW's *Boone County Jamboree*. Listening to the station, Nathan came up with another plan.[38]

"During the war, records were hard to get," he recalled, "and naturally I thought of a brilliant idea, that I could get some hillbilly singers and cut some records and somebody would press them for me. I thought it would be as easy as all that."[39] The first discs by Jones and Travis sold a few hundred copies and were so poorly pressed that they wobbled on the turntable, but this did not deter Nathan. He located space in a former ice factory at 1540 Brewster Avenue in the Evanston neighborhood of Cincinnati where he could house not only offices and (in the late 1940s) a recording studio, but also a record-pressing plant. In *Little Labels—Big Sound*, Rick Kennedy and Randy McNutt described the facility: "Under one roof, Nathan built a truly self-contained independent record company. The King plant had everything he needed except the equipment to make shipping cartons. A singer could walk into King in the morning and leave that night with a new record in his hands."[40]

When the Stanley Brothers and three sidemen arrived at Brewster Avenue on September 30, 1958, for their first recording session at King, they may have been disappointed by what they found. Located in a run-down section of the neighborhood, the brick factory building was painted battleship gray.[41] The industrial Midwest did not feel like home as much as Nashville had. At the same time, recording in the King studio was a big improvement over making records at a radio station.

For the convenience of moving instruments and equipment, Nathan had built the 35-by-20 foot studio next to a loading dock. Squares of white soundproofing tile covered the concrete walls, and light fixtures hung from the twenty-five-foot ceiling.[42] "Although as dark as a garage, the studio produced a clear and funky sound, with depth and presence impossible to define," wrote Kennedy and McNutt. "Funky" referred to the sound of the rhythm and blues performers who were recording hit records at King: the Charms ("Hearts of Stone"), the Royals ("Work with Me Annie"), Billy Ward and the Dominoes ("Sixty Minute Man"), James Brown ("Please, Please, Please") and several others. In the case of Nathan and Brown, the short, near-blind Jewish entrepreneur and the slender, hyperkinetic African American entertainer developed a relationship that "alternated from grudging affection to dislike . . . based on their mutual ambition."[43]

The possibility of mutual respect was not apparent at the outset. Upon hearing Brown and his band in the studio for the first time, Nathan had turned to producer Ralph Bass and said, "The demo was awful and this is worse. I don't know why I have you working here. Nobody wants to hear that noise."[44]

As products of the Scotch-Irish tradition that influenced old-time country music, the Stanley Brothers may not have been aware of James Brown, but knew that King was home to the Delmore Brothers when Alton and Rabon revived their careers in the late 1940s, recording hits such as "Hillbilly Boogie" and "Blues Stay Away from Me."[45] Joining Carter and Ralph in the studio on September 30, 1958, were mandolin player Bill Napier, fiddle player Ralph Mayo, and bass player Al Elliot. Since studio time cost money and the Clinch Mountain Boys were veterans of the recording process, the band quickly completed six songs. Staying overnight in Cincinnati, the group recorded six numbers the next day. These included three instrumental tunes by Ralph and "Train 45," most of which was instrumental. The final two recordings were songs.

Even though King was a step down for a band that had recorded for Columbia and Mercury, the label had attributes that appealed to the Stanley Brothers. With production, marketing, and distribution functions housed in the same building, "King was a working artist's label, a blue-collar music machine"[46]—and Carter and Ralph were hard-traveling musicians whose lives were defined by the demands of each day. They appreciated a company that could deliver the tangible results of their efforts within weeks.

For the Stanley Brothers, signing with King was a matter of good timing. In the same year that their contract with Mercury expired, an overburdened Syd Nathan hired executive Hal Neely from Allied Records in

New York to take over most of King's operations. Neely installed a stereo sound board and tape system in the studio, and doubled the production capabilities of the pressing plant. What mattered most to the Stanley Brothers was that Neely expanded King's country catalogue by signing new artists.[47]

The liner notes to the brothers' 1963 King album *Folk Concert* contained a footnote to their history with the label. In 1946, they had sent a demo tape recorded at WCYB to Syd Nathan. According to the notes, "Carter still tells the story of getting a nice letter from Mr. Nathan telling the boys to practice harder, to learn more about their musical heritage and in a few years to come back and see him."[48]

With the passage of time, bluegrass musicians and fans came to regard King 615—the label number for *The Stanley Brothers and the Clinch Mountain Boys*—with reverence that matched its biblical-sounding label name and number. The cover photograph resembled *Foggy Mountain Jamboree* (banjo player on left, guitar player on right, microphone between them), but the music was as true to the Stanley sound as *Foggy Mountain*'s contents were to Flatt and Scruggs. This was a remarkable result for two short studio sessions. Half of the twelve numbers entered the bluegrass canon: "How Mountain Girls Can Love," "Mastertone March," "She's More to Be Pitied," "Clinch Mountain Backstep," "The Memory of Your Smile," and "Love Me, Darling, Just Tonight." The musicians and their producers had not wasted a track. The material appeared on singles and extended-play 45s as well as on the album.

King 615's liner notes followed almost word for word Don Pierce's "Biography on the Stanley Brothers" in the 1957 songbook *Clinch Mountain Song Review* and included in February 1958 on the sleeve of the Starday LP *The Stanley Brothers: Country Pickin' and Singin'*. Because of the language's presence on two album covers and in a songbook, it played a significant role in defining the Stanley Brothers' public image.

The cover of the Starday LP featured a country landscape, while the notes called attention to the brothers' authentic country roots: "You will notice that these artists use the traditional mountain ballads with harmony singing. Note how these songs tell a story, often sad, of actual things that happen. . . ." Both sets of liner notes mentioned that Carter raised coon dogs and Ralph maintained a herd of Hereford cattle[49]—information that Don Pierce elaborated on in the songbook.

Printed in a slightly larger format than its predecessors, the *Song Review* ran a hefty thirty-six pages contained in salmon pink cover stock.

It cost two cents to mail from WCYB to Abingdon, Virginia, where a devoted fan received her copy.⁵⁰ The songbook contained the lyrics to thir-
ty-one songs. Among fourteen photographs of the band at various venues
were the photos from the Northwest tour taken on both sides of the state
lines of Oregon and Washington.

Crediting Lucy Smith Stanley with having taught Ralph to play banjo,
Carter to play guitar, and both brothers the art of vocal harmony, Pierce's
biography did not mention Lee Stanley. The copy began with the assertion that "The Stanley Brothers . . . front the best banjo, mandolin, and
fiddle band in the nation" and reported that Carter and Ralph "are both
very good song writers and compose a good portion of the songs used on
their recording sessions."

Pierce devoted his longest paragraph to praising Carter's coon dogs:
"Carter Stanley is extremely well known in Southern Virginia, Eastern
North Carolina, Tennessee and Western Kentucky for the very fine pack
of coon dogs that he maintains. Carter breeds and raises the greatest
coon dogs to come out of his part of the country. Some of the nation's
greatest sportsmen come to Carter for their coon dogs and to have him
train their dogs bought from other breeders. It's necessary that Carter re-
fuse a great number of invitations from the nation's foremost sportsmen
for coon hunts because of his personal appearance tours."

One could imagine that at some point in the production of the booklet, Carter put his arm over Don Pierce's shoulders and said, "Now, be
sure to tell all the friends and neighbors about my dogs. You be sure, now!
I guarantee they'll want to know about that."

The younger brother's interest in livestock merited one sentence:
"Ralph's choice of hobbies run more to the dinner table as he breeds, raises, and maintains a fine herd of Hereford cattle on the family farm near
Stratton, Virginia." In the notes to King 615, the farm became "the family
ranch."

Pierce concluded with sentences that were prescient even as they were
hyperbolic. Anticipating by four decades the creation of the "Americana"
genre as a category of popular music, he wrote: "Great entertainers in
their particular field, the Stanleys [sic] sincerity and simplicity continue
to make their type of music our true Americana." He elevated Carter
and Ralph to the status of noble mountain men: "We, at Mercury, are extremely proud of the Stanleys, these hardy men of the hills, who are true
to their heritage."

For reasons of length (perhaps even credibility) some of the song-book's language did not appear in the LP liner notes; but Pierce had accomplished his goal of positioning Carter and Ralph among the hardworking people who tilled the land and herded the cattle. In contrast to Bill Monroe, who was born in western Kentucky near Indiana and whose band wore jodhpurs, and to the smooth professionalism of Flatt and Scruggs, the less polished Stanley Brothers lived in the home place where their music had originated—a heritage that was significant to the rising generation of folk enthusiasts.

14. FOLK TALES

In 1954, 21-year-old Mike Seeger worked in the kitchen of Mount Wilson State Hospital near Pikesville, Maryland, a tuberculosis sanitarium north of Baltimore. He was there as a conscientious objector performing alternative service. Born in New York City, Mike was the child of parents who trained as classical musicians and later became experts in the field of folk music: musicologist Charles Seeger and modernist composer Ruth Crawford Seeger. Raised in suburban Washington, D.C., with his piano-playing sister Peggy, Mike grew up listening to Library of Congress field recordings[1] the way other children listened to "The Bear Went over the Mountain." His half-brother Pete, who taught himself to play banjo, would visit from time to time.

Mike was among the avatars of a generation of old-time musicians who were raised in urban and suburban settings rather than on rural farms. Some would call them "citybillies." Having learned to accompany himself on the autoharp while singing old songs that his parents introduced him to, he took classical guitar lessons for six months in 1951, but his listening tastes ran to old-time country and bluegrass records. A gifted musician, he pursued his passion for the old-time sounds by learning to play banjo, mandolin, and fiddle.[2]

Bob Dylan suggested that Mike had an influence on his becoming a songwriter. "It's not as if he just played everything well," recalls Dylan in his memoir of the New York City folk scene in the early 1960s,[3] "he played these songs as good as it was possible to play them. . . . What I had to work at, Mike already had in his genes, in his genetic makeup. Before he was even born, this music had to be in his blood. Nobody could just learn this stuff, and it dawned on me that I might have to change my inner thought patterns . . . The thought occurred to me that maybe I'd have to write my own folk songs, ones that Mike didn't know."

In 1954, Mike was immersed in old-time music and bluegrass, intent not only on playing the music but preserving it. An important part of his mission was documenting the music of the Stanley Brothers. Whenever they played within driving distance of Pikesville, he would drive to their performances. "I took a tape recorder almost everywhere they were if it was within 50 to 75 miles," he recalled.[4]

I asked him why he had felt drawn to the music of the Stanley Brothers in particular. "Because they were so close to the roots," he responded, "and I just love their singing and Ralph's singing and banjo playing. . . . When I was hanging out with [musicians] Bob Baker and Hazel Dickens, we used to have discussions of who was the best singer." I asked what he and his friends decided. "There were . . . different opinions. These were just discussions, you know."

They sounded like the kind of discussions that young followers of folk music had then: impassioned, argumentative debates over the merits of a particular singer, fiddle player, or band. There were no winners in these arguments, only advocates. Preferences could change after a riveting performance by another individual or group. There was a palpable excitement among audience members listening to the music that often was lost on the musicians themselves, who were going about the business of making a living.

The vanguard of the folk music revival appeared on the Stanley Brothers' doorstep in the mid-1950s: Mike Seeger and others taping of performances at the music parks, and Larry Ehrlich recording old songs and tunes at WCYB. Ralph would tease the music park followers. "I'd look down from the stage while they'd set their tape recorders and their fancy microphones next to our little mic stand: 'I see we got the recording industry again here today.' And they'd get sort of nervous because . . . I wasn't smiling when I said it."[5] Smiling or not, he was pleased they were there. "Back then, that sort of attention was about all we had to keep us going on some days. I'd tell them to sit tight and get the equipment just right, because I wanted to try out a new banjo tune; I'd tell 'em to make sure and get a good recording so I could listen to the play-back tape and see if the new tune was a keeper or not." The tapings began earlier, but it was not until the summer of 1959 that interest in the Stanley Brothers from this devoted coterie of enthusiasts resulted in increased national visibility for the group.

In the second week of February 1959, the group returned to the brick-walled recording studio at King Records. Since Carter and Ralph now called Florida home, the drafty rooms in the former ice factory must have felt chilling to the hands and spirit; yet they had an album to record. The liner notes to King 615 lifted from Don Pierce's biography described the Stanley Brothers as "one of the few acts that consistently experience good sales of country tunes and mountain ballads . . . while at the same time enjoy big demand for their sacred records."

In one of two new sentences inserted in the copy by King's marketing department, a copywriter added: "During a recent interview, Carter remarked that they have noticed more and more requests for sacred songs during personal appearances . . . and, at one point, did almost an hour of encores consisting of nothing but sacred song requests." The brothers had returned to Cincinnati to record their first album of gospel music, *Hymns and Sacred Songs*, which began the pattern of alternating secular and gospel LPs throughout their career on King.

Relocation to Florida resulted in more changes in personnel. Al Elliot was the one sideman remaining from King 615. He had switched from bass to mandolin to replace Bill Napier, who left to join brothers Ray and Melvin Goins of West Virginia. Chubby Anthony, who had played with the Clinch Mountain Boys on *Farm and Fun Time* in 1953, took Ralph Mayo's place on fiddle. On standup bass was a familiar face from the band's recent past, George Shuffler. Late on a fall afternoon forty-five years after the recording of *Hymns and Sacred Songs*, I shut the door to my office at the University of Virginia's College at Wise and picked up the phone to ask George questions about the Stanley Brothers. I had met him just a few weeks earlier at the opening of the Ralph Stanley Museum and Traditional Mountain Music Center in Clintwood, Virginia, where he took part in an on-stage exchange of reminiscences. He was the only musician on stage who had played with both Carter and Ralph; so he brought a singular dimension to the occasion. He made use of his wry sense of humor to keep the audience amused. After the reminiscing, I sought him out to ask if I could call him about his recollections. In hindsight, this was the beginning of my commitment to writing a biography.

When George answered the phone in his slow, mellow drawl, he brushed aside my anxious reminder that we had agreed to talk by reporting that it was a gloomy, rainy day in Valdese, North Carolina, and that all he had been doing was sitting in the chair and watching television. He turned down the volume on the TV and we talked for the better part of an hour. When I broached the subject of Carter, there was an abrupt change of tone in his voice. He said that he would see if he would answer my questions—*would*, not *could*. Even after I reassured him that all I had in mind to ask about the older brother as a songwriter and musician, he remained cautious. "Carter had his life and I had mine," he said.[6] I asked him what he thought of Carter as a singer.

"He was about twenty-five years ahead of his time," he said. "Bill Clifton told me Carter Stanley's the best lead singer he ever heard. I was listening to him every night, so that didn't make much impact on me at the time. The more I heard the old records, the more I woke up to the fact that he was one of the best lead singers that I ever had anything to do with."

What was his opinion of Carter as a songwriter?

"He was a good writer. There's more of his songs being recorded by other groups than any writer that's ever been in bluegrass. He had an awfully smart head on him. He had a memory like an elephant. All he had to do was hear something a time or two and he could do it." He added, "Carter and Ralph were like brothers to me. I didn't feel like I was working for them, I was working with them."

It seemed like time to change the subject to the album of gospel songs that I had in mind. George was unsure to which album I was referring. He seemed to recall it when I praised the vocal arrangement of the song "Daniel Prayed," though he may have been remembering the range of his gospel recordings with the Stanley Brothers.

"There's a song or two on the record where we sing a trio, lead, tenor and bass . . . [and] our harmony was so close you could almost hear an overtone of baritone. Every day we was together for all those years, it paid off in that respect. I think one thing that [could be] attributed to is that we didn't take any words into the studio with us; we just concentrated on harmony and singing, and instead of one trying to outdo the other, we sung together. That's what makes any group good, working together instead of like a pair of mules sawing back and forth."

The brothers wrote seven of the twelve gospel songs that were recorded on February 10 and 11, 1959. Since singing gospel in three and four parts requires tight harmonies and often intricate vocal arrangements, most of the material was well rehearsed. An exception was the first song on the LP, "How Can We Thank Him for What He Has Done," which Carter wrote with Ralph and Al Elliot the night before the session. Carter had written a number of songs on the road, and on the way to Cincinnati, he had an idea for another.

Al Elliot recalled that after the band arrived, ". . . [Carter] sat down and he said, 'I want us to write this song. It's on my mind . . . me, you, and Ralph can sit here and write it.' So we got together and wrote that there that night and had it ready to record the next day. We switched instruments on that. Carter did the recitation and I played the guitar and then we got three-part harmony on it."[7] The recorded version sounds less polished than other songs on the album. On other tracks, the balance between the voices and instruments is off, placing the vocals behind the instruments, especially the fiddle.

Despite uneven production, *Hymns and Sacred Songs* proved to be a worthy counterpart to King 615. Ralph's high tenor singing on "He Said If I Be Lifted Up" was ethereal, anchored in the low range by George Shuffler's sturdy bass vocal. The arrangement to Ralph's "My Lord's Gonna Set Me Free" took advantage of George's booming voice to kick off the number with a "Glory, glory, hallelujah!" Coming second on the LP, "Set Me Free" sounded like a more powerful opening song than "How Can We Thank Him." The running order raised the question of whether the brothers or the label determined the sequence of songs.

Two summer recording sessions for Starday underlined the non-exclusive nature of the Stanley Brothers' contract with King Records. Carter and Ralph were entering a phase of their career in which they would record for several smaller labels in addition to King, which Syd Nathan would grow into the sixth largest record company in the United States.[8]

Radio station WNER employee Bill Savitz engineered the two sessions in Live Oak. "We'd meet Sunday night about six, cut a session, and it'd take about four hours," he recalled.[9] "It was laid back, relaxed. They knew what they were doing. . . . There was no stereo or any mixing to do with it . . . it was straight two mikes right into the [sound] board and then into the recorder." The personnel were the same on both sessions. Bill Napier rejoined the band to play mandolin, and Al Elliot returned to the bass. Chubby Anthony remained on fiddle.

Eight newly recorded songs along with four recorded for Starday the previous summer completed the LP *Mountain Song Favorites Featuring 5 String Banjo*. Starday held the album for December release to capitalize on the holiday market with "Christmas Is Near" and "Holiday Pickin'." At the urging of Savitz, the band recorded a bluegrass arrangement of Wade Mainer's 1930s hit "Maple on the Hill," calling it "Beneath the Maple" and crediting the song to Ralph. Another song credited to Ralph, the driving "Riding That Midnight Train," became one of the brothers' most popular numbers. The songwriting credits for Chubby Anthony's "Highway of Regret" illustrated a common practice among bands working in bluegrass:

assigning half the royalties to the bandleader by listing him as co-author. Considering the size of the market for country recordings in 1959, the amount involved was small.

Yet something momentous was emerging among younger musicians and their followers in 1958–59 that, over the next several years, would retrieve old-time country and bluegrass from the margins where rock and roll and the more orchestrated "Nashville sound" of country music had pushed the older styles.

The roots of the folk music revival in the United States extended back to the late 1910s and early 1920s, when academic collectors such as Englishman Cecil Sharp visited Appalachia and traced many of its songs to Anglo-Saxon origins. The song collectors helped to redefine the region's image from "a haven for rubes and slackers sorely needing modernization"[10] to the repository of a valuable cultural heritage. According to folk revival historian Ronald D. Cohen, "Sharp had spearheaded the romanticization of the rural folk in England, and would do the same while in the United States during the war, connecting Anglo-Saxon traditional ways with quaint, enduring American values and manners."[11] In 1917, Sharp and Olive Dame Campbell published the songs and ballads they had collected in *English Folk Songs from the Southern Appalachians*.

Texas native John A. Lomax began to document an American folk identity apart from British ballads by publishing *Cowboy Songs and Other Frontier Ballads* in 1910. Rather than classifying ballads in terms of lineage and literary criteria, he classified source groups by occupation: songs of miners, lumbermen, railroaders, cowboys, and "the down-and out-classes" such as outcast girl and convict.[12]

Illinois-born poet Carl Sandburg not only collected folk songs throughout his life, but sang them at his readings and lectures, making him one of the first public folk singers. In 1926, he recorded ten songs for the Victor Talking Machine Company, and in 1927 published *American Songbag*, which catalogued 280 songs native to the United States under twenty-four headings such as "Dramas and Portraits," "Minstrel Songs," "Pioneer Memories," and "Blues, Mellows, Balletts."[13]

An important step in the popularization of folk music took place when songs that the publications had legitimized were sung at public gatherings in order to preserve and celebrate them.[14] This marked the beginning of the folk festival movement. In 1928 performer and collector Bascom Lamar Lunsford staged the first Mountain Dance and Folk Festival in Asheville, North Carolina. The American Song Festival in Ashland,

Kentucky, followed in 1930, as did the White Top Folk Festival in south-west Virginia in 1931.

Founded by Annabel Morris Buchanan of Marion, Virginia, the White Top Festival was held on a mountain located near the confluence of Virginia, Tennessee, and North Carolina—seventy-five miles from the Stanley family's home place. For the rest of the decade, the festival was a great success: "Until its demise in 1939, White Top, featuring ballad singers and fiddle contests, attracted thousands, particularly following Eleanor Roosevelt's visit in 1933," Cohen wrote.[15] In that year, an estimated fifteen to twenty-five thousand folk music fans joined the First Lady in attending the festival, which attracted several hundred performers from eight states.

"No better means could be devised for keeping alive such a folk pos-session than this of bringing the singers and fiddlers themselves as com-petitors before expert musicians who value the fine old tunes in their na-tive rendering," Vassar College folklorist Martha W. Beckwith wrote in the *Journal of American Folklore*.[16] "The young suddenly find their elders not outdated and themselves begin to revive the old songs and to give to the tunes their old-time quavers." In addition to the performances and contests, composer John Powell of Richmond, Virginia, delivered nine lectures on "the origin, structure, modality, and recording of English-American folk tunes and their place in American composition"—a schol-arly approach that Beckwith recommended should become a permanent part of the festival.

Since the festivals were intended to be tourist attractions as well as celebrations of tradition, they provoked "controversy about the meaning and value of authenticity."[17] When musicologist Charles Seeger criticized the White Top Festival for its high price of admission and the doubtful authenticity of some of its performers, he took the debate a step further by calling attention to the fact that White Top was open only to white people.[18] A similar situation existed in old-time country music and blue-grass, even though two of the founders of the genres, A. P. Carter in old-time country and Bill Monroe in bluegrass, formed close attachments to African American musicians. These were, respectively, guitarist and singer Leslie Riddle and guitarist and fiddler Arnold Shultz.

Though the young Bill Monroe had backed up Shultz on guitar at square dances and A. P. Carter had taken Riddle with him on song-col-lecting trips (Riddle would memorize the melodies while Carter took down the words),[19] there is no evidence that the Stanley Brothers played with—or were influenced by—African American musicians. Their music is among the least blues-inflected of their contemporaries. Yet with the traditional origins of their material and a home place in the mountains of southwestern Virginia, the Stanley Brothers fit well with the folk revival of the 1950s.

Mike Seeger's enthusiasm for the brothers' music led him to recommend the band to organizers of the first Newport Folk Festival in 1959,[20] modeled after the Newport Jazz Festival that Boston jazz entrepreneur George Wein started five years earlier in Newport, Rhode Island. Aware of the growing interest in folk music, Wein at first considered booking performers such as the Kingston Trio and Odetta into the jazz festival, but decided to establish a separate event. To help produce the new festival, he hired Albert Grossman, co-founder in 1956 of the Gate of Horn folk club in Chicago.[21] Three of the best-known performers of the 1950s—Theodore Bikel, Oscar Brand, and Pete Seeger—made up the board of directors.

Held on July 11 and 12, 1959, the Newport Folk Festival assembled a disparate group of performers from traditional folk music, commercial folk, blues, and bluegrass. Joined by Chicago radio show host Studs Terkel, Brand and Seeger appeared both as performers and masters of ceremonies. They introduced a roster that included folklorist Frank Warner, John Jacob Niles, and the New Lost City Ramblers; commercial folk performers Odetta, Bob Gibson, and the Kingston Trio; blues musicians Sonny Terry and Brownie McGhee, Memphis Slim, and Reverend Gary Davis; and the Stanley Brothers and the Clinch Mountain Boys and Hylo Brown and the Timberliners with special guest Earl Scruggs on banjo.[22]

For the bluegrass musicians and blues performers, especially, the contrast between their places of origin and Newport—summer home of the Astors and Vanderbilts and site of the America's Cup yacht races—could not have been more pronounced. Publicity for the festival was minimal and advance ticket sales small, yet an audience estimated at twelve thousand attended the festival's three concerts, instrumental workshop, and seminar.[23]

This was the second festival appearance for the Stanley Brothers. On May 1, they had performed at the Florida Folk Festival, which began in 1953 at the Stephen Foster Memorial in White Springs, fifteen miles from Live Oak.[24]

At Newport, Carter demonstrated his ability to adapt to his surroundings—what Larry Ehrlich called his intuition "in regard to the individual aura of circumstances." Instead of introducing "Man of Constant Sorrow" as an old ballad from the mountains, he called it a folk song.[25] The band played two commercially oriented songs from King 615 and an upcoming album, "How Mountain Girls Can Love" and "Choo Choo Coming," balanced by the traditional gospel song "Gathering Flowers for the Master's Bouquet." The short festival set aimed not only to please an audience of folk music fans, but also to introduce fans to the band's current recordings.

Ralph's driving banjo did not appear to excite the crowd, though the instrument was an important link between folk and bluegrass music. Pete Seeger had popularized the banjo in urban folk circles during the 1930s and 1940s.[26] The acknowledged master of contemporary players, Earl Scruggs, gave the audience a second opportunity to hear bluegrass banjo when he appeared that evening as the special guest of Hylo Brown and the Timberliners. Scheduled as the festival finale, Scruggs found himself in the awkward position of following the popular Kingston Trio; meanwhile, master of ceremonies Oscar Brand tried to keep pace with audience responses. "We never knew who would reach the audience, who was locally well-known, what traditional singer would be singing country music and pop songs in the hope of extending his or her audience." Brand recalled. "That first program was a wild puzzle."[27]

For example, after performing a couple of songs with his partner Bob (later Hamilton) Camp, Bob Gibson wanted to change partners. He begged Brand to introduce "this girl who was a big deal in Boston. She looked pretty gamy . . . bare feet muddy, black gypsy hair hanging in strings down her face. Then she started to sing 'The Virgin Mary Had a Little Baby.' All the top performers and most of the lesser lights crowded to the stage to see this phenomenon. God, she was great. I almost forgot her name so that I could take her off."[28]

That was the last time Brand would have trouble with the name of Joan Baez, who was making her national debut. "When she went off, the cheers were deafening," he recalled—so loud that the stage manager thought Brand should give Baez an encore, which would put the program further behind a schedule designed to let the audience catch a final ferry. "That part was easy," Brand recalled. "I simply introduced the Kingston Trio, which brought the audience to their feet. They did a delightfully compact performance . . . the audience wouldn't let them off. I was back on the griddle, ending up by promising we'd hold up the ferry and introduce Earl Scruggs.

"Now the crowd was bloodthirsty—they wanted the Kingston Trio." Brand continued. "Who the hell wants a Scruggs? I called [Trio member] Dave Guard out and told him 'Please tell them who Scruggs is.' The crowd still sounded like the Romans at the Colosseum. I announced to Guard's surprise, 'The Kingston Trio will return right after Earl Scruggs shows you why he's called the greatest five-string banjo player in the world.'" On a live recording, it sounded as if Scruggs had difficulty holding the audience's attention.

After Newport, the Stanley Brothers returned to the familiar summer venues of flatbed trailers, roofs of drive-in movie refreshment stands, and stages in music parks. Though the band welcomed the opportunity to play in front of a larger, younger audience, the Newport appearance did not result in immediate bookings in the Northeast. This was not an altogether bad thing. Recording for a Cincinnati label while living in Florida required driving distances that wore a person down. The route from Live Oak to Cincinnati in 1959 took the band north on Route 129 to US 441 near Knoxville, Tennessee, where the Marysville Pike intersected with the Chapman Highway. The driver then followed Chapman downtown along Broadway to US 25W at the intersection of Broadway and Magnolia. From there, the band headed northwest on 25W to Corbin, Kentucky, before the stretch on US 25 to Cincinnati.[29]

The rapid expansion of highways and toll roads such as the Pennsylvania Turnpike throughout the 1950s made the roads better, but the distances did not become shorter. Thirty-four-year-old Carter grew weary and sometimes depressed as he rode in the back seat, gazing out the window at the countryside. He still wrote a few songs on the highway, but often would fall asleep. He had grown all too familiar with roads such as the northern section of Route 11 that ran from Chattanooga, Tennessee, through Virginia and Pennsylvania, and much of Route 19 that extended all the way from St. Petersburg, Florida, to Erie, Pennsylvania. Even as his imagination traveled elsewhere, his eyes wandered from road to buildings to winding rivers that ran alongside the road, taking in picturesque expanses of farms and valleys and the approaching cars and trucks.

Often band members played games of Car and Horse to pass the time. Car was as simple as a game could be: picking a make of automobile, such as Ford or Chevrolet, and counting the number that the players would spot until one player reached eleven. Horse was a little more complicated, awarding three points to the person who spotted a gray horse, two points for a spotted horse, and one point for any other kind of horse. The first

few times they played Horse, the lucky person who spotted a white mule
would win on the spot, except that the players "got to arguing so much"
that they would pull over to see if the mule might have as much as a single
black hair.[30] They decided to count a white mule equal to a gray horse.
Since Ralph and George Shuffler both raised horses, they would make
deals as they drove along to exchange horses, and sometimes would come
across three or four horses in a pasture that they wanted to inspect. If
they found an animal that they liked, one of them might buy it. That involved returning with a horse trailer to pick up the animal, but for musicians who drove all night for business, the personal day trips were lei-
surely and pleasant.

En route from Florida to Cincinnati on a Sunday in mid-September,
Carter was too preoccupied to take part in a game. Though he and the
boys thought that they had done a good job of recording King 615 and
the gospel album, the sales figures had disappointed the people at King.
Syd Nathan made clear to the brothers that they would have to re-au-
dition for the label when they made their next visit to the King studio.[31]
Before leaving for Cincinnati, the musicians discussed ways to make the
sound of the band more commercial. They considered including an autoharp—the instrument that Sara Carter had played with the Original
Carter Family. They abandoned the autoharp idea, but were not sure how
they would proceed as they pulled up to the drab gray building at 1540
Brewster Avenue on the morning of Monday, September 14. They were
booked to record their second secular and gospel LPs for King. There to
meet them in the warehouse-like studio was the short, bald man with the
black-rimmed glasses and ever-present cigar. Syd Nathan knew what he
wanted and what he did not want.

As the musicians took their instruments out of their cases, tuned
up, and prepared to record the first song—the moonshine anecdotes of
"Mountain Dew"—Nathan barked an order. "Just get the damn fiddle out
of here," he said. "I don't want fiddle on this."[32] Gesturing toward a startled
Chubby Anthony, he said, "I want you to go."

Though Nathan's manner was rude, there was a method to it. Drawing
on his experience with the Delmore Brothers, Nathan had learned that
the hillbilly audience liked the twin guitar sound that Alton and Rabon
developed. In the 1930s, the Delmores had been one of the few brother
duets to feature instrumentation other than the familiar mandolin and
guitar format. Nathan intended to push the Stanley Brothers in the same
commercial direction. He thought that by smoothing out the vocals and

reducing the presence of hillbilly instruments such as mandolin and fiddle, he would make the Stanley sound more palatable to a wider audience—and increase record sales.

In the role of producer, Nathan could control the volume of an instrument in the mix. He tolerated a certain amount of banjo because Ralph played it. Ralph was not the leader, but he carried himself with a businesslike sense of purpose that provided a balance to Carter's back-slapping conviviality; and Ralph was willing to adapt his sound and style to the service of the song. After taking control of the recording equipment for "Mountain Dew" to drive home his point, Nathan turned the rest of the session over to his staff engineer.

The concept for the secular album was apparent from its title, *Everybody's Country Favorites.* Even though Nathan had left the studio, his influence remained on the choice of material. Of eight songs that the band recorded on September 14, two were credited to King's first artist, Grandpa Jones, and three were written or made popular by former King artists Hawkshaw Hawkins ("Sunny Side of the Mountain") and Clyde Moody ("Shenandoah Waltz" and "Next Sunday, Darling, Is My Birthday").[33] Nathan had a financial incentive to re-record the songs. Nathan's publishing arm, Lois Music, published most of the songs recorded by King artists, and on "My Birthday," Nathan credited his pseudonym Lois Mann (his wife's maiden name) as co-writer.

On Tuesday morning, September 15, the Stanley Brothers filled out the rest of the album with well-known songs by former Louisiana governor Jimmy Davis ("Shackles and Chains") and the Carter Family ("Weeping Willow"); a sentimental number about a dog, "Old Rattler"; and the second recording of "I'm a Man of Constant Sorrow." On this second version, the brothers added the vocal refrain that was featured forty-one years in a climactic scene of the film *O Brother, Where Art Thou?*

Mandolin player Bill Napier switched to lead guitar on the secular LP and the gospel session that followed, while George Shuffler played bass. Napier's mandolin technique carried over to his guitar playing. "[He] played more like a mandolin-type guitar," Shuffler recalled. "He played real fast with his right hand."[34] Chubby Anthony sat out the sessions, restricted to tapping his fiddle bow against the strings to keep time with the music.

Though at the time the change in sound may have seemed temporary, the sometime producer who happened to own the label converted the Stanley Brothers into a two-guitar band for the rest of their careers. "Syd was most responsible for us starting to use lead guitar," Ralph recalled.[35] "He wanted something that the Delmore Brothers had. They'd been successful with the guitars. They thought we ought to get away from the mandolin because nearly all the bluegrass bands used a mandolin. And they wanted us to get the lead guitar in and get a different sound, which we did."

Song selection on the gospel album continued to reflect Nathan's interest—financial and otherwise—in the material that his artists recorded.[36] Half of the numbers on *For the Good People* had a connection to King. Yet there remained enough latitude for the Stanley Brothers to assemble the material for one of their strongest albums. The LP showcased some of the finest singing of their careers. Recording all twelve songs after completing the secular album that morning, the musicians did not conclude the marathon session until 10:00 that night. Carter's succinct explanation for the remarkable day was "We knew the material better."[37]

The singers were in rare form. After Carter's uncertain-sounding lead vocal on the lament of a prisoner sentenced to death, "My Main Trial Is Yet to Come," voices opened up through the remaining eleven gospel songs, expanding toward full voice on "From the Manger to the Cross" and "Four Books in the Bible." Though George Shuffler's bass vocals could be heard better in the mix of these two songs than on the prior four, it was not until Ralph sang lead on "Purple Robe" and "When Jesus Beckons Me Home" that Shuffler's voice began to resonate clearly on the choruses. It sounded as if the engineer had rearranged the group for Ralph's vocals, perhaps giving George a separate microphone. The new arrangement came together on "Jordan," a rousing song sung as a quartet featuring the bass.[38] When Carter returned to singing lead vocals on the final three songs, he delivered three superior performances that ranged from plaintive ("Pass Me Not") to joyous ("Over in the Glory Land").

With instrumental accompaniment stripped down to two guitars and an almost inaudible bass fiddle, Bill Napier's guitar playing was strong and inventive through the entire set. His nimble mandolin-style playing that began the secular session on "Mountain Dew" settled into a crisp gospel groove. With the exception of "My Main Trial," which dragged, the band's choice of tempo for each song sounded just right. Carter's thumb pick striking a pattern of alternate notes maintained a steady pace on the second guitar.

These twelve songs offer a fascinating opportunity to compare the differences between recording songs live in one or two takes and using the more sophisticated multi-tracking and editing technologies that would arrive in the next decade. As experienced as they were, the band members must have realized that they had captured their harmonies at their best.

After completing the LP projects, Carter and Ralph decided to see if they could record one more song the way they wanted it—a novelty number consisting of questions from a literal-minded traveler and responses from a wise-cracking local. "We hadn't planned on doing it," Carter recalled.[39] "We started doing 'How Far to Little Rock' and somebody in the studio heard it and they said, 'Why not let's record that thing?'"

The brothers first heard the traditional blend of old-time fiddling and repartee known as "Arkansas Traveler" when they were teenagers on Smith Ridge. "We learned that from a feller by the name of Fletcher Moss . . . from Pike County, Kentucky," Ralph recalled.[40] Moss was a carpenter who helped one of their older brothers to build a house. "On weekends when he didn't go home, he would come up and stay with us because we was trying to play a little bit, and he would bring his fiddle . . . and he would do that 'Arkansas Traveler,' and he would ask the questions and answer 'em, too."

Ralph and Carter divided the speaking roles, with Ralph playing the straight man who initiated the conversation. Here are two of the exchanges:

Hello, stranger.
Why, hello again, stranger.
Your corn looks awful little and yellow.
I planted the little yellow kind this year.
Well, you must not be figuring on much more than half a crop, are ya?
That's exactly right, I'm raisin' on the shares—fifty-fifty.
You couldn't be very far from a fool.
Couldn't be what?
Very far from a fool.
That's right, son, just this microphone here between us.[41]

Released as a single, "How Far to Little Rock" cracked the top twenty on the *Billboard* country chart, peaking at number 17 on March 20, 1960, and staying on the chart for twelve weeks.[42] Ralph said that though "Little Rock" was not the brothers' most popular song, it generated the most chart activity in the shortest amount of time.[43]

During the winter before the release of their modest hit, the band members hung out at the Amoco station in Live Oak, drank Royal Crown Cola with or without whiskey, and enjoyed the feeling that the musician's life was treating them better than it had in some time. Lee and Fred Stanley visited Like Oak around this time. "I remember us going fishing," Fred recalled.[44] "Carter had borrowed an outboard engine. There was a small lake there, and he and my dad and I were out there fishing." The expedition was short-lived. "The gas was supposed to have been mixed with oil and hadn't been mixed and the motor locked up. We got somebody to tow us over to back to the dock." Fred's first trip to Florida gave him the opportunity to spend time with Carter Lee and Billy Stanley. He was a month younger than Carter Lee. "Carter always had some kind of joke, and he was certainly the talkative one," he recalled. "Ralph was not very talkative," adding, "Ralph and I share that."

In February 1961 Carter, Ralph, and Bill Napier recorded four gospel numbers at WNER for an extended-play 45 rpm record released by Starday in March. Fiddler Ralph Mayo returned to Florida to replace Chubby Anthony, who had left the group, and Johnny Bonds got his chance to record with the band on bass.

As full-throated as Carter had sounded toward the end of the gospel session for King, his voice sounded strained and thin as he sang into the radio station's microphone. It might have been that the capabilities of the microphone—an ElectroVoice intended primarily for broadcast use—limited the range of sounds that were recorded; or perhaps Carter's vocal cords continued to weaken from the effects of smoking, drinking, and pushing his body to the limit. Six months before his thirty-fifth birthday, he had become living proof of a line spoken by Indiana Jones in *Raiders of the Lost Ark*: "It's not the years . . . it's the mileage."[45] By contrast, Ralph's lead vocal on "In Heaven We'll Never Grow Old" gave striking evidence of what became his signature style: holding notes for long intervals and finishing phrases with a quick upward slur that created a vocal exclamation point.

The tragedy of Carter's decline was its timing. Over the next few years, the Stanley Brothers' newfound status as folk exemplars would take them to the Northeast, Midwest, and West Coast, where they would make their debut at venues ranging from Antioch College in Yellow Springs, Ohio, to the Ash Grove club in Los Angeles. Peers such as Don Reno and Red Smiley who did not seek (or were not able) to develop a following among the folk audience would run the risk of fading into obscurity, while the popularity of the Stanley Brothers would seem assured.[46] Former *Suwannee River Jamboree* host Clarence Parker said, "Once they began playing colleges, they took off like Moody's goose."[47]

15. THE WELL-KNOWN STANLEY BROTHERS

———◆◆×◆●———

In the late 1950s, the band member whose job it was to introduce Carter and Ralph on stage would announce them as "the well-known Stanley Brothers." After a dozen years on the road, the brothers earned the right to claim that modest level of distinction. "Famous" would have been better, but that would have stretched the truth. Flatt and Scruggs were famous. They traveled from city to city in a bus with their name painted on it and starred in their own television show that was syndicated throughout the south. After a similar number of years, the Stanley Brothers still piled into a four-door Cadillac or Packard that hauled a trailer filled with musical instruments. Without the leg room and creature comforts provided by a bus, driving the distances between performances could be brutal, as one weekend in the middle of May 1960 demonstrated.

The village of Yellow Springs, Ohio, is located twenty miles northeast of Dayton in the western part of the state; the town of Rising Sun, Maryland, is fifty miles northeast of Baltimore near the Pennsylvania border. The driving distance from Yellow Springs to Rising Sun is about five hundred miles. In 1960 motorists could cover a third of the distance in the high-speed lanes of the western section of the Pennsylvania Turnpike; they had to negotiate the remaining two thirds on the narrow state roads of Ohio, Pennsylvania, and Maryland. The straight west-to-east route was not particularly challenging—unless the travelers were a group of musicians booked to play a concert at a college near Dayton on Saturday night and first of three sets at a music park north of Baltimore Sunday at noon.

Musicians who spend time on the road sometimes say that they are not so much paid to play as to drive. For the Stanley Brothers, the back-to-back performances in Ohio and Maryland underscored the truth of the saying. The appearances at Antioch College and the New River Ranch earned the band six or seven hundred dollars—about a dollar and a half a mile for the distance between the two gigs. This did not count the 800-mile drive from Live Oak to Yellow Springs, and 880 miles back to Florida. On the positive side, the Antioch booking provided another opportunity to play in front of the audience of northern college students whom the band had encountered at Newport.

The bluegrass scene at Antioch revolved around partners in life and music Jeremy Foster and Alice Gerrard. Gerrard later formed a pioneering female old-time music duo with Appalachian singer Hazel Dickens. Foster had gone to high school with Mike Seeger. When the Antioch student government approved Foster's request for three hundred dollars to hire Dayton-based musicians Bob and Sonny Osborne to perform at the college, it funded the first appearance by a professional bluegrass band in front of a college audience.[1] On March 5, 1960, the Osborne Brothers received a mixed response from students unfamiliar with the rambling introductions and homespun humor of a hillbilly show. The concert was successful enough for the student government to approve additional funds to hire the Stanley Brothers for Saturday, May 14.

Mike Seeger taped both performances, as did Jeremy Foster. A two-release record label doing business as the Vintage Collectors Club issued a bootleg version of the Stanley Brothers concert tapes in 1961, calling it *Live at Antioch College, 1960*. The label's first release was a Flatt and Scruggs compilation. The Stanley Brothers recording included seventeen songs and tunes totaling 44 minutes of music, with abbreviated introductions by Carter. The unedited recording of the performance lasts well over an hour, augmented by additional songs, a sales pitch for the latest songbook, and bass player Lindy Clear's imitations of sounds heard in the country, such as three dogs fighting underneath a porch, a hot rod racing on a bad tire, and a Model T Ford trying to start on a very cold day. Clear performed his impressions in the character of Tennessee Mort. "The only thing more fun than watching Mort onstage was watching Carter's expressions," Ralph recalled.[2] "He enjoyed it more than anybody."

From their early days, the Stanley Brothers drew from traditions other than musical to put together a performance. They incorporated slapstick and country humor into their program along with vestiges of the minstrel show. Carter coordinated the proceedings like a ringmaster, stepping in and out of the spotlight according to the demands of the show. He introduced the music, called attention to a band member who was about to be featured, and served as foil to the comedic personae that materialized during a routine. In addition to Mort, the Stanley Brothers were joined by Ray Lambert's Cousin Wine-Sap and Tom Ashley's black-faced Rastus Jones from Georgia.

When I asked Ralph in 2003 if he wanted to name a quality about Carter that people might not be aware of, he mentioned his brother's extroversion and showmanship. "He was forward," Ralph said. "He never met a stranger. He'd just as soon tell the president of United States what he thought as he did with me. He was just out front that way. I think that was good in a way because he told people what he thought. He was a good crowd-pleaser who could satisfy a Christian on stage or a drunk. . . ."[3]

One aspect of Carter's crowd-pleasing was making use of the full range of talents that band members possessed, whether musical or otherwise. Max Powers took note of Leslie Keith's prowess with a whip. Southwest Virginia native Fred Widener recalled a "seven-foot cowboy" opening for the Stanley Brothers. During a 2002 discussion on a bluegrass listserv, the cowboy's grand-nephew identified his great-uncle as George Osborne, who stood 6' 6" and imitated the voice and style of a popular cowboy singer. Neal Osborne recalled that his great uncle had been a guest at the brothers' shows from early in their careers until 1966. "He would open the programs singing Tex Ritter songs," Neal wrote, "and his standard that he is remembered for was 'Rye Whiskey.'" On one occasion, Ritter himself made a guest appearance on WCYB without identifying himself, followed by George Osborne singing one of Ritter's songs. "Afterward, nobody could tell which was which," Neal wrote.

At Antioch, Carter demonstrated his ability to frame the material for an audience. He introduced some of the numbers as folk songs to meet the college crowd's expectations. When the band's dusty sedan rolled onto the grounds of the New River Ranch on the Sunday afternoon after the Antioch show, the brothers returned to more familiar terrain. "It was a little wooden stage under the trees, next to the creek by the U.S. highway," Ralph recalled,[4] "and they had to string electric lines back in there for the lights and PA system." Their hosts, Bud and Ola Bell Reed, began promoting country and bluegrass music at the outdoor venue in 1951. Ola Belle was a popular regional musician, forming a group with her brother Alex Campbell after he was discharged from the army in 1946. Bud recalled first hearing Carter and Ralph in 1950 or 1951. Bud played music himself and enjoyed getting to know musicians who appeared at the ranch. By 1960, he and the Stanley Brothers had become good friends.

"Carter was the number one guy—no question about that," Bud recalled.[5] "Ralph was a number one guy, too, but Carter was a little more outstanding in many ways because Ralph was a little shy. . . . He would hold back a little bit, you know? I used to fish, and every time Carter would come and I wasn't there, he would ask my wife Ola Belle 'Where is that fisherman at?' But they were great musicians and worked as a team. Carter was one of the best singers that I ever heard . . . he had such a nice voice." When I asked him to elaborate, he answered, "He just had a nice soft voice, a beautiful voice, a soft voice. Have you heard him? Then you know what I'm talking about."

On Sunday after the all-night drive from Ohio, Carter's voice did not have much left. Audibly weary as he introduced the band's first performances that afternoon, he sang the first verse of "So Blue" twice. He said that he did not remember the other verse. After the band played a ragged version of Bill Monroe's tribute to his fiddle-playing uncle Pendleton Vandiver, "Uncle Pen," Carter performed a song that was better suited to a soft treatment. He told the music park audience that he had learned "Come All You Tender Hearted" at backwoods revivals; at other times he said he learned it from an old hymnal. Several people applauded at the start of the song, indicating that New River patrons were more familiar with the brothers' repertoire than the college audience.

After performing the single released the previous week, "Mountain Dew," Carter turned the lead vocal over to mandolin player Curley Lambert, who sang "Baby Blue Eyes." Lambert's lively rendition provided a marked contrast to the singing that preceded it. Carter's voice sounded just plain weak. He and Ralph sleepwalked through a recitation of "How Far to Little Rock" before the group began to wake up with a series of four gospel numbers sung as quartets.

Fiddler Ralph Mayo played energetic breaks during the set, as did Ralph on banjo. Ralph sang lead on "Man of Constant Sorrow" and two other numbers. As a performance, the recorded program of twenty songs (several in shortened form) and two comedy routines offered a clinic on how a group of road-weary professionals could cobble together an acceptable show while running on empty. Ralph liked the show well enough to put it on a CD that he sold years later at appearances.

Helping to make the weekend odyssey to Antioch and the New River Ranch possible was a significant advance in the technology available to television. From its first use by CBS on October 29, 1956, videotape freed performers from having to make television appearances in person. A program recorded at one station could be delivered to others in tape form or fed to a network of stations electronically. For a performance-dependent group such as the Stanley Brothers, videotape was a godsend. It meant that the band could continue to appear on television stations throughout Florida without having to drive all over the state. "After they got videotape, we'd go over to Jacksonville on Wednesday and cut one program and they could send that one wherever they wanted," George Shuffler recalled.[6] "So that left us a lot of fishing time. But then we started touring again, and we could get out and leave on Friday and go north and play the parks."

Shuffler's recollection matched with *Suwannee River Jamboree* musician Arnold Brim's impression that the Stanley Brothers were not often on the *Jamboree* "because they were on the road . . . [and] Jacksonville was their headquarters." Norman Protsman and Clarence Parker had more recollections of Jim and Jesse than they did of Carter and Ralph. Aside from Arnold Brim's crossing paths with Carter at the Amoco station and worshipping with the brothers at the Westwood Baptist Church in Live Oak, little information is available about the personal side of the Stanley Brothers' eight years in Florida.

As of 2006, Ralph's first wife continued to reside in the Live Oak area. I was told that when she and Ralph were married, the former Peggy Camper had worked as a waitress at the Dixie Grill to "make sure the family had what it needed." The family in Florida included a boy whom Ralph had fathered in Ohio, James, and a son, Timothy. Ralph had brought James to Florida to raise him.

Peggy collaborated with Ralph and Carter on the lyrics of two songs that the brothers recorded, "If That's the Way You Feel" and "How You've Tortured My Mind." She was credited as co-author of the songs, which were registered with Broadcast Music International (BMI), and received royalties. In 2009 she was mentioned in the advance reading copy of Ralph's autobiography, *Man of Constant Sorrow*, in a dismissive way.

> *I haven't yet told you I got myself married around this time [mid-1950s] because it don't amount to much. It wasn't a good match. Nobody's fault, really, it just didn't work out. Now she was pretty, yeah boy, but look [sic] don't carry the day. She just wasn't the right woman for me. My mother told me it was going to be a mistake and it wasn't going to last and my mother was right. I don't want to get*

*into the who and the what and the why, but I will tell you this wom-
an, my first wife, was from down by Buzzard's Branch, in between
Bristol and Bluff City.*[7]

The passage did not appear in the published edition in 2010. As a biographer, I made the decision that information about Ralph's first wife
and the two earlier children was important to include. As I listened to the
recordings made in Florida in the first six months of 1960, I thought that
I could hear the arrival of Ralph's mature singing style—finding his voice,
so to speak—in his rendition of the gospel song "Where We'll Never Die"
and re-recording of "Little Maggie," both done for Starday. It might be
trite to attribute musical maturity to being a father, yet the chronological
coincidence is worth noting. Even more pertinent is the information that
Peggy had collaborated and shared writing credit with both Carter and
Ralph on songs they recorded. Ralph discussed his second wife's songwriting in his autobiography.[8]

In 2008 when I called Peggy C. Bland (who had remarried a Florida
highway patrolman), she was tired from having worked the previous
night in the accounting department of large chain store. She said that she
was surprised to receive a phone call about her songwriting because the
same topic had come up in conversation. "Some of girls at work were saying that I should do more with my songwriting," she said.[9] "They don't
understand that as you mature, your mind goes in all different directions."

She said that during the time she was married to Ralph, she wrote
songs and poetry. Country music expert Richard Spottswood told me
that if the song had been recorded properly, "If That's the Way You Feel"
could have become a country music hit. "Carter had the right idea getting [session musician] Pete Drake to play pedal steel guitar," Spottswood
said.[10] "The record was a train wreck because Carter was drunk. Carter
never did get a good cut on it."

Peggy said that she wrote other songs that the brothers recorded, but
was not sure if she received songwriting credit or if the songs had been
released. When I asked if she remembered the title of any of the songs,
she named "So Blue." I asked if she had co-written it. "I did it all on my
own," she said. She said she did not know if the song ever had been recorded. "Elvis wanted the song," she said. "I'm not sure why they didn't go
along with it. I think that maybe they didn't want to be seen as too rock
and roll. I wish he had done it." She said that she regretted not continuing
to write songs: "I should have pursued it more than I did."

In Florida, the professional life of the Stanley Brothers was full of transitions. During the winter of 1959–60, fiddler Chubby Anthony and guitar and mandolin player Bill Napier left the band on short notice to join performer Charlie Moore.[11] The lack of notice angered Carter and Ralph.[12] Anthony's exit was understandable in light of the way Syd Nathan had banished him from the King studio in September. Napier's departure was harder to explain because the versatile musician's guitar playing was at the center of the new sound that the band had adopted.

The fact that their replacements, Ralph Mayo and Curley Lambert, had prior experience with the band softened the blow. Napier still was with the Stanley Brothers at the February session for Starday on which Mayo played. Lambert replaced Napier not long before the Antioch and New River Ranch appearances.[13] At the Antioch show, Carter can be heard cueing Lambert on the part he should sing on a gospel number.[14]

After those shows, the brothers were confident enough in the new lineup to schedule their final session for Starday at Magnum Studios in Jacksonville in late May. Studio owners Tom Markham and Tom Rose had left their business card with Carter and Ralph at a performance in Live Oak. The brothers called soon after to set up a recording session. Despite its impressive name, Magnum was a semi-professional operation built in a wooden garage with a concrete slab floor.

The Stanley Brothers' choice of Magnum provided a small windfall to the owners, who normally charged ten dollars an hour. Starday paid them the union scale of fifty dollars an hour. From the brothers' point of view, the twenty-by-twenty garage offered a roomier place to record than the radio station; and they may have been dissatisfied with the quality of the February tapes. "They came out to the studio three nights and they did probably fifteen or twenty songs," Tom Rose recalled.[15] ". . . They had a mike on the bass and I guess a mike on Ralph and a mike on Carter. They just kind of worked the mikes the way they wanted the sound. They did more of engineering the session than my engineering partner did."[16]

The brothers chose four secular and eight gospel songs to send to Starday. Tom Rose held on to the rest of the material for several years before losing it. Combined with the contents of a four-song EP, the gospel numbers completed an album that was given the same title as the EP, *Sacred Songs from the Hills.* Starday would hold the secular songs until December 1962 to appear on the album *The Mountain Music Sound of the Stanley Brothers.* Starday's Don Pierce maintained a consistent approach to marketing these and others products of his label. "Authenticity, realness, heritage, tradition, and association with the mountains were stressed," wrote bluegrass historian Neil Rosenberg.[17] "The goal was to sell records to people from the mountain regions who appreciated the old stuff by appealing to their sense of identity using positive stereotypes and avoiding the connotations of words like *hillbilly* or even *bluegrass....*"

Pierce's use of cover photographs was consistent with his themes. For the cover of *Sacred Songs,* Carter and Ralph stood outside wearing topcoats on a fall day, with their instruments in their cases. They appear as diminutive human figures against a background of the white pillars and rotunda of a monument that towers behind them. For *Mountain Music Sound,* the cover photograph focuses on the brothers as they sit in dark suits with instruments in their hands in front of a blooming tree. Their relative prominence seemed to vary with each album's material—spiritual and secular.

Pierce's sense of Starday's audience influenced his choice of songs to release as a single. From the twelve available gospel numbers, he chose Albert E. Brumley's "Rank Stranger" backed with "Gathering Flowers for the Master's Bouquet"—a song the Stanley Brothers had recorded for Columbia in 1949. The lyrics to "Rank Stranger" expanded the sentiments of displacement and loss that Carter touched on in his compositions to a sense of complete alienation.

Everybody I met seemed to be a rank stranger
No mother or dad not a friend could I see
They knew not my name and I knew not their faces
I found they were all rank strangers to me

On the first line of each chorus, Ralph sang solo in his piercing tenor, adding oral expression to the song's profound sense of alienation. The feeling would have been familiar to many rural people who had left their farms and the mines in search of better jobs in the cities of north and south. "Rank Stranger" became the Stanley Brothers' most successful single for Starday; rural audiences would request Ralph to sing it well into the next century. In 2008, the National Recording Preservation Board of the Library of Congress added "Rank Stranger" to the National Recording Registry, commenting: "Carter Stanley's masterful handling of the verses and his brother Ralph's soaring tenor refrain produce a distinctive duet. The spare accompaniment . . . and the emotional call-and-response style vocals heighten the emotional anguish of the lyric."

As much as Pierce adhered to a marketing strategy that framed products in the context of authenticity and heritage, Syd Nathan simply wanted his artists to use as many of King's in-house resources as possible—from session musicians to songs published by Lois Music. Nathan and the Stanley Brothers settled into the pattern of recording secular and gospel albums to reach listeners in both markets. The exception was an album of banjo tunes featuring Ralph. On secular albums, Nathan might insist that the brothers include a novelty number as an attempt to broaden their appeal.[18]

The most blatant attempt was a cover of "Finger Poppin' Time" by rhythm and blues artist Hank Ballard. Recorded at the end of the Stanley Brothers' eight-song session on July 11, 1960, this example of the dance craze genre that created the Twist and the Loco-motion raised a few eyebrows when performed by a hillbilly band from rural southwest Virginia. For Nathan, asking the group to record the song was business as usual. Another recording increased his royalties from the number, which had been a hit in the rhythm and blues market and might sell a few records to the country audience.

To create the appropriate ambience on the recording, several employees of King were summoned to the studio to augment the band. George Shuffler recalled, "We had every colored person in Cincinnati a-poppin' his fingers. . . . We was a pickin' and they was poppin' their fingers. We done it up right."[19] He amended the number of finger-poppers in the studio to eight or ten, including a shipping clerk named Roy. King's session report indicated that the finger snaps (perhaps additional ones) were overdubbed rather than recorded with the instruments.

One might think that Carter and Ralph would have resisted a dramatic alteration to their sound that included drums and two overdubbed rhythm guitars. Shuffler did not recall any hesitation. "Naw, they didn't care. Old man Syd thought it'd sell records and that's what we was up there for." However, in the play *Man of Constant Sorrow*, drawn from Ralph's point of view, Ralph refuses to play or sing on "Finger Poppin' Time" until Carter persuades him. Ralph's reluctance is credible in light of his more traditional approach to the brothers' music.

Dropping by the studio that day was Cincinnati disc jockey Wayne Raney, who also was a well-known harmonica player. Raney invited the band to his home studio that night to record for his independent label, Rimrock. The band re-cut "Rank Stranger," which they recorded fourteen months before, and experimented with an arrangement of "Come All Ye Tenderhearted" on which Carter recited the lyrics. During the second number, the musicians were able to release some of the tension that had built up during the day.

"We took about two hours to cut that thing," Curley Lambert recalled.[20] "We laughed ourselves to death, you see. Carter was trying to do the recitation on it. . . . We got so tickled we couldn't do a thing for laughing. So finally we got it cut. Wayne, he was sitting back in the studio . . . working the knobs, big tears running down his cheeks. I never thought it would be released. So some years later I was listening to the radio and heard it. I said, 'Now this just can't be what we done in Cincinnati. . . . .' It was. They put it on one of those package deals, Starday. Oh lord, it was the worst thing I'd ever seen in my life. Everybody was just dying laughing trying to get it cut. It was really a mess."

Though less than enthusiastic about the song, Carter and Ralph knew they had to plug their latest single. After King released "Finger Poppin' Time" on July 25, 1960, the brothers included it in live performances, even receiving requests.[21] Carter introduced the song as "A little tune here that somebody talked us into recording one time. . . ." King released the album that included "Finger Poppin' Time" the following year. While Starday marketed the Stanley Brothers as performers of mountain music, King identified them as country artists, grouping the dozen tracks on *In Person* under the term "country all-time favorites." In fact, only two of them could be considered favorites: "Wildwood Flower" and "Are You Tired of Me, Darling?" recorded by the Carter Family. Though continuing to copyright songs, Carter and Ralph were running out of original material. Both are credited on "Let Me Rest on a Peaceful Mountain."

Thoughts come back from childhood,
Old time memories return.
Let me rest on a peaceful mountain
In the hills near my home sweet home.

To compensate for the lack of original songs, Carter and Ralph relied on several sources for their material: traditional and old-time songs; past or present popular country songs; hymnals and other sources of gospel songs; songs written by the staff at King Records; songs from their existing repertoire; and banjo instrumentals by Ralph, often reworked from traditional material or other artists' tunes. Their (and King's) choices targeted a musical marketplace made up of consumers with an appetite for genuine folk songs performed by authentic musicians. The album titles reflected this: *The Stanley Brothers and the Clinch Mountain Boys Sing the Songs They Like Best, Folk Song Festival, Old Time Camp Meeting, Good Old Camp Meeting Songs, Folk Concert from the Heart of America, The Country Folk Music Spotlight,* and *America's Finest 5-String Banjo Hootenanny.* Only toward the end of their career did the words "bluegrass" and "hymns" appear in the titles of Stanley Brothers' albums on King.

That the folk audience regarded the Stanley Brothers as authentic musicians was apparent when the brothers headlined the first University of Chicago Folk Festival on February 3, 4, and 5, 1961. Their old friend Larry Ehrlich played a key role in bringing the brothers to the Windy City. "I had gone to the University of Chicago and I got out many years before that," Larry recalled, ". . . but I was back in Chicago in '61 and there were a bunch of kids [who] had a folk club. . . . I don't know how I got together with 'em but I suggested the Stanley Brothers to them."[22] The Folklore Society followed Ehrlich's advice and booked the band along with Kentucky ballad singer and banjo player Roscoe Holcomb—a pairing that began the acquaintance between Ralph and Holcomb, who shared a fondness for old hymns.

When the Stanley Brothers took the stage late on the first night, Carter said the band had to drive over ice and snow to get there. "It was worth it," he assured the audience. Perhaps lubricated by alcohol while waiting to go on stage, he seemed unusually garrulous during the introductions, kidding fiddler Vernon Derrick about his small-town origins in Arab (pronounced AY-rab by Carter), Alabama, and mandolin player Curley Lambert for having lost sufficient hair to make room on his head for another face. The latter came under the guise of complimenting Lambert on his good looks. The energy of the music was high, but the performance was uneven. The brothers sang tentative harmony to conclude their latest single, which was by country star George Jones. "We were on some package tours with George, and one time we went to see him play a show in Orlando," Ralph recalled.[23] Jones sang "The Window Up Above," which was new. "We told him how much we liked it and he let us cut a record of it even before he did."

The Stanley Brothers' performances improved each night as the band offered a steady diet of their most folk-oriented material: "Wreck of the Old 97," "The Story of the Lawson Family" (about a North Carolina man who in 1929 murdered his wife and family), and "I'm a Man of Constant Sorrow." In contrast to the recitation that unraveled the Wayne Raney session in Cincinnati, Carter sang "Come All Ye Tenderhearted" well—a gentle solo number that his youngest child would choose forty years later to overdub herself on as a duet with her father.[24]

On the first two nights of the festival, the audience sounded unsure how to respond to bass player Chick Stripling's belligerent brand of country humor, but applauded his skillful tap dancing. With a vaudeville background, the stocky Stripling was light on his feet. On the final night, Carter announced that Mike Seeger would replace Stripling on bass because Stripling was "a little bit under the weather"—a convenient cover for the liquor Stripling had consumed that afternoon at the home of Larry Ehrlich and his needling of Carter and Ralph in regard to the Monroe Brothers, with whom he had worked.[25] "In any case, Chick got out of the way and they asked me to play bass with them," Seeger recalled.

Before leaving the Midwest, the band returned to King studios on February 7 and 8 to record *Old Time Camp Meeting*. The festival was a useful warmup for the album sessions, and the musicians sounded at their best on gospel songs, as they would on May 2 and 3, 1961, when they recorded *Good Old Camp Meeting Songs*. Noticeable on the first number cut in February was the band's mastery of tempo. The tale of death in "Little Bessie" unfolded to a dramatic rhythm, while a remake of "Mother's Only Sleeping" lilted in three-quarter time.

Midway through the session, the band recorded "Working on a Building" with Ralph on lead vocal. The strength of Ralph's voice contrasted with the diminished power of Carter's lead vocals on the other numbers. Carter's once clear, sweet voice had emerged with a naturalness that had been the envy of other singers. Larry Ehrlich recalled sitting next to Lester Flatt and his bass player, Jake Tullock, while Carter sang on stage. Turning to the lead singer whom admirers took to calling The Man, Tullock whispered, "Lester, wouldn't you give your soul if you could sound like that?"[26] Flatt did not respond. By 1961 Carter's voice exhibited a tremor of vibrato and hard edge of effort that would become more pronounced. While still singing most of the lead parts, the older brother was now the less consistent vocalist in the band. The effects of decades of drinking and smoking—in addition to miles of hard travel and nights of no sleep—were stripping Carter of his gift. Though flashes of his voice's former purity and power would appear from time to time over several years, he was losing the unique expressiveness that made him the best natural lead singer that anyone ever heard in old-time country and bluegrass. His accelerating decline threatened the future of the Stanley Brothers.

A family photograph of paternal grandparents Nathan and Stacy Stanley. Courtesy of Fannie Steele.

The Stanley family together before Lee Stanley's departure; from left: Ralph, Lucy, Lee, and Carter. Courtesy of Fannie Steele.

Roy Sykes, left, and Carter Stanley in downtown Norton, Virginia, in 1946. Courtesy of Roy Sykes Jr.

The original WNVA building and tower in the Josephine community of Norton, Virginia. Courtesy of Bill Jones.

Roy Sykes and the Blue Ridge Mountain Boys in 1946; standing, from left, Darrell "Pee Wee" Lambert, Sykes, Carter Stanley, Jack Bevins; crouching, from left, Ray "Pickles" Lambert and Gains Bevins. Courtesy of Roy Sykes Jr.

Roy Sykes shows off his trick fiddling. Courtesy of Roy Sykes Jr.

The core members of the Clinch
Mountain Boys outside WCYB in
1947. Clockwise from top left: Pee
Wee Lambert, Leslie Keith, Ralph, and
Carter. Hazel Lambert photo.

Smartly attired in the early days of *Farm and Fun
Time*. Courtesy of Gusto Records.

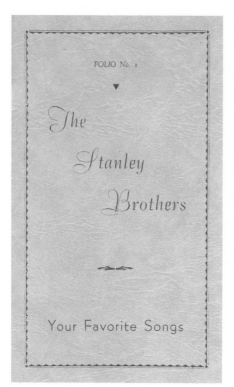

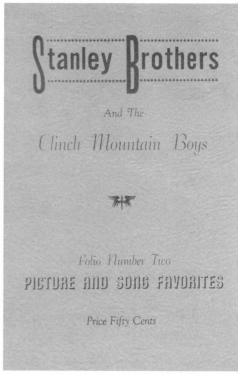

The brothers' first songbook, *Your Favorite Songs*. Courtesy of Don Morrell.

The second songbook, *Picture and Song Favorites*. Courtesy of Don Morrell.

The brothers pose for an early publicity photo in the WCYB broadcast studio. Gusto Records.

Ralph and Carter smile broadly for a King promotional photo. Gusto Records.

Photo proof of a youthful Syd Nathan, founder of King Records. Courtesy of Steve Halper.

The Stanley Brothers' first album, King 615, included several future standards. Gusto Records.

George Shuffler joined the brothers on the cover of *Hymns from the Cross*. Gusto Records.

The brothers perform at the Florida Folk Festival in White Springs in 1959. Robert R. Leahey/State Archives of Florida photo.

Outside King Records on the way to
a recording session. Gusto Records.

Carter confers with a member
of the King studio staff. Gusto
Records.

Ralph works on a banjo lick
in the King studio. Gusto
Records.

Holding one of their "folk" albums on King, *Old Time Camp Meeting.* Gusto Records.

King Records publicity reinforced the brothers' old-time country image. Courtesy of Steve Halper and Brian Powers.

Carter radiates charm as the brothers greet their fans. Gusto Records.

The brothers autograph album covers after a show. Gusto Records.

Ralph and Carter perform at a brisk tempo. Gusto Records.

The Clinch Mountain Boys pose for a potential cover photograph. From left: Chick Stripling, Ralph, Vernon Derrick, Carter, and Curley Lambert. Gusto Records.

On stage circa 1960. John Cohen photo.

Carter playing his well-worn Martin D-28 guitar. John Cohen photo.

Performing a gospel number circa 1960; George Shuffler sings bass next to Carter. John Cohen photo.

Ralph and Carter visit their mother at the home place on Smith Ridge. Courtesy of Fannie Steele.

CYP LANDRENEOU   MIKE SEEGER   ROSCOE HOLCOMB GEORGE SHUFFLER   DON   REVON REED
ADAM LANDRENEOU   CARTER STANLEY   RALPH STANLEY COUSIN EMMY   TRACY SCHWARZ
                                        JOHN COHEN

The American Folk & Country Music Festival touring company gathered for a group photograph. John Cohen photo.

The Stanley Brothers International Fan Club devoted a special newsletter to Carter's final months and funeral. Courtesy of Mary Bruce Mazza.

16. COAST TO COAST

Above the squealing brakes and honking horns of New York City traffic, Japanese businessman Tatsuo Arita thought he heard a voice announcing a bluegrass show that night. This was not the sort of information that Arita expected to drift through the open window of the midtown apartment where he was staying in June 1961—but the announcement caught his attention because he was one of a growing number of Japanese bluegrass fans. Looking for the source of the announcement, he spotted a large sedan bearing Virginia license plates. The Stanley Brothers were driving around the city with their public address system strapped to the top of the car, publicizing that night's show.

The performance on June 9 was the first of four shows Carter and Ralph played in and around New York City during 1961 and 1962—two for the Friends of Old Time Music, including this one. At the second FOTM show on November 30, 1962, and a Long Island performance the following day, the Stanley Brothers shared the stage with the Louvin Brothers—popular *Grand Ole Opry* performers known for their sibling harmony. Accompanying Ira and Charlie Louvin on electric guitar was Claude "Buddy" Hyman, a former member of WCYB's Curly King and the Hilltoppers who had moved from Virginia to New York state to find work.

"There hadn't been any down-home type lead guitar men up there," Hyman recalled.[1] "I joined the union and had plenty of work." The union sent Hyman and a female bass player to back the Louvin Brothers for three shows in New York City. On November 30, Carter recognized Hyman's familiar face from WCYB and suggested a walk between shows. "We hit a bar or two and we got a little tipsy," Hyman recalled. By the time they returned from their walk, Ira Louvin had consumed a few drinks. That led to an argument on stage between Ira and Charlie about which song to perform. Ira announced they would do a song Carter already had sung, prompting Charlie to step to the microphone. "I don't want to do that number," he said. "I want to do another number."

The first Stanley Brothers show led Arita to another, bigger one. Attending the FOTM show at New York University, he heard about an outdoor concert planned for Oak Leaf Park in Luray, Virginia, on July 4. Dubbed Bluegrass Day by its producer, Bill Clifton, the event was one of the first all-day bluegrass festivals.[2]

While staying in New York, Arita met with record collector David Freeman, with whom he had corresponded. "I remember taping some Monroe Brothers 78s for him, and we kept in touch after that," Freeman recalled.[3] Freeman had learned of the Luray festival after writing to Clifton's Blue Ridge Records label in search of more bluegrass records. "I was surprised to get a letter back signed by Bill Clifton, who told me in advance about the Luray festival as well as answering my query about the 45s," he said.

Prior to Bluegrass Day, promoters thought it was unwise to book two of the same type of band on the same day at a country music park. "The logic behind this was that a second bluegrass band would draw no more people than the first," wrote historian Neil Rosenberg, "whereas another kind of country music would attract its own (and different) audiences."[4] On stage on July 4 were Bill Monroe, the Stanley Brothers, Jim and Jesse, Mac Wiseman, the Country Gentlemen, and Clifton himself. Featuring an unplanned reunion of several of Monroe's original Blue Grass Boys, Bluegrass Day foreshadowed a festival four years later that became a milestone in the history of bluegrass.

Taking advantage of his opportunity to rub shoulders with so many well-known musicians, Arita approached Bill Monroe. Dave Freeman watched in fascination as the Japanese businessman carried on a long conversation with the tight-lipped Kentuckian. "Monroe didn't have much to say to most fans around that time, as I recall," Freeman remembered. "I had seen Monroe in person five or six times before then, and had never got much more than a yes or no when trying to talk with him."[5]

Freeman was familiar enough with the personalities of the musicians to follow the direction of their patter between songs. "I had a front row seat and when Monroe was on stage, Carter Stanley was sitting right next to me in the audience, really into the happenings on stage," Freeman recalled.[6] He picked up an undercurrent of animosity between those on stage that day and those who were not—specifically between Bill Monroe and former Blue Grass Boys Don Reno (of the duo Reno and Smiley) and

Lester Flatt and Earl Scruggs. Reno came to listen but turned down an offer to play, and Flatt and Scruggs refused to appear on the same stage as Monroe.[7]

When Monroe took the stage, the bandleader alluded to "bluegrass people . . . [who] don't want to be on a show with you . . . if the folks will think you started them."[8] Joining Monroe on stage for a song, Carter leaped into the fray with both feet: "I guess I'll just break into this kindly blunt like. I understand that they was a group that some of the folks asked to come in here today. They said no, they didn't want to play here because Bill Monroe and the Stanley Brothers was gonna be here. And that was Flatt and Scruggs. You know, we missed 'em a heck of a lot, ain't we?" Savvy members of the audience understood the jibe. They laughed and applauded. Monroe provoked more laughter by taking another run at Flatt and Scruggs. "Now I started the two boys on the Grand Ole Opry, and they shouldn't be ashamed to come on the show and work with us. And I'm sure I wouldn't hurt either one of them."

Neil Rosenberg speculated that Carter made his comments after he took "a few drinks from Clifton's backstage spiked punch bowl and was 'feeling no pain. . . .'" Writer Richard D. Smith repeated the assessment of the situation in his biography of Bill Monroe.

What happened next became one of the most notorious incidents in bluegrass history.

Clifton had provided some backstage hospitality in the form of a spiked punch. That was a mistake, considering that Carter had a serious problem with alcohol. By the time Carter joined Monroe onstage he was merry and feisty.[9]

However, Dave Freeman believed that alcohol had little to do with Carter's comments: "While I have no information regarding what may have gone on backstage, I did not get the impression that Carter was drinking heavily on Bluegrass Day. I did get a chance to talk with him and he was perfectly coherent."

Whether or not Carter was relatively sober that day, the physical effects of years of drinking were about to become more visible. "I think it became clear to many serious Stanley fans that the drinking was really starting to be a health factor soon after that," Freeman said.[10] "Obviously Carter must have had a drinking problem well before that time." Joe Wilson, who followed the Stanley Brothers from the early 1950s, recalled that "the last time I saw them when you could really kind of talk to Carter was in Nashville," adding that the meeting was "the last conversation I had with Carter that kind of made sense." He placed the encounter as far back as 1960 or 1961.[11]

On July 20, 1961, the Stanley Brothers made a stop at King Studios to record four songs for their next album. The cover of *Folk Song Festival* would advertise that they were "award winners" at a hypothetical festival and claim that the collection of studio numbers had been "recorded live." Neither hyperbole nor contrived live albums were uncommon in popular music at the time. The band included veteran sidemen Al Elliot on mandolin and Chubby Anthony on fiddle. George Shuffler doubled on guitar and bass, recording some of his first lead guitar parts for the brothers. Carter and Ralph covered a Delmore Brothers song on this session, "Fast Express."

A month later, the brothers suffered a serious personal loss. Lee Stanley died on August 19. He was buried in a cemetery at Flat Top on Caney Ridge, about eight miles from the home place on Smith Ridge, yet separated from the Smith family cemetery that would be the resting place of his former wife and their two children.

The schedule of summer performances permitted Carter and Ralph little time to grieve the loss of their father. They returned to the studio on September 22 to record the four final tracks of *Folk Song Festival*. The session produced the formulaic "String, Eraser, and Blotter"; a novelty number, "Keep Them Cold, Icy Fingers Off of Me," that used a slide whistle to evoke the supernatural; and a followup to the surprise hit "How Far to Little Rock" entitled "Still Trying to Get to Little Rock." The followup went nowhere. Syd Nathan and his staff took most of the album's material from the King catalogue or wrote it.

The band did not record again until the following May. By that time, Ralph Mayo had replaced Chubby Anthony on fiddle, and the tap-dancing Chick Stripling was back on the bass. George Shuffler remained on guitar and vocals. To make up for the long interval between sessions, the musicians spent May 2, 3, and 4 recording twenty-one songs—twelve for a gospel album and nine for secular projects.

Sometimes a singer's vocal cords can warm up and sound more open as the recording process continues. Whether it was a carryover from the previous day's recording or the chance to get some sleep, all four vocalists (the brothers, Shuffler, and Mayo) sang with full-throated harmony on the five gospel quartets recorded at the beginning of the second day. Carter and Ralph had recorded Carter's "Harbor of Love" for Mercury in August 1954, but the 1962 version with George Shuffler singing bass remains one of the Stanley Brothers' most poignant recordings. For a portion of one day at least, Carter recovered most of his voice. Though the group would continue to make enjoyable albums and record the occasional popular single, its lead singer never would sound this good again.

During the early 1960s, the band members' homes in Live Oak became way stations where the musicians would return between trips to eat a few home-cooked meals and do the laundry. Like acres of undeveloped land, the economic reasons to remain in Florida were vanishing. On December 13, 1961, Ralph encountered his strongest incentive to consider making a change. "The most beautiful vision I ever had was in a bar in Cincinnati, Ohio," he wrote in his autobiography.[12] "It was one of those visions that turned out to be real. The vision was named Jimmie, and I was lucky enough to marry her." The marriage of Ralph Stanley and Jimmie Crabtree did not take place until six and a half years later, but the two of them kept in touch from the night they met at the Ken-Mill Café.

In 1962, Norman Protsman decided to end the *Suwannee River Jamboree* program that he had introduced so successfully in 1958. "TV interrupted it," he said. "People would rather stay home and watch television. Our crowds got smaller."[13] This was less of a loss for the Stanley Brothers than for local musicians because the brothers were touring all the time, much as Jim and Jesse had done after using the radio program as a springboard. "[The reason] why the *Suwannee River Jamboree* went down," musician Arnold Brim explained, "was that every time somebody got to be pretty good, they took to the road."[14]

Of more significant economic impact to the brothers was the end of their relationship with the Jim Walter Corporation. The home-builder's sponsorship had been the brothers' bread and butter since soon after they had moved to Florida; but the shell-home industry was struggling, and the promotional value of a hillbilly band had declined. There were fewer potential buyers at open houses to entertain. In a panicked effort to find another sponsor, Carter collared George Shuffler for support and took to the road. "Carter and I went over to Alabama and talked to a big meat processing company by the name of Bevis that made weiners and bologna and all that stuff," Shuffler recalled.[15] The musicians dressed at their most businesslike for the visit. "They really gave Carter and me the once over

in the office before they took us back through the plant. They wanted to
make sure we wasn't from another meat processing company that was going to try to steal their help."

As mouth-watering as the prospect might have been in lean times, promoting sausages and bologna was not in the band's future. "They wanted
us to move to Alabama," Shuffler recalled. "We went back to Florida and
talked it over and [the brothers] didn't want to move. They had bought
homes and everything. So we just went back on the road. We never did do
anymore of that type [of sponsored] work in Carter's lifetime."

By contrast, Flatt and Scruggs became national celebrities in 1962. The
evening of September 26 witnessed the debut of *The Beverly Hillbillies*,
the CBS television series about an eccentric Appalachian family that mi-
grates from Bug Tussle to Beverly Hills after finding oil on its land. With
personable actor Buddy Ebsen starring as Jed Clampett and wrinkle-
faced Irene Ryan as Daisy "Granny" Moses, the program ran until May
23, 1971—a total of two-hundred-seventy-four episodes. Producer Paul
Henning roughed out a theme song for the series, and Flatt and Scruggs
arranged and performed it. "The Ballad of Jed Clampett" was a hit, reaching number 44 on *Billboard*'s popular music chart in 1962 and becoming
number one on the country chart. Lester and Earl would score a second
country hit with "Pearl, Pearl, Pearl," a comic paean to the charms of Miss
Pearl Bodine, who was the central character in the episode "Jed Throws a
Wingding" in which Lester and Earl made the first of several appearances
on the show.

The spectacular success of their longtime rivals was a bitter pill for
Carter and Ralph to swallow during a period when their own economic
foundation was crumbling. Permanently at odds with his counterpart
Lester Flatt, Carter remained contemptuous toward Lester for the rest of
his life. A year or two after *Beverly Hillbillies* made its debut, Carter un-
leashed this remark during a conversation with country music historian
Bill Malone: "Speaking of Lester Flatt . . . and that's a real good name for
him, because that's the way he sings. . . ."[16] According to Larry Ehrlich,
Carter's "tragedy" was that "he knew how good they were. Carter was
enormously special, and specialness sets you apart."[17]

Already in frail condition, Carter suffered a demoralizing back injury
that summer. According to Roy Sykes Jr.: "He fell off a black horse he had
at the farm in July 1962 and hit a rock. He was in a lot of pain. That was
the reason he started drinking more. He told dad that he was in pain but
he didn't tell Ralph. He and dad were just like brothers."[18]

Carter began to rely on his older daughter for physical and emotional support. "When my sister was born in 1962, Daddy felt I was old enough to help him with his special needs," Doris recalled,[19] "since he was out on the road a lot, ate at odd hours of the night, and Mama had my three brothers and a brand new baby to care for. For the most part afterwards until he died, Daddy became my responsibility as far as cooking special things he needed at the very odd hours he was able to eat, giving his facials, caring for his clothes and suits and hats, nail buffing and clipping and washing, and conditioning his hair so he'd look good on stage."

Even though she had numerous caretaking responsibilities, Doris cherished her personal time with her father. "He took me squirrel hunting, coon hunting, and fishing with him many times those last two or three years he lived," she recalled.[20] "We talked a lot, especially late at night when he could comfortably eat and relax away from the public. Sometimes Mama joined us, but mostly she had a new baby and needed all the sleep she could get."

Before he moved to England in 1963, Bill Clifton noticed that Carter tended to limit his interactions with other musicians. "He was very reticent to introduce himself to another artist," Clifton recalled.[21] "It was up to them to speak to him. . . . [Promoter] Ray Davis came up to me when we were doing a show in Baltimore with Hawkshaw Hawkins and Jeannie Shepard on the bill. He said, 'Could you ask Carter to speak to Hawkshaw and Jeannie? He hasn't spoken to them all evening.' I told Ray I would talk to Carter, and when I did, he said, 'Well, they never spoke to me.'"

The trait seems inconsistent with a personality that was extroverted and personable to fans, friends, and even strangers; but whether from pride, competitiveness, or shyness, the aloof behavior had been present earlier in his career. Clifton recalled that Carter had shown the same attitude toward Bill and Earl Bolick, the Blue Sky Boys, with whom Carter had worked at WCYB. When Clifton asked if he knew the Bolicks, Carter responded "No, I've never met 'em."

"He worked out of the same studio and they were separated by 15 minutes," Clifton exclaimed in our interview. "Surely you must have seen 'em," he said to Carter.

Carter replied, "Sure I've seen 'em, but I never met 'em."

"Bill and Earl never introduced themselves to Carter and he never introduced himself to them," Clifton concluded. "It was an attitude he had that was a bit of a drawback." As the shy younger brother, Ralph often had been perceived as standoffish. Clifton suggested the possibility that

Carter and Ralph might have been emulating Bill Monroe. "They had the attitude that when they worked in schoolhouse or small place when you had to come through the front door, when the show was over, they would just march out the back door without speaking to anybody," he recalled. "That was Bill Monroe's attitude. Maybe they thought that since Bill did it, it would work for them."[22]

Without a sponsor or a regular show, the Stanley Brothers scraped together a living by performing for their longtime fans and capitalizing on their growing popularity within the folk music revival. Though not as lucrative as corporate sponsorship, the folk community's seal of approval created a demand for personal appearances at various centers of the revival, such as colleges. Unfortunately, popularity on campus did not assure good pay. A trip to Ohio demonstrated the point.

On March 17, 1962, en route to a performance at the Dennison Square Theatre in Cleveland, the Stanley Brothers stopped at Oberlin College to play a single set for the Folk Song Club. Future bluegrass historian Neil Rosenberg, who had graduated from Oberlin in 1961, returned for the show from Bloomington, Indiana, where he had begun graduate work in folklore at the University of Indiana. Rosenberg's successor as president of the Folk Song Club, Steve Gibbs, arranged the Stanley Brothers' brief Oberlin appearance after learning of their Cleveland date. "He contacted Carter Stanley and struck a deal—they would play one set at Oberlin the same afternoon for $100," Rosenberg recalled.[23] The venue was Wilder Hall, a men's dormitory with good acoustics where the Folk Song Club hosted hootenannies featuring local performers.

"It was a great show, with good music and comedy work," Rosenberg recalled. "I was impressed at the way in which the band, which I'd never heard in person before, managed their dynamics. Except for solos, the instruments were played at a soft to medium level. This made the singing and the instrumental breaks stand out. They used a single microphone, but I had the sense that they could have done the concert almost as well without it. At the end of the show, the audience worked very hard with applause and shouts to get an encore, but to no avail. I had the sense (confirmed afterwards by Steve Gibbs) that Carter felt we'd gotten our 100 bucks' worth and that was that."

Three decades later, Stanley Brothers historian Gary Reid would share Rosenberg's enthusiasm. He included eight minutes from Oberlin on the first CD issued by his Copper Creek Records label in 1996. *Shadows of the Past* was a compilation taken from Stanley Brothers live performances during the mid-1950s and early 1960s. "I've always enjoyed this particular show," Reid said. "I thought Carter's MC work was good, and the interaction with Chick Stripling was amusing."

The live recording preserves a representative sample of the Stanley Brothers' use of country humor to leaven a show, similar to Lindy Clear's automobile imitations at Antioch. At Oberlin, the bandleader and his argumentative bass player Chick Stripling wrangled over the use of a word. Carter took on the role of professor in front of the college audience, lecturing Stripling on not only the pronunciation of the names of 1960s Communist leaders Nikita Khrushchev and Fidel (not *Fiddlin'*) Castro, but the correct definition of the word in question: *propaganda*. Unfazed by Carter's superior attitude, Stripling asked the bandleader how long he had been married and how many children he had. When Carter responded that he has been married thirteen years but (for purposes of the routine) did not have children, Stripling pounced on the punch line: "That's it right there. There's your propaganda, bubba. That just proves one thing: You got the proper goose, but you ain't the proper gander."[24]

When drinking, Stripling could become a bully. Once in a motel room on the road, Ralph had to pick up a chair to defend himself until Carter arrived. "Carter set down the chair real gentle, like he was tidying up the room for guests," Ralph recalled.[25] "Then he started in on Chick, just ripped him up with his fists flying until poor Chick had blood running off him."

The Oberlin concert produced a nugget of research for folklorist Rosenberg when a former banjo student of his alerted him to a link in the evolution of bluegrass banjo. Rosenberg recalled that student Eric Jacobsen "spoke with Carter, asking him where Ralph learned the three-finger style. Carter told him that Ralph had picked it up from Earl Scruggs when he first came to Bristol. Eric told me about that right away. I later used this information in my 1967 *Journal of American Folklore* article." This influential article, published in what came to be called "the hillbilly issue" of the *JAF*, traced the development of the particular sound of Bill Monroe's Blue Grass Boys into the general style of music called bluegrass.

With its population of rural southerners who had migrated to cities such as Cincinnati, Cleveland, and Dayton, Ohio was familiar territory to the Stanley Brothers. They had performed in the state since the late 1940s. Dayton resident Russell "Mac" McDivitt recalled seeing the brothers on July 4, 1949 or 1950, in Oxford, Ohio, at the town's fireworks celebration. In his early teenage years and without a driver's license, he was pleased that recording stars were coming to his hometown. "I had been hearing 'White Dove' on the radio and I was excited about seeing them," he recalled.

Bookings in the neighboring state of Indiana expanded opportunities to perform in the Midwest. From 1960 to 1964, the Stanley Brothers were annual visitors to Mocking Bird Hill Park in Anderson, Indiana. By now a devoted fan, McDivitt drove to the 1962 show. Closer to home, he remembered attending two shows in Dayton at a Veterans of Foreign Wars post and an American Legion hall on East Third Street—organizations that had supported the army-veteran Stanley Brothers since their earliest days. "These shows would probably have been after 1963 as I remember them doing 'Stone Walls and Steel Bars' and it wasn't recorded until August of 1963," McDivitt said.

Co-written by Ray Pennington, who produced the King session at which it was recorded, "Stone Walls and Steel Bars" was released as a 45 and became one of the brothers' most successful singles in the 1960s. The plaintive quality that had crept into Carter's voice was a good fit to this tale of an inmate on Alcatraz who was being led to his execution "for the love of another man's wife." The first time I heard the song, I did not recognize the lead voice as Carter's. In 2003, when I asked Ralph about Carter's change in tone, he responded, "Oh yeah. Carter failed in the last couple of years. His voice didn't stay as good, but his voice still had that feel. He couldn't use it as well, but he still had the touch."[26]

Typical of the group's most loyal fans, Mac McDivitt tried to see the Stanley Brothers in person whenever they performed within driving distance of his home. In the mid-1960s he heard the band at Dayton's Maple Gardens on West Third Street—a 1930s-style dance hall that later burned down. In the summer of 1964, he drove to Cincinnati to listen to the group at the Ken-Mill on the corner of Kenton and McMillan Streets. During the early to mid-1960s, the Ken-Mill featured bluegrass six nights a week.[27] McDivitt's final opportunity to hear the Stanley Brothers would come at Chatauqua Park near Franklin, Ohio, during its first season of shows in the summer of 1966.

Whenever the brothers performed in Columbus, Carter made a point to keep in touch with old friends Pee Wee and Hazel Lambert, who had moved to the Ohio capital in 1957. Carter and Pee Wee stayed in touch until February 1965, Hazel recalled. "One night about two o'clock the phone rang so Pee Wee said, 'Get up and answer it' and it was Carter. They were . . . somewhere . . . Pee Wee didn't go. They were probably just in a bar or something. Pee Wee talked to him on the phone, and that was the last time he talked to him." Pee Wee died in June of a massive heart attack. Hazel recalled: "he had complained, but you know, it's hard to get some men to a doctor. He just didn't know what it was. . . ."

Hazel heard from a distraught Carter soon after Pee Wee died. "Mommy said that he called over there and he was crying, and then he called me. He couldn't hardly talk. And Mary, Carter's wife, told me, 'I don't think Carter ever got over Pee Wee dying.' Mary said he come home one night and he was telling her about it, and she said 'Oh Carter, shut up'—'cause he was all the time teasing, Carter was . . . and she thought he was just teasing . . . but he wasn't."

On the road, two noticeable effects of these lean years (a period that bluegrass historian Fred Bartenstein termed "the starving-out era") were that Carter and Ralph kept the size of the band flexible and increased the range of their touring. "It was cheaper to pick up musicians at each location," wrote bluegrass historian Bob Artis, "and . . . the Stanley sound had enough adherents among bluegrass musicians that it wasn't hard to find one or two who would fit."[28] Former sideman Lester Woodie re-called a time in August 1962 when Carter and Ralph arrived alone at the Danville, Virginia, fairgrounds. To put together a group for the engage-ment, "Carter called me, and I played fiddle, Allen [Mills] played bass," Woodie said.[29]

After performing in New York City in June, the Stanley Brothers traveled to California for a month during August and September 1962. Their primary destination was a folk club that had opened in July 1958 on Melrose Avenue in West Los Angeles. Founded by 22-year-old gui-tar teacher Ed Pearl, who had taken guitar lessons from folklorist Beth Lomax Hawes, the Ash Grove was one of a handful of folk clubs whose roster of performers became the stuff of legend—from blues singer Son House to jazz composer Charles Mingus, folk singer Joan Baez to folk-rock pioneers the Byrds.

In addition to booking talented West Coast folk musicians such as Barbara Dane and Guy Carawan, Pearl paid attention to suggestions from his East Coast friends John Cohen and Mike Seeger of the New Lost City Ramblers. "The Ramblers turned me on to most of the great country and bluegrass bands," Pearl recalled.[30] Cohen and Seeger's rec-ommendations brought to the West Coast such old-time and bluegrass musicians as Clarence "Tom" Ashley (with little-known Doc Watson on guitar), the Stanley Brothers, and Bill Monroe. The traditionalists were eager to appear at the Ash Grove for one paramount reason: According to Ed's younger brother Bernie, "If you could get a date there, it was a solid enough paycheck to finance a tour of the West Coast."[31]

Booked into the Ash Grove after Tom Ashley but before Bill Monroe, the Stanley Brothers enjoyed the stability of playing two shows a night for two weeks at the club. Recordings from the nights of Wednesday and Thursday, August 29 and 30, document a group dominated by Carter, even more so than at the folk festivals and college concerts. He called the songs, introduced the band, and sorted through a series of requests as fast as an overly persistent audience member could make them: "I don't know whether we remember the words to that or not . . . We had that 'String, Eraser and Blotter' on a little bit ago, Dave. I believe that's the number you're talking . . . I don't know that one . . . I don't know 'Money, Marbles and Chalk' so you're lost there. We'd like to do 'Uncle Pen' for ya."

Bill Monroe's homage to his fiddle-playing uncle Pendleton Vandiver kicked off a series of six Monroe songs that included two Carter sang with Monroe during his brief tenure as a Blue Grass Boy, "The Little Girl and the Dreadful Snake" and "Sugar-Coated Love" ("I helped Bill make that record"). With each introduction, Carter went to lengths to express his admiration for his mentor. "In my opinion there's nobody that can do that bluegrass stuff like Bill Monroe can. . . ." In most cases, he named the year the song had been released.

Poised as Carter always was on stage, a listener could hear that he was losing his air of affability. His once playful wit began to turn acerbic. On-stage comments about band members became more barbed. After introducing an instrumental number by heaping compliments on the show-manship of fiddle player Vernon Derrick, at the tune's conclusion Carter took a gratuitous poke at Ralph's banjo work. "Vern, there's one thing to say," he informed not only Derrick but the audience over the public address system. "Your banjo player let you down there. You're going to have to rehearse him a little bit."

Off stage, Carter's sarcastic barbs created an opening for other members of the band to join in teasing Ralph, whom he nicknamed "Fluffo" when Ralph gained weight and called "Jesus Christ" when the younger brother tried to temper Carter's drinking.[32] On the road, Carter may have been able to consider off limits the topic of his drinking, but at home on Smith Ridge, the family dynamics were different. In a scene from the play *Man of Constant Sorrow*, Lucy Smith Stanley confronts Carter about the drinking's effect on his wife and children.

Carter: I didn't think you'd be here, Ma. Where did you say Mary
was, anyways?
Lucy: She's at work, Carter.
Carter: Work!?
Lucy: She got herself a job at the restaurant—as a waitress.
Carter: Why'd she go and get herself a job for?
Lucy: Your seventy-five dollars a month don't make it with three
young 'uns in the house.
Carter: Seventy-five dollars is all I got left over after I pay the band,
the motel, the gas . . .
Lucy: All you got left after you buy your booze!
Carter: Alright, Ma, I know what you're gonna say, but just hold it. I
already got an earful from Ralph.[33]

Alcohol was not the only presence unwelcome at the Smith Ridge
threshold. On one occasion, a woman came to the door of Lucy's house
to ask if Carter was home. Inside with her children, Mary heard the question. Approaching the door to tell the woman that Carter was on the
road, she continued out the door, where she tore the buttons off the visi-
tor's sweater. Relatives and friends were aware that women were "always
throwing themselves" at Carter. A relative commented that although
Ralph was not as handsome as Carter, women threw themselves at him,
too. "Lot of fun and foolishness on the road, and a lot of temptations,
too . . . ," Ralph wrote in his autobiography.[34] "Now, we used to like pretty
girls, I'll admit it, and there was plenty of pretty girls on the road. . . . Now,
with these girls you'd see on the road, you can look at them and not get
in trouble. But, sometimes, you know, you get with one and maybe go a
little too far."

At the Ash Grove in 1962, Carter and Ralph were pleased to receive
a visit from their former fiddler Leslie Keith. The brothers placed a high
value on loyalty, and Keith had been their mentor at a critical time early
in their career. Members of the Ash Grove audience might not have noticed Keith's presence even though they followed the comings and goings
of these old-time musicians with earnest attention. Many were young
musicians who later would be heard on record: slide guitarist Ry Cooder,
blues singer Taj Mahal, and the blues group Canned Heat. In February
1996 musician and fellow club owner Peter F. Feldmann sat down with
Ash Grove founder Ed Pearl to reminisce about this aspect of the club.[35]
"One thing I remember about the Ash Grove were the audiences," said

Feldmann. "That was a tough audience to play for—they were very astute."
Pearl agreed: "The stage was surrounded by that counter where you had
all these young-ass kids. . . . You never knew who was in the audience. You
had all those musicians listening."

One such listener was 16-year-old Peter Coonradt of Los Angeles,
who would attend Harvard College and participate in the folk scene at
Cambridge's Club 47. "I sat at the counter that wrapped around the stage
barely big enough to hold the band, so I was only a few feet away from
them," he recalled.[36] ". . . I guess the main thing that still resonates for
an LA boy is the nasal twang, the high pitched piercing voices of a rural
America that was vanishing even then. And I think how weird it must
have been for these bib-overall boys to look out into that crowd of beatnik
folkniks and wonder how they wound up in Sodom and Gomorrah."

On September 12, 1962, Carter sent a postcard to his stepsister
Georgia, saying that the brothers would be touring for two more weeks:
"Hi Georgia and all, Hope you're well. We've been here two weeks & still
have two more before we start home. Will be through by sometime in
October. Tell all hello for us. With love, Carter."[37] This included a perfor-
mance in Berkeley around September 20.

The liner notes to the *Folk Concert* album released in June 1963 mention several campus appearances during 1962 and 1963, including performances at the University of Texas, University of Arizona, New Mexico
State University, UCLA, USC, Stanford, and the University of Cincinnati.
The California concerts were organized around Ash Grove appearances
since the Stanley Brothers were invited to return to the club in 1963.[38]
Adding to the miles driven coast to coast in 1962, the group returned to
the Friends of Old-Time Music at New York University on November 30,
followed by shows on Long Island and in Brooklyn on the first two days
of December. Oscar Brand broadcast a tape from the latter show on his
radio program.

Always on the lookout for new material, the brothers learned a song
from the New Lost City Ramblers while they took a break at band member John Cohen's New York City apartment. "Carter told us that they were
recording an album and needed a folk song," recalled Tracy Schwarz.[39]
"So we said 'I'll bet you 'Pretty Little Miss Out in the Garden' would really
be a good Stanley Brothers number' and we played it for them. They all
ran to their instruments and backed us up and got right with it. So that's
how they did it."

In their version, the Ramblers spliced the words of Cousin Emmy to the melody of Roscoe Holcomb—two musicians that both groups would tour Europe with in 1966. According to Mike Seeger, as the Ramblers sang the song for the visitors at John Cohen's, "Carter cracked a joke. 'Pretty fair miss out in the garden, strange young man comes riding by,' and Carter says, 'Strange young man named Phyllis.' What he meant was some gay man, I suppose."[40]

After the holidays, the band drove to Cincinnati to spend January 28 and 29, 1963, in the recording studio completing the *Folk Concert* album. The artificiality of the material represented something of a low point in the brothers' careers. "I Don't Want Your Rambling Letters" and "He Went to Sleep and the Hogs Ate Him" were fake folk titles dreamed up by Syd Nathan, who gave titles to his producers to flesh out as songs.[41] "Rambling Letters" sounded real enough because the writers grafted the lyrics onto the melody of Tom Ashley's popular "Greenback Dollar," but "Hogs" was a surreal representation of the farm life of a hick. Adding to the fakery was the applause overdubbed between studio tracks to simulate a live performance. "The 1960s were treading water, trying to come up with enough content for King," observed musicologist Dick Spottswood.[42] "The King records sounded like made to order product." Most likely *Folk Concert* was an effort to duplicate Flatt and Scruggs's *Live at Carnegie Hall*.[43]

The brothers continued to tour the West during 1963, making the first of two trips to Texas in March. Reduced to a single sideman, they found other musicians to accompany them along the way. One of the pickup musicians was Charles Taylor, a student at Southwest Texas State (now Texas State University) in San Marcos, who recalled:

We were waiting in the parking lot when the Stanleys arrived at their motel. There were only three of them: Carter, Ralph, and Vernon Derrick [on fiddle]. Somehow we met Ralph before meeting the other two. Ralph said that if we knew of an available mandolin player they could use him.

One of us hastily nominated me to be the needed mandolin player. We went to the Stanleys' room an hour or so later, and they had showered and sacked out in order to get a little rest before the show. After we had conversed briefly Carter concluded correctly that I was not the seasoned mandolin player they were looking for. He said that since I wasn't familiar with their material, it wouldn't work out very well for me to play the show with them. He added that instead they would just have me come out on stage during the show and do a couple of numbers with them. I have always felt that Carter was very tactful and kind in making that decision. I have also sometimes wondered whether or not Carter chastised his brother for diving in too deeply before gathering all the facts.[44]

From Taylor's vantage point backstage, the fiddle player stole the show.

In my opinion, Vernon Derrick was Carter and Ralph's ace in the hole the night they performed in San Marcos in '63. The audience, for the most part, was not well schooled in bluegrass music. Most of them had probably never heard "Are You Tired of Me My Darling" and "Voice from on High." Most of them, however, had heard the "Orange Blossom Special" and they really dug it when Derrick played it early in the show. The crowd also liked Derrick's vocal imitations of country singers.[45]

Taylor was persistent in reminding Carter of his presence. "The main thing I remember is that on at least two and probably three occasions, I implored Carter not to forget to call me out and each time he assured me that they would call me out."[46] At last Carter brought the young amateur on stage to play "Bile Them Cabbage Down" and "Ragtime Annie" with the professionals. Taylor took his turn on mandolin as Ralph and Derrick shared instrumental breaks. He also remembered an onstage spat:

At one point in the show Carter and Ralph did a little sparring. The way I remember it is that when Carter was introducing "Cumberland Gap," someone in the crowd called out for 'Mountain Dew.' Ralph started picking "Mountain Dew" while Carter was going on with his intro. I think Carter said something like "Let's do Cumberland Gap" and Ralph answered that they had a request for "Mountain Dew." After a couple more little exchanges, Carter relented and the three of them took off on "Mountain Dew." When Carter sensed that the audience was digging the "Dew," he seemed to warm up to it. The audience sort of enjoyed the little bit of brotherly sparring.[47]

"Bill Malone and I both felt that the Stanleys would have been better off with another lead instrument," Taylor added, "but in spite of [their] being understaffed, we truly enjoyed the show." Malone had been part of the welcoming committee that had met the band at the motel. While attending the University of Texas, he hung out at Threadgill's—a Gulf station turned beer joint just outside Austin—with a small group of students who were fans of bluegrass and old-time country music. By 1963 Malone was a faculty member at Southwest Texas State, where his colleague and friend Bill Pool persuaded a student organization to sponsor the Stanley Brothers. He recalled:

I had become an ardent fan of the Stanleys in the early or mid-fifties, bowled over by their soulfulness and "authenticity." I was so delighted that people still sounded that way, even in the days of rock and roll and country pop. And, of course, I identified with them personally, thinking that they could be brothers or cousins.

The auditorium was packed at SWT, and the response from most people was pretty enthusiastic. I do recall at least one faculty colleague, though, who was repelled by their show, particularly by their corniness and sometimes crude humor. She insisted that this was not "folk music" and that the brothers were not "folk." I countered that their show (humor, stage patter, music, et cetera) was exactly the kind of thing that "real" country people did. Needless to say, the whole event was wonderful to me. Their singing was soulful and their playing was exciting. They were doing songs like "Six Months Ain't Long" and "Hills of Roan County," which had recently come out on their Folk Concert *LP.[48]*

After the concert at Southwest Texas State, Malone rode with the musicians to the University of Texas for a performance sponsored by the campus folk song club. En route he became aware of Carter's need for alcohol. "Carter insisted on stopping at a liquor store on the outskirts of town to get a pint of Jack Daniels or something like that," he recalled. "The audience in the [UT] student union was very small, and Carter took the opportunity to 'lecture' the club on the poor advertising and promotion that had taken place. The president of the club . . . was deeply offended." Malone was not sure if liquor had fueled Carter's remarks because "he in fact made his comments in a rather good-natured but direct way."

From Texas the musicians traveled to Colorado for a week, where they were accompanied by an electric bass player. They then headed home to Florida. Family photographs taken around that time show Carter, his wife

Mary, and their three youngest children: Doris, Bobby, and Jeanie. In her pink sunsuit and bright red sneakers, little Jeanie is the center of attention. The daughter of two dark-haired, pale-skinned parents, Doris is strikingly blond and tanned, taller than her mother's shoulder. Bobby, who is close to Doris in height, wears blue jeans and a light blue western-style shirt. His belt sports a good-sized buckle. In one picture, Bobby stands in front of the family's brick and shingle home, holding Jeanie's shoulders as if to rock her in her wooden rocking chair. In the photos of Mary, she holds one or both of her daughters and looks directly at the camera. In his pictures, Carter wears light blue slacks, a white short-sleeved shirt, and large sunglasses. He appears to be looking outside the frame of the photograph. In one picture, he cradles Jeanie in the crook of his right arm and puts his left hand on Bobby's shoulder. He is looking toward the sky. The only full-fledged smile in the photographs appears on the face of Doris as she looks at Jeanie being held by her mother. Parked in the driveway is the white Cadillac with trailer hitch that the band took on the road.

In the late summer of 1963, the musicians squeezed into the Cadillac for trips to King Records on August 13 and 14 and September 16 and 17 to record the two dozen songs and tunes that appeared on the albums *The Country Folk Music Spotlight* and *America's Finest 5-String Banjo Hootenanny. Spotlight* included "Stone Walls and Steel Bars"—an excellent example of shorter, catchier songs designed for jukebox play—and *Hootenanny* consisted entirely of instrumentals featuring Ralph on banjo, George Shuffler on lead guitar, and Ralph Mayo on fiddle.

In a public radio series on bluegrass produced in the mid-1970s, producer Jeff Mills reported: "Ralph was asked to put together a banjo album for King Records. According to the story, Ralph took his banjo to a hotel room and returned in three hours with twelve songs ready to record."[49] In fact, the tunes were recorded in two separate sessions on August 13 and September 16. Syd Nathan took a personal interest in the banjo project, designed to capitalize on the popularity of the banjo during the folk music revival. Nathan shared production duties with Ray Pennington on all but one track. "We just put some old tunes together and named 'em," Ralph recalled.[50] A highlight was a moody, reverb-laden rendition of Grayson and Whitter's "Train 45," which was based on the tune "Lonesome Reuben." To record enough material to round out the album, Ralph reached back in his repertoire to the clawhammer style of "Shout Little Lulie"—the first tune he learned from his mother when he was 11. His career was coming full circle.

17. STARVING OUT

By October 1963 Carter and Ralph had been professional musicians for seventeen years. They had something to show for their efforts: Carter owned a modest house and Ralph a small farm. With help from the earnings of their wives, they were able to support their families. Yet the financial pressure was constant, and the musicians were starved for work. Around Baltimore, where many transplants from Appalachia had migrated, promoter and radio show host Ray Davis was the man who could provide the work. Davis was well established in the Baltimore country music market. He had begun broadcasting as an amateur on a Delaware station before becoming a professional in 1948 after his mother agreed to let him leave home on May 2—his fifteenth birthday. Soon he was in a position to hire old-time country and bluegrass performers on a regular basis. He loved the Stanley Brothers.

Davis met Carter in 1951 when the older brother was a member of Bill Monroe's Blue Grass Boys. He met Ralph after the brothers reunited. By that time Davis was hosting a country and bluegrass program on WBMD-AM six afternoons a week, sponsored by Johnny's Used Cars at 900 East Fayette Street. He hired the Stanley Brothers and other bands by the week to have them play shows in the Baltimore area while appearing on his program.

Between promoting the brothers' performances and hosting them on the radio show, Davis became good friends with the brothers. Ralph would be his best man. When Carter was taking care of the band's bookings, all he had to do was call up Davis and say, "We need a week's work." The arrangement worked well for both parties. "We just had one contract," Davis recalled.[1] "Carter wrote it in red pencil on the back of one of my [promotional] pictures . . . something to the effect that 'It is hereby agreed that the Stanley Brothers agree to work for Ray Davis in and around Baltimore for such-and-such an amount for one week.' . . . I still have it."

Davis's radio studio was housed on the second story of a building that overlooked the lot at Johnny's Used Cars. In 1962, he began to use the studio to make recordings for a small label he started, Wango Records. He named the label after his home town, which was located between Salisbury and Ocean City, Maryland. In December 1963, at the end of one of their weeks working for Davis in Baltimore, the Stanley Brothers agreed to record an album of gospel songs for Wango. In deference to his sponsor Johnny Wilbanks (advertised as "The Walking Man's Friend"), Davis called the group John's Gospel Quartet. The name changed to John's Country Quartet for the next Wango album—a collection of songs including Bill Carlisle's "No Letter in the Mail Today" and the traditional ballad "Pretty Polly."

In the liner notes to a reissue of the series by County Records in 1973, Bill Vernon of *Muleskinner News* praised the four albums (the final two were gospel) and its producer:

> *They were produced and recorded by a man who didn't want the transitory trivia that large record companies frequently foist upon their artists. Ray Davis wanted the Stanley Brothers to record the old tried-and-true songs that he knew they did best. . . . Carter and Ralph, and their various sidemen, were able to record under the best possible conditions, minus any of the pressures, commercial or otherwise, that usually rob recording sessions of the human element so vital to their success.*[2]

Davis had a marketing strategy in mind when he recorded John's Gospel Quartet. While working in 1955–56 at radio station XERF in Del Rio, Texas—the same station on which the Carter Family achieved North American fame in the 1930s[3]—Davis discovered the power of a radio station to sell in-house products directly to its audience. This was the reason, Bill Vernon wrote, why Davis "made little attempt to distribute these four albums . . . beyond his own listeners."[4]

XERF's business office was in the United States, but the studio and transmitter were located across the border in Ciudad Acuña, Mexico, beyond the regulatory reach of the Federal Communications Commission. This enabled the station's owners to build a transmitter capable of generating a 250,000-watt signal—five times the power allowed in the United

States. The transmitter was so powerful that the owners had to build their own diesel plant because the town did not have enough power to generate the station's signal.

In the 1930s, Joe Carter, the youngest child of A. P. and Sara Carter, could hold a tin can against the wire fence that surrounded the station and listen to the program that was being broadcast.[5] When Davis was at XERF, the station broadcast at night because the signal was too weak during the day. As he entered the facility, which was secured by a guard, Davis would see the gardener hosing down the grounds in order to boost the signal at night.

Arriving at XERF, Davis found song sheets left over from the Carter Family's shows in the studio. He later regretted that he did not save this historic material from the trash, but remembered the lessons in marketing.

I learned about mail order in Del Rio. We would record and put out whatever people wanted. Each record had a different color label because in mail order, you needed to pack in a hurry. I learned from Wayne Raney that you didn't need [individualized] covers. . . . Del Rio would play the actual hit, but often there were different musicians on the record. The musicians on the record would sound as close to [the original] as they could. I can tell you why they did it. They did it because they were paid to do it.[6]

In December 1963 Carter's voice was absent from the first John's Gospel Quartet session except for the chorus of one song. The reason given over the years was that he had laryngitis;[7] but holiday drinking may have contributed. The session took place at the end of a week in which Davis had asked the Stanley Brothers to produce twenty-four fifteen-minute radio shows for WBMD and other area stations in addition to making personal appearances. At the end of this exhausting schedule, Johnny Wilbanks had the musicians play for an on-air Christmas party in the lobby of the business.[8] Only after the party could Davis and the musicians settle into the task of recording an album. By that time, Carter appears to have been incapacitated by alcohol and overwork.[9] Fortunately the strong voices of the Stanley Brothers' bass-playing neighbor from southwest Virginia, Jack Cooke, and guitarist George Shuffler were able to take the lead or harmonize with Ralph so that the lead singer's absence hardly was missed. At one session, after Ralph had sung a lead vocal at

Davis's suggestion, Carter joked that Davis liked Ralph's voice better than his. The versatile Cooke recalled singing "all over" the recordings, from lead to high harmony.[10] Often employed as a bass singer, Shuffler proved to be a stirring baritone lead singer on three gospel numbers, and Cooke's casual delivery was serviceable on two more.

The Stanley Brothers' next album for King, *The Country Folk Music Spotlight*, was released the same month that the quartet album was recorded. *Country Folk Music Spotlight* was the first of several bare-bones productions the brothers recorded for King and smaller independent labels. The reasons were economic. As Mike Seeger recalled, "Bluegrass was doing very poorly at this time in general."[11] George Shuffler was the sideman, overdubbing bass fiddle after recording lead guitar in a trio with Carter and Ralph.

In contrast to the Wango sessions, whose material was taken from the Stanley Brothers' early repertoire and the hymnbooks of gospel songwriter Albert E. Brumley (whom Davis had known at XERF), King provided the musicians with more commercial material from its publishing company, Lois Music. Producer Ray Pennington and R. Marcum co-wrote a country song, "Don't Cheat in Our Home Town," which was a successful followup to their "Stone Walls and Steel Bars." Pennington contributed "Standing Room Only (Outside Your Heart)." The song combined clever lyrics with a pop melody and could have been a Buddy Holly composition—though by this time the young rock and roll star who wore geeky black-framed eyeglasses had been dead for four years.

In England, where Buddy Holly and the Crickets had toured in 1958, the American group was recalled in name by a British group called the Silver Beatles, soon shortened to the Beatles. From February 1 to April 4, 1964, three songs by the Beatles held the number one position on the *Billboard* popular music charts. For old-time country musicians, the starving out had become a famine. During the winter of 1964, the Stanley Brothers toured again in Texas with George Shuffler accompanying them. Ironically, near-poverty coincided with an increased awareness of the importance of their music. On February 6, South Texas State College faculty member Bill C. Malone interviewed Carter and Ralph for a project that began with his doctoral dissertation at the University of Texas and would become his groundbreaking book *County Music U.S.A.: A Fifty-year History.*

Not all the itinerary was musical. "I remember sitting around in [colleague] Bill Pool's living room, and the subject of deer came up," Malone recalled.[12] ". . . There are a huge number of those critters in the surrounding hill country. George and Carter decided to drive out into the country in the hopes of spotlighting some deer and killing them. I don't know whether they carried a gun with them or not, or whether they just wanted to blind the poor critters." Like Malone a history professor, Pool brought the musicians to then President Lyndon Baines Johnson's LBJ Ranch west of Johnson City; both faculty members took their visitors to dinner at a local restaurant, where shenanigans ensued. "I don't remember how many people were involved," Malone recalled,[13] "but Bill Pool's wife, Jeanette, and daughter were present. Jeanette was a very proper and dignified lady who taught at the Baptist Academy. You should have seen her reaction when Ralph and George began making small balls out of the dinner rolls and then throwing them at each other." In addition to jack-lighting deer and food fighting, the musicians performed at the college and the San Marcos Baptist Academy where Jeannette Pool taught.

Perhaps because groups were in fashion, a more dignified George Shuffler posed with Carter and Ralph on the cover of the King gospel album *Hymns of the Cross*, recorded on April 1 and 2, 1964. Wearing dark suits and ties, the brothers and Shuffler clasped their hands at their waists. A white cross dominated the background. Shuffler's name appeared in small type under the Stanley Brothers written large. Decades later Ralph remained proud of *Hymns of the Cross*, released in July 1964. He remembered the album for its cover as well as its contents: "I think this right here is one of our best, the one with George Shuffler's picture with Carter and me. We'd go along a lot of times riding in the car of a night, late at night, sometimes we'd drive all night and sing, seemed like we just happened to get on hymns, sing that more than anything else, so I guess that led us to record a lot of gospel songs."[14]

In the studio, the Stanley Brothers had become a gospel group as much as they were a bluegrass band. They had gained a reputation in the genre as the best singers of sacred songs. Their recording of "Beautiful Star of Bethlehem" introduced into the bluegrass repertoire a Christmas hymn that would be covered by Emmylou Harris. With origins in the English ballad tradition, "O Death" featured alternating lead vocals by the brothers that allowed a direct comparison of their voices. As Carter's voice had become thinner and unable to sustain a note as it once had, Ralph's voice had grown stronger and more confident. Ralph's a cappella recording of "O Death" on the soundtrack album of the film *O Brother, Where Art Thou?* would win a 2001 Grammy award for best male country vocal.

Time would testify to the enduring quality of the Stanley Brothers' music, but in 1964 *Hymns of the Cross* was just another gospel album. The hyperbolically titled *The Remarkable Stanley Brothers Play and Sing Bluegrass Sounds for You*, recorded on July 16 and 17, was another workmanlike secular album. The brothers were struggling to stay afloat in a diminishing market. The sizeable segment of the United States audience that had embraced country music now watched performers such as Johnny Cash, Buck Owens, and Porter Wagoner on television rather than listening to old-time sounds. Country became "countrypolitan."

Though Carter and Ralph found themselves confined to a niche market, the power of television endowed two of their contemporaries, Lester Flatt and Earl Scruggs, with genuine celebrity. Because of their regional radio and television shows, Virginia neighbors Jim and Jesse had celebrity status in Georgia and Florida. Their sponsor, Martha White Mills, continued to sponsor a segment of the *Grand Ole Opry*. The McReynolds brothers appeared as guest hosts, paving the way for the sweet-voiced duo to join the *Opry* cast on March 2, 1964. They moved to Gallatin, Tennessee, to be close to their new base of operations. The Stanley Brothers had relocated from Dickenson County as well, but to rural Florida rather than to Nashville. Had they missed the opportunity to move to the center of a growing industry?

Flatt and Scruggs survived the rock and roll era by playing the role of hillbilly musicians on television and covering rock songs on record. Jim and Jesse modernized their sound by adding electric guitars and drums. In November 1965 they released *Berry Pickin' in the Country*—an album composed entirely of their versions of songs by rock songwriter Chuck Berry. Developments such as these signaled what some thought might be the last days of bluegrass.

In the King studio, Carter and Ralph made an effort to adapt their style, recording "Finger Poppin' Time," but as musicians who were born into the tradition of string-band music and cut their professional teeth on the sound of Bill Monroe, their options were limited. On *Hymns of the Cross*, session musician Earl Taylor added quavering vibrato harmonica to the sacred number "The Robe He Wore," yet this was done to duplicate another recording rather than try something new. An anonymous drummer played on several tracks of *Bluegrass Sounds*, yet stayed in the background by using brushes. He picked up drumsticks only to lay down a martial tempo on "How Bad I Do Feel"—an old folk song. Recorded on July 16, 1964, "How Bad I Do Feel" required twenty-one takes—a record for musicians who prided themselves on being efficient in the studio. "We spent eight hours one time at a session because they wouldn't give it up," engineer Ron Lenhoff recalled.[15] "It was just a bad tune right from the very start. They just wouldn't let go of it. That was one of the first things they did. That just put everybody in a bad mood."

A series of black-and-white photographs from the session provides a glimpse of the Stanley Brother at work in the recording studio.[16] Ralph appears focused, while Carter looks bone-tired and overweight—a pack of cigarettes bulging his shirt pocket. Color photographs taken outdoors for the album's cover are equally unflattering. Carter appears pale, unsmiling, and distracted.[17] Once careful about his appearance, he had tucked the sunglasses he had been wearing in his shirt pocket and stares heavy-lidded into the distance, looking like a fragile version of actor Robert Mitchum. George Shuffler is included in the photo, but was cropped out when the image appeared on the cover of *Bluegrass Songs*.

The Stanley Brothers would go more than a year before recording again for King; yet the period is well documented, thanks to the three additional John's Gospel/Country Quartet recordings for Ray Davis. The brothers recorded their fourth and final project for Davis in November 1964. There is some question whether the third and fourth albums were recorded separately or together. The fourth sounds more like a full band than the third, with Red Stanley (no relation) on fiddle and Baltimore-area musician Barry Glickman on bass.[18] Fred Bartenstein notes another difference: "If George Shuffler is present, he is not playing guitar and only singing quiet baritone."

After an absence from the festival calendar, the Stanley Brothers were invited back to the Newport Folk Festival in summer 1964 and played a return engagement at the University of Chicago Folk Festival in January 1965. The brothers brought Red Stanley and a 17-year-old guitarist to Chicago—a significant drop in the experience level of their sidemen since the 1961 Chicago appearance with Vernon Derrick on fiddle and Curley Lambert on mandolin. The new guitarist, Larry Sparks, was a promising instrumentalist and singer who would mature into the International Bluegrass Music Association's male vocalist of the year in 2004 and 2005; but in 1965 the most accomplished guitar player on stage was Chicago's Old Town School of Folk Music faculty member and future director Ray Tate, who sat in on bass to complete the quintet.

The difference in the Stanley Brothers' energy level between 1961 and 1965 was pronounced. Gone was the full-throated folk duo of the late

1950s and early 1960s. Carter sounded weary and depleted, though Ralph compensated with crisp vocals and crackling banjo. Despite Carter's audible decline and sometimes inaudible reading of the lyrics, he had written a clever new song, "Sharecropper's Son," that he introduced at the festival. "Now I'd like to do one that I wrote about two weeks ago," he told the audience. "This is not a folk song, I guess. . . . It might be a folk song. . . . It's not an old song; I'll put it that way."[19] Despite the uncertain introduction—strained by Carter's attempts to relate all the material to a folk audience—the song showed a considerable amount of craft in four verses and a two-line chorus: "Daylight 'til dark and the work's never done / The Lord'll have mercy on a sharecropper's son."

There was a more personal contrast between the Chicago performances in 1961 and 1965. At the earlier appearance, Carter had been a genial emcee who was respectful of the band members. He asked Ralph if he would satisfy a festival organizer's request for the banjo instrumental "Big Tilda," and responded to the ovation Ralph received by saying that his brother would perform an additional number later in the set. Carter's only barb was a good-natured jibe directed at Curley Lambert after Lambert flubbed the notes of the mandolin break to "Rabbit in a Log." In mid-song Carter told Curley: "play it again—and play it right. . . ."

By 1965, the onstage relationship between the brothers showed signs of strain. After "Sharecropper's Son," Carter announced that it "comes time now to punish everybody"—a sarcastic way of saying he was going to ask Ralph to play a song. His remark drifted into a complaint that Ralph would change musical keys on his featured songs every night. "According to how I feel," Ralph explained into a microphone. The musical explanation was that Ralph would change the key of a song to fit the most comfortable pitch for his (or Carter's) voice on a particular night. Maintaining his composure, Ralph introduced "Man of Constant Sorrow" as a song for which he received a lot of requests and had been playing for fifteen or twenty years—to which Carter felt bound to add, "At least." Ralph sounded as if he was asserting not only his standing in the band but his popularity as well. His performance drew sustained applause.

Unlike in 1961, when Carter acknowledged Ralph's important role in the band, in 1965 Carter followed "Man of Constant Sorrow" with a wandering introduction to the song he was about to perform—the Carter Family's "Single Girl, Married Girl." By referring to the personal connection he felt to his folk-icon neighbors in southwestern Virginia, Carter was playing to the audience; yet if one song and performance

8

encapsulated the lethargic depression into which Carter had fallen, it was "Single Girl." He sang it as a spiritless lament rather than as the brisk, pre-feminist recording Sara Carter had popularized in 1927. The instrumental breaks meandered as much as Carter's rendition of the verses.

Most at the University of Chicago Folk Festival were unaware of any underlying drama. It was four years since the band had appeared at the festival, and many audience members were new; they followed the lead of the older members of the Chicago folk crowd, who held the Stanley Brothers in high esteem approaching cult status. For longtime fans who looked closer, a problem was apparent.

Editor and folklorist Judith McCulloh recalled that after the Stanley Brothers' shows in 1965, people crowded around "like groupies," waiting for a chance to have a word with the musicians. She thought that the brothers were fine on stage, but was disturbed by behavior that she and others observed at a party after one of the performances. "Everyone there was concerned about Carter because of his drinking," she said.[20]

It is difficult to imagine the effect that Carter's drinking had on Ralph over the years. Privately Carter disparaged the value to the band of the younger brother's banjo playing, nicknamed Ralph "Little Jesus" in response to Ralph's attempts to moderate his drinking, and now embarrassed him in public. This behavior had been going on for a while. Bill Malone recalled that at one of the Texas appearances, "Ralph made a little flub on his banjo, and Carter criticized him. Ralph wryly responded with 'Why don't you play it then?' knowing full well that Carter could not play the passage."[21] Malone thought the interchange was more cute than critical, but by 1965, the criticism was more pointed.

As bluegrass historian Bob Artis wrote in 1975, "By the middle of the 1960s, Carter was clearly not a well man. It was a sad thing to see the Stanley Brothers . . . and saddest for those who loved their music the most."[22] By this measure—and because Carter's condition threatened his livelihood—Ralph must have been the saddest of all.

These poignant and traumatic years for the Stanley Brothers came at a time when the economic future of bluegrass was about to begin a slow recovery. The key contributor to the recovery would be a festival movement modeled after the multi-day folk festivals such as those held at Newport and the University of Chicago.

In early 1965 promoter and agent Carlton Haney planted the seed for the movement in a dressing room of the *Grand Ole Opry*, where he pitched an idea he had for a festival to Bill Monroe.[23] Haney had noted the success of two daylong outdoor festivals, both called Bluegrass Day, in 1960 and 1961. The first was held on Sunday, August 14, 1960, at Watermelon Park in Berryville, Virginia. Washington, D.C., media personality and musician Don Owens and his partner John U. Miller produced the first Bluegrass Day. Presenting a half dozen of the most popular acts, the show drew an estimated 3,000 people.[24]

The second Bluegrass Day was the concert Bill Clifton promoted on July 4, 1961, at Oak Leaf Park in Luray, Virginia. Haney wanted to go a step further. He envisioned an entire weekend of bluegrass music, culminating on Sunday with Monroe at the center of "The Bluegrass Story." In Haney's vision, musicians who had played with Monroe's Blue Grass Boys and now had groups of their own—as so many of them had—would join Monroe on stage in performances that would pay tribute to his pioneering the music.

Monroe had come a long way toward overcoming his resentment toward "imitators" as his new northern supporters helped him realize that many people acknowledged him as the originator. Central to Monroe's increasing self-awareness of his role in what had become a genre of music was his business relationship and eventual friendship with Ralph Rinzler, the son of a New Jersey doctor, who had graduated from Swarthmore College in 1956 and become an active participant in the folk revival.

If Rinzler built the bridge, Carter helped put the cornerstone in place. His involvement came out of necessity. Accompanied by Mike Seeger, Rinzler traveled to Sunset Park to try to introduce himself to Monroe and interview him for the folk music magazine *Sing Out!* In March 1962 the magazine had published an article on Earl Scruggs that pronounced Scruggs "the undisputed master of Bluegrass music."[25] Rinzler wanted to set the record straight on the origin of the style.

"Ralph Rinzler wanted very much to help Bill Monroe get some recognition for his role in bluegrass because he didn't have that recognition in 1960–61," Seeger recalled.[26] The immediate problem was that Monroe refused to talk to Rinzler and Seeger because he was upset about Seeger's having sent a tape to Scruggs's wife Louise of the music from the second Bluegrass Day that included Monroe and Carter's remarks on the absence of Flatt and Scruggs.

Seeger came up with the solution. "I knew Ralph and Carter were [performing] at the New River Ranch," Seeger recalled. "I had the idea to ask Carter to talk to Bill to get him to talk to us. So we went down during Bill's show [at Sunset Park] to get Carter and Ralph to come up." Quick to grasp the dynamics of the situation and wanting to do anything he could to help his mentor, Carter agreed.

When I interviewed him in 2006, Seeger remained appreciative of Carter's cooperation and diplomacy. "Carter went way out of his way after doing a whole day's program to come up and talk to Bill and help both me and Ralph and help Bill understand what was going on," Seeger recalled. ". . . I think Carter understood what was going on, what we were trying to do, and he trusted us." According to Monroe's biographer, Richard D. Smith, "Monroe didn't agree to anything right away. But on a warm June night in an empty country music park some very thick ice had been broken."[27]

In August 1962 Rinzler was able to conduct his interview with Monroe in Galax, Virginia; and his article, "Bill Monroe—the Daddy of Bluegrass," appeared in the February-March 1963 issue of *Sing Out!* The article's appearance in a folk music magazine showed the split that had developed between bluegrass and country music. In January 1963, at a party in the New York home of Oscar Brand, the alliance was formalized: Rinzler became Monroe's manager.[28]

Rinzler introduced Carlton Haney to the Newport Folk Festival, where Haney was impressed by the combination of main-stage shows and small workshop programs.[29] Coupled with Haney's interest in the all-day bluegrass events in Berryville in 1960 and Luray in 1961, Newport was the inspiration for what became a milestone in the history of bluegrass, often identified by a single word: Fincastle.

In Haney's view, the time had come for a new way to market the music.[30] He arrived at this conclusion from observations he made while booking the duo of Don Reno and Red Smiley into movie theaters. Often they performed to perhaps fifteen or twenty people a night. The familiar format called for the musicians to follow the movie, so the size of the audience was determined by the popularity of the film as well as that of the musicians. In Haney's opinion, the format had become a commercial dead end because of the economic challenge to movies by a relatively new medium. "Television was killing theaters," Haney said.[31]

For the venue of the first multi-day festival in the history of bluegrass, Haney settled on "a horse farm north of Roanoke"—Cantrell's Horse Farm in Fincastle, Virginia. For the dates, he chose Labor Day weekend. For the performers, he hired a half dozen bands and a number of individual performers. He recalled paying Bill Monroe $400 and the Stanley Brothers $250. He argued with the frugal Monroe over a 50-cent difference ($3.50

versus $3) in the price of motel rooms; Monroe thought he could get the lower rate.[32] Admission for the three days was $6, or $2.50 per day. Following in the footsteps of Newport, Haney advertised a workshop and talent contest in addition to the stage shows.

He chose the horse farm because it was close to the center of his business rather than accessible to a potential audience. This proved to be a mistake. Fincastle was more than 230 miles from Washington, D.C., and remote from the folk music capitals of Philadelphia, New York, and Boston. Only 500 or so bluegrass pilgrims made the trip. What they got for their money was the opportunity to sit for three days in a pasture, use outhouses, and soak in the performances that took place on a rickety flat-roofed stage. Film of the festival taken by a camera crew from WDBJ television in Roanoke shows seven or eight microphone bristling in front of the performers.[33] Wearing a madras jacket, Carlton Haney darts to and from the stage as he makes introductions and announcements.[34]

What the pilgrims also received for the price of admission was, from the perspective of the history of the genre, priceless: many of the original performers of bluegrass assembled in one place—Flatt and Scruggs being the notable exception. On the program with Bill Monroe and the Blue Grass Boys and the Stanley Brothers and the Clinch Mountain Boys were Don Reno and the Tennessee Cutups, Red Smiley and the Bluegrass Cutups, Jimmy Martin and the Sunny Mountain Boys, former Monroe fiddler Benny Martin, former guitarists and lead vocalists Clyde Moody, Mac Wiseman, and Jim Eanes, former banjo player Larry Richardson, and special guest Doc Watson. Though advertised, the Osborne Brothers were unable to perform.

Perhaps because of the small audience, the feeling of kinship at Fincastle was palpable. Richard Smith writes, "There was a sense of solidarity . . . a shared identity and commitment, the wonderful feeling of being able to look around and think: Here are all these people who love this music just like me."[35]

One of the pilgrims was photographer Phil Zimmerman. He described his sense of community as he and a friend arrived at the festival:

It was a long, straight shot down I-81 to the Route 220/Fincastle exit. . . . We took the . . . exit and began looking for Carlton Haney's First Annual Roanoke Bluegrass Festival. We found the turn-off and followed the dusty tire tracks across a pasture toward the tree line in the distance. Even before we reached the makeshift parking lot, we heard the thump of a stand-up bass wafting across the field on the hot late-summer breeze. Moments later we were navigating between small groups of musicians picking away. Back at school there were barely enough players to scrape together one band, but there we were, surrounded by bluegrass![36]

According to Fred Bartenstein, musicians and fans thought Fincastle would be "the Irish wake of bluegrass music." Instead, it came to be recognized as a moment of reawakening and—in Haney's subsequent festival presentations of "The Bluegrass Story"—the beginning of a movement that would provide bluegrass with a desperately needed new marketing format.

Bartenstein's memory of the Stanley Brothers and the historic multi-day festival remains clear:

I was 14 at the time, but I remember George Shuffler's dark glasses, gum chewing, and beautiful guitar leads on a beat-up sunburst Gibson instrument. I remember Carter wandering off to the rail at the side of the stage, transfixed by the mountain scenery and unready to sing the next verse of the song at the end of an instrumental break. Mainly, I remember how excited I was to see my heroes live and in person after so many times hearing them on the radio and on record.[37]

"The Stanley Brothers were very cool," recalled Phil Zimmerman. "They wore dark suits and ties, dark sunglasses, and loafers with white socks."[38] One of his photographs captures Carter and Ralph looking like rustic versions of the Blues Brothers.

The performers were aware that the focus of the festival was Bill Monroe. While introducing the hymn "Mansions for Me" during one of the band's festival sets, Carter paid a heartfelt tribute to Monroe, who was backstage:

That's one of the great Bill Monroe tunes. And I don't know if his name's been mentioned here today or not, but . . . [laughter] . . . No, I'm serious. I mean that. It should be . . . very often . . . a lot of places that it isn't. I'm always happy to mention it anywhere. And I think as far as I'm concerned, the way Carlton said it a while ago when he opened the show, that he's the pappy of the bluegrass, and as far as I'm concerned, he's the pappy of the country music. And I think

there's millions now instead of thousands that agree with me all over
the country. I believe that. I really do.[39]

The audience responded with applause.

On the concluding Sunday of the festival, Carlton Haney stage-man-
aged the centerpiece "Story of Bluegrass" with help from Ralph Rinzler,
who wrote the script and served as offstage consultant. Upon revisiting
the tapes, Fred Bartenstein wrote that "Carlton is negotiating some tricky
musical politics in his first Monroe-centric explication of the story of
bluegrass."[40]

The format of the two-hour narrative (consisting of songs and their
introductions plus periods of repartee among the musicians) called for
identifying various sounds that came into the genre as a way of bringing on stage the musicians who had contributed to the genre's evolution.
Musically speaking, some sounds were a reach, such as Haney crediting
Clyde Moody with a new picking style Haney called "flogging the guitar."
Monroe needed to remain at the center of the narrative, but the revital-
ization of his career had begun only recently; sizeable musical egos had to
be appeased because several of the performers were more popular than
Monroe.

In a singular move, making clear that the Stanley Brothers had a successful band before meeting Bill Monroe, Haney gave Carter and Ralph
their own two-song set during the narrative. The brothers chose to sing
their first hit, "Little Glass of Wine," and one of Carter's most enduring
originals, "The White Dove." Neither song was connected to Monroe. On
tape, Haney can be heard urging Monroe and his bass-playing son James
off stage before the Stanley Brothers came on, but the elder Monroe said
he would stay put.

While the situation was awkward for Haney, who told Monroe that he
could take the Stanley segment "out of the tape" later, Carter accommo-
dated Monroe's presence with characteristic ease. After introducing the
band, he said that he would not introduce the person on stage who wasn't
doing anything. With the timing of a comedian, he said that he didn't
know the man's name and paused before saying that it was Bill Monroe,
of course. In so doing, he simultaneously gave Monroe the needle and
provoked general laughter in which Monroe could join.

At the conclusion of the narrative, Haney brought the Stanley Brothers
back on stage—Carter as a former Blue Grass Boy and Ralph for his contribution to the bluegrass sound on banjo. While Monroe and Carter's

duets on "Cabin of Love" and "Sugar Coated Love" were serviceable, Ralph's two banjo numbers—"Clinch Mountain Backstep" and "Big Tilda"—were masterful. Having praised Carter for his lead singing and guitar work, both of which had diminished, Monroe announced that Ralph got the best sound out of the banjo of anyone he had heard. Given the opportunity by Haney, Carter declined to tell any stories on Monroe, treating his former boss with careful respect.

Though no longer in good voice, Carter sounded as if he were in good humor throughout the weekend. Phil Zimmerman recalled that, during the band's show on Saturday night, hundreds of moths were attracted to the bare lightbulbs and small floodlights that lit the stage. "At one point, Carter opened his mouth to sing and inhaled one of the moths," Zimmerman said. "He gagged and coughed it out, exclaiming, 'Them chocolate bugs is alright, but them vanillers, I cain't hardly stand them!'"[41]

Another attempt at humor was less successful. At a point in the show when Carter needed to buy time for Ralph to retune his banjo, he decided to tell a joke that he had heard from George Shuffler that morning. One can hear in his hesitation that he had doubts even as he began. The setup was a freedom march in Alabama on which a "little colored boy" asked Dr. Martin Luther King Jr. how he could get his picture in the paper. King told the boy that he would need to do something extraordinary. As an example, he directed the boy's attention to people in "Arabia and the Buddhist countries" who "put their clothes on, soak 'em with gasoline, set theirselves [sic] afire and burn up." Puzzled, the boy responded: "These freedom marches, I'm all for 'em . . . these sit-ins, I'll sit just as long as you pay me . . . but that cookout business, I ain't foolin' with that a-tall."[42]

Rooted as it was in bleak news of the mid-1960s, the "civil rights joke"[43] was a reminder that the culture of bluegrass was almost exclusively white—and remains so. Upon meeting the one person of color attending Ralph Stanley's annual Memorial Day festival in 2002, Jimmy Martin exclaimed, "If I could have gotten you people to buy my records, I'd have sold another million."[44]

From Fincastle the Stanley Brothers drove northwest to Cincinnati, where they recorded half of their final album for King on September 8. Returning to the studio on September 20, they completed the project. For the second time in their King career, they recorded as a trio, with George Shuffler overdubbing the bass.

Reflecting the influence of the war in Vietnam, the album included two patriotic songs: "Pray for the Boys," which had been recorded by Flatt and

Scruggs during the Korean War, and "Searching for a Soldier's Grave," written and recorded in the early 1940s.[45] After the sessions, Carter expressed satisfaction with the results: "I felt like the last time we was there, we got the best sound we've ever got at King."[46] But when the album was released in 1966, it sported a gaudy cover at odds with its contents. Its title was *The Greatest Country & Western Show on Earth by the One and Only Stanley Brothers . . . Hearing Is Believing.*

Tellingly in terms of Carter's physical and emotional condition, it was Ralph who corrected the marketing mistake. "I got Syd Nathan to see into this," he recalled, ". . . a gospel album and he calls us 'the greatest country and western show on earth,' and I told him that would never do and he changed the cover. . . . He agreed with me real quick on that. He probably wasn't paying attention to the songs."[47] The new cover showed a church interior with stained-glass windows and bore the title *A Collection of Original Gospel & Sacred Songs.* Reviewing the album in August 1966 for the new magazine *Bluegrass Unlimited,* Dick Spottswood called it "the best from the Stanleys in years."[48]

Carter and Ralph closed out 1965 in December with sessions for Wayne Raney's Rimrock label that completed what would be released as two gospel albums: *An Empty Mansion* and *A Beautiful Life* and. In the notes to the first, Ralph described the circumstances of the recordings:

I don't remember the exact date, but we met a very dear friend by the name of Wayne Raney. We had heard and admired him since we were all very young, but when he started spinning the country records on WCKY in Cincinnati, Ohio, we had the privilege of meeting him. We began to visit him in his home each time we were in that part of the country. It was on one of these visits that he told us we were his favorites when it came to singing hymns, and asked if we would record some hymns that he could someday release on this album. This we did . . .[49]

Perhaps mindful of copyright, the musicians kept to public domain material taken, for the most part, from books of hymns. Old-time music historian Ivan M. Tribe observed of *A Beautiful Life*: "Most [of the songs] . . . likely date from the late 19th and early 20th century, and, while virtually all can be found in the hymn books, some are seldom performed in bluegrass arrangements." He singled out J. B. F. Wright's "Precious Memories" and A. P. Bland and Mrs. A. S. Bridgewater's "How Beautiful

Heaven Must Be" as examples.[50] The pace of several performances suggests that the singers might have been reading from the hymnals as they
sang the material.

Though the bottom line was business, the results were as if the en-
trepreneurs behind the Wango and Rimrock labels had joined forces to
lift the Stanley Brothers above the inconsistent material they were being given to record by King. Both Ray Davis and Wayne Raney were
musicians, though Davis gave up performing "because I couldn't sell records."[51] Perhaps they had a musician's understanding of what it was that
the Carter and Ralph did best at a point in their careers when the older
brother's voice was failing.

On occasions when Carter's voice sounded something like its old self,
several of these "quickie" recordings are among the brothers' best. Wayne
Raney's harmonica contributes to several Rimrock recordings, notably
"Where the Soul Never Dies."[52] Particularly moving on the spare-sound-
ing third Wango album is a slow duet between the brothers on the hymn
"Lord, I'm Coming Home."

18. WHAT THE DOCTOR SAID

———◆◆✕◆●———

Bruce William Mongle did not fit the mold of how a doctor should look or act. When he was five, his mother taught him to play clawhammer banjo; when he was older he rode bucking broncos. He chewed tobacco and spat juice wherever he could while visiting patients in the Bristol Memorial Hospital. "Whenever there was an ashtray and wastebasket during rounds, he would spit into it," recalled his nephew Joe Mongle.[1] "You always could tell his car because there would be tobacco juice on the driver's side." The doctor's daughter, Mary Bruce Mazza, said of her father, "If you had been in a room with a hundred people and been asked who the general surgeon was, you would have picked the janitor before you picked him."[2]

His own father had died when Mongle was eighteen, but he was able to graduate from Emory and Henry College—a reputable Methodist-affiliated school in Emory, Virginia, twenty miles north of Bristol. He earned his medical degree from the Medical College of Virginia in Richmond. After a residency in surgery at Carraway Methodist College in Birmingham, Alabama, he rose to captain in the army, serving as examining physician for the Selective Service before returning home to Bristol to establish a practice in general surgery and gynecology. In 1943, the former country boy bought two hundred acres of sprawling farmland near Blountville, Tennessee, and became something of a country squire—in the words of the local paper at the time of his death, "one of the most respected and influential citizens the county seat has ever known."[3]

Even as Doc Mongle maintained his practice and raised his daughter and son (his wife Mary Pauline died in 1955 when Mary Bruce was 10), he found time to enter banjo and fiddle contests and play in bands. He raised coonhounds and ran fox hunts. He owned not only a Cadillac but one of the first horse trailers in Bristol—an acquisition that made news when it broke loose; yet in the doctors' parking spaces at the hospital, his vehicle of choice might be his pickup truck.

With many similar interests—coon hunting, horses, clawhammer banjo, and country music—it was not surprising that Doc Mongle became more than a physician to Carter and Ralph Stanley, especially to the older brother. "He and Carter were best of buddies," recalled Joe. When the time came that the urgings and pleadings of his mother, wife, and brother persuaded Carter to see a doctor about his drinking, it was natural that he would take his problem to Doc Mongle.

No one in the Mongle family remembers when Doc became the Stanley Brothers' physician. For patient privacy reasons, his appointment books and medical records were destroyed after he died. The lack of records leaves uncertain how often he counseled Carter, yet it appears to have been on a number of occasions. In his interview with Terry Gross, Ralph recalled:

> We got a doctor up in Bristol, Tennessee, that we went to all the time, and he liked us. He played the banjo a little bit. And when we moved down in Florida, the doctor came down there one Christmas on vacation, and he had his doctor instruments with him. [In his autobiography, Ralph wrote "Carter wasn't feeling well . . ."][4] And he took Carter in his house and examined him, and he told Carter, he said, "If you don't quit what you're doing . . . you won't last another year." And that was the twenty-sixth of December [1965], and he passed away the next year on the first of December.[5]

The advice that Doc gave to his patient seems to have been common knowledge among Bristol musicians. When I interviewed former *Farm and Fun Time* performer Joe Morrell in December 2004 in his music store on State Street, he was emphatic on the point. "I knew the man who told Carter he had to quit [drinking] or it would kill him," Morrell said. "That was Doc Mongle. He didn't quit, and it killed him." A member of the Stanley family summarized the opinion of Carter's generation: "Carter drank himself to death."

In the United States, the concept of alcoholism as a disease dates back as far as 1784.[6] Yet even after the founding of Alcoholics Anonymous in 1935, many people—including some physicians—considered chronic use of alcohol to be the result of personal weakness. In 1960 Dr. Elvin Jellinek of the Yale Center of Alcohol Studies further defined alcoholism in his book, *The Disease Concept of Alcoholism*. He wrote that alcoholics were individuals with a tolerance for liquor who experienced withdrawal symptoms and either loss of control or inability to abstain from alcohol.[7] Such individuals could not drink in moderation; and with continued drinking, the disease was progressive and life-threatening. According to Jellinek, some features of the disease, such as inability to abstain and loss of control, were shaped by cultural factors.

In the mountains of far southwestern Virginia, cultural factors acting on Carter and Ralph as they grew from boys to young men were considerable. Appalachia's combination of isolation, independence, and poverty created a society in which the manufacture of moonshine liquor was commonplace. Many in the population met personal and local demand by distilling their own "mountain dew."

If Carter had not tasted moonshine earlier, he would have when he and Carl Hammons became best friends in high school, because Hammons' father Ballard ran a still. According to medical studies, moonshine is much more of a health hazard than commercially distilled liquor. Both contain ethanol—the grain-derivative type of alcohol found in alcoholic beverages. The consumption of ethanol is not intrinsically destructive to the body, but its unregulated consumption with moonshine is toxic. In a study of the effects of moonshine published in 1961, a group of researchers explained how the paraphernalia used in making 'shine jeopardized a drinker's health:

> *Much of this alcohol is fermented by small producers in ground stills using barrels, soldered pipes and employing automobile radiators and multiple copper tube units sealed with solder as condensers. As a result of the use of this equipment, there is a considerable quantity of lead in the distillate.*
>
> *The product of such a distillation process, euphemistically termed whiskey or "white lightning", is actually a lethal compound in which the ethanol present merely serves as a vehicle for the poisonous lead ions contained in the distillate.*[8]

Half a century later, the problem continues in the region. Leading a recent research study into alcoholism associated with moonshine was Dr. Christopher Holstege, director of the Division of Medical Toxicology at the University of Virginia Health System. Dr. Holstege described two differences between moonshine and commercial liquor:

> *Whether the person with alcoholism drinks moonshine or liquor from the store, the ethanol will cause the same disease pattern and clinical effects in that alcoholic. Moonshine is different from commercial liquor in that the content of ethanol drunk is not known. Our studies of moonshine showed concentrations ranging from 10– 66% ethanol. The other unique characteristic of moonshine is the risk of contaminants, with lead being the most commonly described contaminant.[9]*

The news release announcing the study concluded, "This lead content, Holstege suggests, can lead to toxic levels in those who abuse moonshine."[10]

High ethanol content and presence of contaminants were characteristics of the liquor that Carter began to drink as a teenager in the late 1930s and early 1940s. In the early 1950s Carter consumed more of the same in advance of the Stanley Brothers' regular Saturday night performances in Grundy, Virginia. As many who knew him observed, Carter continued to drink heavily throughout his adult life. According to those closest to him, he tried to quit several times and managed to do so for three or four months before a friend or fan would put a drink in his hand. "Everybody wanted to drink with Carter," Ralph recalled.[11] "After the show, before the show, anytime. And that was hard for him to turn down. He just had a weakness, you know, and he just got too far gone."

The drinking had an effect on his children. Doris Stanley Bradley recalled: "I was . . . the child who accompanied him on concert tours as often as school allowed during his last year on earth. He needed and wanted someone to look after him as he became sicker and I considered it my duty and my honor to do that."[12] Carter's second son William, known as Bill or Billy, accompanied the group on the road in the summer of 1966. "It was tough," Bill recalled.[13] "There were no buses. We traveled in cars. After I got through with that, I didn't want any part of the bluegrass music business."

Though twenty-one months apart in age, Bill and his older brother, Carter Lee, both graduated in May 1966 from Suwannee High School in Live Oak. Bill was a very good student and had skipped a grade. Their

schoolmate Garth Nobles, who later became mayor of Live Oak, recalled that "Billy and Carter were both very popular in school. . . . They
were very personable and nice-looking young men."[14] Both were active in
school sports and activities. Carter Lee played basketball in the eleventh
grade and ran track as a senior. Bill played basketball as a junior. Carter
Lee belonged to the science, pep, and thespian clubs. Bill belonged to the
science club and "worked in the school office as part of a work/study program to make money."[15] As seniors, Carter Lee was voted best dancer and
Bill was voted best dressed. Their graduation brought their father home
from the road. Still recovering from a big party the night before, Carter
Lee drove to the airport in Jacksonville. It was his first trip to the city.
Not finding his father at the Eastern Airlines ticket counter, "I waited and
waited," Carter Lee recalled.[16] "The woman at the counter said 'Can I help
you?' I said I was waiting for my father. She asked what his name was
and had him paged." Five minutes later, Carter strode down the aisle of
the terminal, wearing an overcoat, a brown hound's tooth hat "like Bear
Bryant used to wear," and carrying a briefcase. On or off stage, Carter
Stanley cut a figure that caught people's attention. In the briefcase, he had
two bottles of Johnny Walker Red scotch for his sons. As a graduation
present, he bought them a 1962 Ford Falcon Futura.

On the road, Carter's alcohol consumption required a combination of
understanding and maintenance from those working with him. Today we
might call it enabling, but in the mid-1960s, keeping alcoholic members
functional was a fact of life in more bands than the Stanley Brothers. The
band member who attended most to Carter's needs was the newest member of the Clinch Mountain Boys: lanky, loquacious Melvin Goins from
West Virginia. Melvin joined the band on January 18, 1966. Since bookings still were difficult to obtain, it helped that this fast-talking musician
could double as an agent for the group.

Melvin had known the Stanley Brothers for years, working with
them in shows that packaged bluegrass bands and in music parks. He
met Carter and Ralph during their WCYB days when the band drove
a green 1950 Packard with the bass fiddle strapped to the top.[17] Melvin
and his older brother Ray performed as the Goins Brothers with fiddle
player Joe Meadows on WHIS in Bluefield, West Virginia, from August
to November 1953. As did most bluegrass groups, the Goins Brothers
and Stanley Brothers often crossed paths. When Melvin and Ray joined
cousins Curley Ray and Ezra Kline in a popular West Virginia band, the
Lonesome Pine Fiddlers, Meadows found work with the Stanley Brothers.

The Lonesome Pine Fiddlers hosted a radio show in Pikeville, Kentucky, from 11:30 to noon six days a week. When the Stanley Brothers' itinerary brought them near Pikeville, they would stop by the station to make an appearance.

By the time Melvin became a Clinch Mountain Boy, preparations for a package tour of Europe in March 1966 were under way. "I joined them a week too late for the trip," he recalled. "They already had gotten their passports" and immunizations. Hired to play bass on the tour was the entertaining but unreliable Chick Stripling. On fiddle was quiet newcomer Don Miller, who wore a moustache that gave him a resemblance to the 1950s television detective Boston Blackie. George Shuffler played lead guitar.

It did not take Melvin long to realize that Carter was in fragile condition for a tour that involved international travel. He barely was able to keep to the group's schedule in the United States. "He wasn't eating," Melvin recalled. "You know he was drinking. He wouldn't do some of the things he needed to do. I would try to get him to eat. When a man drinks, he doesn't eat. He sometimes wouldn't eat until late of a night."

Melvin believed that Carter's drinking did not affect him when he was on stage. "Carter was a pro," he said. On February 24, 1966, Carter's stage presence held up under the scrutiny of television cameras during the Stanley Brothers' appearance with 1930s country star Cousin Emmy on Pete Seeger's regional program *Rainbow Quest*. Recorded live in the studios of the new ultra-high-frequency television station WNJU in Newark, New Jersey, the show's format showcased Seeger on vocals and banjo as he welcomed guest artists from various genres of music, including folk, country, and blues. Over the course of thirty-eight programs broadcast in 1965 and 1966, guests ranged from country performer Johnny Cash to the folk duo of Richard and Mimi Farina. Mimi was Joan Baez's sister.

In deference to Ralph Stanley and Cousin Emmy, who both were skilled banjo players, Seeger played only the show's theme song on his customary banjo, switching to twelve-string guitar for most other numbers. A videotape of the Stanley Brothers' performance provides one of the few video documents of the brothers working together. When Carter and Ralph stepped forward to sing "It Takes a Worried Man," their vocals were in complete sync. A genial Carter handled the emcee chores, while Ralph appeared less comfortable on the sparse set, whose design fell between that of a country kitchen and pickin' porch. Vaudeville veteran Chick Stripling seemed the most at home of the quintet, performing a shortened version of his tap-dancing routine. George Shuffler beamed and picked clean guitar breaks, while Don Miller stepped out of the background to take his turn on fiddle. The band's low-key style was in marked contrast to the high-energy antics of Cousin Emmy, who not only played "Turkey in the Straw" by puckering her lips and tapping her cheeks, but inflated a rubber glove to the size of a cow's udder to play "You Are My Sunshine" with the escaping air. Carter closed the Stanley Brothers' featured numbers with a relaxed version of "Single Girl." Heavy-lidded and moving slowly, he looked tired.

The Stanley Brothers had traveled to New York City by car, stopping to fix a flat tire on their instrument trailer. The full touring company previewed and rehearsed with appearances in New York and Boston on Friday and Saturday, February 25 and 26. The New York concert for the Friends of Old Time Music took place at the Fashion Institute of Technology. A well-meaning listener told Roscoe Holcomb that his music hit "too close to home." Not a professional musician, Holcomb took offense. "I was singing it for myself, buddy, not for you," he replied.[18]

In Boston, the Stanley Brothers opened the Saturday night concert of the First Boston Folk Festival (dubbed Winterfest) at the War Memorial Auditorium in downtown Boston. According to the *Broadside of Boston*, the group "started off the evening with a brilliant 'Worried Man' and followed it up with a bit of good-humored buck-and-wing by Chip[*sic*] Stripling, the bass player. If it was unorthodox, it was entertaining and the full house enjoyed it. They ended their set with a good performance of the old standard, 'Rank Strangers.'"[19] The next stop would be Germany.

Organized by promoters Horst Lippmann and Fritz Rau, who began to bring package tours of U.S. artists to Europe with the American Folk & Blues Festival tours in 1962, the American Folk & Country Music Festival began its tour in Baden-Baden on March 1, 1966.[20] For the musicians, the early signs were promising. The first venue was a television studio, and accommodations were excellent. "The hotel at Baden-Baden was the nicest place many of us had even seen," recalled John Cohen of the New Lost City Ramblers,[21] "but once we left there it was bus travel and tight hotel rooms for the next 20 days." After three days of taping on the television station's set, designed like a European's idea of an American country store, the musicians performed every night through March 20—twice with afternoon shows as well as evening. Eleven of the fifteen concert venues were in German cities such as Hamburg, Frankfurt, and Munich; the tour also went to London, Stockholm, Copenhagen, and Basel, Switzerland.[22] There was some air travel, but most was by bus.

As with other intense experiences shared in close quarters, the tour produced both bonding and irritation. When asked what he remembered of the tour, George Shuffler answered tersely, "It was long."[23] Mike Seeger took advantage of the opportunity to get to know the Stanley Brothers. In the group photograph appearing on the cover of a boxed CD and book set issued in 2008, Seeger stood next to Carter. With his dark slicked-back hair, he looked as if he could be Carter's son. Ralph stood next to Roscoe Holcomb, who would become his gospel-singing partner on the tour, sometimes accompanied by Carter. In keeping with their supporting roles, George Shuffler and Don Miller stood behind the group. By the time the photo was taken, Chick Stripling had been sent home. The tap-dancing bass player had become "more obnoxious than the tour directors could tolerate," according to Tracy Schwarz of the New Lost City Ramblers.[24] George Shuffler summarized: "He got drunk and wouldn't sober up."[25] Schwarz replaced Stripling on bass.

On Friday, March 11, the ensemble arrived at London's Royal Albert Hall. Old friend Bill Clifton was in London, having moved to England in 1963. He and the Stanley Brothers had exchanged letters about touring England, but Clifton had been unable to find enough work to finance the trip. "They really wanted to come," Clifton recalled. "They were willing to do it down to the bone, but were barely able to eke out expenses in America."[26] Clifton paid a visit to Carter and Ralph at their hotel. What he saw was unsettling. "Carter was so depressed at the time that I was really worried about him," he said.[27] The performance was a qualified success. "The attendance was bigger than first expected," David Brassington wrote to the fan club newsletter, "but sad considering it was such a good show. . . . Carter is a real fine singer, and even a sore throat didn't trouble him until the end."

Some of the musicians recognized that Carter was in the advanced stages of alcoholism, but audiences would not have known. When the promoters taped an entire evening of music in Bremen on March 17, Carter handled emcee work on his own and split an introduction with Mike Seeger. Only those who had heard Carter earlier in his career would have noticed the considerable difference between the subdued man on stage at Bremen's Die Glocke concert house and the vibrant entertainer who had charmed audiences from the WCYB studios to the Ash Grove.

After opening the show with the crowd-pleasing "How Mountain Girls Can Love" and two band numbers, Carter and Ralph joined Roscoe Holcomb for an unusual rendition of the hymn "Village Churchyard." They performed the hymn as it would have been sung in the Old Regular Baptist churches of Appalachia—unaccompanied by instruments in an arrangement called lining out (in local vernacular, "say a line, sing a line").[28] In this tradition, the leader quickly chants the line to be sung, and the congregation follows at a slower pace, singing the actual melody. The sound is stately and archaic—the Appalachian version of Gregorian chant.

In Bremen, Holcomb lined out the words and the brothers joined in on the verses. Their voices rose and fell in mournful repetition. As it did after listening to other unfamiliar elements of the music, the audience applauded though it did not know what to make of what it was hearing. The styles and sounds of the country music tour were quite different from those of the blues tour. Promoter Fritz Rau recalled: "The German audience expected white blues music but that was neither the music of the Stanley Brothers nor of Cyp Landreneau or Cousin Emmy. Roscoe Holcomb even read his lyrics from a sheet of paper."[29]

Back home in Daisy, Kentucky, Holcomb made a living as a construction worker. John Cohen of the New Lost City Ramblers had encountered him in 1959 while collecting songs around Hazard, Kentucky.[30] "At the first song he sang for me, with his guitar tuned like a banjo and his intense, fine voice, I was deeply moved," recalled Cohen,[31] "for I knew this was what I had been searching for—something that went right to my inner being, speaking directly to me." Despite Cohen's enthusiasm for Holcomb, some of the musicians were not sure that an amateur belonged on the tour. To Shuffler, Holcomb was "just a little mountain man afraid of everything."[32] But once in Europe, Holcomb and Ralph formed a friendship that Mike Seeger believed might have influenced Ralph's future musical direction: "More and more toward the end of the tour, Roscoe and Carter and Ralph would get together as we traveled and sing some of the Old Regular Baptist songs. I sometimes wonder if those sessions might have influenced Ralph Stanley's move towards the older songs and way of singing. . . ."[33]

To close the second half of the show, the Stanley Brothers would return to the stage with the Clinch Mountain Boys. In Bremen the band performed eight numbers, including "Riding on that Midnight Train" from a recent album and favorites such as "Stone Walls and Steel Bars" from 1963, "Rank Stranger," and the gospel song "Jordan."

After flying back to the United States on March 21, the brothers made the thousand-mile drive home to Florida. "We were glad to get back home," recalled Shuffler. He admitted that he—like Holcomb—was afraid of air travel.[34] While the band had been hop-scotching around Europe, Melvin Goins had booked the Stanley Brothers into what Shuffler called "little matinee dates" in schoolhouses. That was the only work available. "Bluegrass was at a low ebb,"[35] Shuffler said. The musicians performed two and sometimes three shows a day for schoolchildren. "We taught them the basics of bluegrass music, the old-time tunes," Melvin Goins recalled,[36] "and me and Carter would tell little stories and I'd do comedy. . . . then Ralph would explain about the banjo. . . ."

I asked George if playing in rural schoolhouses after headlining in European concert halls felt like a letdown. He responded that the only letdown would have been not working. As for the schools, "You got used to it."[37] On April 8 and 9 the Stanley Brothers left the schoolhouses to make a weekend trip to the Midwest. The band performed at Purdue University's Memorial Union in West Lafayette, Indiana, and the Majestic Theatre in Monroe, Michigan.

Just as musicians and venues needed to adapt to survive during the 1960s, so did radio programs. The popular *Wheeling Jamboree* on Wheeling, West Virginia's WWVA relocated four times during the decade, settling from January 1966 to December 1969 into the Wheeling Island Exhibition Hall, which could seat 3,000 fans.[38] When a new program director from the West Coast, Arlen Sanders, modernized WWVA's format to Top 60 country, the hiring of bluegrass veteran Mac Wiseman in May 1966 to manage the station's talent agency and booking provided a valuable connection for those who played the old-time country sounds.[39] Wiseman proved a good friend to the Stanley Brothers. On May 20 they began three weeks of almost nightly appearances in West Virginia, Ohio, and Kentucky that were bracketed by performances on WWVA on May 21 and June 11.[40]

In Europe, Carter had displayed some humor, telling the occasional joke on stage and misinforming audiences that George Shuffler's regular group was John's Gospel Quartet;[41] but veteran showman that he was, he was putting up a front. According to Shuffler, the truth was that "Carter'd been in declining health for a year, really. You could tell he didn't feel good. He just wasn't himself, you know. He slept a lot and he didn't feel like driving."[42] The last was evident because driving "was the mainstay with just the three of us . . . getting to places. They was taking us farther and keeping us longer . . . So Carter, he just didn't feel up to going on the stage part of that time. He was going downhill."

Ironically, business was improving. Melvin overheard Carter tell a fan in Kentucky, "We've worked more this year than we have in years."[43] The schoolhouse bookings meant steady if low-paying work that kept the band busy. " . . . Carter and Ralph, they was lucky if they got to go back to Live Oak once a month then," Melvin recalled.[44] "And when summertime come on, then we would play the drive-in theaters," where the musicians climbed on top of concession stands and sacrificed themselves to mosquitoes as they played forty-five-minute shows to earn a hundred dollars on a Saturday night. During the week, drive-in owners would deduct the cost of the movie and advertising posters from ticket sales and split the remainder with the band.[45]

Advertised appearances around this time included performances at the American Legion Park in Culpeper, Virginia, on June 26; Guy's Drive In Theatre in Richlands, Virginia, on July 2; the Greenbrier Drive-In in Hinton, West Virginia, on July 22; and Ontelaunee Park in New Tripoli, Pennsylvania, on August 28.

On Sunday, October 2, the group appeared at WWVA Day at Sunset Park in Oxford, Pennsylvania, along with announcers and other performers from the station. The WWVA affiliation had increased the Stanley Brothers' popularity among the station's widespread listening audience. "When we went into Wheeling, that opened a lot of good dates for us up in the New England states," recalled Melvin.[46] "We could play parks and things. . . . And so, with the schools then about three to four days a week, and then the drive-in theaters and then our park shows on Sunday, man we really thought we was doing great."

On Saturday, October 15, the Stanley Brothers made an appearance on the *Wheeling Jamboree* before embarking on a zigzag trip through Ohio, Indiana, Tennessee, and Kentucky. The musicians left Wheeling for performances on Sunday afternoon and evening at a venue in Beanblossom, Indiana, called the Brown County Jamboree. Traveling in Carter's green and white 1966 Mercury, they stayed overnight at the home of their friends Homer and Faye Elam in Dayton, Ohio. The Elams accompanied the musicians from Ohio to Indiana. Faye Elam was glad when the big Mercury pulled over to a roadside stand so that Carter could buy fruit. She thought that if he had an appetite, his health must be improving.

On stage in Indiana, he coughed between numbers. He incorporated the cough into his patter, telling the audience that he caught a cold the previous night at the chilly "Elam Motel."[47] The motel scenario set up a one-liner that the motel walls "were so thin I heard a fella in the next room change his mind." This was followed by more country humor. In character as the buffoonish Big Wilbur, Melvin Goins complained about not being able to sleep because newlyweds in the next room kept him up all night by eating candy. As straight man, Carter asked how he knew they were eating candy. "The lady kept saying 'O Henry . . . O Henry' all night," deadpanned Melvin.

In the latter half of their careers, the Stanley Brothers depended too much on comedy for some listeners' tastes. "In the last ten years . . . they have had a number of comedians, but most tell the same old worn out jokes," recalled Mrs. Doris Ball.[48] "Even if they had a fresh routine every time, we would prefer more music and less comedy." Though Carter thrived on the comic interludes, they could make for an uneven show. Following the Big Wilbur routine at the Brown County Jamboree, the group performed "Searching for a Soldier's Grave" from its most recent King album. Carter announced that the brothers would play for the troops in South Vietnam for six weeks beginning in January 1967. He asked listeners to spread the news to friends and relatives who might be stationed there.

Leaving Indiana, the band drove 250 miles to Nashville for a fan club convention organized by the *K-Bar-T Country Roundup* magazine to coincide with the annual disc jockey convention. Carter and Ralph were the fan club convention's guests of honor for bluegrass, and "Texas Troubadour" Ernest Tubb was honored for country music. Presiding over the Stanley Brothers Fan Club was Fay McGinnis from Wyandotte, Michigan, who heard the Stanley Brothers on radio station WRVA and thought, "That's got to be the prettiest music I ever heard in my life."[49] After she and her husband, Roy, listened to Carter and Ralph in person at a union hall in Detroit, she bought a new record player and her first album: *The Stanley Brothers*, King 615. She began to report bluegrass news in her area to the fan club newsletter. When the woman who ran the club quit, the brothers asked Fay to take her place.[50]

"I had no idea in the world what I was doing," she recalled. "Nothing. . . . Carter told me one thing I never forgot. He said, 'Write anything you want to as long as it's the truth, because you might have to face it or we might have to face it. Make it truthful.' And I always stuck to that."[51]

With Fay in charge, the club resumed activity in November 1965 and became the Stanley Brothers International Fan Club. By May 1967 an

86-page edition of its newsletter, the *Stanley Standard*, listed representatives in thirteen states and the District of Columbia as well as Canada, Czechoslovakia, England, Japan, and Sweden.[52] Fay and vice president Norma Fannin of Columbus, Ohio, introduced a tape swapping club for members. Fans behind the Iron Curtain sent "minerals and rocks and different things" to pay for memberships.[53] When Carter asked her to book the band, Fay asked a friend to accompany her into Detroit bars, where she negotiated bookings for $200 to $250 a night.

At the fan club banquet on Wednesday, October 19, Carter and Ralph received plaques. "Very humbly the boys accepted the award for twenty years of wonderful country bluegrass entertainment," wrote an attendee.[54] Carter's plaque depicted a guitar, and Ralph's a banjo. For the brothers and the fans who were close to them, emotions rose to the surface. From the podium, Fay McGinnis "caught a glimpse of Carter on my left and he was just looking at me and had tears in his eyes. . . ."[55] No sooner had Fay and Norma Fannin returned to their seats than convention organizer Blanche Trinajstick called them back to the stage to receive plaques and boxes of red roses. "Tears filled their eyes . . . ," the attendee wrote.

"[Carter] was very ill at that time," recalled Norma Fannin, "but he never let on. When we were given our awards, there was no speech on stage, but the one he said to Fay and I in the car later that evening are words I will forever treasure. They were of pride toward the club and the fans and to each of us who had devoted so much of our time to the promotion of the Stanleys."[56]

Fay's husband and another musician had booked studio time that night to make a bluegrass record with George Shuffler. When the three men stood up to leave the banquet, the bluegrass guests of honor surprised their hosts by following the trio, telling Fay "They might need us."[57] Fay and Norma rode to the studio with Carter and Ralph. Carter drove and became lost. "Do you think I'll spend the rest of my life just going around in a circle in Nashville?" he asked.[58] At the studio, Carter offered to play any instrument except bass, but was not needed. He spent his time in the hall plucking Fay's antique banjo. Ralph supervised the session.

After recording, the group visited the Black Poodle and two or three other music clubs before returning to the hotel. The next morning Carter was sick. He stayed in bed all day, even when his companions went to a club that night to see George Jones. The following morning when Fay and Roy were about to leave Nashville, Fay thought Carter looked worse: "Carter looked so thin, and he had just a strap tee-shirt [on] . . . when he was lying in bed. And he had these red blotches on him." Fay asked why he had the blotches. Carter said he didn't know and asked for his guitar case. He reached in and took out a stick of wood that he had been whittling on. He gave it to Fay, extolling the soothing effects of whittling.[59] When Fay and Roy left, he found the strength to get up and go to the hotel lobby to say goodbye.

On Friday, October 21, Carter, Ralph, and George rejoined Melvin Goins in Hazel Green, Kentucky, for the first of two weekend engagements that Melvin had booked. As they had done so many times, the Stanley Brothers took the stage at the Red River Valley School and began to play. Four decades later, Melvin displayed his remarkable memory. He recalled that "At the time, we were opening with 'How Mountain Girls Can Love,' 'Stone Walls and Steel Bars,' and 'Rank Stranger.'"[60]

After three numbers, Carter began to bleed from the nose. He left the stage, leaving the other three musicians to carry on without him. He told Melvin that barbecue sauce he had eaten in Mountain City, Virginia, had made him sick, but Melvin knew better: ". . . he had been drinking."[61]

The next engagement was Saturday night at the courthouse in Frenchburg, Kentucky. Melvin said, "Boys, I'll meet you there."[62] The other musicians planned to drive to Cincinnati to pick up records at King. They did not make it. According to George Shuffler, "Carter was bleeding all the time and we left there and got up on the Mountain Parkway . . . Carter was in the back and he said, 'Pull off. I'm sick.' We pulled off. . . . We heard the awfullest sound."[63] Carter had opened the back door and vomited onto the ground. Ralph said, "My God, what's the matter?" When he and George turned on the interior light, they saw that Carter had vomited blood. Their first thought was to rush Carter to the hospital in Lexington, Kentucky, but his bleeding subsided enough for him to say, "Just turn around and take me back up to Ma's. I feel better now."[64] Ralph reversed direction and sped southeast through the mountains along Route 23 until he reached the back roads to Smith Ridge. He covered the 125 miles in about two and a half hours.

When Melvin met the group in Frenchburg on Saturday, he asked where Carter was. "I thought I'd let Carter set this one out," said Ralph. "He wasn't feeling too good."[65] The show went on as scheduled. Melvin headed home, while Ralph and George drove back to Smith Ridge. They had covered ninety miles to Wayland, Kentucky, when a police car with flashing lights and wailing siren pulled pull them over. "I didn't know what in the world I'd done wrong," recalled George, who had been driving.[66]

The police officer approached the driver's side and asked if one of them was Ralph Stanley. George answered, "Yes." The officer said, "Well, you better get to Bristol quick as you can. You got a brother just at the point of death."

19. SMITH RIDGE

———◆◆◆◆◆◆———

After Ralph and George had left Carter with Lucy Smith Stanley on Smith Ridge, his hemorrhaging resumed. The family called the ambulance to take him to Bristol Memorial Hospital, where the medical staff in the emergency room and intensive care unit gave him frequent blood transfusions to keep him alive.[1] When his condition failed to improve after a week, Doc Mongle decided that he needed to transfer Carter to the University of Virginia Hospital in Charlottesville, 250 miles to the northeast, if he was going to have a chance to live.

Ralph and George were in Carter's hospital room in Charlottesville when a doctor came in to tell him that he would need an operation. "You stand about a fifty-fifty chance with that," the doctor explained. "You're going to have to stay in here about six to eight weeks 'til we can build you up before you can start thinking about playing."[2] According to George, "We left him in pretty good hopes. The bleeding stopped while we were there . . . no trace of blood whatsoever. And he was real pleased and he got up, set on the side of the bed and everything."

Hattie Rasnick, a Stanley cousin from the coal-mining community of Trammel, went to the hospital to visit her sister, who was being treated for cancer. When Hattie visited Carter in his room, he looked terrible. "Hattie," he said, "I had the awfullest surgery in my life."[3] In his autobiography, Ralph wrote that the operation was a success. "The surgery went fine and the bleeding stopped and doctors told him he needed to rest there for a few weeks," he recalled.[4] Carter's brother-in-law, Roy Sykes, who was police chief of Pocahontas, Virginia, took time off from his job to stay a motel room near the hospital. Staying with him and his son Roy Jr. was Carter's oldest son, Carter Lee. Just as his father had joined the Army Air Corps after high school, Carter Lee had entered the Air Force on October 18, 1966.[5] He was an airman in basic training at Lackland Air Base near San Antonio, Texas, when he was called out of class to be told that his father was dying. Flying to Tri-Cities Regional Airport near Blountville, Tennessee, he met his mother and other family members. When Doc Mongle arranged for Carter to be transported to the University of Virginia Hospital, Carter Lee called Lackland Air Base to request permission to extend his leave. He, Roy Sykes, and Roy Jr. followed the ambulance to Charlottesville. Mary Stanley returned to Florida to take care of her young children.

According to Dr. Christopher Holstege of the University of Virginia Medical Center, the surgery recalled by Ralph and Hattie Rasnick was likely to have been a procedure that was tried first at UVA Hospital in 1964.[6] Carter Lee remembered Doc Mongle telling him that Carter's liver had become enlarged and hard like a football. The doctor said that he had "nothing to work with." Dr. Holstege characterized the procedure as "a desperate act to save a life"; he added that "most patients have bad outcomes."

From my description of Carter's symptoms, Dr. Holstege concluded:

I suspect that due to his alcoholic liver disease, Carter developed portal hyptertension and subsequent varices. Bleeding from his esophageal varices could certainly cause him to vomit and defecate blood. He would have had a poor prognosis and doctors might have used balloon tamponade with the Sengtaken-Blakemore tube.

Tamponade simply means compression. With liver disease, the veins in the esophagus become engorged due to resistance by the liver and subsequently enlarge and finally break. As a result, many alcoholics with liver disease die from bleeding into their gastrointestinal tract. You cannot manually compress a vessel's bleeding into the esophagus, so doctors developed a balloon to do it (by inserting a tube down the throat to the esophagus and then blowing up an attached balloon to compress the bleeding vessel).

The procedure worked. Carter regained some strength. Roy Sykes Jr. remembered that Carter was allowed to receive calls at a pay phone outside his room.[7] Country star Buck Owens would call around 4:00 p.m. Norma Fannin called several times. She reported that ". . . each time he had one main desire—to be out on the road doing shows with Ralph, to be with his family, to get back his strength so he could have gone to Vietnam in January."[8] Bill Monroe and Jim and Jesse McReynolds kept in touch with their friend and fellow musician.

Toward the end of November, musicologist Richard Spottswood heard that Carter "was fighting for his life." He, Alice Gerrard, and a friend drove together from Washington, D.C., to offer their support. "We pleaded with him to stay put at the UVA Hospital," Spottswood recalled.[9] "He had blinders and wanted to get up and do the gig. None of us had any idea of how badly his health had deteriorated from drinking. This was the wake before he died. Nobody else was coming to see him." Asked how Carter looked, Spottswood said, "He looked dead." Carter Lee's leave had ended in the fourth week of November. Communication from Carter's hospital room to his home in Live Oak was difficult because the family had no telephone.[10] His daughter Doris recalled receiving three calls at school. "He would call the school office and they would come get me from class and allow me to go into the teachers' lounge to use the telephone in there where it was more private," she recalled, "and because Daddy usually wanted to talk a while. . . . Those telephone calls as he lay dying in the hospital meant the world to us both and kept him connected to his wife and children."

Composing on a pad of paper, Carter wrote lyrics to three new songs, including a wistful season's greeting to his wife, "Merry Christmas, Mary." The family did not discover the other two until after Mary's death on November 4, 1990. Written on thin, faded pieces of paper, they were in the suitcase Carter had taken to the hospital. Their titles were "Two Sides to a Story" and "Jesus Is Precious." Both since have been recorded. His daughter Jeanie and nephew Ralph Stanley II recorded "Two Sides" in 2004 for Jeanie's album *Baby Girl* with a melody written by producer Joe Isaacs. Ralph recorded "Jesus Is Precious" for the same project as an unaccompanied vocal, singing the lyrics to the melody of a gospel song.

During Carter's absence, Ralph, George, and Melvin performed as a trio, fulfilling a grueling schedule of appearances between November 1 and November 18 that took them from the schools and theaters of Virginia and Kentucky to the Erie County Fairgrounds administration building in Sandusky, Ohio; theaters in North Carolina and Georgia; the Southern Louisiana Hayride in Ponchatoula, Louisiana; and back to Kentucky and Virginia. On Saturday, November 19, they drove to Wheeling for an appearance on WWVA. They looked forward to a much-needed break. The following Thursday would be Thanksgiving.

Ralph drove George Shuffler home to North Carolina and continued south for the holiday. "I was feeling some relief about everything, and I went back down to Florida for Thanksgiving," Ralph recalled.[11] On

Wednesday, November 30, he collected George and returned to Smith Ridge because they needed to go back on the road.[12] In the meantime, Carter's determination to leave the hospital had gotten the better of him. Around Thanksgiving, he insisted that his half-brothers Doc and Lance come to Charlottesville and take him to his mother's house. Pronouncing himself recovered, he checked out of the hospital and returned to Smith Ridge. When Ralph and George arrived around 10:00 p.m. on Wednesday of the following week, he was there to meet them.

The brothers and George exchanged greetings. Ralph conveyed best wishes to Carter from his family and friends in Live Oak, including an offer from a local car dealer that he would be glad to work with Carter whenever he wanted to trade in his Mercury. Carter was not amused. "Well, it's a funny thing that you have to get down just about on your deathbed before people will show sympathy and lend a helping hand," he responded.[13]

Ralph and George wanted to go to sleep—Ralph having driven from Florida and George having taken over the wheel from Valdese, North Carolina, so that Ralph could get some rest. They had to leave the next morning. "But Carter, he was sitting on the couch, and he kept begging us not to go to bed," George recalled.[14] "He said, 'Let's set up and talk a while.' He said, 'Up here it's just me and Ma.' He said, 'I'm lonesome and I want to talk.'" As always, he was persuasive. The three men talked for an hour ... until Carter began vomiting blood. All Lucy Smith Stanley could find for her son to throw up into was a box—". . . and he's just . . . spewing just the awfullest," recalled George. ". . . looked like a gallon of blood there, you know."

The sudden reoccurrence of symptoms pointed to the likelihood that the balloon procedure had given way. To Ralph and George, who were groggy from travel and lack of sleep, the scene must have seemed like a bad dream. For Lucy Smith Stanley, it was a mother's worst nightmare. Almost two decades later, George recalled the trip to Bristol Memorial Hospital.

And they [sic] was just an old blue frozen snow on the ground and we called the ambulance over at Clintwood and Harold Stanley came in the ambulance and we carried him out of the house in the snow and put him in the ambulance. And Carter asked me would I ride with him in the ambulance to the hospital. And I said I'd be glad to. And Ralph followed us in the truck and we got him checked in. When we

got to the hospital I had on a white kind of coat and it was specked
with blood all over and they opened the back door of the ambulance
and the blood was running out the back of it. And they got him back
in the hospital and he had less than a pint of blood, they said. Veins
collapsed. They went into his foot and finally found an artery there,
a big vein or something, and they got the blood started and he kindly
leveled off.[15]

By this time, it was eight in the morning. An exhausted Ralph said, "George, I believe Carter has eased off some."

"He's a-resting," said George. "Let's go out and get us a little bite of breakfast and some coffee."

Thirty minutes later, they came back to the intensive care unit. Since George was smoking, Ralph told him to finish his cigarette while he checked on his brother. Within seconds Ralph reappeared, looking white as a sheet. "George, Carter's a-dying," he said. There was commotion as nurses paged a doctor. When the doctor arrived, he and the nurses went into Carter's room. They came out and gave Ralph and George a solemn look before returning to the room. Five minutes later at around 10:45 a.m. on December 1, 1966, a nurse came out again to tell the two men that Carter had died. He was 41. "He was calling for Ralph," Carter Lee recalled being told. "It was an awful death."

Ralph, George, and others began making phone calls and funeral arrangements. George called a neighbor of Lucy Smith Stanley on Smith Ridge to ask her to break the news to Lucy that Carter had died "and kindly get braced for us to come in there."[16] Roy Sykes and Roy Jr. had driven from Pocahontas during the early morning hours. The elder Sykes had spoken with Carter before his death and took on the painful task of calling Carter's wife Mary with the news.[17] Ralph notified the Miller Funeral Home in Clintwood, from which ambulance driver Harold Stanley returned to pick up the body. Ralph's wife Peggy called Carter Lee at Lackland Air Base. Numerous relatives needed to be told, including half-sister Ruby Rakes Eubanks, who lived in Michigan.

Later that day, Mary Bruce Mongle was surprised to find her father at home so early and to see him so upset. She sat down with him and had a conversation. "He came home and told me how that [Carter] had been hemorrhaging," she recalled.[18] "He talked about how many pints of blood he had given him. He kept giving him blood, but there was nothing that could be done for him. He was upset because it was not only a doctor-patient relationship but a friend relationship." The transfusions required between 85 and 125 pints of blood.[19]

Though Carter's death came as a shock to family, friends, fellow musicians, and fans, it would be difficult to characterize it as unexpected. He had been very sick throughout his final year, and close to death in October. Even Ralph would acknowledge it. "In the last few years of his life, Carter was unhappy, because he knew he was sick, but he was a fella who wouldn't give up," Ralph told an interviewer in 1976.[20] "He thought he could conquer anything, and he wouldn't admit . . . he knew it was coming, and still he wouldn't admit it." Painful though it must have been, family members may have considered the possibility of making arrangements for the event.

Planning for Carter's funeral moved quickly. Co-owned by brothers Robert and R. C. Miller, the Miller Funeral Home stood on a bluff near the center of Clintwood. The building was a three-story Victorian mansion with twin columns on either side of its front door. In 2003 it would become the home of the Ralph Stanley Museum and Traditional Mountain Music Center. Living as they did in the middle of a region that had developed with the lumber and coal industries, the Miller brothers were more accustomed to arranging funerals for the families of owners and managers than for the family of the working man. Now they would arrange the funeral of a working man who had become a music star.

To the residents of Dickenson County, Carter was much more than a well-known musician. He had been a popular friend, neighbor, and benefactor. There were Christmases "when we'd hear of a neighbor or a family in our town who wouldn't be having much of a Christmas, and Daddy would have us kids pack up boxes with fruit, nuts, candy," daughter Doris recalled,[21] "and he'd come up with a few appropriate toys from somewhere. We had to deliver part of our own Christmas to some needy family . . . before we had any visit from Santa Claus at our house."

A family named Childress lived on a narrow dirt road that Carter took on the way to his mother's house. The Childress children would holler when his Cadillac passed. One of the children was stricken with polio. "Daddy always had something for that young crippled boy who was confined to a wheelchair," Doris recalled.[22] "Be it a candy bar, a new record, a comic book, or whatever he'd been able to get."

On Friday and Saturday, December 2 and 3, hundreds of people climbed the steep front steps into the funeral home to view the body of Carter Glen Stanley and offer sympathy to his family. Surviving Carter were his mother Lucy, wife Mary, five children, five brothers, four sisters, and numerous kinfolk.[23] On Saturday afternoon, funeral home personnel moved his body to the home of his mother on Smith Ridge to give the family the opportunity to mourn in private. Someone lifted up four-year-old Norma Jean Stanley so that she could look into the casket to say goodbye to her father.

Winter weather in southwest Virginia generally does not clamp down until after the first of the year, but the day of Carter's funeral was unseasonably cold. Hundreds had paid their respects at the funeral home, and on the morning of December 4 more than two thousand people overflowed the Ervinton Elementary School gymnasium in Nora. Attendance was estimated to be 2,300 to 2,500.[24]

The appropriateness of the funeral's location was evident. "It was conducted in a place which was highly significant to the life of Carter for two reasons . . . ," wrote Pete Richardson in the *Bluegrass Bulletin*.[25] "It was a high school gymnasium . . . the same high school where Carter went to school. . . . But the fact that Carter and Ralph had presented their music on so many high school gymnasium floors in their career makes it so very, very significant." He concluded: ". . . it was right and fitting that this great man of our music should lie in state in such a humble environment."

Carter's death came so suddenly that many family members, friends, and fans were in denial. On her way to the funeral from Ohio, Norma Fannin recalled that "I kept telling myself 'It's not true, he was just sick,' but on the airplane to Bristol, I knew this was no dream. . . ."[26] Some who could not make the funeral conveyed their feelings through others. Buck Owens called Fay McGinnis to tell her that in his heart, he would never forget how Carter had encouraged him when he "so greatly needed it."[27] Those who could find a way to make it to Dickenson County did. Mike Seeger traveled all the way from New York. Carter's first cousin Kenneth Stanley drove to the funeral from Illinois.

There was an awkward delay. Those assembled in the gymnasium, including Rev. Landon Colley and Rev. Stewart Owens, who officiated, had to wait for an hour for Bill Monroe to arrive. Carter's former bandleader and mentor was flying in from Louisiana.[28] Under another circumstance, there might have been unrest; but this was a respectful gathering that knew how to entertain itself. Fred Sullivan remembered the singing in the gymnasium. He grew up in Haysi, where he helped his father run two sawmills. The better quality softwoods went to Johnson City, Tennessee, for furniture, and to Pulaski, Virginia, for caskets. The rough grade of wood was used as beams to support wooden roofs in mines. During the wait for Monroe, Sullivan recalled that no sooner would one group finish singing the Monroe favorite "Six White Horses," which made reference to a funeral, than another group would stand up to sing it again.[29]

Monroe finally arrived in the gymnasium. He and Carter had such a close bond that he promised Carter that if the necessity arose, he would sing the hymn "Swing Low, Sweet Chariot" at his funeral. On this sad day he fulfilled his promise. "He stood at the head of the coffin and sung the whole thing with his hands on the coffin," George Shuffler recalled.[30] "Sung the whole thing. It was tear-jerking time, I tell you. It was sad and pitiful." Yet as Pete Richardson wrote in the *Bluegrass Bulletin*, ". . . to Bill Monroe it was pure, simple, humble and deep LOVE."[31] Monroe told the assembled mourners that Carter was the best natural lead singer he ever had heard.

The service continued into the afternoon as the weather worsened. It was "sleeting and snowing and freezing . . . colder than a kraut rock," recalled George Shuffler, who was a pallbearer.[32] "We took him back up on the mountain to bury him at the old home place. . . . But it was so cold. We had to carry him up from down there in front of the house up to the graveyard, and I thought I would freeze to death." The other pallbearers were George's brother John, who had played bass with the Stanley Brothers; Lonnie Boland, Gene Duty, Homer Elam, and Jack Lynch. "That was the six of us. I was right up at the head of the coffin. Harold Stanley was in charge of the funeral. . . . He put me up there beside [Carter's] head. He told me this is where the most important one walks."

Carter was laid to rest in the suit he had bought in October in Norton, Virginia, to wear at the fan club banquet in Nashville. "He thought that was the finest suit in the world," said George Shuffler, who was with him when he bought it.[33] "And it was. It cost a ton of money back then even. He said, 'It's the best suit I ever owned.'"

The Smith family cemetery sits on a knob on Smith Ridge. Members of Lucy Smith Stanley's family had been buried there for decades. Their headstones nestled among half a dozen trees. Carter's stone was a mixture of traditional and contemporary. Etched into it was a scene of the sun rising between two pine trees, identifiable as such by the two large pinecones at the base of each. Affixed to the stone above the trees was a black-and-white photograph of Carter seated—thoughtful, with hands folded, wearing a shirt and tie. To the left of the scene was his first name and dates of birth and death; to the right was the image of a guitar. The name Stanley was carved below the scene in large letters; and below that was the phrase "Farewell Carter for a little while." A footstone laid in the ground honored Carter's service in the Army Air Forces during World War II.

An undated photograph taken after the burial shows Carter's widow, Mary, and older daughter, Doris, standing behind the headstone. Mary wears a black dress, Doris a light-colored sweater. Both wear sunglasses. Between headstone and footstone is a large flower arrangement in the shape of a guitar, with a smaller guitar arrangement to the headstone's left. Two cars and a group of men talking at the chain-link fence are visible in the background. The picture is peaceful. Carter was at rest.

Ralph had a decision to make. The question had been on his mind for some time. "I don't know what to do," he told George Shuffler.[34] "All I know is music." After a pause, he said, "I'm going to try to go on." He cancelled several appearances to give George and himself a brief rest. George returned home to Valdese, North Carolina. When Ralph called a few days later and asked if he was ready to resume personal appearances, George said that he was.

"I just can't stand sitting here no longer," Ralph explained.[35] "The suspense of the thing's killing me. So let's just hit the road and see what happens."

Though he sounded matter of fact, Ralph must have had to come to terms with serious insecurity about his ability to succeed without his brother. In November, when Carter was in the hospital, he told an audience at the Erie County Fairgrounds in Ohio that being on stage without his brother was "just like losing my right arm."[36] Recalling instances where Carter had left the stage during their performances together, Ralph came to believe that Carter had been pushing him into the role of emcee as preparation for the day when he would no longer be there.[37]

Some aspects of the transition would be simple. Ralph had taken charge of much of the booking and all of the bookkeeping. More difficult—and personally complicated—was the task of selecting the musicians with whom he wanted to work.

Melvin Goins was available if Ralph wanted him to stay—and he did. "I stayed on three more years with Ralph because I didn't know what the situation would be," recalled Melvin.[38] "I knew Ralph wasn't going to quit but I knew it was going to be rough on him to go on after Carter's passing on because Ralph and Carter worked close together . . . and of course Carter done all the emcee work."

Curly Ray Cline was an affable old-time fiddler who had played with Melvin in the Lonesome Pine Fiddlers. He had joined the Stanley Brothers on weekend dates after they returned from Europe. During the week, he ran a coal mine that he owned in Kentucky. "It was getting on my nerves so I had to quit one," he recalled.[39] "I couldn't handle them both." As they drove to a performance in Virginia while other band members rode in a separate car, Ralph offered Cline a job. "I don't know how well I'm going to do," Ralph said. "But I'd like to have you regular . . . just so we'd take a chance at it."[40] Ralph said he would try to give Cline enough work to earn a living. He made good on his offer, and soon Cline was able to sell the mine.

By the middle of January, George Shuffler's future with the Clinch Mountain Boys was limited. After Carter's death, he and Ralph had sung together in the car and performed occasional duets on stage, "but it just wasn't the blend" Ralph was looking for, Shuffler recalled.[41] In his private way, Ralph had decided that the band needed a new lead singer. Regardless of Shuffler's past service, Ralph's first priority was to continue the vocal and instrumental sound that had been successful for him and Carter since 1946.

As with his decision to continue, Ralph moved quickly. On February 7, 1967, while playing at Tom's Tavern in Dayton, Ohio, he paid close attention to the house band during its set. He was considering the band's lead singer, Roy Lee Centers, who sounded a lot like Carter. On the same night, he auditioned a young guitar player who had played with the Stanley Brothers on occasion. Larry Sparks came to the club at the suggestion of Ralph's friend and temporary bass player Jack Lynch.[42] Sparks had played with the house band from time to time. During the band's set, "They called me up to sing with them," Sparks recalled.[43]

That's what people would do at that time. After I sang the songs, Ralph came up to me and we talked and he asked me to step outside. I didn't know if he wanted to fight. So we stepped outside and sat in his brand new Pontiac wagon and he asked if I wanted to sing with him . . . join the band. I said I would like do that. I didn't know how well I would do, but I would try. I guess he liked what I did. I guess I had a little feel that he always was used to. That's my opinion.

Realizing that Sparks needed a more professional guitar and stage costume, Ralph offered him Carter's Martin-D45 guitar and black leather slip-on boots.[44] By this time George Shuffler—the "third Stanley Brother" of the 1960s—had left the group. "I didn't stay too long after that because seem like it . . . was on Ralph's mind . . . ," George recalled. "We didn't fall out or have no fights or cussing battles or nothing, but I could just tell that I was out of place. It wasn't the same, in other words. So I just excused myself and came [home]."[45]

As Ralph returned to the road with a reorganized band, Carter's family found itself in desperate financial circumstances. As a relative put it, "Carter died a poor man." Carter Lee was serving in the air force, and the other children were not in a position to contribute much to the family income. Mary got work as a waitress. A loyal friend to the last, Doc Mongle waived Carter's medical expenses. "That was a big relief," recalled Ralph.[46] Musicians and fans responded to the financial crisis by organizing benefits. Planned while Carter was in the hospital, the first took place at Cousin Nick's in Washington, D.C., on Saturday, December 4, 1966— the same day as Carter's funeral. The club owner contributed fifty dollars. A number of people in the area donated blood to offset the cost of the transfusions that Carter had received.[47]

By far the largest benefit was held on Sunday, April 9, 1967, at the University of Maryland's basketball venue, Cole Field House, in College Park. Before the performances Walter Saunders—one of the Stanley Brothers fan club's Virginia representatives—asked Ralph if he planned to continue playing the old-time mountain music that had become the band's trademark. "He answered with an emphatic 'Definitely,'" Saunders reported.[48] Co-sponsored by the University of Maryland's Campus Chest and the year-old magazine *Bluegrass Unlimited,* the concert brought together a variety of performers from the bluegrass and old-time country fields: Jim Greer and the Mac-O-Chee Valley Folks; Washington veteran Buzz Busby and Bill Emerson's new group; George Winn and the Bluegrass Partners; North Carolina's Doc Watson and his son Merle; New River Ranch proprietors Alex and Ola Belle Campbell's New River Boys (though Alex and Ola Belle were not present); the Washington area's popular progressive bluegrass band, the Country Gentlemen; Mac Wiseman leading a group of first-generation bluegrass performers (the others were Don Stover and Tex Logan); and a group led by Mike Seeger that included Alice Gerrard, Hazel Dickens, Tex Logan, and Lamar Grier.[49]

An appearance by Roy Sykes caught even knowledgeable fans by surprise. Walter Saunders wrote, "I had no idea he was still actively engaged in bluegrass music." Richard Spottswood reported: "He still has a fine band that all enjoyed hearing." Sykes told the audience about meeting Carter at Fort Meade and their first concert (Ervinton High School) and radio show (WNVA in Norton). In tribute to his brother-in-law, Sykes performed a song he had written years before that had been recorded by Flatt and Scruggs, "Will the Roses Bloom Where She Lies Sleeping?" Walt Saunders recalled, "They did it with a lot of feeling and it brought a lump to my throat." Patsy Stoneman—daughter of old-time music recording artist Ernest V. Stoneman—"made a surprise appearance during the Sykes portion, accompanying herself on the autoharp."

When Ralph Stanley and the Clinch Mountain Boys appeared, "It was very saddening to come on the stage without Carter," Saunders wrote. "It was almost like I expected him to walk out and join them at any moment." Noticing that George Shuffler was no longer with the group, Saunders approved of Larry Sparks as his replacement: "His voice blends perfectly with Ralph's and they retain much of the original sound of the Stanley Brothers."

Ralph told the audience what he had told Saunders: He would continue to play the old-time songs that he and Carter always had done. To drive home the point, he sang a medley of three of them, including "Little Maggie" and "Pretty Polly." The audience responded with "thunderous" applause. Saunders was ecstatic. "His voice was in perfect control, and I have never heard him sing more beautifully. The running banjo background for his singing was the best I have ever heard him do." Ralph's rendition of "Man of Constant Sorrow," which was to become his signature song, "nearly brought the roof down."

Closing the show were Bill Monroe and His Blue Grass Boys. As would be the case for many years, Monroe was in the process of putting together an ensemble of younger musicians, including fiddle player Byron Berline. According to Richard Spottswood, ". . . there were few spots in their appearance when it showed, and the considerable talents of all on hand were able to smooth over the rough spots nicely." Their performance reached a peak when Monroe asked Mac Wiseman to sing with him on "Can't You Hear Me Callin," which they had recorded for Columbia years before. The emotional climax would come next when Monroe called Ralph Stanley, Curly Ray Cline, and Melvin Goins on stage to join him in singing "Swing Low, Sweet Chariot." An emotional Walt Saunders reported:

Bill said this was the hardest song he ever had to sing when he did it at Carter's funeral. He invited the audience to join them on the chorus. It was a stirring experience for me as I sat there joining the two legendary men of the music, Bill Monroe and Ralph Stanley, in a tribute to the memory of an equally legendary figure, Carter Stanley. Tears dimmed my eyes again as I sang along with them, and to say it was an emotional moment would be putting it mildly.[50]

During and after the show, emcees made an appeal for blood donations. Walt Saunders pledged a pint. He looked at his watch; it was past 9:00 p.m. He had been listening to music for seven hours. The University of Maryland Campus Chest and *Bluegrass Unlimited* sent the proceeds of the benefit to Mary Kiser Stanley so that she could pay some of her family's bills.[51]

During twenty years in the music business, the young men who had their pictures taken at the Cumberland Gap became pioneers in their own way. They smoothed the rough, angular edges of the music of the mountains to make it more commercially viable. Though never as successful as they hoped to be, they became perhaps the most influential of the old-time country bands that also played bluegrass.

Carter and Ralph began as imitators of Bill Monroe and his Blue Grass Boys and rivals of Flatt and Scruggs, yet achieved enduring success comparable to both groups. As Carter always insisted, they played real country music in the original sense of the term: music from the rural country. At their best, as on the first Mercury recordings, they were as compelling as any acoustic country band before or since.

The central question hanging over the Stanley Brothers' career is: How successful would they have been if Carter had remained healthy? Carter Lee once asked his uncle Ralph what might have happened if his father had lived. Ralph replied, "We couldn't play the shows and we couldn't spend the money." Yet attention to health was neither in Carter's makeup nor the nature of the country music business during the decades from 1946 to 1966. As Richard Spottswood wrote in a recollection of his visit to Carter at the UVA Hospital, "As long as he was stuck in a hospital bed, he was relinquishing control over his life and he was determined to regain it at the first opportunity, seemingly without a thought about how long he'd survive on his own."[52]

From the perspective of many of Carter's contemporaries, alcoholism was an occupational hazard. Carter succumbed to it. On the other hand, a resilient Ralph carried on for more than sixty years, keeping his and Carter's music alive until another pair of brothers—Joel and Ethan Coen—would include Ralph's "O Death" and the Stanley Brothers' "Angel Band" in the Grammy award–winning soundtrack of the film *O Brother, Where Art Thou?* Then the music of the Stanley Brothers was heard more widely than the two young men at the Cumberland Gap ever could have imagined. All of their studio recordings remain in print, as do many live performances. Their names have become synonymous with the notion of authenticity in old-time country music and bluegrass.

NOTES

---·◆·▸×◂·◆·---

Chapter 1

1. John Mack Faragher, *Daniel Boone: The Life and Legend of an American Pioneer*. New York: Henry Holt, 1992, 89–90.
2. *Ibid.*, 92–93.
3. www.dickensonctyva.com/
4. Stanley Brothers, *Folio No. 1*, collection of Don Morrell, Abingdon, Virginia.
5. John Alexander Williams, *Appalachia: A History*, Chapel Hill: UNC Press, 2002, 1–18.
6. www.dickensonctyva.com/html/history___heritage.html
7. *Ibid.*
8. Ralph Stanley with Eddie Dean, *Man of Constant Sorrow: My Life and Times*, New York: Gotham Books, 2009, 17.
9. Fannie Steele and Ina Jean Dotson, *The Crabtree-Stanley Collection: A Memorial*, Midlands, VA: I. J. S. Dotson, 1996, 302.
10. www.houseofnames.com/xq/asp.fc/qx/standly-family-crest.htm.
11. When I asked about the discrepancy, Stanley genealogist Fannie Steele explained to me, "I do know that years ago some did not know the exact date of birth as there was no birth certificates. A lot of older people guessed their age."
12. Steele and Dotson, *The Crabtree-Stanley Collection*, 307.
13. *Ibid.*, 308.
14. Lillian Gobble and Rhonda Robertson, *Between Brothers: Civil War Soldiers of Wise and Dickenson Counties*, Wise County Historical Society, 2004.
15. In 2001 at the Russell County Fair, Ralph Stanley II introduced his father and his contemporaries as having "come out of the hollers to invent their own music." Author's notes from event, September 2001.
16. James Abel Smith, written statement regarding family, January 31, 1942, Clintwood, Virginia.
17. Doris Stanley Bradley, posting to BGRASS-L listserv, June 4, 2004.
18. John Wright, "Ruby Rakes Eubanks," *Traveling the High Way Home: Ralph Stanley and the World of Traditional Bluegrass Music*, Urbana: University of Illinois Press, 36.
19. Steele and Dotson, *The Crabtree-Stanley Collection*, 365.
20. Gary B. Reid, booklet to *The Stanley Brothers: The King Years 1961–1965*, 4.
21. Ralph Stanley interview with Mike Seeger, March 1966.

22. Douglas Pote, *Man of Constant Sorrow*, Barter Theatre, Abingdon, Virginia.

23. Ralph Stanley interview with Terry Gross, *Fresh Air*, July 15, 2002.

24. Ken Ringle, "The Natural King of Bluegrass: Virginia's Ralph Stanley, the Old-Timey Singer Whose Time Has Come," *Washington Post*, March 20, 1993.

25. Wright, "Ralph Stanley," *Traveling the High Way Home*, 45.

26. James A. Baker, Stanley Brothers *Folio No. 1*, collection of Don Morrell.

27. Fran Russell, "The Stanley Brothers," *The Stanley Brothers and . . . The Clinch Mountain Boys* (songbook), collection of Don Morrell.

28. Ralph Stanley interview with Mike Seeger, March 1966.

29. Tony Russell, *Country Music Records: A Discography, 1921–1942*, Oxford, UK: Oxford University Press, 2004, 142.

30. Susan A. Eacker and Geoff Eacker, "A Banjo on Her Knee—Part I: Appalachian Women and America's First Instrument," *Old-Time Herald*, Vol. 8, No. 2.

31. Ralph Stanley interview with Mike Seeger.

32. Ralph Stanley with Eddie Dean, *Man of Constant Sorrow: My Life and Times*, New York: Gotham, 2009, 50–51. Hereafter abbreviated *MCS*.

33. Jim Owens, e-mail to author, May 19, 2005.

34. David W. Johnson, "Lonesome Melodies: Conversations with Ralph Stanley," *Mars Hill Review*, Issue 22, 2004.

35. Trulah Taylor interview, fall 2004.

36. June Suthers interview, February 18, 2007.

37. Jeffrey Fox, "Clinch Mountain Schooldays," *Ralph on Ralph:* The Clinch Mountain Express *Interviews Dr. Ralph Stanley*, third edition, May 2002.

38. Wright, "Ralph Stanley," *Traveling the High Way Home*, 47.

39. *Ibid.*

40. Johnson, "Lonesome Melodies," *Mars Hill Review*, 2004.

41. Russell, *Country Music Records*, 50.

42. Jack Tottle, "The Stanley Brothers on WCYB Bristol," notes to *Live Again! WCYB Bristol Farm and Fun Time*, Rebel CD-2003, 1997.

43. Loyal Jones, *Country Music Humorists and Comedians*, Urbana: University of Illinois Press, 2008, 124.

44. Wright, "Ralph Stanley," *Traveling the High Way Home*, 49.

45. Ralph Stanley interview with Mike Seeger.

46. Wright, "Ralph Stanley," *Traveling the High Way Home*, 46.

47. *Ibid.*, 49.

48. John Cohen, "Ralph Stanley's Old Time Bluegrass," *Sing Out!*, Vol. 23, No. 6, 1975.

49. Ralph Stanley interview with Terry Gross.

50. Fox, "Growing up in the Clinch Mountains," *Ralph on Ralph*, 2002.

51. Wright, "Benny Steele," *Traveling the High Way Home*, 40.

52. Cohen, "Ralph Stanley's Old Time Bluegrass," 3.

53. Eddie Dean, "Carter Stanley: The Sibling That 'O Brother' Forgot," *Washington Post*, May 28, 2004.

Notes

Chapter 2

1. Doris Stanley Bradley, post to BGRASS-L listserv, June 4, 2004.
2. E-mail to the author.
3. Fox, "Growing Up in the Clinch Mountains," *Ralph on Ralph*, 2002.
4. Carl Hammons interview, October 7, 2007.
5. *MCS*, 63.
6. A relative quoted Ralph as advising, "If there ain't money in it, don't do it."
7. *MCS*, 86.
8. Steele and Dotson, *The Crabtree-Stanley Collection*, 369.
9. *MCS*, 69–70.
10. *MCS*, 68.
11. Fred Stanley interview, May 25, 2009.
12. *MCS*, 27.
13. *MCS*, 27.
14. *MCS*, 42.
15. *MCS*, 43.
16. Cohen, "Ralph Stanley's Old Time Bluegrass," 1975.
17. Russell, *Country Music Records*, 703–4.
18. Carter Stanley interview with Mike Seeger, March 1966.
19. Wright, "Ralph Stanley," *Traveling the High Way Home*, 48.
20. *Ibid.*, 48.
21. Ralph Stanley interview with Terry Gross.
22. *Ibid.*
23. Cohen, "Ralph Stanley's Old Time Bluegrass," *Sing Out!*, 1975.
24. *Ibid.*
25. Charles K. Wolfe, *Kentucky Country: Folk and Country Music of Kentucky*, Lexington: University Press of Kentucky, 1982, 19–21.
26. *Ibid.*, 176. In addition, here is an excerpt from the interview transcript in Wolfe's article, "Man of Constant Sorrow—Richard Burnett's Story," *Old Time Music*, No. 10 (Autumn 1973), 8. CHARLES WOLFE: What about this "Farewell Song"—"I am a man of constant sorrow"—did you write it? RICHARD BURNETT: No, I think I got the ballet [*sic*] from somebody—I dunno. It may be my song . . .
27. Wolfe, "Man of Constant Sorrow—Richard Burnett's Story," *Old Time Music*, No. 10 (Autumn 1973), 22.
28. Wolfe, booklet to *Burnett & Rutherford: Complete Recorded Works in Chronological Order (1926–1930)*, Document Records, 1998.
29. Russell, *Country Music Records*, 65–66.
30. Ringle, "The Natural King of Bluegrass."
31. Carter Stanley interview with Mike Seeger.
32. Ivan M. Tribe, "Wade Mainer" in Barry McCloud, ed., *Definitive Country: The Ultimate Encyclopedia of Country Music and Its Performers*, New York: Perigee, 1995, 498–99.
33. Wade Mainer interview, December 2005.
34. Tribe, "Wade Mainer," 498–99.
35. *Folk Ways* television program hosted by David Holt on UNC-TV.

36. Carter and Ralph recorded more than a dozen songs recorded by Mainer's Mountaineers, including "Little Birdie" and "Little Maggie" that are closely identified with Ralph.
37. Nolan Porterfield, *Jimmie Rodgers: The Life and Times of America's Blue Yodeler*, Urbana: University of Illinois Press, 1979, 98–99.
38. *Ibid.*, 99.

Chapter 3

1. Kenneth W. Noe, *Southwest Virginia's Railroad: Modernization and the Sectional Crisis*, Urbana: University of Illinois Press, 1994, 11.
2. Steele and Dotson, *The Crabtree-Stanley Collection*, 305.
3. www.battlesatwise.com/cranesnest.html. Accessed May 18, 2009.
4. Carter Stanley interview with Mike Seeger.
5. Ringle, "The Natural King of Bluegrass."
6. Herb E. Smith, *The Ralph Stanley Story*, video, Appalshop, 2000.
7. Russell, "The Stanley Brothers."
8. Fox, "Growing Up in the Clinch Mountains," *Ralph on Ralph*, 2002.
9. *Ibid.*
10. Russell, "The Stanley Brothers."
11. Wright, "Ralph Stanley," *Traveling the High Way Home*, 50.
12. *Ibid.*
13. Johnson, "Lonesome Melodies."
14. Wright, "Ralph Stanley," *Traveling the High Way Home*, 50.
15. *Ibid.*, 51.
16. Baker, *Folio No. 1.*
17. Bluegrass historians Walter Saunders and Gary B. Reid recall hearing Sykes say this during their interview with him.
18. Richard Blaustein, "WOPI—the Pioneer Voice of the Appalachians," *Journal of Country Music*, Volume VI, Number 3, Fall 1975.
19. www.teachingamericanhistorymd.net.
20. E-mails from Joy McReynolds, wife of Jesse McReynolds, and Roy Sykes Jr. to the author.
21. I asked James Alan Shelton, Ralph Stanley's lead guitar player from 1994 onward, to explain cross-picking to me:

   The cross-picking technique is a way of playing a roll pattern with the flat pick much the way a banjo player would do it except that he would be using three fingers. The correct picking pattern is down-down-up. You pick out any three strings that are side by side and play this roll while working the melody of the song into the roll. . . . A good way to start would be to hold a D chord while playing the roll on the fourth, third and second strings. Hit the fourth string with a downstroke of the pick, then hit the third string with a downstroke and finally, hit the second string while using an upstroke with the pick. The way to do it is to just keep repeating the roll pattern over and over. DDU-DDU-DDU-DDU and make it flow into a rhythmic pattern.

22. Wayne Erbsen, "Wiley & Zeke—the Morris Brothers," www.nativeground.com.
23. Brian Golbey, booklet to *That Old Train* by the Delmore Brothers, British Archive of Country Music, 2002.

24. Carter's term.
25. *Bristol Herald Courier,* October 11, 1936.
26. Nolan Porterfield, *Jimmie Rodgers,* 226.
27. Carter Stanley interview with Mike Seeger.
28. Charles K. Wolfe, *In Close Harmony: The Story of the Louvin Brothers,* Jackson: University Press of Mississippi, 1996, 22–23.
29. *Ibid.,* 61–62.
30. The Stanley Brothers recorded only one Delmore Brothers song, "Fast Express," possibly at the urging of King Records owner Syd Nathan.
31. *An Evening Long Ago,* recorded March 24, 1956, by Larry Ehrlich, Columbia/DMZ/Legacy, 2004.
32. "Blue Sky Boys" artist biography, www.CMT.com.
33. Carter Stanley interview with Mike Seeger.
34. www.roanetnheritage.com/research/m&m/05.htm.
35. Gary B. Reid, booklet to *The Stanley Brothers, the King Years, 1961–1965,* 12.
36. Gillian Welch interview, May 26, 2006.
37. Wolfe, *Kentucky Country: Folk and Country Music of Kentucky,* 98.
38. Date based on Ralph's recollection of Clyde Moody having joined the Blue Grass Boys just before he saw them, and Neil Rosenberg's date for Moody joining the group.
39. Wolfe, *Kentucky Country,* 97.
40. Carter Stanley interview with Mike Seeger.
41. Wright, "Joe Wilson," *Traveling the High Way Home,* 82.
42. *Ibid.,* 82–83.
43. *Ibid.,* 83.
44. Illustration of concert poster in Richard D. Smith, *Can't You Hear Me Callin': The Life of Bill Monroe, Father of Bluegrass.* Boston: Little, Brown, 2000.
45. Wright, "Joe Wilson," *Traveling the High Way Home,* 83.

Chapter 4

1. *MCS,* 83–84.
2. Gary B. Reid e-mail to author, February 24, 2007.
3. Gary B. Reid e-mail to author, February 24, 2007.
4. This and other photos of Carter Stanley and Roy Sykes are from the collection of Roy Sykes Jr., and used with his permission.
5. Charles K. Wolfe, booklet to *Old-Time Music from Southwest Virginia,* County Records CO-CD-3253, 2001, 3.
6. Carter Stanley interview with Mike Seeger.
7. Johnson, "Lonesome Melodies."
8. Bill Jones of Norton, Virginia, in e-mail to author, October 13, 2006. According to the station's log, the locally produced programs during the time the Stanley Brothers played on WNVA were *Hillbilly Roundup* (6:00–6:30 a.m.), *Lonesome Pine Jamboree* (6:30–7:00 a.m.), *Mid-Morning Musicale* (9:30–10:00 a.m.), *Checkerboard Jamboree* (1:00–1:45 p.m.), *Jamboree* (7:00–8:00 p.m.), and *Lonesome Pine Jamboree* from Jenkins, Kentucky (9:45–10:15 p.m.). It is possible that the Saturday show was not listed.
9. *Folio Number Two, Picture and Song Favorites* songbook, collection of Don Morrell.

10. Fox, *Ralph on Ralph*, 2002.
11. *Folio Number Two.*
12. Exie Rose interview, February 4, 2006.
13. Also from West Virginia, Curly Ray Cline played fiddle with the Stanley Brothers in the mid-1960s, continuing with Ralph Stanley for more than twenty years.
14. Johnson, "Lonesome Melodies."
15. Reader of this book in manuscript.
16. Johnson, "Lonesome Melodies."
17. Gary B. Reid, e-mail to the author, July 29, 2006.
18. Fox, *Ralph on Ralph*, 2002.
19. Bob Sayers, "Black Mountain Odyssey: Leslie Keith," *Bluegrass Unlimited*, Vol. 11, No. 6, December 1976.
20. Carter Stanley interview with Mike Seeger.
21. Gary B. Reid e-mail to the author, July 29, 2006.
22. Fox, *Ralph on Ralph*, 2002.
23. Hazel Lambert, unpublished interview, November 25, 2006. Courtesy of Gary B. Reid.
24. Fox, *Ralph on Ralph*, 2002.

Chapter 5

1. Ralph Berrier Jr., *If Trouble Don't Kill Me: A Family's Story of Brotherhood, War, and Bluegrass*, New York: Crown, 2010, 67–68, 81–82.
2. It appears that KDKA's owner, the Westinghouse Broadcasting Company, was able to win the public relations battle to the claim of being first. KDKA received the first limited commercial license, though the history of radio reveals that other broadcasters were on the air earlier.
3. Blaustein, "WOPI—the Pioneer Voice of the Appalachians," 122.
4. *Ibid.*
5. Ralph Peer interview with Lillian Borgeson, 1959.
6. Nolan Porterfield interview, 2002.
7. Berrier, *If Trouble Don't Kill Me*, 67–68, 81–82.
8. Judith McCulloh e-mail to the author, March 3, 2006.
9. Berrier, *If Trouble Don't Kill Me*, 73–74.
10. *MCS*, 92.
11. Carter Stanley interview with Mike Seeger.
12. From description in East Tennessee State University's WCYB archives.
13. *MCS*, 111.
14. *MCS*, 111.
15. Ralph Stanley interview with Terry Gross.
16. Successor to the Federal Radio Commission.
17. Blaustein, "WOPI—the Pioneer Voice of the Appalachians," 123.
18. *Ibid.*, 125.
19. *Ibid.*
20. *Ibid.*, 128. Daughter June would marry Johnny Cash.
21. In 1954, after WCYB beat out WOPI for a television license, W. A. Wilson began to think about getting out of the broadcast business, selling Bristol's first radio station in 1959 to a group of local businessmen.

Chapter 6

1. "Bristol Honors Radio History," *The Bluegrass Blog*, www.thebluegrassblog.com/bristol-honors-radio-history/. Posted by Richard Thompson, September 24, 2007. Accessed June 3, 2009.
2. *1947–49 Bristol City Directory.*
3. Bass player Ray Lambert had not joined the group or was not playing on air at the time.
4. Carter Stanley interview with Mike Seeger.
5. *Live Again! WCYB Bristol Farm and Fun Time*, Rebel Records, REB-CD-2003, 1997.
6. Smith, *Can't You Hear Me Callin'*, 89.
7. Ralph Stanley interview, May 2005.
8. Johnson, "Lonesome Melodies."
9. *Ibid.*
10. cass.etsu.edu/ARCHIVES/ARCHIVES/Hardwoods.
11. Johnson, "Lonesome Melodies."
12. *Ibid.*
13. Max K. Powers interview, fall 2001.

Chapter 7

1. Wade Mainer interview, December 2005.
2. Gary B. Reid, booklet to Stanley Brothers, *Earliest Recordings: The Complete Rich-R-Tone 78s (1947–52)*, Rounder Records 11661-1110-2, 2005, 4.
3. Fred Congdon e-mail to the author, May 9, 2005.
4. *1947–49 Bristol City Directory.*
5. Reid, booklet to *Earliest Recordings*, 6.
6. *MCS* advance reading copy, New York: Gotham Books, October 2009, 101.
7. Fred Bartenstein, notes to *Banks of the Ohio* radio program No. 161.
8. Carter Stanley interview with Mike Seeger.
9. Neil V. Rosenberg, *Bluegrass: A History*, Urbana: University of Illinois Press, 1985, 84.
10. Rosenberg, *Bluegrass: A History*, 84.
11. Revolutions per minute.
12. Reid, booklet to *Earliest Recordings*, 7.
13. *Ibid.*
14. Carter Stanley interview with Mike Seeger.
15. Reid, booklet to *Earliest Recordings*, 10.
16. Ralph Stanley interview, March 2005.
17. His unaccompanied rendition of "O Death" on the soundtrack of *O Brother, Where Art Thou?* received the Grammy Award for best male country vocal in 2002.
18. "Don't Forget This Song," credited to A. P. Carter and recorded February 15, 1929.
19. Rosenberg, *Bluegrass: A History*, 84.
20. Neil V. Rosenberg, "From Sound to Style: The Emergence of Bluegrass," *Journal of American Folklore*, Vol. 80, No. 316 (April–June, 1967), 146.
21. *Ibid.*, 145.
22. Ralph Stanley interview, March 2005.

Chapter 8

1. *MCS*, 111–12.
2. Carter Stanley interview with Mike Seeger.
3. Fox, "Clinch Mountain Travel," *Ralph on Ralph*, 2002.
4. *Ibid.*
5. Johnson, "Lonesome Melodies."
6. Kerry Hay e-mail to the author, September 9, 2006.
7. I asked Kerry Hay about signs of professionalism. "The reason that I made that comment was that Carter had the same easy-going bandleader approach for a stage show, at that early time, that he exhibited throughout his career. Both Carter and Ralph appeared totally at ease on stage, as if they had been doing that type of thing for years." E-mail to the author, January 2, 2007.
8. Gary B. Reid e-mail to Kerry Hay and the author, September 11, 2006.
9. Gary B. Reid e-mail to Kerry Hay and the author, September 9, 2006.
10. *MCS*, 118–19.
11. Hazel Lambert, unpublished interview, November 25, 2006. Courtesy of Gary B. Reid.
12. *Ibid.*.
13. Carter Stanley interview with Mike Seeger.
14. *MCS*, 169.
15. Rosenberg, *Bluegrass: A History*, 27.
16. Sandra Poulimenos interview, March 24, 2007.
17. Thelma Easterling Bruzdowski interviews, February 2007.
18. *Bluegrass Mandolin Home Page* www.users.waitrose.com/~john.baldry/mando/jesse .html. Accessed January 24, 2007.
19. Ann Fessler, *The Girls Who Went Away: The Hidden History of Women Who Surrendered Children for Adoption in the Decades before Roe v. Wade*, New York: Penguin, 2006, 139.
20. *Ibid.*, 143.
21. Sandra Poulimenos e-mail to the author, July 9, 2005.
22. *Ibid.*
23. Fox, "Clinch Mountain Travel," *Ralph on Ralph*, 2002.
24. Gary B. Reid, booklet to *The Stanley Brothers & the Clinch Mountain Boys 1949–52*, Bear Family Records BCD 15564 AH, 1991.
25. *Ibid.*
26. *Ibid.*
27. Ralph Stanley interview with Mike Seeger.
28. *Ibid.*
29. *MCS*, 136.
30. Bill Clifton interview, February 21, 2006.
31. Ralph Stanley interview with Mike Seeger.
32. John Wright, *Didaskalia* Vol. 3, No. 3 (Winter 1996), University of Warwick, Sallie Goetsch and C. W. Marshal, eds.
33. Wayne Erbsen, "Lester Woodie: Coming Up the Hard Road," *Bluegrass Unlimited*, March 1980, 45.
34. Ralph Stanley interview with Mike Seeger.
35. Wright, "Ralph Stanley," *Traveling the High Way Home*, 54.

36. Carter Stanley interview with Mike Seeger.
37. Wright, "Ralph Stanley," *Traveling the High Way Home*, 54.
38. Reid, booklet to *The Stanley Brothers & the Clinch Mountain Boys 1949–52*.
39. *Ibid.*
40. Notes to *The Rich-R-Tone Story*, Rounder Collective, 4.
41. Ralph Stanley interview with Mike Seeger.
42. Jim McReynolds interview with Neil Rosenberg, February 5, 1965, as quoted in *Bluegrass: A History*, 82–83.

Chapter 9

1. Reid, booklet to *The Stanley Brothers & the Clinch Mountain Boys 1949–52*
2. Carter Stanley interview with Mike Seeger.
3. Ralph Stanley interview with Mike Seeger.
4. John Wright, "Ralph Stanley," *Traveling the High Way Home*, 55.
5. *MCS*, 143.
6. Gary Marmorstein, *The Label: The History of Columbia Records*, New York: Thunder's Mouth Press, 2007, 84.
7. *Encyclopedia of Country Music*, Country Music Hall of Fame and Museum, 470.
8. Bob Sayers, "Black Mountain Odyssey: Leslie Keith," *Bluegrass Unlimited*, Vol. 11, No. 6, December 1976.
9. As reported in *Billboard*, November 1949.
10. Carter Stanley interview with Mike Seeger.
11. Reid, booklet to *The Stanley Brothers & the Clinch Mountain Boys 1949–52*.
12. Lester Woodie e-mail to author, March 5, 2007.
13. *Ibid.*
14. Carter Stanley interview with Mike Seeger.
15. Ralph Stanley interview with Terry Gross.
16. Rosenberg, *Bluegrass: A History*, 88.
17. Carter Stanley interview with Mike Seeger.
18. The vocal slide became such a signature of the Stanley sound that when Keith Richards of the Rolling Stones sang a similar vocal phrase while rehearsing a tribute to the late Gram Parsons, he turned to fellow musician Jim Lauderdale and said "Stanley Brothers!" Quoted by Jim Lauderdale at the concert before the opening of the Ralph Stanley Museum and Traditional Music Center, October 2004.
19. Wright, "Ralph Stanley," *Traveling the High Way Home*, 47.
20. *Ibid.*
21. Ralph Stanley interview with Mike Seeger.
22. Joe Morrell interview, December 11, 2004.
23. A. P. suffered from a lifelong tremor.
24. Erbsen, "Lester Woodie: Coming Up the Hard Road," *Bluegrass Unlimited*, March 1980, 44.
25. John Wright, "Lester Woodie," *Traveling the High Way Home*, 101.
26. Lester Woodie e-mail to author, October 30, 2006.
27. John Wright, "Lester Woodie," *Traveling the High Way Home*, 101–2.
28. Ivan Tribe, *Mountaineer Jamboree: Country Music in West Virginia*, Lexington: University Press of Kentucky, 1984. Paperback afterword 1996, 138–39.

29. Lester Woodie e-mail to the author, May 30, 2007.

30. Ivan Tribe, *Mountaineer Jamboree*, 139.

31. Lester Woodie e-mail to author, October 19, 2006.

Chapter 10

1. Tracey E. Laird, *Louisiana Hayride: Radio and Roots Music Along the Red River*, New York: Oxford University Press, 2005, 94–95.

2. Laird, *Louisiana Hayride*, 7, 95.

3. Lester Woodie e-mail to the author, June 14, 2008.

4. Laird, *Louisiana Hayride*, 4.

5. *Ibid.*, 13.

6. *Ibid.*, 17.

7. *Ibid.*

8. *Ibid.*, 32.

9. *Ibid.*, 37.

10. Erbsen, "Lester Woodie: Coming Up the Hard Road," 48.

11. Ralph Stanley interview with Mike Seeger.

12. www.allmusic.com.

13. Gary B. Reid, notes accompanying *The Stanley Brothers, the Definitive Collection (1947–1966)*, Time Life, 2007, 11.

14. George Shuffler interview, May 14, 2007.

15. Hazel Lambert, unpublished interview, November 25, 2006. Courtesy of Gary B. Reid.

16. In his autobiography, Ralph said Art Satherley flew to Nashville "direct from Los Angeles." *MCS*, 146.

17. Gary G. Reid, booklet to *The Stanley Brothers & the Clinch Mountain Boys 1949–52*, Bear Family Records BCD 15564 AH, 1991, 6.

18. Lester Woodie e-mail to the author, October 19, 2006.

19. According to Roy Sykes Jr., Keith composed this popular fiddle tune in late 1939 when the car carrying Roy Sykes and the Blue Ridge Mountain Boys became stuck on top of a mountain between Norton, Virginia, and Pikeville, Kentucky. Keith, who was a member of the group at the time, remained inside the car while the rest of the band pushed it out of the deep snow.

20. *MCS*, 147.

21. Lester Woodie e-mail to the author, October 9, 2006.

22. Wright, "Lester Woodie," *Traveling the High Way Home*, 99.

23. Wright, "Ralph Stanley," *Traveling the High Way Home*, 56.

24. *MCS*, 151.

25. *Ibid.*, 153.

26. Hazel Lambert, unpublished interview.

27. *MCS*, 153.

28. Wright, "Ralph Stanley," *Traveling the High Way Home*, 56–57.

29. Hazel Lambert interview, June 21, 2007.

30. Jeffrey Fox and Janice Wallen, "An Odd Career Move," *Bluegrass Adventures I: Then . . . and Now (A Mountain Music Storybook)*, Ja Vi Publishing, 2000.

31. Jack Tottle, "Ralph Stanley: The Stanley Sound," *Bluegrass Unlimited*, May 1981, 16.

32. Lester Woodie e-mail to the author, March 6, 2007.

Chapter 11

1. Wright, "Joe Wilson," *Traveling the High Way Home*, 77.
2. *MCS*, 155.
3. *Ibid.*, 156.
4. Fox, "Clinch Mountain Travel," *Ralph on Ralph*, 2002.
5. Wright, "Ralph Stanley," *Traveling the High Way Home*, 56.
6. www.birthplaceofcountrymusic.org. Accessed April 29, 2007.
7. Wright, "Joe Wilson," *Traveling the High Way Home*, 77–78.
8. Wright, "Ralph Stanley," *Traveling the High Way Home*, 57.
9. Gary B. Reid, notes to *The Stanley Brothers, The Definitive Collection (1947–1966)*, 11.
10. Rosenberg, *Bluegrass: A History*, 100.
11. *Ibid.*
12. Bill Clifton interview, February 21, 2006.
13. Rosenberg, *Bluegrass: A History*, 85.
14. *Ibid.*, 81.
15. Ironically, Jim and Jesse were invited to become cast members of the *Grand Ole Opry*, while the Stanley Brothers never received an invitation. Ralph joined the *Opry* in 2000.
16. Bill Clifton interview, February 21, 2006.
17. Gary B. Reid e-mail to author, May 14, 2007.
18. Smith, *Can't You Hear Me Callin'*, 96.
19. Bill Clifton interview, February 21, 2006.
20. *Ibid.*
21. Reid, booklet to *Earliest Recordings*, 18–19.
22. *Ibid.*, 20.
23. *MCS*, 175.
24. June Suthers interview, February 18, 2007.
25. *MCS*, 174.
26. *Ibid.*
27. George Shuffler interview, April 21, 2005.
28. Reid, booklet to *The Stanley Brothers & the Clinch Mountain Boys, 1953–58 & 1959*, Bear Family, 7.
29. Bob Artis, *Bluegrass*, New York: Hawthorn, 1975, 34.
30. www.bluegrasslyrics.com.
31. Adapted for the stage, *Lonesome Pine* has become the state pageant of Virginia, produced each summer in Big Stone Gap.
32. Carter Stanley interview with Mike Seeger.
33. Artis, *Bluegrass*, 38.
34. Johnson, "Lonesome Melodies." 35. www.countrymusichalloffame.com.
36. Article at www.nashvillepost.com dated June 29, 2000.
37. *Ibid.*
38. www.countrymusichalloffame.com.
39. Revolutions per minute.
40. Johnson, "Lonesome Melodies."
41. Carter Stanley interview with Mike Seeger.
42. Johnson, "Lonesome Melodies."

43. Lester Woodie e-mail to the author, October 30, 2006.
44. www.bluegrasslyrics.com.
45. Erbsen, "Lester Woodie: Coming Up the Hard Road," 48.
46. www.bluegrasslyrics.com.
47. Laird, *Louisiana Hayride*, 121.
48. *Ibid.*, 124.
49. Recollection of D. R. Hutchinson, Abingdon, Virginia.
50. George Shuffler interview, fall 2004.

Chapter 12

1. *The Encyclopedia of Country Music*, 247.
2. Larry Ehrlich e-mail to the author, July 15, 2011.
3. Larry Ehrlich interview, May 27, 2008.
4. *Ibid.*
5. Ehrlich, booklet to *The Stanley Brothers: An Evening Long Ago*, Columbia/DMZ/Legacy, 2004.
6. Ehrlich, booklet to *An Evening Long Ago*.
7. Larry Ehrlich interview, August 17. 2006.
8. Larry Ehrlich e-mail to the author, September 23, 2011.
9. Posted to the BGRASS-L listserv, January 23, 2005.
10. Though the brothers might not have thought much about the recording in 1956, Ralph duplicated it on CD as a "gift" to fans attending his performances around 2001. The price was $20.
11. Joe Morrell interview, December 11, 2004.
12. Reid, booklet to *The Stanley Brothers & the Clinch Mountain Boys, 1953–1958 & 1959*.
13. Reid, notes to *The Definitive Collection (1947–1966)*, 14.
14. *Country and Western Jamboree*, December 1955.
15. Tottle, "Ralph Stanley: The Stanley Sound," *Bluegrass Unlimited*, May 1981, 17.
16. Bill Clifton interview, February 21, 2006.
17. Carter Stanley interview with Mike Seeger.
18. Reid, booklet to *The Stanley Brothers & the Clinch Mountain Boys, 1953–1958 & 1959*.
19. *Ibid.*
20. *MCS* advance reading copy, 197.
21. *Ibid.*
22. Wright, "Joe Wilson," *Traveling the High Way Home*, 84.
23. Charlie Louvin interview with British country singer Hank Wangford for a United Kingdom Channel 4 television series, "A–Z of Country Music." Accessed June 26, 2007 on YouTube.
24. *Ibid.*
25. Neil Rosenberg, "From Sound to Style," 146.
26. Wright, "Ron Thomason," *Traveling the High Way Home*, 157.
27. Joe Morrell interview, December 11, 2004.
28. Information on the Northwest tour provided by Gary B. Reid. *Clinch Mountain Song Review* from the collection of Don Morrell.
29. Joe Morrell interview, December 11, 2004.

30. Kermit K. Keeter, Steven Businger, Laurence G. Lee, and Jeff S. Waldstreicher, "Winter Weather Forecasting throughout the Eastern United States. Part III: The Effects of Topography and the Variability of Winter Weather in the Carolinas and Virginia," *Weather and Forecasting*, Vol. 10, Issue 1 (March 1995), 42–60.
31. Dean, "Carter Stanley: The Sibling That 'O Brother' Forgot."
32. Reid, booklet to *The Stanley Brothers & the Clinch Mountain Boys, 1953–1958 & 1959*.
33. Nathan D. Gibson, *The Starday Story: The House That Country Built*, Jackson: University Press of Mississippi, 2011, 71.
34. Jerry E. Powers interview, May 27, 2006.
35. www.bluegridgeinstitute.org/ballads/floodsong.html.
36. *MCS*, 123–24.
37. *Ibid.*, 123.
38. As quoted in Gibson, *The Starday Story*, 72.
39. "Beneath the Big Sandy," *Time*, March 10, 1958.
40. Excellent Records number EX-400 A.
41. As quoted by Rick Kennedy, co-author with Randy McNutt, *Little Labels—Big Sound: Small Record Companies and the Rise of American Music*, Indiana University Press, 1999, 71.

Chapter 13

1. Arnold Brim interview, June 27, 2007.
2. Norman Protsman interview, July 13, 2007.
3. Clarence S. Parker interview, August 11, 2007.
4. www.floridamemory.com.
5. Norman Protsman interview, July 16, 2007.
6. Protsman enforced similar standards at WNER. "Sometimes one of the boys would play a record I didn't like, and I would go into the station and I'd say, 'Could I have that record?' and I would break it. I was a mean old bugger." He recalled breaking two or three records.
7. www.jimandjesse.com.
8. Stanley Brothers, *Shadows of the Past*, Copper Creek Records, CCD-0101.
9. Gary B. Reid, "The Stanley Brothers in Florida," *Florida Bluegrass News*, March–April 1985, Vol. 1, No. 2.
10. Bill Clifton interview, February 21, 2006.
11. *Ibid.*
12. www.foodreference.com/html/f-martha-white-flour.html. Accessed June 29, 2007.
13. Rosenberg, *Bluegrass: A History*, 101.
14. *Ibid.*
15. *Ibid.*
16. *Ibid.*, 106–7.
17. *Ibid.*, 107.
18. *Ibid.*, 135, 177.
19. Bill Clifton interview, February 21, 2006.
20. Ralph Stanley interview with Mike Seeger.
21. As quoted by Reid, "The Stanley Brothers in Florida."

22. *Ibid.*

23. Stanley Brothers, *On Radio*, Rebel Records CD 1115.

24. *MCS*, 203.

25. *Ibid.*, 202.

26. George Shuffler interview, July 6, 2007.

27. Arnold Brim interview, June 27, 2007.

28. *MCS*, 202.

29. Rosenberg, *Bluegrass : A History*, 134–35.

30. *Ibid.*, 138.

31. *Ibid.*

32. Gary B. Reid, booklet to *The Stanley Brothers: The Early Starday King Years 1958–1961*, Starday/King Records, 1993, 1.

33. Gary B. Reid, notes to *Shadows of the Past*.

34. In a little more than a decade the LP would bring about major changes in the concept of popular music, as recording artists such as the Beatles, with the release of *Sgt. Pepper's Lonely Hearts Club Band* in June 1967, designed their projects to take advantage of the longer format.

35. John Wright e-mail to the author, March 6, 2007.

36. Fox, *King of the Queen City*, 10, and Kennedy and McNutt, *Little Labels—Big Sound*, 62.

37. As quoted in Fox, *King of the Queen City*, 8.

38. Fox, *King of the Queen City*, 8–9.

39. Kennedy and McNutt, *Little Labels*, 62.

40. *Ibid.*, 60.

41. *Ibid.*, 57.

42. *Ibid.*, 66.

43. *Ibid.*, 69.

44. As quoted in Kennedy and McNutt, *Little Labels*, 57.

45. Kennedy and McNutt *Little Labels*, 64.

46. *Ibid.*, 69.

47. *Ibid.*, 67.

48. As quoted in the booklet to *The Stanley Brothers: The Early Starday King Years 1958–1961*, 2.

49. Rosenberg, *Bluegrass: A History*, 140–41.

50. *Clinch Mountain Song Review*, collection of Don Morrell.

Chapter 14

1. Mike Seeger, "About the Performers" notes to *Mountain Music Bluegrass Style*, Smithsonian Folkways CD 40038, 1991.

2. *Ibid.*

3. Bob Dylan, *Chronicles: Volume One*, New York: Simon & Schuster, 2004, 70–71.

4. Mike Seeger interview, June 22, 2006.

5. *MCS*, 197.

6. George Shuffler interview, fall 2004.

7. Reid, booklet to *The Stanley Brothers: The Early Starday King Years 1958–1961*, 5.

8. www.bsnpubs.com/king/kingstory.html. Accessed July 14, 2007.

9. Reid, booklet to *The Stanley Brothers: The Early Starday King Years 1958–1961*, 5.

10. Ronald R. Cohen, *Rainbow Quest: The Folk Music Revival and American Society, 1940–1970*, Amherst: University of Massachusetts Press, 2002, 10.

11. *Ibid.*

12. *Ibid.*, 12.

13. *Ibid.*, 11.

14. *Ibid.*, 13.

15. *Ibid.*, 14.

16. Martha W. Beckwith, *Journal of American Folklore*, Vol. 46, No. 182 (October–December 1933), 416.

17. Cohen, *Rainbow Quest*, 14.

18. *Ibid.*

19. Smith, *Can't You Hear Me Callin'*, 24; Mark Zwonitzer with Charles Hirschberg, *Will You Miss Me When I'm Gone?: The Carter Family and Their Legacy in American Music*, New York: Simon & Schuster, 2002, 131.

20. Oscar Brand e-mail to the author, July 22, 2007.

21. Rosenberg, *Bluegrass: A History*, 152.

22. Cohen, *Rainbow Quest*, 145.

23. *Ibid.*, 146.

24. fpc.dos.state.fl.us/folklife/fp516175.jpg and www.floridamemory.com/collections/folklife/festival.cfm.

25. *Newport Folk Festival: Best of Bluegrass 1959–66*, Vanguard CD 187/89-2, 2001.

26. Bruce Winkworth, booklet to *Newport Folk Festival*, 4.

27. Oscar Brand e-mail to the author, July 29, 2007.

28. *Ibid.*

29. Robert V. Droz, www.us-highways.com, in an e-mail to the author, August 2, 2007.

30. Ralph Stanley interview with Mike Seeger.

31. Gary B. Reid e-mail to the author, August 5, 2007.

32. George Shuffler as quoted by Gary B. Reid in booklet to *The Stanley Brothers: The Early Starday King Years 1958–1961*, 7.

33. Reid, booklet to *The Stanley Brothers: The Early Starday King Years 1958–1961*, 7–8.

34. George Shuffler interview, fall 2004.

35. Reid, booklet to *The Stanley Brothers: The Early Starday King Years 1958–1961*, 7.

36. Kennedy and McNutt, *Little Labels*, 66.

37. Reid, booklet to *The Stanley Brothers: The Early Starday King Years 1958–1961*, 8.

38. In an e-mail to the author on July 5, 2007, Gary Reid wrote: "I think a lot of these songs were trios, with Shuffler alternating between bass and baritone vocal parts. Napier was kept busy providing the bulk of the instrumental work on the guitar."

39. Reid, booklet to *The Stanley Brothers: The Early Starday King Years 1958–1961*, 10.

40. Ralph Stanley interview with Mike Seeger.

41. Ruby Rakes, "How Far to Little Rock."

42. Reid, booklet to *The Stanley Brothers: The Early Starday King Years 1958–1961*, 10.

43. *Ibid.*

44. Interview with Fred Stanley, May 25, 2009.

45. From Lawrence Kasdan's script to *Raiders of the Lost Ark*, 1981.

46. Paraphrase of Fred Bartenstein introducing one such group on his *Banks of the Ohio* radio program.
47. Clarence Parker interview, August 11, 2007.

Chapter 15

1. Rosenberg, *Bluegrass: A History*, 155.
2. *MCS*, 189.
3. Johnson, "Lonesome Melodies."
4. *MCS*, 185.
5. Bud Reed interview, spring 2006.
6. Reid, "The Stanley Brothers in Florida."
7. *MCS* advance reading copy, 196–97
8. *MCS*, 266.
9. Peggy C. Bland interview, March 20, 2008.
10. Richard K. Spottswood interview, July 11, 2011.
11. Reid, booklet to *The Stanley Brothers: The Early Starday King Years 1958–1961*, 11.
12. Gary B. Reid e-mail to the author, August 7, 2007.
13. *Ibid.*
14. *The Stanley Brothers Live at Antioch College*, Vintage Collectors Club ZK 002.
15. Reid, booklet to *The Stanley Brothers: The Early Starday King Years 1958–1961*, 12.
16. *Ibid.*
17. Rosenberg, *Bluegrass: A History*, 141.
18. Reid, booklet to *The Stanley Brothers: The Early Starday King Years 1958–1961*, 14.
19. *Ibid.*
20. Interview with Doug Gordon and Roy Burke III as quoted by Gary B. Reid in booklet to *The Stanley Brothers: The Early Starday King Years 1958–1961*, 15.
21. Reid, booklet to *The Stanley Brothers: The Early Starday King Years 1958–1961*, 14.
22. Gary B. Reid, booklet to two-CD set *Folk Festival*, ST-CD-5003, 2001, sold by Ralph Stanley at personal appearances, 2.
23. *MCS*, 205.
24. In the manner of Natalie Cole overdubbing herself singing on her father Nat "King" Cole's recording of the song "Unforgettable," years after he died.
25. Reid, booklet to *Folk Festival*, 6, and booklet to *The Stanley Brothers: The King Years 1961–1965*, King Records, 2003, 2.
26. Larry Ehrlich interview, August 7, 2007.

Chapter 16

1. Claude Hyman interview, May 6, 2008.
2. According to Fred Bartenstein, "A similar event was held at Watermelon Park in Berryville, Virginia, on August 14, 1960."
3. David Freeman, e-mail to Fred Bartenstein, July 24, 2007.
4. Rosenberg, *Bluegrass: A History*, 178.
5. David Freeman e-mail to Fred Bartenstein, July 24, 2007.
6. David Freeman e-mail to the author, January 18, 2008.

7. Rosenberg, *Bluegrass: A History*, 178.
8. *Ibid.*, 179.
9. Smith, *Can't You Hear Me Callin'*, 152–53.
10. David Freeman e-mail to the author, January 18, 2008.
11. Wright, "Joe Wilson," *Traveling the High Way Home*, 81.
12. *MCS*, 260–65.
13. Norman Protsman interview, July 13, 2007.
14. Arnold Brim interview, June 27, 2007.
15. Gary B. Reid, "The Stanley Brothers in Florida."
16. Bill Malone e-mail to the author, January 12, 2008.
17. Larry Ehrlich interview.
18. Roy Sykes Jr. interview, January 6, 2007.
19. Doris Stanley Bradley e-mail to the author, September 15, 2007.
20. *Ibid.*
21. Bill Clifton interview, February 21, 2006.
22. *Ibid.*
23. Neil V. Rosenberg e-mail to the author, January 25, 2008.
24. Stanley Brothers, *Shadows of the Past*.
25. *MCS*, 216–17.
26. Johnson, "Lonesome Melodies."
27. According to Bgrass, Inc. on the Miami University Hamilton Web site. Accessed February 1, 2008.
28. Artis, *Bluegrass*, 38.
29. Lester Woodie e-mail to the author, December 17, 2006.
30. Ed Pearl interview with Peter F. Feldmann, *Old-Time Herald*, Vol. 5, No. 8, 1996.
31. Bernie Pearl as quoted by Rebecca Kuzins, "The Last Coffeehouse," *Los Angeles*, February 1985, www.ashgrovemusic.com. Accessed September 26, 2011.
32. Dean, "Carter Stanley: The Sibling That 'O Brother' Forgot."
33. Pote, *Man of Constant Sorrow*, Barter Theatre, Abingdon, Virginia, 27–28.
34. *MCS*, 169.
35. Ed Pearl interview with Peter F. Feldmann.
36. Peter Coonradt e-mail to the author, 2007.
37. Card belonging to Jeanie Stanley Allinder. Text courtesy of Gary B. Reid.
38. Gary B. Reid e-mail to the author, January 27, 2008.
39. Reid, booklet to *The Stanley Brothers: The King Years 1961–1965*, 15.
40. *Ibid.*
41. *Ibid.*, 11.
42. Richard K. Spottswood interview, July 11, 2011.
43. Reid, booklet to *The Stanley Brothers: The Definitive Collection (1947–1966)*, Time Life, 2007, 21.
44. Charles Taylor e-mail to the author, Jan. 15, 2008.
45. Charles Taylor e-mail to the author, Jan. 26, 2008.
46. Charles Taylor e-mail to the author, Jan. 31, 2008.
47. Charles Taylor e-mail to the author, Jan. 26, 2008.
48. The Stanley Brothers performed the numbers on this tour, though the album was not released until June 1963. Bill Malone e-mail to the author, Jan. 11, 2008.

49. Reid, booklet to *The Stanley Brothers: The King Years 1961–1965*, 14.
50. *Ibid.*

Chapter 17

1. Ray Davis interview, April 23, 2008.
2. Bill Vernon, booklet to *Long Journey Home*, Rebel CD-1110, 1990.
3. The call letters were XERA when the Carters were on the air.
4. Bill Vernon, booklet to *Long Journey Home*.
5. Joe Carter interview, December 2002.
6. Ray Davis interview, April 23, 2008.
7. Gary Reid, liner notes to *Uncloudy Day*, County Records 753, originally issued as Wango 103.
8. *Ibid.*
9. I came to this conclusion this after separate conversations with two people who were familiar with the session.
10. Jack Cooke interview, May 23, 2008.
11. Interview with Mike Seeger, June 22, 2006.
12. Bill C. Malone e-mail to the author, January 11, 2008.
13. *Ibid.*
14. Reid, booklet to *The Stanley Brothers: The King Years 1961–1965*, 17.
15. *Ibid.*, 22.
16. *Ibid.*, 20–21.
17. *Ibid.*, 22–23.
18. Bill Vernon, notes to LP reissue of Wango 106, titled *That Little Old Country Church House*, County Records 738.
19. Stanley Brothers, *Folk Festival*, ST-CD-5003, 2001.
20. Judith McCulloh interview, March 2007.
21. Bill C. Malone e-mail to the author, January 12, 2008.
22. Artis, *Bluegrass*, 37.
23. Smith, *Can't You Hear Me Callin'*, 200.
24. Notes to Don Owens's nomination as a candidate for the International Bluegrass Music Association Hall of Fame, 2008.
25. Smith, *Can't You Hear Me Callin'*, 169.
26. Mike Seeger interview, June 22, 2006.
27. Smith, *Can't You Hear Me Callin'*, 171.
28. *Ibid.*, 172–73.
29. *Ibid.*, 201.
30. Carlton Haney interview, January 3, 2008.
31. *Ibid.*
32. Smith, *Can't You Hear Me Callin'*, 202.
33. Recordings courtesy of Fred Bartenstein.
34. Photographer unknown, www.youtube.com. Accessed May 2, 2008.
35. Smith, *Can't You Hear Me Callin'*, 202.
36. www.bluegrasstime.com.
37. Fred Bartenstein e-mail to the author, May 29, 2007.

38. www.bluegrass.time,com.
39. Appalachian College Association Central Library's Digital Library of Appalachia, www .aca-dla.org.
40. Fred Bartenstein e-mail to the author, August 5, 2008.
41. www.bluegrasstime.com.
42. www.aca-dla.org.
43. As it is identified in the Digital Archives of Appalachia.
44. Overheard by the author, who was in the same line to meet Jimmy Martin.
45. Reid, booklet to *The Stanley Brothers: The King Years 1961–1965*, 24.
46. *Ibid.*, 22.
47. *Ibid.*, 23.
48. *Ibid.*
49. Notes to CD reissue of *An Empty Mansion*, Old Homestead Records, OHCD 118.
50. Notes to CD reissue of *A Beautiful Life*, Old Homestead Records, OHCD 119.
51. Ray Davis interview, April 23, 2008.
52. Recordings courtesy of Gary B. Reid.

Chapter 18

1. Joseph B. Mongle Jr. interview, December 2007.
2. Mary Bruce Mazza interview, December 2007.
3. Undated newspaper clipping courtesy of Mary Bruce Mazza.
4. *MCS*, 238.
5. Ralph Stanley interview with Terry Gross, July 15, 2002.
6. Mary Bruce Mazza interview, October 20, 2008.
7. Thomas R. Hobbs, "Managing Alcoholism as a Disease," *Physician's News Digest*, February 1998. Accessed on www.physiciansnews.com/commentary/298wp.html.
8. *Ibid.*
9. Eskew, Crutcher, et al., "Lead Poisoning Resulting from Illicit Alcohol Consumption," *Journal of Forensic Sciences*, Vol. 6, January–October 1961, 337, 342.
10. Dr. Christopher Holstege e-mail to the author, August 27, 2007.
11. "Lead Toxicity Can Occur Among Chronic Abusers," University of Virginia Health System news release, May 28, 2003.
12. *MCS*, 170.
13. Doris Stanley Bradley e-mail to the author, September 15, 2007.
14. Conversation with William B. Stanley, July 30, 2011.
15. Garth Nobles e-mail to the author September 9, 2010.
16. *Ibid.*
17. Carter Lee Stanley interview, November 28, 2011.
18. Melvin Goins interview, October 27, 2007.
19. *American Folk & Country Music Festival* book accompanying two-CD set of the same name, Bear Family Records, 2008, 17.
20. Ralph Earle, "Folk at Winterfest," *Broadside of Boston* Vol. 5, No. 2, 6.
21. *American Folk & Country Music Festival* book, 2, 11–12.
22. *Ibid.*, 17.
23. *Ibid.*, 2.

24. George Shuffler interview, October 8, 2008.

25. Tracy Schwarz e-mail to the author, September 23, 2008.

26. George Shuffler interview, October 8, 2008.

27. Bill Clifton interview, February 21, 2006.

28. Bill Clifton interview, February 21, 2006.

29. Vernacular courtesy of Dr. A. Denise Stanley of Emory and Henry College, Emory, Virginia.

30. *American Folk & Country Music Festival* book, 13.

31. John Cohen, booklet to *Mountain Music of Kentucky*, Smithsonian Folkways CD 40077, 1996, 22–24.

32. *Ibid.*, 29.

33. Mike Seeger interview, October 8, 2008.

34. *American Folk & Country Music Festival* book, 21.

35. George Shuffler interview, October 8, 2008.

36. *Ibid.*

37. Wright, "Melvin Goins," *Traveling the High Way Home*, 109.

38. George Shuffler interview, October 8, 2008.

39. Tribe, *Mountaineer Jamboree*, 66.

40. *Ibid.*, 67.

41. Stanley Brothers performance dates for 1966 courtesy of Gary B. Reid.

42. Wright, "George Shuffler," *Traveling the High Way Home*, 92–93, and George Shuffler interview, October 8, 2008.

43. Wright, "George Shuffler," *Traveling the High Way Home*, 93.

44. Wright, "Melvin Goins," *Traveling the High Way Home*, 112.

45. *Ibid.*, 109.

46. *Ibid.*, 110.

47. *Ibid.*, 112.

48. James Alan Shelton, notes to *Brown County Jamboree*, CD released by Ralph Stanley, circa 2004.

49. "Our Favorite Star Has Gone Out," *Stanley Standard*, May 1967, 22.

50. Wright, "Fay McGinnis," *Traveling the High Way Home*, 175.

51. *Ibid.*, 176–77.

52. *Ibid.*, 177.

53. *Stanley Standard*, May 1967, 1.

54. Wright, "Fay McGinnis," *Traveling the High Way Home*, 178.

55. Letter from Kitty of the KCZT Tape Club, *Stanley Standard*, May 1967, 12.

56. Wright, "Fay McGinnis," *Traveling the High Way Home*, 181.

57. Norma Fannin, "He Was That Kind of Guy," *Stanley Standard*, May 1967, 4.

58. Wright, "Fay McGinnis," *Traveling the High Way Home*, 181–82.

59. *Ibid.*, 182.

60. *Ibid.*, 182–83.

61. Melvin Goins interview, October 21, 2007.

62. *Ibid.*

63. Wright, "Melvin Goins," *Traveling the High Way Home*, 112–13.

64. Wright, "George Shuffler," *Traveling the High Way Home*, 93.

65. *Ibid.*

66. Wright, "Melvin Goins," *Traveling the High Way Home*, 113.
67. Wright, "George Shuffler," *Traveling the High Way Home*, 93–94.

Chapter 19

1. Wright, "George Shuffler," *Traveling the High Way Home*, 94.
2. *Ibid.*
3. As quoted by Hattie Rasnick's daughter June Suthers, February 18, 2007.
4. *MCS*, 243.
5. Carter Lee Stanley interview, November 28, 2011.
6. Dr. Christopher P. Holstege e-mail to the author, December 9, 2011.
7. Roy Sykes Jr. e-mail to the author, February 18, 2007.
8. Fannin, "He Was That Kind of Guy," 4.
9. Richard K. Spottswood interview, July 11, 2011.
10. Doris Stanley Bradley e-mail to the author, September 15, 2007.
11. *MCS* advance reading copy, 243–44.
12. Wright, "George Shuffler," *Traveling the High Way Home*, 94.
13. As quoted in Wright, "George Shuffler," *Traveling the High Way Home*, 94.
14. *Ibid.*, 94–95.
15. *Ibid.*, 95.
16. *Ibid.*
17. Roy Sykes Jr. interview, January 6, 2007.
18. Mary Bruce Mongle interview, February 9, 2008.
19. Walter Saunders, "The Carter Stanley Memorial Concert," *Stanley Standard*, May 1967, 24; Roy Sykes Jr. interview, January 6, 2007.
20. Bob Cantwell, "The Lonesome Sound of Carter Stanley," *Bluegrass Unlimited*, June 1976, 16.
21. Doris Stanley Bradley e-mail to the author, September 7, 2007.
22. *Ibid.*
23. "Famed Gospel Singer Stanley Buried in Native Dickenson," reprinted from *Cumberland Times*, December 15, 1966.
24. *Cumberland Times*, December 15, 1966, and *Stanley Standard*, May 1967.
25. "In Memoriam . . . Carter Stanley," *Bluegrass Bulletin*, Vol. 2, No. 3, January 1967, reprinted in *Stanley Standard*, May 1967.
26. Fannin, "He Was That Kind of Guy," 4.
27. "In Memoriam . . . Carter Stanley."
28. George Shuffler interview, April 21, 2005.
29. Fred Sullivan interviews, November 19, 2004, and February 16, 2005.
30. George Shuffler interview, April 21, 2005.
31. "In Memoriam . . . Carter Stanley."
32. George Shuffler interview, April 21, 2005.
33. Wright, "George Shuffler," *Traveling the High Way Home*, 96.
34. *Ibid.*
35. *Ibid.*
36. Rosa M. Merideth, "Standing Room Only . . . The Stanley Brothers," *Stanley Standard*, May 1967, 39.

37. *MCS*, 234.

38. Wright, "Melvin Goins," *Traveling the High Way Home*, 113.

39. Wright, "Curly Ray Cline," *Traveling the High Way Home*, 131.

40. *Ibid.*

41. Wright, "George Shuffler," *Traveling the High Way Home*, 96.

42. *MCS*, 255.

43. Larry Sparks interview, August 13, 2008.

44. *MCS*, 257–58.

45. Wright, "George Shuffler," *Traveling the High Way Home*, 96.

46. *MCS*, 256.

47. Dianne Sims, "Washington D.C. Reporter," *Stanley Standard*, 23.

48. Saunders, "The Carter Stanley Memorial Concert," 24.

49. *Ibid.*, 25.

50. *Ibid.*, 27.

51. Roy Sykes Jr. interview, January 6, 2007.

52. Richard K. Spottswood recollection, July 13, 2011.

BIBLIOGRAPHY

———◆▶◆◀◆———

"Famed Gospel Singer Stanley Buried in Native Dickenson," *Cumberland Times*, Clintwood, Dickenson County, Virginia, December 15, 1966. Reprint.

Fresh Air interview with Ralph Stanley. Terry Gross, host. National Public Radio, July 15, 2002. Transcript produced by Burrelle's Information Services, Livingston, New Jersey.

Artis, Bob. *Bluegrass*. New York: Hawthorn Books, 1975.

Baker, James A. *Folio No. 1* songbook. From the collection of Don Morrell, Abingdon, Virginia, no date.

Bartenstein, Fred. "The Ralph Stanley Story: An Interview with Fred Bartenstein." *Muleskinner News*, March 1972, 6–18.

———. "Bluegrass Generations." Presented at the Bluegrass Music Symposium at Western Kentucky University, September 9, 2005. www.fredbartenstein.com/bluegen.html.

Beckwith, Martha W. "The White Top Folk Festival." *Journal of American Folklore*, Vol. 46, No. 182, October–December 1933, 416.

Berrier, Ralph, Jr. *If Trouble Don't Kill Me: A Family's Story of Brotherhood, War, and Bluegrass*. New York: Crown, 2010.

Blaustein Richard. "WOPI—The Pioneer Voice of the Appalachians." *Journal of Country Music*, Vol. VI, No. 3, Fall 1975, 122–29.

Cantwell, Robert. *Bluegrass Breakdown: The Making of the Old Southern Sound*. Urbana: University of Illinois Press, 1984.

———. "The Lonesome Sound of Carter Stanley." *Bluegrass Unlimited*, Vol. 10, No. 12, June 1976, 10–16.

Cohen, John. "Ralph Stanley's Old Time Bluegrass." *Sing Out!* Vol. 23, No. 6, 1975, 2–8.

Cohen, Ronald D. *Rainbow Quest: The Folk Music Revival and American Society, 1940–1970*. Amherst: University of Massachusetts Press, 2002.

Dean, Eddie. "Carter Stanley: The Sibling that 'O Brother' Forgot." *Washington Post*, May 23, 2004.

Delmore, Alton. *The Delmore Brothers: Truth Is Stranger than Publicity*. Charles K. Wolfe, ed. Nashville: Country Music Foundation Press, 1977, 1995.

Durand, Loyal, Jr. "'Mountain Moonshining' in East Tennessee." *Geographical Review*, Vol. 46, No. 2, April 1956, 168–81.

Dylan, Bob. *Chronicles: Volume One*. New York: Simon & Schuster, 2004.

Eskew, Anne E., James C. Crutcher, M.D., et al. "Lead Poisoning Resulting from Illicit Alcohol Consumption." *Journal of Forensic Sciences*, Vol. 6, No. 3, July 1961, 337–50.

Eller, Ronald D. *Miners, Millhands, and Mountaineers: Industrialization of the Appalachian South.* Knoxville: University of Tennessee Press, 1982.

Erbsen, Wayne. *Rural Roots of Bluegrass: Songs, Stories, & History.* Asheville, NC: Native Ground Music, 2003.

———. "Lester Woodie: Coming Up the Hard Road." *Bluegrass Unlimited,* March 1980, 41–48.

Faragher, John Mack. *Daniel Boone: The Life and Legend of an American Pioneer.* New York: Henry Holt, 1992.

Fessler, Ann. *The Girls Who Went Away: The Hidden History of Women Who Surrendered Children for Adoption in the Decades before Roe v. Wade.* New York: Penguin, 2006.

Fowler, Gene, and Bill Crawford. *Border Radio.* Austin: Texas Monthly Press, 1987.

Fox, Jeffrey. *Ralph on Ralph:* The Clinch Mountain Express *Interviews Dr. Ralph Stanley,* 3rd ed. Dayton: Ralph Stanley Fan Club, May 2002.

Fox, Jeffrey, and Janice Wallen. *Bluegrass Adventures I: Then . . . and Now (A Mountain Music Storybook).* Williamsburg, KY: Ja Vi Publishing, 2000.

Fox, John, Jr. *The Trail of the Lonesome Pine.* New York: Grosset & Dunlap, 1936.

Fox, Jon Hartley. *King of the Queen City: The Story of King Records.* Urbana: University of Illinois Press, 2009.

Gibson, Nathan D. *The Starday Story: The House that Country Built.* Jackson: University Press of Mississippi, 2011.

Gobble, Lillian, and Rhonda Robertson. *Between Brothers: Civil War Soldiers of Wise and Dickenson Counties.* Wise County Historical Society, 2004.

Grundy, Pamela. "'We Always Tried to Be Good People': Respectability, Crazy Water Crystals, and Hillbilly Music on the Air, 1933–1935." *Journal of American History,* Vol. 81, No. 4, March 1995, 1591–1620.

Harrison, Don. "Old-Time Man." *Virginia Living,* June 2008, 54–57.

Holstege, Christopher P., M.D., et al. "Analysis of Moonshine for Contaminants." *Journal of Toxicology,* Vol. 42, No. 5, 2004, 597–601.

Johnson, David W. "Lonesome Melodies: Conversations with Ralph Stanley." *Mars Hill Review,* Issue 22, 2004, 139–54.

———. "'We Thought We Had Reached the Top': The Stanley Brothers' Early Radio Shows and Recordings." *Journal of Country Music,* Vol. 25.2, 2007, 8–14.

Jones, Loyal. *Country Music Humorists and Comedians.* Urbana: University of Illinois Press, 2008.

Kennedy Rick, and Randy McNutt. *Little Labels—Big Sound: Small Record Companies and the Rise of American Music.* Bloomington: Indiana University Press, 1999.

Kingsbury, Paul, ed. *The Encyclopedia of Country Music.* New York: Oxford University Press, 1998.

Laird, Tracey E. *Louisiana Hayride: Radio and Roots Music along the Red River.* New York: Oxford University Press, 2005.

Leyburn, James G. *The Scotch-Irish: A Social History.* Chapel Hill: University of North Carolina Press, 1962.

Lornell, Kip. "Early Country Music and the Mass Media in Roanoke, Virginia." *American Music,* Vol. 5, No. 4, Winter 1987, 403–16.

Marmorstein, Gary. *The Label: The Story of Columbia Records.* New York: Thunder's Mouth Press, 2007.

McDonald, James J. "Principal Influences on the Music of the Lilly Brothers of Clear Creek, West Virginia." *Journal of American Folklore*, Vol. 86, No. 342, October–December 1973, 331–44.

McGinnis, Fay, ed. *Stanley Brothers International Fan Club News Letter*. September 1966.

——, ed. *Stanley Brothers International Fan Club Bulletin*, October 1966.

——, ed. *International Stanley Brothers Fan Club Journal: The Stanley Standard*, late 1966.

——, ed. *Stanley Brothers International Fan Club: The Stanley Standard, Memorial Issue*. Vol. II, No. II, May 1967.

Meade, Guthrie T., Jr. "Copyright: A Tool for Commercial Rural Music Research." *Western Folklore*, Vol. 30, No. 3, July 1971, 206–14.

Meade, Guthrie T., Jr., with Dick Spottswood and Douglas S. Meade. *Country Music Sources: A Biblio-Discography of Commercially Recorded Traditional Music*. Chapel Hill, NC: Southern Folklife Collection, 2002.

Noe, Kenneth W. *Southwest Virginia's Railroad: Modernization and the Sectional Crisis*. Urbana: University of Illinois Press, 1994.

Otto, John S., and Augustus M. Burns. "Black and White Cultural Interaction in the Early Twentieth Century South: Race and Hillbilly Music." *Phylon*, Vol. 35, No. 4, 1974, 407–17.

Peterson, Richard A. *Creating Country Music: Fabricating Authenticity*. Chicago: University of Chicago Press, 1997.

Phillips. V. N. (Bud). *Bristol, Tennessee/Virginia: A History*. Johnson City, TN: Overmountain Press, 1992.

Porterfield, Nolan. *Jimmie Rodgers: The Life and Times of America's Blue Yodeler*. Urbana: University of Illinois Press, 1979.

Pote, Douglas. *Man of Constant Sorrow*. Barter Theatre, Abingdon, Virginia. May 5, 2006. Final script.

Price, Steven D. *Old as the Hills: The Story of Bluegrass Music*. New York: Viking, 1975.

Reedy, Dennis, ed. *School and Community History of Dickenson County, Virginia*. Johnson City, TN: Overmountain Press, 1994.

Reid, Gary B. *Stanley Brothers: A Preliminary Discography*. Roanoke, VA: Copper Creek Publications, 1984.

——. "The Stanley Brothers in Florida." *Florida Bluegrass News*, Vol. 1, No. 2, March–April 1985, 6–7.

Ringle, Ken. "The Natural King of Bluegrass: Virginia's Ralph Stanley, the Old-Timey Singer Whose Time Has Come." *Washington Post*, March 20, 1993.

Roberts, Leonard, and C. Buell Agey, eds. *In the Pine: Selected Kentucky Folksongs*. Pikesville, KY: Pikesville College Press, 1978.

Rorer, Kinney. *Rambling Blues: The Life and Songs of Charlie Poole*. Danville, VA, McCain Printing, 1982.

Rosenberg, Bruce A. *The Folksongs of Virginia: A Checklist of the WPA Holdings, Alderman Library, University of Virginia*. Charlottesville: University of Virginia Press, 1969.

Rosenberg, Neil V. *Bluegrass: A History*, Urbana: University of Illinois Press, 1985.

——. "From Sound into Style: The Emergence of Bluegrass." *Journal of American Folklore*, Vol. 80, No. 316, April–June 1967, 143–50.

Russell, Fran. "The Stanley Brothers." *The Stanley Brothers and . . . The Clinch Mountain Boys* [songbook]. From the collection of Don Morrell, Abingdon, Virginia, no date.

Russell, Tony. *Country Music Records: A Discography, 1921–1942.* New York: Oxford University Press, 2008.

Sayers, Bob. "Black Mountain Odyssey: Leslie Keith." *Bluegrass Unlimited,* Vol. 11, No. 6, December 1976, 13–17.

Scruggs, Mrs. Earl (Louise). "Earl Scruggs: The Legend and the Man." *Muleskinner News,* Vol. 3, No. 1, January 1972, 2–9.

Smith, L. Mayne. "An Introduction to Bluegrass." *Journal of American Folklore,* Vol. 78, No. 309, July–September 1965, 245–56.

Smith, Richard D. *Can't You Hear Me Callin': The Life of Bill Monroe, Father of Bluegrass.* Boston: Little, Brown, 2000.

Spottswood, Richard K. "The Carter Stanley Memorial Concert." *Bluegrass Unlimited,* Vol. 1., No. 11, May 1967, 1–2.

Stanley, Ralph, with Eddie Dean. *Man of Constant Sorrow: The Life and Times of a Music Legend* (advance reading copy). New York: Gotham, 2009.

——. *Man of Constant Sorrow: My Life and Times.* New York: Gotham, 2009.

Steele, Fannie Lane, and Ina Jean Johnson. *The Crabtree-Stanley Collection: A Memorial.* Midlands, VA: I. J. S. Dotson, 1996.

Sturgill, Roy L. "'Fiddlin' Cowan Powers and Family: Pioneer Recording Artists of Country Mountain Music." *Historical Sketches of Southwest Virginia, Publication No. 17.* Abingdon, VA: Historical Society of Southwest Virginia, 1985, 54–65.

Tottle, Jack. "Ralph Stanley: The Stanley Sound." *Bluegrass Unlimited,* May 1981, 14–21.

——. "The Stanley Brothers on WCYB Bristol," notes to *Live Again! WCYB Bristol Farm and Fun Time,* Rebel CD-2003, 1997.

Tribe, Ivan M. *Mountaineer Jamboree: Country Music in West Virginia.* Lexington: University Press of Kentucky, 1984. Paperback afterword 1996.

——. *The Stonemans: An Appalachian Family and the Music That Shaped Their Lives.* Urbana: University of Illinois Press, 1993.

——. "Wade Mainer." In Barry McCloud, *Definitive Country: The Ultimate Encyclopedia of Country Music and Its Performers.* New York: Perigee, 1995.

West, John Foster. *The Ballad of Tom Dula.* Durham, NC: Moore Publishing, no date.

Wilgus, D. K. "An Introduction to the Study of Hillbilly Music." *Journal of American Folklore,* Vol. 78, No. 309, July–September, 1965, 195–203.

Williams, John Alexander. *Appalachia: A History.* Chapel Hill: University of North Carolina Press, 2002.

Wilson, Joe. "Bristol's WCYB—Early Bluegrass Turf." *Muleskinner News,* Vol. 3, No. 8, October 1972, 8–12.

Wolfe, Charles K. *A Good-Natured Riot: The Birth of the Grand Ole Opry.* Nashville: Country Music Foundation Press and Vanderbilt University Press, 1999.

——. *Kentucky Country: Folk and Country Music of Kentucky.* Lexington: University Press of Kentucky, 1982.

——. *In Close Harmony: The Story of the Louvin Brothers.* Jackson: University Press of Mississippi, 1996.

——. "Man of Constant Sorrow: Richard Burnett's Story." *Old Time Music,* No. 9, 6–9; "Man of Constant Sorrow: Richard Burnett's Story 2," No. 10, Autumn 1973, 5–11.

——. Booklet to *Burnett & Rutherford: Complete Recorded Works in Chronological Order (1926–1930),* Document Records, 1998.

Wright, John. *Traveling the High Way Home: Ralph Stanley and the World of Traditional Bluegrass Music.* Urbana: University of Illinois Press, 1993.

——, ed. *It's the Hardest Music in the World To Play: The Ralph Stanley Story in His Own Words.* Chinacum, WA: Beaver Valley Press, 1988.

Zwonitzer, Mark, with Charles Hirschberg. *Will You Miss Me When I'm Gone?: The Carter Family and Their Legacy in American Music.* New York: Simon & Schuster, 2002.

DISCOGRAPHY

———————◆◆✖◆●———————

Acuff, Roy. *King of Country Music.* Proper Properbox 70 P1377-1380, 2004.

Arthur, Emry. *I Am a Man of Constant Sorrow, Volume One.* Old Homestead OHCD 4190, 2001.

Ashley, Clarence. *Greenback Dollar: The Music of Clarence "Tom" Ashley 1929–1933.* County CO-CD3520, 2001.

Blue Sky Boys. *The Blue Sky Boys.* JSP Records JSP7782A, 2007.

Blue Sky Boys. *Farm and Fun Time Favorites, Volume One and Volume Two.* Copper Creek CCCD-0125 and 0126, 1994.

Blue Sky Boys. *On Radio, Volume Three and Volume Four.* Copper Creek CCCD-0145 and 0146, 1997.

Burnett, Richard D., and Leonard Rutherford. *Burnett & Rutherford: Complete Recordings in Chronological Order (1926–1930).* Document DOCD-8025, 1998.

Callahan Brothers. *The Callahan Brothers.* Old Homestead OHCD 4031, 2000.

Carter Family. *The Carter Family 1927–1934* and *The Carter Family, Volume 2, 1935–1941.* JSP Records JSPCD7701A, 2001, and JSP7708A, 2003.

Carter Family. *The Carter Family on Border Radio, Volume 1.* Arhoolie CD 411, 1995.

Coon Creek Girls. *Early Radio Favorites.* Old Homestead OHCD 4142, 2006.

Delmore Brothers. *That Old Train.* British Archive of Country Music BACM CD D 044, 2002.

Delmore Brothers. *Classic Cuts 1933–1941.* JSP Records JSP7727, 2004.

Fiddlin' Powers and Family, et al. *Rural String Bands of Virginia.* County CD-3502, 1993.

Fiddlin' Powers and Family, et al. *Old-Time Music from Southwest Virginia.* County CO-CD-3523, 2001.

Flatt & Scruggs. *The Complete Mercury Recordings.* Mercury B0000070-02, 2003.

Flatt & Scruggs. *Lester Flatt & Earl Scruggs and the Stanley Brothers: Selected Sides 1947–1953.* JSP Records JSP7724A, 2003.

Flatt & Scruggs. *Foggy Mountain Jamboree.* Columbia/Legacy 82876 77627 2, 2005. Originally released in 1957.

Georgia Yellow Hammers. *Johnson's Old Grey Mule: Classic Old Time String Band from North Georgia.* British Archive of Country Music BACM CD D 073, 2004.

Grayson, G. B., and Henry Whitter. *Early Classics, Volume I and II.* Old Homestead OHCD 157 and OHCD 165, 2004.

Grayson, G. B., and Henry Whitter. *The Recordings of Grayson and Whitter: Recorded 1928–1930*. County CO-CD-3517, 1998.

Holcomb, Roscoe. *The High Lonesome Sound*. Smithsonian Folkways SF CD 40104, 1998.

Holcomb, Roscoe. *An Untamed Sense of Control*. SFW CD 40144, 2003.

Jim & Jesse. *Jim & Jesse 1952–1955*. Bear Family BCD 15635, 1992.

Jim & Jesse. *Dixie Hoedown: Their Complete Starday Recordings*. Starday King KSCD-0120, 2003.

Jim & Jesse with Larry Roll. *The Virginia Trio: Their First Historical Gospel Recordings*. Old Dominion OD 498-18, no date.

Karl and Harty. *Karl and Harty with the Cumberland Ridge Runners*. Old Homestead OHCD 4137, 2003.

Kazee, Buell. *Legendary Kentucky Ballad Singer*. British Archive of Country Music BACM CD D 027, 2002.

Lilly Brothers and Don Stover. *Bluegrass at the Roots 1961*. Smithsonian Folkways SFW CD 40158, 2005. Originally released as FA 2433.

Lonesome Pine Fiddlers. *Windy Mountain*. Bear Family BCD 16351 AH, 1992.

Louvin Brothers. *Tragic Songs of Life*. Gusto GTCD-0105, 2003. Originally released in 1956 as Capitol LP T769.

Louvin Brothers. *Ira and Charlie*. Gusto GT-0112-2, 2003. Originally released in 1958 as Capitol LP T910.

Louvin Brothers. *Radio Favorites '51–'57*. The Country Music Foundation CMF-009D, 1993.

Macon, Uncle Dave. *Early Recordings 1924–1925*. Old Homestead OHCD 4184, 2001.

Macon, Uncle Dave. *Go Long Mule*. County CO-CD-3505, 1994.

Maddox Brothers and Rose. *America's Most Colorful Hillbilly Band: Their Original Recordings 1946–1951*. Arhoolie CD 391, 1993.

Mainer, J. E., et al. *The Early Years 1935–1939*. JSP Records, JSP77118A, 2009.

Mainer, J. E., et al. *Classic Sides 1937–1941*. JSP Records, JSP77124, 2009.

Mainer, Wade. *Early and Great Sacred Songs*. Old Homestead OHCD 4013, 1998.

Mainer, Wade and J. E. *Wade and J. E. Mainer and the Mainer's Mountaineers, Volume II*. Old Homestead OHCD 4044, 2007.

Monroe, Bill. *Bill Monroe: Blue Moon of Kentucky 1936–1949*. Bear Family BCD 16399 FL, 2002. Compact discs and book. Essay and biography by Charles K. Wolfe. Discography by Neil V. Rosenberg.

Monroe, Bill. *Bill Monroe and His Bluegrass Boys: All the Classic Releases 1939–1939*. JSP Records JSP7712A, 2003.

Monroe, Bill. *The Father of Bluegrass: The Early Years 1940–1947*. ASV Living Era CD AJA 5298, 1999.

Monroe Brothers. *Volume One: What Would You Give in Exchange for Your Soul?* Rounder 82161-1073-2, 2000.

Monroe Brothers. *Volume Two: Just a Song of Old Kentucky*. Rounder 82161-1074-2, 2001.

O'Day, Molly. *Radio Favorites: Sacred and Secular Songs*. Old Homestead OHCD 140, 2004.

Old Regular Baptists. *Songs of the Old Regular Baptists: Lined-Out Hymnody from Southeastern Kentucky, Volumes 1 and 2*. Smithsonian Folkways SF CD 40106, 1997, and SFW CD 50001, 2003.

Poole, Charlie. *Charlie Poole and the North Carolina Ramblers: Old-Time Songs*. County CO-CD-3501, 1993.

Roane County Ramblers. *Complete Recordings 1928–1929.* County CO-CD-3530, 2004.

Skillet Lickers. *The Skillet Lickers: Old-Time Fiddle Tunes and Songs from North Georgia.* County CD-3509, 1996.

Stanley Brothers, et al. *Live Again! WCYB Bristol Farm and Fun Time.* Rebel CD-2003, 1997.

Stanley Brothers. *Earliest Recordings: The Complete Rich-R-Tone 78s (1947–1952).* Rich-R-Tone Revenant 203, 1997.

Stanley Brothers. *Earliest Recordings: The Complete Rich-R-Tone 78s (1947–1952).* Rounder 116611-1110-2, 2004.

Stanley Brothers. *The Complete Columbia Stanley Brothers.* Columbia/Legacy CK 53798, 1996.

Stanley Brothers. *Angel Band: The Classic Mercury Recordings.* Mercury 314-528 191-2, 1995.

Stanley Brothers. *The Stanley Brothers and the Clinch Mountain Boys 1949–1952.* Bear Family BCD 15564, 1991. Discography by Gary B. Reid.

Stanley Brothers. *The Stanley Brothers and the Clinch Mountain Boys 1953–1958 & 1959.* Bear Family BCD 15681, 1993. Discography by Gary B. Reid.

Stanley Brothers. *The Early Starday King Years 1958–1961.* Starday/King KBSCD-7000, 1993. Discography by Gary B. Reid.

Stanley Brothers. *The King Years 1961–1965.* King KG-0950-2, 2003. Discography by Gary B. Reid.

Stanley Brothers. *The Definitive Collection (1947–1966).* Time Life B0007833-02, 2007.

Stanley Brothers. *Stanley Brothers and the Clinch Mountain Boys.* King KCD-615, 1988.

Stanley Brothers. *Hymns and Sacred Songs.* King KCD-645, 1988.

Stanley Brothers. *An Empty Mansion: In Memory of Carter Stanley.* Old Homestead OHCD-118, 1999. Originally Rimrock RLP 153, 1967.

Stanley Brothers. *A Beautiful Life.* Old Homestead OHCD-119, 2007. Originally Rimrock RLP 200, 1967.

Stanley Brothers, et al. *American Folk & Country Music Festival.* Bear Family BCD 16849 BK, 2007.

Stanley Brothers. *Bluegrass Gospel Favorites.* Cabin Creek 203, 1981.

Stanley Brothers. *That Little Old Country Church House.* County 738, August 1973. Originally released as John's Gospel Quartet, Wango 103, 1966.

Stanley Brothers. *Long Journey Home.* Rebel REB-CD-1110, 1990. Released as County 739, 1973. Originally released as John's Country Quartet, Wango 104, 1966.

Stanley Brothers. *Uncloudy Day.* County 753, 1977. Originally released as John's Gospel Quartet, Wango 105, 1966.

Stanley Brothers. *Stanley Brothers of Virginia, Volume Four.* Country 754, 1976. Originally released as John's Gospel Quartet, *Songs of Mother and Home,* Wango 106, 1965.

Stanley Brothers, et al. *The bluegrass story.* Unreleased live recording narrated by Carlton Haney. Roanoke Blue Grass Festival, Fincastle, Virginia, September 5, 1965. Courtesy of Fred Bartenstein.

Stanley Brothers. *An Evening Long Ago.* Columbia/DMZ/Legacy CK 86747, 2004. Recorded March 24, 1956 at WCYB in Bristol, Virginia. Originally released as a private pressing to be sold at concerts, *Old-Time Songs,* ST-CD-5001, 1999.

Stanley Brothers. *Live at Antioch College.* Vintage Collector's Club ZK-002, circa 1981. Recorded May 14, 1960, in Yellow Springs, Ohio. May have been released as a limited edition.

Stanley Brothers. *Folk Festival.* ST-CD-5003, 2001. Released as a private pressing to be sold at concerts.

Stanley Brothers. *Brown County Jamboree: The Last Show of the Stanley Brothers,* 2004. Recorded October 16, 1966, in Bean Blossom, Indiana. Released as a private pressing to be sold at concerts.

Stanley Brothers. *Live at the New River Ranch.* Recorded May 15, 1960, in Rising Son, Maryland, no date. Released as a private pressing to be sold at concerts.

Stanley Brothers. *Shadows of the Past.* Copper Creek CCCD-0101, 1996.

Stanley Brothers. *Stanley Series, Volume 1, Number 4.* Copper Creek CCSS-V1N4, 1984. Recorded October 16, 1966, at the Brown County Jamboree in Bean Blossom, Indiana.

Stanley Brothers. *Stanley Series, Volume 2, Number 4.* Copper Creek CCSS-V2N4, 1987. Recorded August 30, 1962, at the Ash Grove, Los Angeles, California.

Stanley Brothers. *Stanley Series, Volume 3, Number 2.* Copper Creek CCSS-V3N2, 1989. Recorded August 29, 1962, at the Ash Grove, Los Angeles, California.

Stanley Brothers, et al. *Newport Folk Festival: Best of Bluegrass 1955–66.* Vanguard 187/89-2, 2001.

Stanley, Ralph. *Poor Rambler: His Complete King and Gusto Recordings.* K3CD-0951, 2002.

Stanley, Ralph. *Ralph Stanley and the Clinch Mountain Boys 1971–1973.* Rebel REB-4001, 1995.

Stanley, Ralph. *Short Life of Trouble: Songs of Grayson and Whitter.* Rebel REB-CD-1735, 1996.

Stanley, Ralph, et al. *The Ralph Stanley story.* Unreleased live recording narrated by Fred Bartenstein. Camp Springs, North Carolina, September 8, 1969. Courtesy of Fred Bartenstein.

Stoneman, Ernest V. *Edison Recordings—1928.* County CD-3510, 1996.

Various artists. *Old-Time Music of West Virginia, Volume One and Volume Two.* County CO-CD-3518 and CO-CD-3519, 1999.

Various artists. *Music from the Lost Provinces: Old-Time Stringbands from Ashe County, North Carolina & Vicinity, 1927–1931.* Old Hat CD-1001, 1997.

Various artists. *Early Country Radio.* JSP Records JSP 7757, 2005.

Various artists. *Mountain Music of Kentucky.* Smithsonian Folkways SF CD 40077, 1996.

Various artists. *American Banjo Three-Finger and Scruggs-Style.* Smithsonian Folkways CD SF 40037, 1990. Originally released as Folkways 2314 in 1957.

Various Artists. *Mountain Music Bluegrass Style.* Smithsonian Folkways, CD SF 40038, 1991. Originally released as FA 2318 in May 1959.

Various artists. *Old-Time Mountain Banjo.* County CO-CD-3533, 2005.

Various artists. *Black Banjo Songsters of North Carolina and Virginia.* Smithsonian Folkways SF CD 40079, 1998.

Various artists. *Classic Bluegrass from Smithsonian Folkways, Volumes 1 and 2.* SFW CD 40092, 2002, and SFW CD 40163, 2005.

Various artists. *Classic Mountain Songs from Smithsonian Folkways.* SFW CD 40094, 2002.

Various artists. *Are You From Dixie? Great Country Brother Teams of the 1930's.* RCA 8417-2-R, 1988.

Various artists. *O Brothers! Family Harmony in Old-Time Music & Bluegrass.* ASV Living Era 5467, 2003.

WPAQ: The Voice of the Blue Ridge Mountains: Radio Recordings from Mount Airy, NC 1947–1950. Rounder CD 0404, 1999.

Recorded Contemporary Interviews

Keith, Leslie. Interview by Mike Seeger, November 23, 1964. Field tape FT-5638. (20009) Mike Seeger Collection, Southern Oral History Project, University of North Carolina at Chapel Hill. Used by permission.

Stanley, Carter. Interview by Mike Seeger, March 1966. From field tapes FT-8815 and FT-8816. (30001) Southern Folklife Collection, University of North Carolina at Chapel Hill. Used by permission.

Stanley, Ralph. Interview by Mike Seeger, March 1966. From field tapes FT-8815 and FT 8816. (30001) Southern Folklife Collection, University of North Carolina at Chapel Hill. Used by permission.

Videotaped Television Appearances

Featured artists on *Pete Seeger's Rainbow Quest*. Recorded at WNJU, Newark, New Jersey, February 24, 1966. Shanachie 605 DVD, 2005.

Guest artists on Don Reno and Red Smiley's *Top o' the Morning* show, WDBJ-TV, Roanoke, Virginia. *Bluegrass 1963*. Man-do-lin Productions DVD, 2008.

Index

283

blackface, 38, 47
Bland, Peggy C., 140, 150, 178–79, 241
Bloomington, Indiana. *See* Indiana
Blountville, Tennessee. *See* Tennessee
Blue Grass Boys. *See* Monroe, Bill
Blue Ridge Mountain Boys. *See* Sykes, Roy
Blue Sky Boys, 35–36, 92, 193
Bluefield, West Virginia. *See* West Virginia
Bluegrass Bulletin, 243–44
Bluegrass Day, 187–88, 214
bluegrass music: business, 225; characteristics, 37, 70, 81, 90, 116; culture, 219; festivals, 36, 188, 213–16; genre, 25, 37, 44, 70, 108, 131, 164, 214, 216, 218; origins, 23–25, 53; popularity, 47, 81–82, 163, 231; relationship to folk music, 166; revival, 213, 217; split from country music, 215; standards, 99, 123, 155, 208–9
Bluegrass Unlimited, 131, 220, 247, 249
Bluff City, Virginia. *See* Virginia
Bolick, Bill, 35–36, 193
Bolick, Earl, 35–36, 193
Bonds, Johnny, 150–51, 172
Boone, Daniel, 4–6
Boone, North Carolina. *See* North Carolina
Boone County Jamboree. *See* radio shows
Bowman, Ralph, 141
Bradley, Doris Stanley, 8, 18, 101, 129–30, 149, 193, 204, 225, 233, 239, 242, 245
Bradley, Harold, 118–19
Bradley, Owen, 118–19
Bradley Studio, 116, 118–19, 121, 132
Brim, Alan, 143–45, 150, 178, 191
Bristol, Tennessee. *See* Tennessee

Bristol, Virginia. *See* Virginia
Brooklyn, New York. *See* New York
Brown, Hylo (and the Timberliners), 165–66
Brown, James, 154
Brumley, Albert E., 181, 208
Buchanan, Annabel Morris, 164
Bumgarner, Samantha, 10
Bundy, Bill, 59
Burnett, Dick, 23–24
Busby, Buzz, 247

California: Berkeley, 200; Los Angeles, 197, 200
Camp Gordon, Georgia. *See* Georgia
Campbell, Alex, 176
Campbell, Olive Dame, 163, 176, 247
Camper, Peggy. *See* Bland, Peggy C.
Caney Branch, Tennessee. *See* Tennessee
Canton, Ohio. *See* Ohio
Carbo, Virginia. *See* Virginia
Carfax, Virginia. *See* Virginia
Carter, A. P., 26, 51, 91, 110, 139, 164
Carter, Joe, 206
Carter, Maybelle, 21, 26, 51, 56, 87, 111
Carter, Sara, 26, 168, 207, 213
Carter Family, 21, 26–27, 51–52, 56, 65, 68–70, 79, 85, 91, 94, 110–11, 126, 128, 139, 168–69, 183, 206–7, 212
    Works: "Can the Circle Be Unbroken?," 52, 69; "The Cyclone of Rye Cove," 139; "Keep on the Sunny Side," 52, 169; "The Wildwood Flower," 52, 183
Carterton, Virginia. *See* Virginia
Carver, Cynthia May. *See* Cousin Emmy and Her Kinfolk
Cash, Johnny, 210, 227
Castle Studios, 103
Castlewood, Virginia. *See* Virginia
Chance, Floyd T. "Lightnin'," 121

Lynch, Jack, 244, 246
Lynchburg, Virginia. *See* Virginia

Maces Springs, Virginia. *See* Virginia
Macon, Uncle Dave, 33
Mainer, J. E., 24, 33
Mainer, Wade, 24–26, 33, 38, 64, 69, 89–90, 135, 162
Mainer's Mountaineers, 21, 24, 64, 68, 254
Malone, Bill C., 192, 202–3, 208–9, 213
Mamou Cajun Band, 83
Man of Constant Sorrow (play), 84, 110, 182, 198
Marcum, R., 208
Marion, Virginia. *See* Virginia
Martha Gap, Virginia. *See* Virginia
Martin, Ben E. "Benny," 140, 216
Martin, Jimmy (and the Sunny Mountain Boys), 115, 216
Maryland, 32, 131, 135, 174, 249; Baltimore, 174, 205; College Park, 247; Fort Meade, 31; Glen Burney, 146; Middle River, 32; Ocean City, 206; Pikesville, 158; Rising Sun, 146, 174; Salisbury, 206
Mauldin, Bessie Lee, 121
Mayo, Ralph, 128, 133, 154, 160, 172, 177, 180, 190, 204, 226
McClure, Virginia. *See* Virginia
McDivitt, Mac, 195–96
McGinnis, Fay, 233–34, 243
McMichen, Clayton, 34, 53
McReynolds, Jesse, 32, 76–77, 82, 109, 115, 145, 210, 238
McReynolds, Jim, 76–77, 82, 90, 115, 145, 210, 238
McReynolds brothers (Jim and Jesse), 32, 77, 82, 115, 145, 178, 188, 191, 210, 238
Meadows, Ralph "Joe," 122, 131–33, 226
Melbourne, Florida. *See* Florida
Melody Mountain Boys, 92, 115

Memphis, Tennessee. *See* Tennessee
Mercury Records, 81, 113, 115–16, 118–23, 130–33, 139–41, 146–48, 151, 154, 156, 191, 232, 240, 249
Michigan, 113–15, 241; Detroit, 114, 233–34; Flint, 25; Monroe, 231; Wyandotte, 233
Middle River, Maryland. *See* Maryland
Miller, Don, 227–29
Mills, Allen, 197
minstrelsy, 38, 47, 63, 98, 175
Mississippi Sheiks, 99
Mongle, Bruce William, 130, 222–23, 227–28, 241, 247
Monroe, Bill: and the Blue Grass Boys, 37, 41, 47, 65, 67–68, 79, 85, 88, 90–91, 103, 105, 107, 111, 134, 188, 195, 205, 214, 216, 248–49; fishing, 172, 177, 193; and Lester Flatt, 65, 90–91, 111, 147, 188–89; *Grand Ole Opry*, 37; image, 41, 102, 157; imitation by the Stanley Brothers, 37, 42, 58–59, 67–68, 70, 79–80, 85, 88–90, 105, 108, 111–12, 133–34, 136, 194, 210, 214, 249; minstrelsy, 38; musical education, 36–37; musicianship, 82; personality, 188, 194; pioneer of bluegrass music, 25, 31, 195, 213–15, 217; playing with African American musicians, 164; and Elvis Presley, 119–21; rivalry with the Stanley Brothers, 80; and Earl Scruggs, 65, 90–91, 111, 147, 188–89; and Carter Stanley, 105, 116, 136, 189, 198, 205, 214, 217–18, 238, 243–44, 248–49; as Stanley Brothers' producer, 120–21, 130; success, 47
Works: "Blue Moon of Kentucky," 59, 119–20, 130, 132; "Cabin of Love," 109, 219; "Can't You Hear

Raleigh, North Carolina. *See* North
Carolina
Ralph Stanley Museum and
Traditional Music Center, 43, 125,
160, 242
Raney, Wayne, 183, 185, 207, 220–21
RCA (Radio Corporation of America),
31, 81, 83–84, 100, 118–19, 130,
133, 140, 144, 198, 212
records. *See* phonograph records
Red Smiley and the Bluegrass Cutups,
216
Reed, Bud, 176
Reed, Ola Bell, 176
Reno, Don, 127, 152, 172, 188, 215–16;
and the Tennessee Cutups, 216
Republican Party, 14
Richard Cox and the Harvesters, 94
Richardson, Larry, 216, 243–44
Richlands, Virginia. *See* Virginia
Richmond, Virginia. *See* Virginia
Rich-R-Tone label, 65, 67–70, 81,
84–85, 109, 111, 122
Riddle, Leslie, 164, 166
Rimrock Records, 183, 220–21
Rinzler, Ralph, 214–15, 218
Rising Sun, Maryland. *See* Maryland
Ritter, Tex, 176
Robinson, Russ, 66
rock 'n' roll, 84, 90, 120, 124, 132, 151,
163, 179, 203, 208, 210
rockabilly, 151
Rodgers, Jimmie, 34, 52, 85, 100
Rose, Exie, 43–44
Rounder Records, 66
Rouse, Ervin, 53
Rouse, Gordon, 53
Roy Hall and His Blue Ridge
Entertainers. *See* Hall, Roy
Roy Sykes and the Blue Ridge
Mountain Boys. *See* Sykes, Roy
Rutherford, Leonard, 23

Salisbury, Maryland. *See* Maryland
San Antonio, Texas. *See* Texas
San Marcos, Texas. *See* Texas
Sandburg, Carl, 163
Sandusky, Ohio. *See* Ohio
Satherley, Art, 84–86, 92, 102–3
Saturday Night Jamboree. See radio
shows
Sauceman, Carl, 81, 84
Saucemen, J. P., 81
Savitz, Bill, 162
Schwarz, Tracy, 200, 229
Scott County, Virginia. *See* Virginia
Scruggs, Earl, 26, 59, 65, 76, 79–82, 85,
89–92, 100, 109, 111, 113, 134–35,
146–48, 152, 155, 157, 165–67,
174–75, 189, 192, 195, 201, 210,
214, 216, 220, 248–49
Seeger, Charles, 158, 164
Seeger, Mike, 29, 34, 83, 87, 89, 118, 133,
152, 158–59, 165, 175, 185, 197, 201,
208, 214, 229–30, 243, 247
Seeger, Pete, 10, 158, 165–66, 227
Sharp, Cecil, 163
Shelton, James Alan, 32, 254
Shepard, Jeannie, 193
Shouns, Tennessee. *See* Tennessee
Shreveport, Louisiana. *See* Louisiana
Shuffler, George, 32, 83, 92, 101, 104,
109–11, 115–16, 124–25, 136–37,
145, 148, 150–51, 160, 162, 168–70,
182, 190–92, 204, 207–9, 211, 217,
219, 227–31, 234–35, 239, 244–48
Shuffler, John, 92, 105
Shultz, Arnold, 36, 164
Sing Out!, 14–15, 214–15
Skaggs, Ricky, 123
"Sleep, Baby, Sleep," 52
Slim, Texas (and His Prairie
Buckaroos), 94
Smiley, Red, 152, 172, 215–16

Smith, Fiddlin' Arthur, 46
Smith Ridge, Virginia. *See* Virginia
"Soldier's Sweetheart, The," 52
Sons of the Pioneers, 92
Sparks, Larry, 211, 246, 248
square dancing, 44, 115, 164
St. Petersburg, Florida. *See* Florida
Stamper, Art, 112, 115–16, 133
Stanley, Bobby, 150, 204
Stanley, Carter: adolescence, 18–22,
    27; alcohol use, 19, 75–76, 130,
    140, 146, 172, 184–85, 189, 192,
    198, 207, 213; alcoholism, 130,
    189, 203, 207, 223–27, 229, 235,
    238–39, 250; back injury, 192;
    birthplace, 5; childhood, 9–17;
    criticism of Ralph Stanley,
    134–35, 198, 213; death, 223–25,
    235–36; diminished vocals, 172,
    185–86, 196, 209, 212; Ervinton
    High School, 14; fishing, 172,
    177, 193; friendship with Carl
    Hammons, 10, 29, 224; friendship
    with Roy Sykes, 31–32, 73, 192,
    237; funeral, 242–45; genealogy,
    6–8; grudge against Lester Flatt,
    79–80, 189, 192, 249; hunting,
    29, 150, 156, 193, 223; illegitimate
    daughter, 76–77; marriage to
    Mary Kiser Carter, 73–74; mili-
    tary service, 27, 29–31, 33, 39–40,
    43, 99; and Bill Monroe, 105, 116,
    136, 189, 198, 205, 214, 217–18,
    238, 243–44, 248–49; personality,
    12, 44–45, 127–28, 176, 193–94,
    198; physical description, 72, 75;
    relationship with his children,
    101–2, 129–30, 203–4; relation-
    ship with his parents, 18–20, 29,
    74, 198–99; relationship with
    Ralph Stanley, 127–28, 198, 213;
    songwriting, 45, 77–79, 81, 84,

93, 96, 103, 134, 138, 161; woman-
    izing, 75–76, 199
Stanley, Carter Lee, 149–50, 172,
    225–26, 237–39, 241, 247, 249
Stanley, Doris. *See* Bradley, Doris
    Stanley
Stanley, Fred, 20, 172
Stanley, Jeanie, 77, 101, 150, 204, 239,
    243
Stanley, Lee, 8, 15, 18, 20, 23, 40, 46, 48,
    62, 74, 105, 156, 190
Stanley, Lucy Smith, 8–9, 11, 18, 20–22,
    29, 40, 74, 102, 114, 156, 198–99,
    237, 240–41, 243–44
Stanley, Mary Kiser, 73–74, 101–2,
    149–50, 197, 199, 203–4, 238–39,
    241, 243, 245, 247, 249
Stanley, Peggy. *See* Bland, Peggy C.
Stanley, Ralph: adolescence, 18–22, 27;
    birthplace, 5; car accident, 107–8;
    childhood, 9–17; criticism from
    Carter Stanley, 134–35, 198, 213;
    Ervinton High School, 14; geneal-
    ogy, 6–8; Grammy Award, 209;
    influence of Earl Scruggs, 89–90,
    134, 195; "Little Jesus" nickname,
    198, 212; *Man of Constant Sorrow*
    (autobiography), 16, 24, 178–79,
    191, 199, 223, 237; marriage to
    Peggy C. Bland, 178–79; mar-
    riage to Jimmie Crabtree, 191;
    military service, 27, 30–31, 33,
    39–40, 42–43, 99; personality, 12,
    44–45, 93, 127–28, 198; physical
    description, 72; relationship with
    his children, 178–79; relation-
    ship with his parents, 18–20, 29,
    74, 198–99; relationship with
    Carter Stanley, 127–28, 198, 213;
    tattoos, 40; traditional approach
    to music, 182
Stanley, Ralph, II, 239

WSAZ-TV, 94
WSM. *See* radio stations
WTOB. *See* radio stations
WVLK. *See* radio stations
WWNC. *See* radio stations
WWVA. *See* radio stations
Wyandotte, Michigan. *See* Michigan

XERA. *See* radio stations
XERF. *See* radio stations

Yellow Springs, Ohio. *See* Ohio